Julian Maclaren-Ross
Collected Memoirs

FITZROVIA

PART OF SOHO

A   Finch's The One Tun
B   L'Étoile
C   Schmidt's
D   The Duke of York
E   Bertorelli's
F   Plumbing Supplies
G   The Fitzroy Tavern
H   Pogiolli's
I   The Marquis of Granby
J   Le Tour Eiffel
K   Mrs Buhler's First Café
L   The Wheatsheaf
M   The Bricklayer's Arms
N   Winsor & Newton
O   The Black Horse
P   W. R. Loftus

Q   "The Two-thirty House"
R   The Highlander
S   The Pillars of Hercules
T   The Shanghai
U   Bakery
V   All Night Café
W   The Gargoyle Club
X   The Mandrake Club
Y   Patisserie Valerie
Z   The Swiss
AA Mrs Buhler's Second Café
BB F. Denny, outfitters for
    Chefs and Waiters
CC The York Minster
DD St. Anne's
EE Zwemmer's Bookshop
FF The Colony Club

JULIAN MACLAREN-ROSS
Collected Memoirs

with an introduction by Paul Willetts

BLACK
SPRING
PRESS

Published in 2004 by Black Spring Press Ltd
Burbage House
83–85 Curtain Road
London EC2A 3BS

www.blackspringpress.co.uk

The Weeping and the Laughter first published by Rupert Hart-Davis,
1953 ('Monsieur Félix' first published in different form in *Penguin
New Writing*, 30 May 1947); 'Monsieur L'Abbé' first published in
Encounter, December 1953; 'The Gondolier of Death', 'My Father
was Born in Havana', 'Old Ginger', 'Adventures in Film' (parts 1
and 2) and 'Bop' first published in *The Funny Bone*, Elek Books,
1956; 'The Bird Man' first published in *Encounter*, January 1956;
'A Visit to the Villa Edouard Sept' first published in the *London
Magazine*, June 1955; *Memoirs of the Forties* first published as a
collection by Alan Ross, 1965 (individual stories serialised in the
London Magazine between November 1964 and March 1965);
'Are You Happy in Your Work' first published in *The Saturday Book*,
October 1943; 'Second Lieutenant Lewis' first published in *Penguin
New Writing*, April 1946; 'In Their Black Books' first published in
Punch, 25 November 1953; 'The Night Bathers' first published in
Punch, 1 January 1958; 'Some Time I Shall Sleep Out' first published
in the *Times Literary Supplement*, 20 December 2002.

ISBN 0-948238-30-5

A full CIP record for this book is available from the British Library

Cover design Hanna Sundén; front cover: Berwick Street Market,
1932, © Museum of London; back cover: Julian Maclaren-Ross,
sitting in the garden of Greenleaves, Bognor Regis, 1940,
© C.K. Jaeger; map opposite title page, showing the pubs of Soho
and Fitzrovia, by Ruthven Todd, taken from the catalogue of the
exhibition 'Fitzrovia and the Road to York Minster', The Parkin
Gallery, London, 26 September to 27 October 1973, © Michael
Parkin.

Typeset in Minion by Dexter Haven Associates Ltd, London
Printed and bound in Great Britain by Cox and Wyman Ltd, Reading

CONTENTS

Publisher's Note

Aspects of the style in originals of some of the author's stories are idiosyncratic, and we have preserved these idiosyncracies. Often speech is not rendered in quote marks, and words like 'can't' and 'won't' are set without the apostrophe. Equally, where the source we have used follows conventional style we have stayed faithful to the original.

The stories are not presented entirely chronologically, as might seem logical, because we wanted to present them still grouped together in the collections in which they originally appeared (or were intended by the author to appear). This presents few problems in the first three sections of the book, which cover, in order: childhood; adolescence and early adulthood; the late thirties, forties and fifties. But the final section is a miscellany of individual pieces which cover periods throughout his life, and in one case before it. The section is broadly chronological, but individual stories deal with periods already covered in the other collections, and within the section stories which it seems natural to place together have been, even where that interferes with the strict chronology of events.

We would like to thank Paul Willetts for his invaluable help in the preparation of this volume.

Soho pub scene, drawing by Ruth Willetts, c. 1952. Courtesy of Paul Willetts.

Introduction
Paul Willetts

FEW SIGNIFICANT TWENTIETH-CENTURY WRITERS HAVE LED A stranger, more bohemian existence than the flamboyant, self-destructive Julian Maclaren-Ross. Like Jack Kerouac and Charles Bukowski, whose lives were comparably chaotic, he used his adventures as the basis for much of his work. Despite the abundant problems he faced, not least alcoholism, debt, homelessness and drug-induced psychosis, he maintained an impressive literary output. This encompassed short stories, novels, memoirs, criticism, translations, screenplays, parodies, radio drama and essays on popular culture, his productivity contradicting the myth of him as a bar-room dilettante who devoted less energy to writing than to talking about it. As you'd expect from someone so prolific in so many genres, someone whose precarious finances frequently compelled him to write with exceptional rapidity, his work *is* uneven, but the best of it matches, and from time to time surpasses, anything produced by his more celebrated contemporaries. No wonder, then, that his writing garnered often lavish praise from prominent figures on the London literary scene, among them Evelyn Waugh, Graham Greene, Cyril Connolly, Anthony Powell and John Betjeman, who believed that he possessed 'genius'.

Many of the personality traits that made his life so difficult can be traced back to other members of his extraordinary, widely dispersed family. His nomadic mother was the child of an Anglo-Indian officer in the British army who served not only on the subcontinent but also in Burma and Africa, later staving off bankruptcy by producing a series of hair-raising memoirs of life as a soldier and big-game hunter. Maclaren-Ross's similarly rootless father hailed from a wealthy part-Scottish, part-Cuban family who owned a shipping-line as well as plantations in Cuba and the southern states of America. Yet Maclaren-Ross himself was born in the far from exotic surroundings of suburban south London where, during the summer of 1912, his parents had lodgings. In tribute to the midwifery skills of their landlady Mrs McLaren, his parents baptised him James McLaren Ross.

JULIAN MACLAREN-ROSS COLLECTED MEMOIRS

Over the next few years, supported by the income from his paternal grandfather's sizeable investments, he and his parents made their home in a succession of south-coast seaside resorts. While they were living in Bournemouth, they were joined by his much older sister, who had been away at school, and his brother, who had been in the army. Unfortunately, his cosy family life was disrupted by his sister's elopement to Canada and his brother's death from tuberculosis.

In 1921 his father transplanted what remained of the family to the French Riviera, where they had relatives and where they'd be able to enjoy a much higher standard of living. Instead of enrolling the young James—routinely addressed as 'Jimmy'—in an English-speaking school, his father insisted on him joining the French education system. As a result, he was soon bilingual. But his education ended at the age of only sixteen when, following an argument with a teacher, he was expelled from a school in Paris. He then returned to live with his parents on the Riviera, where he acquired a taste for its thriving café society, devotees of which ranged from French aristocrats to penniless White Russian exiles. Fixated by Oscar Wilde, who had moved in the same circles as his father, he adopted the outmoded sartorial style of an 1890s fop. Besides sporting a malacca cane and a long cigarette-holder, he dropped his baptismal christian name in favour of the more suave 'Julian'. It was an integral part of the process of reinventing himself as a droll, imperturbable dandy.

Already arousing his parents' disapproval by harbouring ambitions to become either a painter or a writer, he felt that he could only attain his goals by returning to England. Towards the end of 1933, he left behind his parents and, thanks to an allowance from his paternal grandfather, settled in Bognor Regis, scene of a brief, idyllic childhood interlude. By mid-1935 or thereabouts, he had succumbed to the lure of London. It was then that he made his earliest forays into the louche world of Soho's pubs and clubs, with which he would become associated. There he courted a struggling actress. Still no closer to realising his creative ambitions, he married her and took her back to Bognor, where his elderly, ailing parents were ensconced. But the marriage foundered after about six months.

The demoralised Maclaren-Ross—as he had taken to calling himself, the double-barrelled surname accentuating his haughty persona— sought solace by lodging with a sympathetic, artistically inclined married couple whom he'd befriended. They encouraged him to concentrate on his writing. As well as producing short stories, he penned innovative radio plays, a couple of which were purchased by the BBC.

His life was, however, thrown into disarray by the sudden termination of his allowance at the beginning of 1938. To support himself, he worked as a door-to-door vacuum-cleaner salesman, his choice of job influenced by its potential as literary raw material. That same year he befriended Graham Greene, about whom he would later produce a vibrant memoir. Inadvertently highlighting the fundamental untrustworthiness of a genre in which supposed facts can be warped by flawed memory and the need to tell a good story, he claimed that Greene was responsible for giving him the idea of writing about his antics as a salesman.

Sacked by Electrolux and then Hoover, he ended up working as a gardener, defiantly clad in his foppish costume while he mowed lawns. When that venture culminated in failure, he drew unemployment benefit.

Not long after the Second World War had begun, he succeeded in selling one of his short stories—entitled 'A Bit of a Smash in Madras'—to *Horizon*, the influential new magazine. When the story appeared in the June 1940 issue, its use of obscenities toned down, it made a strong impression on readers such as V.S. Pritchett, who found its colonial Indian backdrop so convincing that he assumed Maclaren-Ross must have been writing from experience. On the strength of 'A Bit of a Smash in Madras', the firm of Jonathan Cape offered to publish a collection of his stories. Before Maclaren-Ross could seize this important opportunity, he was conscripted into the army.

Diagnosed with a chronic knee problem that rendered him a liability on the parade ground, he was consigned to clerical duties in a sequence of drab coastal garrisons. From January 1942 onwards, he channelled his frustrations into a stream of atmospheric, often wryly amusing short stories about life in the army, sending up bureaucracy and incompetence. By using fictional techniques to present factual material, these stories anticipated the so-called New Journalism of the 1960s, epitomised by Hunter S. Thompson's *Hell's Angels*. Though Maclaren-Ross's army stories were usually written in laconic, vernacular, first-person prose, indebted to American writers such as Ernest Hemingway, Dashiell Hammett, James M. Cain and Damon Runyon, they captured the distinctive rhythms of English speech. In the words of the future literary critic Anthony Cronin, who encountered them as a schoolboy, they were 'so spare and unerring as to constitute, in however small a way, almost a new kind of writing'. By the end of the year, they were a widely read feature of *English Story*, *Lilliput*, and other high-circulation literary magazines that were flourishing in wartime conditions. They were to exert a far-reaching, if seldom acknowledged influence on English fiction, popularising the demotic way of writing that would, several decades afterwards, appear ubiquitous. So instantly identifiable was Maclaren-Ross's deceptively casual style that it even became the subject for a parody in *Pie*, a well-known literary quarterly.

During August 1942, he was commissioned by John Lehmann, editor of *Penguin New Writing*, to produce a documentary account of his day-to-day life as a Despatch Clerk in Felixstowe for the magazine's 'Report Today' section. The result was a vivid, melancholy piece called 'Are You Happy In Your Work', the revised version of which is included here. When Lehmann declined to publish it, a rival editor came to the rescue.

Maclaren-Ross's reputation as a rising literary star failed to offset his growing disillusionment with the army, which hadn't, he felt, allowed him to make a meaningful contribution to the war effort. He responded by deserting from the depot in Southend where he was stationed. With the aid of Scotland Yard, he was tracked down and arrested. Slung into a military prison, he suffered a breakdown, prompting the authorities to transfer him to a psychiatric hospital just outside Birmingham, where his suitability for a court martial could be assessed. After three nightmarish months there, he was sentenced to twenty-eight days in the army's tough Detention Barrack at Colchester. On his release, he was sent back to Southend to await his imminent discharge from the military.

It wasn't until August 1943 that he resumed civilian life and headed for London, where he'd already found accommodation. Assisted by a friend, he landed a job as a screenwriter for a company producing short, government-funded propaganda films. His boss assigned him to work in tandem with the poet Dylan Thomas, who became a frequent drinking partner. Maclaren-Ross soon established himself as a conspicuous figure in the Wheatsheaf, a fashionable bohemian pub located to the north of Oxford Street in the area known at that stage as 'North Soho'. It was a district that would later be dubbed 'Fitzrovia' in honour of the nearby Fitzroy Tavern's former pre-eminence. Dressed in either a camel-hair coat or an astrakhan-collared alternative, together with a pale suit and brightly patterned tie, augmented by a cane, cigarette-holder, snuff-box and dark glasses, Maclaren-Ross staked out his favourite spot at the bar. From there, he routinely held forth to a crowd of acolytes, attracted by his growing renown, vaguely Latin good looks, and outlandish costume—part fin-de-siècle dandy, part Riviera playboy, part Hollywood gangster.

Only a few months after he had been hired as a screenwriter, the company employing him folded. He was temporarily saved from penury by an advance payment from Jonathan Cape for *The Stuff to Give the Troops*, a collection of his army stories which went on to enjoy both critical and commercial success. Once the advance ran out, he tried to raise money from Jonathan Cape for another book, the company's refusal precipitating what was to be the first of many bust-ups with publishers. He was then forced to sell the rights to a second book of short stories, subsequently titled *Better Than a Kick in the Pants*, to a small, recently founded firm for a knockdown price. He also sold *Bitten by the Tarantula*, a sub-standard, nostalgia-tinged novella written earlier in the war, to André Deutsch, who had just set up his own imprint. So convinced was Deutsch by the commercial potential of Maclaren-Ross's writing that further advance payments were handed over for the rights to a full-length novel and a collection of short stories. But Maclaren-Ross's fondness for drinking and expensive hotels, where the management would sometimes be forced to impound his laundry in lieu of payment, ensured that the cash didn't last long. He was now spending so much time in the Wheatsheaf both at lunchtime and in the evenings that his writing had to be squeezed into the early hours, tiredness held at bay by copious quantities of powerful amphetamines.

By the time the war ended, Maclaren-Ross had, as John Lehmann put it, 'already established a reputation, not only as a wit and a character, but as the author of some brilliant short stories... Everything seemed within his grasp, and he was tipped as one of the most promising young authors, likely to make his mark in films... and on the air as well.' His boozy, spendthrift way of life was, however, beginning to undermine his burgeoning literary career. To satisfy his incessant need for ready cash, he took on a flurry of journalistic assignments, demonstrating his versatility as a writer. For *Penguin New Writing*, he produced 'Second Lieutenant Lewis', a sensitive memoir of his fleeting friendship with Alun Lewis, the Welsh poet and short-story writer, whom he'd met while stationed in Felixstowe. What's more, he provided the magazine with four perceptive, ground-breaking essays on the cinema, covering topics such as American film noir and the work of Alfred Hitchcock. Meanwhile, *Better Than a Kick in the Pants* and *Bitten by the Tarantula* were published, the latter chalking up substantial sales. But its commercial impact was limited by Deutsch's inability to secure additional supplies of stringently rationed paper on which to print a rapid second edition.

Lack of money and amphetamine-induced paranoia making him more prickly than ever, Maclaren-Ross clashed with André Deutsch. Before he could find a new publisher, he was obliged to fulfil his contract by supplying Deutsch with the promised novel. He decided to rework the manuscript of a book he'd been writing about his days as a vacuum-cleaner salesman. When he revealed his plans to Deutsch, he was offered another advance. Holed up with his much younger girlfriend in a vast, luxurious hotel overlooking Russell Square, he spent the summer of 1946 sculpting the material into *Of Love and Hunger*, a tragi-comic masterpiece in which his alter ego becomes entangled in an affair with the glamorous wife of a friend. Shortly after he had delivered the finished manuscript, his publisher released *The Nine Men of Soho*, his third collection of stories. As the title implies, many of the stories were about the bohemian milieu which he knew so well, yet the book also featured other characteristically autobiographical pieces set else-where. The collection was padded with 'My Father was Born In Havana', a jokey, surprisingly accurate description of his colourful antecedents, their true indentities concealed behind pseudonyms. In her review for *The Tatler and Byestander*, Elizabeth Bowen proclaimed that Maclaren-Ross was a 'writer due for the first rank'.

He was, nonetheless, still afflicted by recurrent financial problems. These forced him to neglect his long-term plans as a novelist in pre-ference for projects that would yield short-term cash dividends. Through a friend at the BBC, he obtained work as a bit-part actor in radio drama. And he accepted a commission to translate Raymond Queneau's *Pierrot mon ami*. But he soon spent the fee. At that point in mid-1947 he was bailed out by his old friend Graham Greene, who was the Managing Director of Eyre & Spottiswoode, a well-established publishing house. For the rights to Maclaren-Ross's long-mooted novel based on the crimes of the 1930s German serial killer Eugen Weidmann, Greene stumped up a generous advance. While Maclaren-Ross laboured over the novel, *Of Love and Hunger* was published. Its appearance elicited some enthusiastic reviews, notably from Anthony Powell, who bracketed it with the latest books by Patrick Hamilton and Scott Fitzgerald. Again, its healthy but potentially huge sales were restricted by paper-rationing.

Such was Maclaren-Ross's imprudent extravagance that he was running out of money by December of that year. With his serial-killer novel still unfinished, his faith in it dwindling, he found work first as an anonymous book reviewer for the *Times Literary Supplement*, then as a screenwriter on an adaptation of a 1916 bestselling weepie, set in the snowbound Canadian wilderness. His screenwriting assignment proved so unsuitable that he recruited a friend to pen the majority of the film, later released as *The Naked Heart*.

The new decade, which he would dismiss as 'a decade I could well have done without', began no more promisingly than its predecessor had ended. He combined book reviewing with a discouraging stint as a script doctor on a creaky British B-feature called *Four Days*. By 1951, financial necessity had compelled him to accept more screenwriting work, this time providing an updated, never-to-be-produced adaptation of Robert Louis Stevenson's *The Suicide Club*. On completing that, he managed to persuade the publisher Hamish Hamilton to stump up an advance for a fictionalised version of his experiences in the film industry. But his plans were stymied by an attack of writers' block, not helped by psychological problems stemming from his prolonged dependence on amphetamines to help him work, often for marathon spells.

In a bid to regain lost literary momentum, he switched from fiction to non-fiction. Not that it's always easy to differentiate between his contributions to each genre. During the late summer of 1952, he began a childhood memoir, focusing on his itinerant life from birth until the age of ten. To this he gave the title *The Weeping and the Laughter*, a quotation from the Decadent poet Ernest Dowson, also used in *Laura*, one of Maclaren-Ross's favourite movies. Resisting the temptation to leave the flat he shared with his latest youthful girlfriend, who had been accompanying him on his wanderings since 1949, Maclaren-Ross worked so relentlessly on the book that he'd finished it by the penultimate week of September. Yet there's no hint of haste in its elegant, serpentine sentences, which contrast with the laconic style of so much of his previous work.

The book represented a broadening of his literary range, affording readers a sustained view of the wistful, tender, and unexpectedly vulnerable side of his personality, sometimes glimpsed through the flippant façade of his army stories. Nowhere is this more evident than in the touching postscript to the section about the period when he and his family were living in a rented house on the outskirts of Bournemouth. 'Looking back,' he wrote, 'it is not surprising that with the passage of time I should recall that house so clearly when other places I've lived in since have faded in memory: for there I first made acquaintance with the few interests, both work and play, that were to absorb me throughout my adult life ... even, in a rudimentary form, with that game for two players called love, in which, in after years, I was always to be the ultimate loser.'

Like so many of his other memoirs, *The Weeping and the Laughter* is punctuated by references to incidents that appear more fictional than factual. Despite their improbability, they can, whenever possible, usually be verified. Take the example of his shady Uncle Bertie: in a typically casual aside, Maclaren-Ross refers to his uncle, who appears elsewhere in this collection, being involved in 'a case that achieved international publicity'. The case stemmed from a breach of the Official Secrets Act, resulting in Uncle Bertie and an unnamed Syrian being sentenced to a spell of hard labour in Malta.

Because Maclaren-Ross had already alienated most of the leading publishers, he was forced to sell *The Weeping and the Laughter* to a small firm, devoid of the distribution and marketing muscle that would enable the book to reach the audience that it deserved. In the interval between delivering the manuscript and its publication, he kept himself afloat by working on scripts for the newly created independent television channel, as well as on essays and book reviews. He also worked on the first in a series of literary parodies for *Punch* which were admired by P.G. Wodehouse, William Faulkner and Malcolm Muggeridge, who regarded him 'as the best living parodist'.

When *The Weeping and the Laughter* was released in March 1953, it received a fulsome reception, bringing him recognition as 'one of the most gifted writers of his generation'. But its disappointing sales triggered a bitter dispute with his publisher. Over the ensuing months, he wrote two pieces for *Punch*. Of these, 'Bop'—a waspish account of a trip to a be-bop club—was the first to appear in print. Unlike Colin MacInnes, author of *Absolute Beginners* and fellow Soho-ite, who was fascinated by London's embryonic youth culture, Maclaren-Ross despised its conformity. His evocation of the be-bop club, patronised by young, black-clad existentialists is a witty forerunner of a comparable scene in *The Rebel*, one of two feature films starring the comedian Tony Hancock.

Maclaren-Ross's next memoir, written for *Punch*, was called 'In Their Black Books'. It's a slight, sketchy piece about an occasion on which he'd been mistakenly arrested, his reference to being 'a marked man' betraying a whiff of the paranoia that periodically threatened to engulf him. Along with some of his short fiction, 'In Their Black Books' probably started life as a bar-room anecdote, trotted out on numerous occasions until it was ready to be set down on paper.

Undeterred by the commercial failure of *The Weeping and the Laughter*, Maclaren-Ross was planning a sequel entitled *The Rites of Spring*. He envisaged it forming part of a four-volume sequence. Courtesy of a commission from *Encounter*, the magazine co-edited by the poet Stephen Spender, he was able to finance the composition of a lengthy chapter about his early days at school in France, presided over by a stern, autocratic Catholic priest. This continued the tone and style of *The Weeping and the Laughter*. On its publication in December 1953, it appeared under the title of 'Monsieur L'Abbé: A Memoir'. Just prior to that, Maclaren-Ross persuaded BBC radio to fund the writing of a chapter about the bullying that had flourished at that same school. He called it 'The Gondolier of Death'. Entertaining and poignant though it is, the piece was never broadcast.

His disappointment over *The Weeping and the Laughter* was compounded by the unforeseen departure of his girlfriend, with whom he had enjoyed a semblance of domestic stability. Deprived of her influence, the impoverished and indebted Maclaren-Ross returned to his previous hotel-hopping existence, but the hotels in question were no longer the grand establishments he had formerly inhabited. He raised some much-needed money by obtaining a commission from John Lehmann's recently launched *London Magazine*. The commission was for 'A Visit to the Villa Edouard Sept', another section from *The Rites of Spring*, in this case describing an ill-fated 1930 invitation to the home of the notorious Frank Harris. Out of what must have been an embarrassing, not to say painful, incident, Maclaren-Ross fashioned a delightful, self-effacing memoir. In his later incarnation as a successful radio playwright, he would dramatise 'A Visit to the Villa Edouard Sept' for BBC radio, the programme's producer casting him in the rôle of his own cantankerous father. No recording of his performance has, regrettably, survived.

Still floundering in the absence of his girlfriend, he retreated to Oxford in August 1954. Initially, he stayed with close friends, his alcoholism, belligerence and egomania making him an awkward guest. He then moved into a nearby bedsit, the rent on which he paid by not only writing more magazine articles and television scripts, but also by translating Georges Simenon's *Maigret and the Burglar's Wife*. In between all this, he managed to complete 'The Bird Man', an account of his boyhood acquaintance with an eccentric bird-breeder who lived in an abandoned windmill. It was, like the Frank Harris memoir, destined to form part of the follow-up to *The Weeping and the Laughter*, a volume that was never completed. On the evidence of the surviving sections, brought together here for the first time, *The Rites of Spring* would have been a worthy successor.

From Oxford, Maclaren-Ross made periodic trips to London, during which he'd revisit old haunts, meet friends and call on people who had commissioned work. Drinking in the Wheatsheaf one afternoon in November 1955, he bumped into George Orwell's flirtatious, once-beautiful widow, Sonia, whom he'd known years earlier when she was working as an assistant on *Horizon*. He developed an instant obsession with her which she briefly encouraged. Soon he was stalking her and contemplating a move back to London in order to be near her. With the proceeds from the sale of *The Funny Bone*, a compilation of his recent work, he bankrolled his return to London at the beginning of 1956. To avoid the bailiffs, creditors and taxmen pursuing him, he switched addresses on a regular basis. As his financial position worsened, he sought help from friends who provided him with accommodation. He was even reduced to sleeping on a park-bench and in the waiting-room at Euston Station. Always alert to the literary potential of his experiences, however unpleasant, he described his sojourn at Euston in 'Some Time I Shall Sleep Out'. He submitted this remarkably unself-pitying piece to the London *Evening Standard*, but its rejection resulted in it remaining unpublished during his lifetime.

The downward trajectory of his career was paralleled by his deterio-rating mental health, which culminated in the belief that his personality had been taken over by the fictional character of the villain from *Dr Jekyll and Mr Hyde*. In keeping with this rôle, his continued fixation with Sonia Orwell led him to contemplate her murder. Luckily, he was distracted by a reciprocal infatuation with the tearaway niece of the publisher Leonard Woolf. Together they dodged from hotel to hotel, one jump ahead of their creditors, their troubled romance punctuated by rows, reconciliations and, for Maclaren-Ross, further periods of homelessness.

Midway through the first summer of their relationship, *The Funny Bone* was published. It gave him a chance to salvage some of his literary journalism, along with various uncollected stories and memoirs. The memoirs consisted of 'Second Lieutenant Lewis', 'The Bird Man', 'In

Their Black Books', 'The Gondolier of Death', 'Old Ginger', 'Bop', and 'Adventures in Film', the concluding section of which told the story of his earlier stint as a script-doctor. In the wake of the book's publication, Maclaren-Ross received a writ from a barrister acting on behalf of H.E. Bates, one of the writers whose work he'd gently parodied. The case was heard in the High Court, where the judge censured the absent Maclaren-Ross.

Though he found steady employment as a journalist and as the scriptwriter on three low-budget films, not to mention a six-part radio series fictionalising his obsession with Sonia Orwell, he continued to be beset by money problems. These compelled him to take up residence in a Turkish bath in Russell Square, described with his usual precision and mordant wit in 'The Night Bathers'. The piece, which appeared in *Punch*, projects an appealing air of hardboiled resilience far removed from the vulnerability of *The Weeping and the Laughter*.

Just before the birth of his only child, he married his girlfriend and supported his family by cranking out popular, critically well-received radio plays, most of them thrillers, earning him the tag of 'radio's Alfred Hitchcock'. In addition to scripting these, he also acted in them and, on one occasion, crooned an accompanying song. But his relationship with the BBC was wrecked by his repeated failure to fulfil commissions for which he'd already been paid. As one of his producers pointed out, he treated the BBC more like his bank than his employer.

At the start of the 1960s, he relaunched his career as a novelist with the novelisation of his first radio series, the ominously titled *Until the Day She Dies*. Sales of the book justified both a prompt reprint and a couple more such novelisations of his radio scripts, published as *The Doomsday Book* and *My Name Is Love*, the second of these harking back to his unrequited attraction to Sonia Orwell. For a novelist capable of producing *Of Love and Hunger*, these final novels, which steered his talent in an unsuitable direction, represent a feeble anti-climax.

After a catastrophic period in Brighton, heralding the end of his second marriage, he went back to London, where he resumed his old semi-destitute routine, protracted sessions of writing juxtaposed with afternoons and evenings in smokey pubs and drinking clubs. In the final months of 1962, the new editor of the prestigious *London Magazine* recruited him as a contributor. He supplied a string of astute articles on everything from Sexton Blake to American pulp fiction, for which he had a pioneering passion.

Most likely inspired by *A Moveable Feast*, Ernest Hemingway's reminiscences of bohemian Paris, Maclaren-Ross resolved to write his own memoirs of London in the 1940s. Since these were, appropriately enough, earmarked for serialisation in the *London Magazine*, he adopted the episodic format used to such good effect in *The Weeping and the Laughter*. Unsurprisingly, the chapter-plan for *Memoirs of the Forties* omitted any reference to the military psychiatric hospital where he'd been incarcerated, his failure to live up to his chosen self-image as a wisecracking Hollywood hard-man providing a source of enduring shame.

The first published instalment, depicting his friendship with Dylan Thomas, featured in the magazine's November 1964 edition. That same month, having celebrated the arrival of an unexpected royalty payment by guzzling a bottle of brandy, he suffered a fatal heart attack, his health eroded by years of stress, alcoholism, drug abuse and heavy smoking. Before he died, aged only fifty-two, he just had time to gulp a few parting words to his current girlfriend.

In the weeks leading up to his death, he had written thirteen of the planned thirty-eight chapters of *Memoirs of the Forties* which continued to appear in the *London Magazine*. Several of these focused on the Fitzrovian pub scene which he'd first sampled around thirty years earlier. Yet—presumably in pursuit of a neater, more self-contained and dramatic story—he merged his discovery of Fitzrovia with his account of an epic wartime pub-crawl led by the dissolute Singhalese poet, J.M. Tambimuttu. He was also guilty of other minor distortions and omissions, conveniently forgetting the private income that he'd enjoyed for most of the 1930s.

Had he lived to complete the book, it would have included potentially fascinating and revealing reminiscences of Anthony Powell, George Orwell, Nina Hamnett, Henry Green, Eric Ambler, Joyce Cary, Brian Howard and others. Even so, it provided what the critic John Davenport described as 'an unrivalled picture of those almost mythical 1940s'. Just under a year after his death, it was published in book form, minus the now restored epilogue to the chapter about Dylan Thomas, a supplementary selection of his other work compensating for the book's relative brevity.

Many of the people depicted in it complained about the way he'd caricatured them and about his perpetuation of certain apocryphal anecdotes, but the critics, V.S. Pritchett among them, applauded its re-creation of the period. Its vivacity, descriptive richness and novelistic use of dialogue make it an antecedent of the type of memoirs that would achieve such popularity in the 1990s. 'There is nothing else that so conveys the atmosphere of bohemia and fringe-literary London under the impact of war and its immediate hangover,' wrote one reviewer. 'The book is comic, nostalgic and at times even moving, all without the least sense of strain.'

Though his career as a writer had been brought to a premature but triumphant conclusion, Maclaren-Ross went on to enjoy a uniquely productive parallel career as the model for characters in other people's novels. During his lifetime, he had already provided the template for five thinly disguised characters. Death removing the threat of libel action, both Olivia Manning and Anthony Powell felt free to redeploy aspects of his bizarre life, idiosyncratic personality and sartorial panache in their work. While Manning transplanted him into her *Balkan Trilogy* as the impecunious, dandified Prince Yakimov, Anthony Powell famously cast him as the wayward writer X. Trapnel in *A Dance to the Music of Time*.

Without the need for such disguises, he has also made unforgettable appearances in the classic memoirs of many writers, notably Dan Davin and Anthony Cronin, both of whom portray him with appalled fascination. Again and again, he has been characterised as a tragic embodiment of bohemian excess, of squandered talent. Admittedly, he might have achieved a lot more had he been less self-destructive. But he still succeeded in leaving behind a substantial, varied, and influential body of work. His talents—admired by current writers as diverse as Michael Holroyd, Harold Pinter, Virginia Ironside, Jonathan Meades, Chris Petit and D.J. Taylor—can be best appreciated in *Of Love and Hunger*, his short stories, essays, parodies and memoirs. The *Collected Memoirs* offers an affecting and often amusing introduction to the life and work of a man whose literary gifts have tended to be eclipsed by the romantic allure of the self-image that he so energetically projected.

Paul Willetts
July 2004

THE WEEPING
AND THE LAUGHTER:
A CHAPTER OF AUTOBIOGRAPHY

For
Barbara
This part of my childhood

They are not long, the weeping and the laughter,
   Love and desire and hate:
I think they have no ~~prison~~ *portion* in us after
   We pass the gate.

They are not long, the days of wine and roses,
   Out of a misty dream
Our path emerges for a while, then closes
   Within a dream.

Ernest Dowson

AUTHOR'S NOTE

This is the first part of an autobiography. All the incidents which it contains are, perforce, factual; and I have attempted to tell the truth, to the best of my ability, throughout. To avoid, however, giving pain to persons figuring in these pages who may still be alive today, I have substituted fictitious names for those borne by the characters in real life: including, for the most part, members of my own family.

The book is concerned with my childhood alone: the more formative years of adolescence will be the subject of further volumes in the future.

J.M.-R.

The Coloured Alphabet

*   *   *

SOON AFTER MY BIRTH, WHICH TOOK PLACE AT MIDNIGHT AND during a thunderstorm, war broke out, and one of my earliest memories is of being snatched from my cot and carried out in my father's arms on to the lawn of our house at Ramsgate, just in time to see a German Zeppelin cast its shadow on the rooftop from the vast moonlit menace of the sky.

I am told that I crowed with glee and stretched out my hands towards that long bright silver cigar, but this I cannot confirm; I recall the sight vividly as one which afforded me considerable pleasure, but not my physical reactions to it. The Zeppelin did not appear in the least threatening: to represent, rather, the promise of a shining toy too large for me to handle at the age I was then but which, with luck, I might be given later. The immense stretch of emptiness above, on the other hand, was daunting as I stared up into those stars that blinked back at me a message which I could not read; the cold remote globe of the moon seemed to swim backwards through clouds out of the Zeppelin's way as it passed safely over, and perhaps the silent consternation of those grouped around me on the lawn communicated itself, for suddenly I set up a howl of terror.

A memory of this irrational fear may have left its mark, since I am increasingly a prey to fits of agoraphobia when confronted, alone, with large expanses of night sky in an open space, and when there is moonlight.

I was born with red hair. Later on this fell off and brown hair, which became progressively darker, took its place. My father had started life with auburn hair and my mother's was black, so presumably both parents were satisfied: though not always with my subsequent conduct.

3

Indeed there were times, as I grew older, when my father expressed the opinion that the Devil had got into me, and my mother that I took after my uncle Bertie: a relative (her brother, incidentally) for whom a bad end had frequently been predicted, and who did finally figure in a case that achieved international publicity.

I wish my early days could have been more exciting. My father had been born in Havana, as a baby he had been surrounded by tarantulas and vampire bats; my mother's birthplace was Calcutta: the sight of a rogue elephant trampling one of her brothers to death had been a highlight of her childhood, and later she lived on an island in the Azores dominated by a smoking volcano; I was born prosaically at South Norwood and have little but the Zeppelin to look back upon. As a very small boy even my diabolical instincts and rumoured resemblance to Uncle Bertie had not yet had time to develop, and certainly I did not attain to the heights of naughtiness previously scaled by my brother, who liked when little to lead my parents a dance by disappearing suddenly if taken for a walk, and had to be exercised on reins or strapped in a push-cart to combat this wanderlust; nor, like my sister, did I clear a path through crowds by the use of both elbows, or exclaim, when descending in a department-store lift, Oh Mummy are we going to Hell? Any such tendencies would in any case have been ruthlessly curbed by my Nanny, who was Belgian and whom I called Nana. She had an accent in speaking English not dissimilar from that of the French governess in *Uncle Silas*, if what she said were phonetically rendered, and though her disciplinary methods did not resemble those of this fictional prototype, they were at the same time quite severe enough to keep me in check. She also had a moustache which prickled unpleasantly when she kissed me; this did not happen often, luckily, as all demonstrations of affection were kept for public exhibition only: in private our relations were on a strictly practical plane.

In Ramsgate Nana had a gentleman-friend: he was a sergeant in some unit stationed nearby and had an even thicker moustache than Nana herself; only I knew of his existence and we used to meet him in parks and tea-shops when the rest of the family was not present. Consequently she was most distressed when a Zeppelin did in fact bomb our house and reduce it to ruins: this happened whilst we were on holiday elsewhere, but her narrow escape from death did not console Nana for her separation from the sergeant when we moved, temporarily, to a furnished house in another seaside town. She could of course have resigned her charge and remained behind, but she was prevented from doing so by her fear of my father, whom she always called 'Mon Capitaine': possibly her connection, by proxy, with the British army caused her to adopt this military form of address.

The new town, whose name I cannot now remember, had streets paved with cobblestones and leading down-hill; these streets were full of Belgian refugees whom, because they spoke Flemish among themselves, I mistook for German spies. Nana was not slow in correcting this error; she too spoke Flemish and carried on long conversations with her compatriots: they swapped atrocity stories by the hour, some of which (those not actually concerned with rape) were afterwards repeated to me, and I thus became familiar with the fabled cruelty of the Crown Prince, Nana's especial hate. I remember my indignation both at his sadism towards British soldiers and at the fact that by a baptismal coincidence he should have the same name and be called by the same diminutive as my own brother, now serving as a private in H.M. Forces, for he was a socialist and had insisted on enlisting in the ranks: a great disappointment to my father, coming at a time, too, when my brother's earlier choice of the priesthood as a career had seemed safely a thing of the past.

In the long wartime winter evenings, as the nursery light burnt low, Nana crouched at a table writing, I presume, to the sergeant; and in the mornings she would watch impatiently for the arrival of the postman. I watched with an equal anxiety, for Nana's attitude towards me was apt to vary from day to day according to whether or not a letter from the sergeant had arrived. The sergeant alas proved to be a less and less assiduous correspondent as time went on; restraints and punishments became more stringent during these periods of uncertainty, and worst of all Nana discovered the existence of a private fear of mine, which she used to hold over my head both as a guarantee of good behaviour and a means of enforcing her will.

This fear centred around a man called Nathan, who sold ice-cream for a living and was frequently to be seen pushing the machine which contained his wares about the cobbled, crooked streets of the town, which may possibly have been Teignmouth. There was nothing outwardly sinister about Nathan: in appearance he was gaunt, dark and hollow-eyed, with a faint look of Robert Louis Stevenson or Mischa Auer; the panic which the sight of him engendered in me went deeper than that, and it was what he represented rather than the man himself that was the cause of it.

A short time before there had been a case reported in all the papers which dealt with the arrest and conviction of a group known as the Hokey-Pokey Men. Hokey-Pokey was a sort of miniature barber's pole made of ice-cream and striped in different colours according to the various flavours which went to its composition, and the Hokey-Pokey Men were Italians domiciled in London responsible for its manufacture. Police had descended suddenly upon their factory, which proved to be a basement in Soho, and the raid disclosed that Hokey-Pokey was mixed in chamber-pots which had not been disinfected after use; many children had developed typhoid fever after consuming the ice-cream thus manufactured, and the prison sentence imposed upon the Hokey-Pokey Men was severe. I could not read at this time, but somehow I became acquainted with the details of the affair; my sister may have read the newspaper report aloud, anyway I cut out a press photograph of a Hokey-Pokey Man standing beside his tricycle; and though he in no way resembled Nathan, the horror and obscure sense of shame with which the whole incident filled me were now symbolised in the person of this latter, whose customer, before the case, I had often been. I was also terrified lest some well-meaning grown-up should stop him and buy me an ice which, being at that time very polite, I would be obliged to eat in order to avoid hurting the feelings of the donor, and consequently die of typhoid. I therefore made every effort to escape encountering Nathan, and was grateful for the bell which he rang to herald his approach; for though sweat broke out on me at the sound of it, the warning it gave considerably lessened the chances of meeting him face-to-face.

Unfortunately I made the mistake of preserving the cutting and the photograph, which I hid in an oak chest in the hall and used sometimes to produce, shivering, from its hiding-place when no one was looking, to remind myself, perhaps, of the ever-present danger. Nana caught me doing this one day; in next to no time she had extracted the whole story, and triumphantly threatened that, if I did not promise instant obedience in the future, she would not only take me direct to Nathan, but would also buy me ice-cream, and Hokey-Pokey, if it could still be obtained, at that. This threat was often reiterated when letters from the sergeant became more and more infrequent and Nana's nerves were increasingly on edge: why I did not go to my parents and make a clean breast of my fears is quite incomprehensible to me now; I can only say that the recollection of my stupidity does not make me any more tolerant of those preposterous situations which arise in films and radio plays when characters given cause for alarm fail to take their problems to the proper quarter, i.e. the police.

Then the sergeant's letters ceased altogether, enquiries elicited the information that he'd been posted overseas; Nana was sure that he would write from France but he did not. I found that to whistle 'Mademoiselle from Armentières' at this time caused Nana to fly at once (as I did not put it then) off the handle, but I found also that the consequences were not worth the brief satisfaction I derived from seeing her transformed, at a second's notice, from her starched, severe calm into a foreignly shrieking fury; corporal punishment was not resorted to, as my father disapproved strongly of that and never, himself, struck any of us, but there were other, equally effective ways of subduing me when Nathan was not immediately at hand; and one of these, twice put into practice during the first days of the sergeant's defection, was to drop me bodily into the huge black leather trunk inseparable from my parents' travels, and close down the lid. This trunk stood in the hall not far from the oak chest which was the repository of the Hokey-Pokey cutting, and a few seconds' immersion in the musty dark of its interior were sufficient to reduce me to an outward state of sobbing contrition, though inwardly I harboured thoughts of revenge. Incidentally these experiences should have induced claustrophobia, but in fairness to Nana I must state that they did not, since, as I've already indicated, it is the reverse rather that I suffer from.

Nana herself, however, had a complex: it was arachnoid in origin, and my sister Carol shared it to an even greater degree, being able to detect the presence of a spider on entering a room in which one lurked otherwise invisible, as Lord Roberts of Kandahar was said to do with cats. I often brooded on the possibility of introducing a spider into Nana's presence but they did not seem easy to come by; and then one day my opportunity of getting even was presented to me, as it were, on a platter.

I was seated on my pot at the time. Nana always burnt a form of incense called Ruban de Bruges in the nursery when I was engaged in doing what she euphemistically described by a sound best rendered as hein-hein, and she was bending, with her back turned, over the saucer in which the incense was ignited, when, glancing idly about, I observed a magnificent specimen of the type known as Drain Spider on the wall directly above my head. Squatting there, spreading the shadow of its long hairy legs, it seemed to me as large as those tarantulas which I had never seen but which figured so prominently in my father's early life in Havana. My cry of triumph made Nana jump round; it so happened that Carol chose this moment to make an entrance; the gesture which I sketched, and the gleeful yell accompanying it, startled the spider, which got into motion with a speed of which, from its original immobility, it had seemed incapable; and the upshot was, that when the women had finished screaming and climbed down from their respective chairs, I spent so protracted a spell in the trunk that on re-emergence I had to be given sal volatile to soothe me and prevent my parents, shut-off by a green baize door from this part of the building, from overhearing the din we made and arriving with awkward questions on the scene. My own clamour was caused by rage rather than fear, for I felt myself unjustly treated: after all, I had not imported the spider but merely drawn attention to its presence, and I resented particularly my sister's participation in my punishment, since I had not meant to frighten her and she had been in favour of sitting on the lid of the trunk. I remember that I rejected all attempts at reconciliation, and lay awake for some time grinding the few teeth I had at that age; my only satisfaction was that Nana too would spend a disturbed night, for she couldnt be certain that the spider would not reappear, suddenly, from its secret bolthole.

Unbeknown to me, however, Nana's days with us were numbered. It was her passion for atrocity stories that finally earned her the sack. This had increased lately, and there was perhaps a hope in the back of her mind that the sergeant might fall into the hands of Little Willie himself and suffer as a punishment for his faithlessness some of the tortures which she now seemed to take an active relish in recounting, though I may be doing her an injustice here.

My father by contrast hated all talk of Frightfulness, as they called it then; he discouraged even in wartime anything likely to promote hatred between nations and would not countenance the use of the term Boche nor allow me to draw the Kaiser's head on the shell of my breakfast-egg and then smash it in with a spoon, as other children did. This attitude, combined with his dislike of all militarism, which as an ex-officer wounded in the Boer War he felt entitled to express whenever he liked, was apt to be misunderstood when aired in public, and led to his half-strangling a man in a bus who accused him of being unpatriotic and pro-German. Nana naturally was aware of his views, having already received more than one warning in this connection, but he so seldom entered the nursery that she felt comparatively safe within its walls, forgetting that my father, like many big men, and despite his limp, could move silently when he chose and she was in the middle of one of her favourite stories, in which Little Willie, wearing of course the full-dress uniform of the Death's Head Hussars, was about to blind ceremoniously a group of Allied prisoners selected for his personal attention—the soldiers were all set, stoically, for the sacrifice: the bayonet, or it may have been a sword, was being drawn from its scabbard—when a voice from the doorway cut the narrative short and brought Nana to her feet, rigid as though herself on parade.

My father spoke in French, which I did not at that time understand, but in a tone which left his meaning beyond doubt; and my mother, who had followed him into the room, moved anxiously forward, fearing perhaps that he might fall in a fit, as had happened many years before in France, when he'd observed, from an upstairs window, the butcher boy, delivering the joint, drop it accidentally in the dust and attempt to wipe it clean on the seat of his pants.

With a sweeping gesture of the hand that clutched his stick, and on which the veins, like those at his temples, showed darkly swollen, he set Nana's protestations aside and at the same time motioned my mother to remove me from the scene: so that to my disgust I was unable to witness the sequel, nor was I allowed to watch Nana's departure, which took place half an hour later and without saying good-bye. These disappointments, however, did not prevent me from indulging, first, in a war-dance which brought plaster down from the ceiling and, sub-sequently, in behaviour that caused my father to advance his theory of demoniacal possession; for I had it firmly in mind that Nana's discomfiture had come about because of her recent harshness to me: a sort of divine judgment or retribution such as I'd often been threatened with but which had recoiled, through her wickedness, upon her own head. Providence, I felt, was on my side—also I knew that nannies were scarce just then, and that a new one would not easily be found to replace her. So it proved, and a housemaid, bribed with a promise of bigger wages, was brought in to cope, but in my new mood of emancipation I speedily disposed of her, for she lacked knowledge of Nathan and was too timid to try the trunk; moreover she smelt, and to tell her so reduced her easily to tears.

My sister, a tougher proposition altogether, and much against her will, was then assigned to take charge of me: it'll occupy the girl's mind, my father said; give her something to do.

For some time past my sister, too, had been causing parental anxiety. Her flat refusal to compromise with conventional standards had led to her expulsion from two schools and a convent: 'wilful' and 'wayward' had been the adjectives used most frequently, in head-mistresses' reports, to describe her; now she was seventeen, and sat about the house all day long, devouring milk chocolate by the block and sensational novels by the score. A close companionship had existed between Carol and my brother, whom she adored: there was but a few years difference in age instead of the big gap which separated me from them both, and now without him she felt lost; the move had also uprooted her from her friends, and she was in no mood to make new ones at the moment. Then, too, in Ramsgate she had been responsible for the arrest of a spy, and this had gone considerably to her head.

The spy was one of the sort who by flashing lights signals to the enemy: Carol, who'd seen him at it had at first been laughed at by the local authorities; then, furiously, had lodged a complaint higher up, which led to investigation by the War Office and the apprehension of the German agent, whose real name proved to be Schwob: we were not told whether they shot him, but Carol always hoped so, which was not unnatural, since he, or someone like him, may have brought about the eventual destruction of our home. Anyhow it was all very exciting, and Carol now felt herself cut out for a career in the Intelligence Department, like those beautiful pantherine women in the books she read; but the Department showed no desire, so far, to make use of her services, and she often talked of enlisting, as a makeshift, in the Waacs or applying for a job in a munitions factory: both of which projects were frowned upon and, indeed, actively opposed by my father.

Altercations with him became at this period an almost daily occurrence, a constant bone of contention being a béret of pillarbox red, to which Carol was particularly attached, but which my father thought too flamboyant. it therefore disappeared one day, and Father, accused point-blank of having confiscated it, stroked his beard blandly and declined to commit himself. My sister then swore that she'd go hatless until the scarlet béret, or one identical with it, was returned to her. So far a stalemate had been reached, and Carol strode about the town from sweetshop to circulating library, her cloud of hair blowing out in the breeze to match the tight canary-yellow jumper which had been selected for that reason and was her favourite at the time.

Over the question of wearing stays she also proved adamant in her refusal; and my mother, who still owned a waist little larger than my father's collar measurement, was grieved, for she felt that her daughter was letting herself run to seed; though the crowd of admiring men who followed Carol about the streets, undeterred by the contemptuous rebuffs with which their advances were received, did not appear to be of this opinion. Now that I was obliged to share my sister's sorties, I became extremely popular with these gallants, who sidled up and offered me gifts as a means of approach to Carol whenever she left me waiting outside Timothy White's, an establishment from which I'd been barred for scraping my shoes on the polished library floor. These perquisites I always accepted, though holding out in all fairness no hope of return: for although Carol strictly disapproved, in principle, of my doing so, she was not above sharing in the spoils if these happened to be, as she called them, chocs.

The admirers were for the most part uniformed young men on leave, but there was one more sinister figure who dogged us from a distance, never actually approaching but raising his hat and smiling toothily if we glanced back at him. This was an elderly gentleman, wearing spats and, in wet weather, galoshes, who was known to us as the Old Civvy, to distinguish him from the others. Carol felt she could cope with the servicemen, and indeed did so, as I've said, devastatingly; but the Civvy was an altogether different cup of tea, belonging as he evidently did to the category of roués: notoriously dangerous, according to all accounts, and capable of anything, even assault. His stealthy rubber-shod pursuit and the ingratiating gleam of his teeth, obviously artificial, began to prey on my sister's nerves, and gradually he became to her what Nathan still was to me.

My father, called at last into consultation, said grimly that he'd soon put a stop to that, and took up his stance in a doorway close to the spot where the Civvy was most likely to appear. For once we dawdled to lead the quarry on, and it so happened that the Civvy, seeing us at a standstill, chose this morning to open a frontal attack by commenting, with what surely seemed a frightful leer, upon the state of the weather. My father stepped out from his hiding-place with a menacing cough, his stick poised suggestively; the Civvy whipped round smiling: and instead of a red-handed roué, Father found himself confronting our landlord, Mr Foxe, who having recognised my sister (though he was not known, by sight, to either of us) thought it only polite to acknowledge her whenever they met, and finally to pass the time of day. There can be little doubt as to the innocence of his intentions, but it was an embarrassing moment for all concerned; and in order that Mr Foxe should not interpret correctly the angle of his stick, my father was forced to pretend he had been scratching his neck with the ivory handle of it: a gesture in which he would not ordinarily have indulged, and the outcome of the incident was that Mr Foxe was asked to tea.

He accepted, and proved himself on the very first occasion to be a fearful bore, but one extremely hard to get rid of, since after all we were living in his house. He came to tea, he came to lunch, he came to dinner: he was a widower and compared my mother to his own dear spouse, now laid, alas, to rest. My sister, who was not compared with his daughter, at present in the Land Army, and who still found his intent sunken stare disturbing, was able to escape the worst of it by pleading me as an excuse: but this meant she was obliged to spend the evening trapped in the nursery, for the only way out lay through territory expansively occupied by Mr Foxe. I welcomed this situation, for like our landlord I was lonely: but I fear that Carol found my company an almost equal strain, since much of my time was spent in teasing her, as far as I dared without risking the trunk, unmercifully.

I'd become tired, lately, of my toys: most of these had been, formerly, of German manufacture, but now with the war we had Japanese goods instead, which I did not find up to the mark: the heads of the tin soldiers came off too easily, the bricks were too light and failed to make a loud enough noise in falling when a fort built of them was bombed during a battle; the legs of the horses, too, were brittle and would not stand up to a cavalry charge. My oldest favourite was a model motor-car made in Berlin, with a miniature leather hood which could be raised or lowered at will, but this had disintegrated with age, and the new kind, which when wound up with a key ran in circles, were never as satisfactory, piling up, as they did, on the fringe of the carpet and overturning with a fizz of sharp wheels in which I caught my fingers painfully.

So, bored and at a loose end, forbidden to blow soap bubbles because of the mess they made, I embarked on a steady persecution of my sister, revolving chiefly around the fact that she now had to sleep in the nursery, which contained, of course, the spider, always present in spirit as a potent weapon in the war of nerves, though it never in reality reappeared during the rest of our stay, having probably been scared to death by the fuss which greeted its initial emergence. Carol had the trunk as a counter-measure, but the after-effects of this on me were so severe that she hesitated to employ it except when, driven to desperation after a long day, she wanted to curl up quietly on the bed with a book and a box of chocolates. I had the sense to respect her peace at such moments: though sometimes, since I could not read myself, I would plague her to read a passage aloud, a request rarely granted owing to the nature of the books she preferred.

It was nightmares which ultimately brought this period to a close. Both of us suffered from them and had to sleep with the light on; the worst of mine was concerned with an object which I called the Little Bit of Linoleum, and recurred roughly once a week. In shape it resembled a finger-stall or condom, and might really have been made out of rubber; as in a modern ghost-story, it did not do anything: the mere fact of its appearance was sufficient to bring me shrieking and sobbing out of my sleep, disturbing Carol who in all probability had just settled down to a dreamless respite from her own terrors.

Then I had a respite also; the Little Bit of Linoleum did not materialise for over a fortnight; on the other hand my sister had just read *Dracula*, and the result was such that on the first night my father had to be sent for: his comment, when he had calmed her down, being one of surprise; for having met Bram Stoker in the days when this author was Sir Henry Irving's manager, he found it strange that such a dim little man could write a book capable of giving a grown-up girl hysterics. Nonetheless, the effect of *Dracula*, like the flavour of the Spearmint gum that Carol had of late begun to chew, was a lasting one: to add to it all, my sister, once fully awake, began to insist that I join her in a search for the spider, slipper in hand; and since neither of us was getting any sleep, it was decided we should separate.

So my sister returned to her savage daydreams upstairs, flicking impatiently over the pages of *Sapper* and *Victoria Cross*, or consuming Mackintosh's Toffee-de-Luxe (Full Cream) as an alternative to Cadbury's Milk; and, as no nanny had yet answered our advertisement, it was my mother's turn to look after me in person.

My mother had only one valve to her heart. As a girl in Portugal she had been fond of deep-sea diving and swimming for long periods below the surface, to avoid the Portuguese men-of-war that infested these waters, and her condition had developed as a result. The men-of-war referred to above were not, by the way, an Iberian fleet, but a species of poisonous amoeba able, so Mother told me, to electrify the current in which they float; and the vivid description she gave of those iridescent jellies, trailing their glamour and terror through the tropical blue, a shoal of rainbow-coloured shock, remains with me still: though with time and distance I may well have got the details wrong.

My mother's girlhood in other ways too had been adventurous. Like my father she was much travelled. First there was India: my grandfather being a colonel in the Madras Staff Corps no doubt accounts for her birth in Calcutta, and she grew up in a family of five brothers, all of whom were now distributed in appropriately numbered corners of the earth; not including the one who'd died under the elephant's hoof, and who, incidentally, was believed by the natives to be a reincarnation of Buddha. Another brother, Uncle Harry, had been abducted as a child by an eagle, and carried off to its eyrie: this story was always a favourite of mine, as the protagonist at the time of his abduction must have been about my own age; the details elude me now, but his rescue was effected somehow, since he later reappeared, combating illicit diamond buyers in Kimberley, apparently unscathed by his early upbringing in the eagle's nest.

In India there was also another elephant, and this one could count. He was fed on chapattis, sort of pancakes made of flour and water, which I have often eaten since in Indian restaurants, though they strike me now as a surprisingly light diet for so large an animal. It may be for this reason that he counted them so carefully; of course the number of chapattis allotted to him was astronomical and he could only count in tens: but by tapping each one lightly with his trunk and using the metric system he arrived at a correct estimate, and then, satisfied, settled down to his meal. Unfortunately the boy who looked after him, perhaps it is called a *sais*, anyway he died, and the new one who took over was dishonest. He stole from the stack of chapattis, selling them on the side to other elephant-boys or perhaps eating them himself, not realising that his charge could reckon up the deficiency. Every day the elephant was given shorter and shorter measure; he counted and re-counted with growing bewilderment and anger, until one morning it was scarcely necessary to count at all, for the pile had been cut down brutally by half. When this happened, the elephant, who'd stood enough, backed his keeper against a convenient wall and by leaning his weight crushed the man flatter than a chapatti before help could be summoned: a sad end to this tale being that the accomplished beast was himself executed for taking the law, so to speak, into his own hands, instead of being exported to a circus, where his mathematical ability would probably have earned him a fortune.

Then there was a jackal. The jackal was mad and bit almost everybody in the village; this seemed to take place up-country; the natives who were bitten went mad in their turn and ran amok, whereupon my grandfather was called upon to shoot them down: a task he did not relish. He determined to shoot the jackal instead, but this was elusive, and none of the tricks which as a shikari he'd tried successfully on man-eating tigers seemed in this case to work. Finally, however, the jackal was lured into the open and despatched with two bullets, but in its death agony managed to sink its teeth in my grandfather's leg, he having incautiously approached, believing the brute to he dead. My grandfather gave himself up for lost: there was no medical man within miles; but luckily my grandmother, then the reigning Belle of Bangalore or some such place, happened upon the scene, and proved herself to be practical as well as pretty: for without further ado she sucked the poison from the wound, not contracting, I'm glad to say, hydrophobia in the process.

It must have been soon after this that the colonel was posted to Africa in the line of duty; and while he and his men fought the Masai and pygmies with poisoned arrows who infected their water-wells, his family embarked on a tour of the East. During this period my mother developed the Aleppo Boil and, later, ophthalmia in Egypt: she also learned to speak Arabic. An interlude in Spain followed: bullfights and fandangos and a fonda with stains of dried blood on the walls (my grandfather, presumably on leave, reappeared in this episode and confounded with his service revolver an inn-keeper bent on robbery and maybe murder); then on to Portugal: swimming and diving, the electric jellyfish and the marvels of the sea-bed; the volcano cropped up somewhere here; it never actually erupted though showers of hot rock fell from time to time on the fishermen while prayers were offered up: I was shown a snap-shot of it, taken by my uncle Hugh, and was surprised to see snow on the top.

At this stage my mother might have given promise of turning out a tomboy: a convent in Pau corrected all that, adding French to the five languages she already spoke; but certainly her athletic prowess was notable upon the volcanic island, though as a child she'd suffered from anaemia and been given iron to remedy the lack of red corpuscles. For years I imagined this tonic to have been conveyed in the form of unyielding bars, and often stole a furtive glance at her teeth, but these, while strong and white and still her own, seemed too small for such a feat of mastication. The treatment however had been triumphantly successful, for despite her heart condition she was a woman of enormous energy, though in appearance the opposite of an amazon, being slim, dark and sedate, and giving an impression of great repose. When I knew her she almost invariably wore a small scarlet watch decorated with fleurs-de-lys pinned to her blouse, the face turned inward against her breast, and a high lace collar with a whalebone rim. Her hair was arranged in the fashion of her youth, high on her head with a fringe in front, and only in very late years did it start to turn grey. In face I am supposed to resemble her, as my brother did to a greater degree: we got our height from my father, to whose shoulder Mother, when standing, scarcely reached.

Like all members of our family, on both sides, she was an expert story-teller: I naturally listened to her tales with enchantment, and it may have been then that I conceived, subconsciously, the ambition to be a writer. For writing, Mother said, ran in the family: her father had written a book, in fact several books, though I only saw one, a copy of which he gave—for he died before I was born—to my brother on his tenth birthday. It had as a frontispiece a photograph of my grandfather in full regimentals and with all his medals on: with his bushy black sidewhiskers and dark eyes staring directly and with a shade of defiance into the camera, he seemed formidable and severe; the upper part of my face is believed to be like his, and also the way I stand, erect and with the head thrown back, though in his case this may have been adopted to give an illusion of increased height, for he was not, I am told, a tall man. Across the photograph was written the inscription to my brother, and this particular copy, which after my mother's death I had for some years but later, alas, lost, had illustrations in water-colour by the author himself, one of them depicting a superb Bengal tiger stalking through the jungle, with my grandfather perched in a tree above it preparing to shoot.

My mother used to read to me as an especial treat from this book, which was published by Messrs Chapman and Hall; the parts I liked best were those which dealt with pig-sticking and of course the tiger.

There was also a section dealing with the time when he built a lighthouse in the Andaman Islands with the aid of native convict labour, and some experiences on the Gold Coast where he served, before retiring, as a commissioner; a bit which was not read to me told of his visit to a Maharajah: dancing girls were brought out for his entertainment, and he was later invited to choose one as a companion for the rest of the evening, but the girls, on closer examination, turned out to be boys.

These readings took place before I myself could read; my mother now taught me, and in a very simple way: she would read aloud until an exciting incident was reached, then put the book down and leave the room on some household pretext, whilst I awaited her return in an agony of suspense, occasionally snatching up the volume to puzzle at the indecipherable symbols on the page. One day these were indecipherable no longer, and she returned to find me halfway through the next chapter: so it came about that the first book I ever read was *The Coral Island* by R.M. Ballantyne, an experience, I'm sure, shared by many.

Before this I had been given an alphabet made up of cachous, each letter a different colour, with which I used to trace patterns. Though they smelt nice, I never ate them, for I had been told they were poisonous: I treated them therefore with the respect due to a dangerous commodity which I was, unaccountably, allowed to handle, unlike matches. Now that I could read, I understood more fully their purpose: the patterns which I formed with them became words, and I developed on the spot a spelling mania. I spelt all the longest words I could think of, my favourite was Pantechnicon, with Rhododendron a runner-up, and used to lay siege to my sister, whenever she entered the nursery, to provide me with even longer words: an importunity which she resented, not being herself a resoundingly good speller.

Writing followed on swiftly, and I used to record lists of all the long words in blue exercise books called the Prodigious, that had a picture of an airship on the cover and extremely coarse fibrous yellow paper, made, according to Mother, from rags: though by its texture sacking seemed a more likely material. Thus I learned to write, but pothooks and all the other paraphernalia I found tiresome; and then, and for many years afterwards, I printed everything in small block letters intended to resemble the print of a book, and executed with a pencil named, if I remember rightly, the Koh-i-noor. These pursuits took the place of the toys I'd tired of, I ceased to be bored and fretful, and for a time even ate my food without the fuss I usually made, for I was very fastidious, and anything such as a black speck in a bowl of bread-and-milk would immediately put paid to my appetite: butter, which during that war had the taste of train oil being the only substance I still baulked at. Bent over my cachous and Koh-i-noors, I became so absorbed and quiet that my father, on his rare visits to my domain, got quite concerned and enquired whether I felt ill.

Change, however, was in the air. We'd been enjoying lately a reprieve from the company of Mr Foxe, who'd hurried to the bedside of a sick relative from whom he perhaps expected a legacy, and my father proposed to move quickly, before he returned, to another furnished house in a town too far away for him to follow us. Such a house had presented itself in the columns of *Dalton's Weekly*, correspondence between my father and the owners had been initiated; now a rental satisfactory to both parties had been agreed upon; also the house was situated outside Bournemouth, a place where Father had lived before, and where my brother, from his latest letters, expected to be stationed on his return from overseas. The prospect of seeing him again roused even Carol from her sullen apathy, though for some reason she was not actually with us when we arrived, one afternoon, in the streets of what must have been Boscombe.

It was winter. My mother and I waited in an arcade, with strict instructions to stay where we were until my father returned: we saw him strike out, stumping heavily with his stick, into a stream of traffic and disappear from sight along the opposite pavement, in search of the suburb, called Southbourne, where the new house had its location. We went into a tea-shop, for I was hungry, and when we emerged the day had darkened above the green glass roof, which diffused downwards an aquarium light. There was no sign of Father. We paced up and down, staring into shop windows like fish through the glass of their tank. We looked at the clock. I suggested that Father might have got lost, and was sharply rebuked: Father had been a sailor, he never got lost. Neither of these statements was strictly true, though he had certainly been to sea, and after two hours had gone by it began to look as if I'd been right; another possibility was that Father had met with an accident and perhaps been killed: this must have occurred to my mother, though not to me, for I naturally imagined him to be immortal.

She now became very nervous, I sensed this though she did not let it appear, and a search was decided upon. We in turn struck out into the current of the main street, almost at random, for Mother had even less idea than my father where to look, never having been in the place before. By now it was almost night and a sort of sand-storm was blowing up. We arrived at some kind of dunes; these were desolate; there was a smell of pines and the sand blew in my eyes. I burst into tears. We turned about and were blown back in the direction of the arcade, where my father, who'd arrived meantime, was angrily awaiting us: he brushed aside our relief; why the devil hadn't we stayed where he told us?

He'd had a terrible time, there was coal to be got in unless we all wanted to freeze, then the maid engaged by letter had not turned up and another had to be procured at short notice, now he was tired and wanted his tea. He interrupted these complaints to tell me to stop crying and stood by impatiently pulling at his beard while Mother with the corner of a handkerchief removed grit from my eye. Then our luggage had to be fetched from the station and my erstwhile dungeon, the Trunk, was lashed on the top of a taxi. I'd never been in one of these before and swiftly recovered my spirits with the ride, though it was too dark to see the town and both parents told me to sit quiet. In this fashion, and I must finally have fallen asleep, we arrived at our new home.

Gaudelier and Partridge

*　　　*　　　*

MY FATHER, OR SO HE SOMETIMES CLAIMED, WAS NEVER WRONG. But no sooner had we settled in at the new house than his assertion, at any rate in this one instance, was exploded; it argues much, however, for his usual infallibility that I remember the exception so well: it came about in the following manner.

Travelling upset my father, he hated trains, and even the shortest railway journey—while ours had been long—tended to result in one of the headaches from which he suffered and which, since the fit brought on by the French butcher-boy, were complicated by vertigo. The attacks had been caused, originally, by a horse kicking him in the head at the age of six, when his life had been despaired of, as I've already told in a piece of family history entitled 'My Father was Born in Havana': but for the benefit of readers unacquainted with that work (and they must include almost the entire population of the British Isles) it is necessary to re-state this, and other facts about him while trusting not to bore by this recapitulation those who have read the earlier account and who must, in any case, form a select minority. Anyhow a headache had now come on in earnest; it was the first one I'd known at close quarters: blinds were drawn in his bedroom, I was told to walk on tiptoe, and Maud our new maid was ordered downtown to get a prescription made up.

My father had a store of such prescriptions for combating his various ailments; they were tattered pieces of paper which had to be handled with the utmost care lest they came apart altogether, and there was always great difficulty in finding the right chemist to cash them, since all contained vast doses of poison and resulted in bottles labelled in scarlet and stamped with the most sinister devices imaginable. The one for headaches was particularly lethal: most chemists rejected it with cries of horror and thoughts of Scotland Yard; but in Bournemouth my father knew of one who, years ago, had not hesitated and whose mixture had been most effective in its cure.

Perhaps he'll be dead, my mother ventured timidly from the bedside.

Nonsense, he was quite a young man, Father said sniffing at his green bottle of smelling salts; Now Maud listen to me and mind what I say. Yessir said Maud. Don't interrupt, my father told her, the shop you want is down by the arcade you cant miss it, the name is Gaudelier. Got it? Gaudelier.

Yessir said Maud and off she went. But in an hour she was back: Please sir there's no chemist by that name, there is a shop sir where you said, but it's called Partridge.

Rubbish Father roared, I tell you it's Gaudelier and I am never wrong. Now go and don't come back without that medicine, d'you hear. Maud almost in tears again sallied forth and this time returned with the bottle clutched in her hand: You see? Father said snatching it from her; Gaudelier! I told you.

Beg pardon sir but it aint said Maud pointing to the name on the label, it's Mr Partridge sir, he says he knows you quite well; you didn't have a beard then but you was in the army, Captain Ross he said oh yes and how is he keeping.

This was irrefutable proof, for my father never used his former rank, except occasionally abroad where it impressed foreign officials and got him quickly through the customs: Maud was unaware that he had ever been commissioned and it had certainly not been on the prescription. He was stumped, but quickly recovered with a growl: Oh well, what does it matter about the fellow's name, here's something for your trouble and close the door quietly as you go out; dont slam it now.

But my mother, though wise enough to say nothing at the time, had not failed to notice the slip, and in after years, during one of their rare arguments she was wont to murmur Gaudelier and Partridge as a come-back to the claim with which my father sought to subdue all opposition. Nobody ever found out why or how this error came about, perhaps not even my father; he may have confused, in his anguish, the Bournemouth chemist with some other obliging pharmacy in France: and certainly the name Gaudelier suggests a foreign origin.

It occurs to me that, in these immediately preceding sections, I may have laid undue emphasis upon my father's irascibility: actually, though he was never a man to trifle with, these outbursts were by no means typical, and it is the control which as a rule he kept on what had been in his youth a notoriously uncertain temper, rather than his occasional loss of it, that impresses me now. For looking back I see, as I did not then and only imperfectly later, that he spent most of his days in varying degrees of physical discomfort: since, added to the constant trial that his wounded leg was to him, there was also the hernia, to counteract which he had to wear a peculiarly tight truss, not to mention the outbreaks of nettlerash and hay-fever to which he was subject, regularly, every summer. Coming, therefore, on top of all this, the headaches must have seemed the last straw.

Mr Partridge's draught was successful in relieving, however, the worst of the pain—though perhaps not all of it, for my father was seldom, thereafter, without his smelling-bottle close by him; and it is with the aromatic savour of the salts, and the smell of cherrywood that may have been the soap he used, with which, as children do, I came to associate him; for he had given up tobacco years before, and, nowadays, rarely drank. These odours permeated what was always, wherever we lived, known as his study, to which later on I was summoned for lectures on acts of disobedience; to this room, on the ground floor front in the Southbourne house, he retired once the headache subsided to work on the translations that were sent him from Whitehall and were his contribution to the war effort; also to add to the accumulation, already vast, of notes on his biography of Napoleon Bonaparte, which he had spent much of his middle age in planning but which remained, at the end of his life, still unwritten.

There was a third occupation which seemed at variance with the semi-olympian figure he had made himself into, and this was the backing of horses and study of racing form: almost the only habit left over from the days when as a young masher, unbearded then, he had worn a curly-brimmed bowler with tight narrow-lapelled checks instead of the characteristic suits that I knew him in, mostly cut from black broadcloth, bales of which must have been used in making them up, he was so big, and looped across their waistcoats the massive chain of the gold hunter (given him by his maternal grandfather) whose top he used to snap open to look at the time.

In his study, however, he wore looser fitting coats of black or, when it was very hot, white alpaca; here he sat in an easy chair specially made for him, since even then he must have weighed all of eighteen stone and, in his time, twenty. By him on the desk was the monogrammed tin which had once contained his own blend of cigarettes but was now filled with the liquorice pastilles which he sucked incessantly instead of smoking; and beside the desk itself was the revolving globe of the world which like the big black trunk accompanied him everywhere and had somehow escaped the blitzing of our Ramsgate home: continents of different colours with vivid blue between; the very stuff of romance to be spun whirling at a touch, though I was not allowed until much later to set it in motion, or, indeed, to enter the study at all.

I was also barred from the kitchen, presided over then by an exceedingly grim cook, who left, much later, in high dudgeon over a question of honesty; but a small playroom was fixed up for me near the top of the house, where Maud deputised as a nanny, for having a largish house now to set in order my mother was not so readily available as a companion. Maud also took me for walks and wheeled me about, when tired, in the push-cart to which my brother had formerly been strapped and which I had inherited by right of succession. I remember her as gentle and sweetly pretty, with violet eyes: the only ones I have ever seen. This was a time free from care, but I might have known it could not last; suddenly Maud was whisked back to her ordinary duties and her place taken by a truly appalling woman called Nurse.

In life, I have learned, there is always worse to come, so that one's past, in the light of the present, never seems as black as it did at the time. Thus when I was in the army I looked back on my days as a vacuum-cleaner salesman almost with nostalgia; and now, though I know this will sound hard to believe, there are times when even the Service itself appears preferable to the vicissitudes of a professional writer's life. In this way, then, Nana, all her faults notwithstanding, became—and with reason—a figure infinitely desirable by comparison with Nurse. I will not go into all she did, the recollection is more painful to me than even that of a certain sergeant-instructor, since eaten by sharks; just one instance of her régime will suffice: it is like Nana and Nathan only worse, for Nana did no more than turn to her own advantage a fear already in existence, while Nurse created one of her own.

In the arcade at Boscombe there was in those days (and may be still for all I know) a phrenologist's shop, which had in its window the outline of a human head cut up like an orange in varicoloured quarters, with arrows pointing to various centres of mental activity. This diagram, whenever I was taken into the town, used to fascinate me (for I knew what a phrenologist was, having him in my list of long words) until Nurse, noticing my interest, turned it into a terror. She made out I was secretly mad, an 'idiot' was the word she used: only she and I shared this knowledge, but the phrenologist could find out any time by reading my bumps, if not on sight, and then I'd be put away behind padded walls, a strait-jacket, which she lovingly described, being reserved for particularly bad behaviour. If, however, her slightest word were obeyed, and I did not 'give any trouble', she would keep silence, not take me into the shop, and no one else need ever know.

How long this sinister blackmail might have continued is hard to say, had illness not supervened to save me. One's life forms patterns which can after a time be recognised; and just as pneumonia snatched me away from that sergeant-instructor in 1941, so bladder trouble now formed a means of escape from Nurse. Like the pneumonia it began with a sharp pain that grew suddenly worse, until I was almost in convulsions: cold may have been the cause, but the doctor feared a stone might be forming; there was talk of an operation, but this I did not hear, for by that time I was delirious. In the wild stuff I shouted, fear of the phrenologist must have been predominant: anyway my parents got to hear and as a result Nurse was out of the house, as that later enemy of mine might have put it, 'without her feet had time to touch the ground'.

No sooner had she left than, as if there'd been some connection, the pain disappeared too: dissolved with the stone the doctor said; luckily for me, since he had come prepared, and a catheter was half out of his instrument case. Oddly enough, when I became fully conscious, the first person I asked for was Carol: it must have been the vague memory of being said good-bye to, through a mist of pain, that made me call for her, and I broke into a bitter lament on being told she had Gone To Do Her Bit. How she finally persuaded my father to allow her to enlist, I never found out; though I believe Mr Foxe's daughter being a Land Girl had something to do with it: Father was well known to shiver if our former landlord was mentioned, and even a Waac uniform would be preferable, in his opinion, to Carol's going about with a pitchfork, in breeches and top boots.

But my grief at her departure was tempered by my joy at that of Nurse; and so, in that house, I first became aware of happiness as I know it now: a calm between two crises, like a cloud lifting to let through sun, though my being a child then the period of respite was longer; seemed, in fact, as though it might last for ever.

For now a blissful convalescence set in: a time symbolised to me by Mrs Beeton's Cookery Book. There was a copy of this in the house, though I am certain that the grim cook downstairs never made use of it, judging by the boiled and solid fare served up to us; and though I did not read the recipes, the paintings of food that formed the illustrations, besides being appetising, entranced me by their bright colours and the exotic names given to the dishes, so different from what we got that they seemed the sort of meal eaten not so much abroad as on another planet: maybe by those Green Men of Mars one read about a year or two later in the novels of Edgar Rice Burroughs. I used to pore over its pages for hours, and thus the first few words of French I learned to speak were *faisan à la financière*, a delicacy which I supposed for some years to be reserved solely for financiers and which I somehow never came to order in after-life.

Then there were games: even my father came up for an occasional set of dominoes, without moreover making me put the pieces back tidily in the box afterwards, as he would have insisted upon had I been well; and besides this, Mother now taught me to play cards: Beggar My Neighbour first, and then what is still a favourite game—Bézique. Cards became a passion ousting everything, even the Cookery Book. I have always been a creature of crazes, and when my mother was not there to play (for I was never able to teach Maud), I used to deal endless hands upon the counterpane against an unseen opponent whom I called She: this title must have been meant to represent Mother and not the dream of a future female partner, since at that time I regarded all girls, if I thought about them at all, as soppy.

During the reign of Mrs Beaton and the Bézique markers, I must have neglected my alphabet of cachous and the Prodigious exercise books: one reason for this being that I hated to encounter, in my list of long words, the profession Phrenologist, since it was a reminder of the bad time I'd been through. My father discovered that this shadow of the terror still persisted, and decided that it could only be dispelled by a visit to the shop in the arcade itself. There I was duly taken, when well enough to walk, and as my father steered me by surprise through the door, I started to scream, thinking I was about to be certified at last. But the phrenologist, a reassuring figure, not unlike a thin Pickwick if that is possible, soon allayed my fears once Father had explained them to him, and we had a relieved laugh together when my bumps were read and no signs of lunacy could be found: though my father laughed rather less and was thoughtful on the way home, for the phrenologist had diagnosed predominant artistic tendencies, and I had just begun to paint.

Towards the close of my convalescence my mother had given me, it may have been a Christmas present, a box of water-colours, the flat sort: not in tubes, though I had these later. Their very names were magic: cobalt, ultra-marine, rose madder, and they at once took precedence over the card-games; I had always been fascinated by colours: when not even old enough to talk, so I'm told, what I liked to play with were the reels of brilliant cotton or silk which my mother used for embroidery, until these had to be taken away I got them so grubby; and now here was a chance to employ colour myself. The paintbox was accompanied by a book which led to the development of another craze, though painting did not go by the board because of it, since the two interests were interdependent.

This book was of butterflies and moths, showing on one side of the page specimens already coloured as they should be, to serve as models; and on the other, outlines only, to be filled in by the prospective artist. One in particular took my fancy: the Privet Hawk Moth, and this was not only due to the delicate pink of the under-wings, rose madder indeed, but in part to the strangeness of its caterpillar, also represented, hanging upside down on a twig, the colour of the privet leaves on which it fed, not unlike the one in Alice, with a peculiar horn on its tail: a sort of sting but harmless in reality, even to the predatory birds it was intended by nature to scare.

I soon learned to use a brush, filling in the outlines carefully so as not to slop over the edges as happened at first, when I used to cry inconsolably until another book was bought, to start in again; and from painting these lovely insects to becoming interested in their actuality was but a step. I have never had more than a few interests; but when I take up something I always learn about it thoroughly, and soon I was stumbling over the Latin names of species, I learned to say Lepidoptera; and not long after I was equipped with butterfly-net and killing-bottle —less cruel than squeezing the heads of those I caught to make life extinct—and with my mother roamed through the meadows in pursuit of Peacocks and Red Admirals, which I pinned out on cork in a glass case, like a real collector. Purple Emperors were what I was really after, it was slightly disgusting that these alighted for preference on dung; but whether because my mother had a disinclination to be led in the direction of mounds of manure, or because they were scarce in those years (as Red Admirals were not), I never caught one. (Some time later, adolescent in the South of France, when other crazes had eclipsed entomology, I saw clouds of them surrounding a tree bearing plums the colour of that iridescent stain on the wings that gave them their name; and a peasant who was shooing them off as pests told me they feasted on the fruit: a habit I do not remember seeing recorded in any of the textbooks that I read as a child, nor had I supposed their mandibles strong enough to bite pieces out, as in the plum the peasant showed me; perhaps wasps really did it and the Purple Emperors got the blame.)

Moths were the biggest problem, since they came out only at night and I, not unreasonably, was forbidden to stay up so late. Sometimes on those long summer evenings I persuaded Mother to remain out with me until the first droop of dusk, when the air became blue enough for some small specimen, such as a Cinnabar, to emerge from wherever it slept by day. But these soon ceased to satisfy me; what I hungered after were the big Hawks, especially the Privet; though I also aspired to the Death's Head itself, the migrant king of moths, marked with a skull-and-crossbones similar to that on my father's medicine bottles, which was supposed to squeak like a mouse if touched, much as a mandrake is supposed to scream like a man when uprooted—though I've no means of knowing the truth of these assertions, since I never found either Death's Head or mandrake root.

My mother had a brainwave about this; she suggested that it was easier to look for the larvae, keep them until they turned into chrysalids, and then wait for the moths to hatch out. Boxes of caterpillars shortly filled the kitchen: much to the disgust of the cook they were placed on shelves above the range, to speed up the processes of nature by artificial warmth; they were principally the Woolly Bears which turned into Tiger Moths and brought out a rash on the hands if picked up without gloves, but once I got hold of a Goat Moth caterpillar—enormous in size and feeding, I think, on rotting logs—that stank like the animal after which it was named and had eventually to be condemned, for Cook simply would not stand it and my father backed her up. I was furious at what seemed an act of vandalism, but the emergence of the Tiger Moths, whose black and orange wings soon began to batter, still wet from birth, on the walls of their boxes, consoled me somewhat: it was sad that they should be popped so soon into the killing-bottle, before they were even able to fly, but I told myself that their life would have been short anyway, which cannot be denied.

There were also traps to be set in the back garden with lanterns and sheets of paper smeared with treacle for the moths, lured by the light in the first instance, to stick to or else drop off, drunk with sweetness, to be picked up and despatched with cyanide next morning: but this was too messy by far, the treacle got on my clothes, the delicate scales came off in the goo; also the lantern was unwise in wartime and, a rumour having got around that we were spies, this method had to be discontinued.

This must have been about the first time that the war touched us down there: a German plane did fly over, got out of control, crashed into some trees, and came down in flames in a clearing not far from the bottom of our road, the pilot and crew being, I believe, burnt alive, though I was not encouraged to ask about their fate or, indeed, to talk about the incident at all. I suppose I was too young then for the war to interest me much; battles must have been taking place and by rights I should have been anxious for my brother's safety, for he was still overseas and his leave, long overdue, kept on being cancelled; but like my father he seemed too splendid and remote a figure ever to die: besides he had been away so long he seemed scarcely real. All the same my parents must have been worried not only for him but for my sister, now stationed near Woolwich Arsenal; and how futile my butterfly-nets and paintboxes must have appeared to them, and how kind they were not to let me see it.

Mother was pleased about my painting, for it seemed that I was taking after her father, but my father was more than a little perturbed: the entomology he didn't mind, except when it became a nuisance as in the case of the Goat Moth, for he himself had collected birds' eggs at school and grown out of it; but the painting, taken in conjunction with what the phrenologist had told us, caused him at times to stroke his beard and say he hoped the boy wasnt going to turn out an artist. He had no objection to art itself, indeed even admired its more traditional examples; but he had known artists, Beardsley had been a protégé of my grandmother's: anyway he didnt fancy it as a career for his younger son, the elder having so narrowly missed becoming a priest.

Undeterred, for once, by his disapproval, I continued to paint, especially in winter when the days drew in, there were no butterflies, and country walks with my mother or Maud were made impossible by rain. This pattered on the glass roof of the conservatory in front of the house where I painted; there were no plants that I can recall except geraniums in pots, but under the sort of draining board on which my brushes and tubes were set out was an area of earth and stones rich in insect life: especially two kinds of woodlouse, one which rolled up like a small armadillo at a touch, the other flat and sometimes white, which had not the ability to protect itself with armour; I believe the correct name for these to be silverfish. In the intervals of observing them, as became a true aurelian, I made sketches in charcoal on blocks of cartridge paper, and painted a small picture of two yellow cows couchant on crimson grass (though I had not then seen a Gauguin). I also attempted a still life à la Mrs Beeton, intended as a present for Carol's birthday, but this was not a success, for I could not get the pheasant right, so she was sent the cows instead.

In this way time passed until I was first six and then seven.

On my seventh birthday my father sent for me in his study and said, Now my boy you are seven years old, and if you commit any offence that deserves it, you can be sent to prison just like a grown-up person.

I dont know why he said this but he did, perhaps it was to instil in me a feeling of manly responsibility in which he felt I was sadly deficient: anyhow it produced, as he should have known, the very opposite. I retired to the back garden, where I was now allowed to play, to a secret hide-out I had there, and thought over his pronouncement. My dominant feeling was one of curiosity about prison: what could it be like? It was often mentioned in books I read, the villain was always being sent there and sometimes the hero, though he of course was innocent, but there were no descriptions except of mediæval times, with portcullises and dungeons; and I now determined to try it for myself.

I'd long ago discovered that I could escape from the garden, there was a tradesmen's entrance at the side which was left unlocked in the mornings when they called, but I was in honour bound never to use this; and indeed had never, until now, had the nerve to do so. I lifted the latch, watching, like the felon I meant soon to become, to see if I were observed from the house, but all was clear; and in a moment I was out and speeding down the road in the direction of a house owned by a Mrs Bradlaw.

Mrs Bradlaw was the widow of a sea-captain, I'd heard my father say she drank, and she did smell oddly like a barber's shop. She used to lie in wait at the window of her drawing-room until Father limped heavily into sight, when the door would burst open and she'd come bustling out to pass the time of day. My father hated her, but his native courtesy would not let him show it: he would doff his broad black hat and stand shifting his weight from his bad leg on to his stick until, after a reasonable interval, he could politely escape. As Mr Foxe did with my mother, only reversing the process, Mrs Bradlaw was wont to compare my father to her dear departed hubby, a real gentleman if ever there was one, the very spitting image of yourself Mr Ross, she'd say; and once Father was dragged into the house to inspect a portrait of the deceased; actually this supposed double could not have been more unlike, but the incident put him in a bad temper for two days afterward, at the thought that this, perhaps, was how he seemed to other people.

I came round the corner, spied up at the house, but again I was in luck, nobody about and Mrs B not, this morning, at her post. I stooped for a stone, and coming up took careful aim at that window from which brilliant light flashed dazzling back into my eyes: so that when with the crash of glass, the crack appeared on the pane, the flash went out as though I had shivered the sun itself; smashed a star-shaped hole in its shining face. This shocked me and I dived back, running all the way without meeting anyone, until, inside with the gate latched, I could lean back against it to let the stitch in my side abate. Now I had begun to fear, not prison, but punishment for having left the garden: another worry was whether once behind bars, they would let me paint.

Nerving myself to be a man, for after all I was seven and old enough to go to gaol, I entered the house and knocked on the door of my father's study.

He was seated at his desk in his white alpaca coat, for this was one of the hottest Julys on record, and as I came in he laid down the powerful magnifying glass, almost microscope, which he used instead of spectacles, and leaned back, closing his eyes for a moment to adjust the temporary squint it gave him. I trembled as, stroking one hand down the length of his face to the point of his beard, with the action of one removing a mask, he turned on me, from under tufted brows, the intense blue battery of his stare: but his voice was mild as he said Yes my boy, for it was still my birthday and he didnt know yet about Mrs Bradlaw's window.

Father, I said, I shall have to go to prison now; and drawing a deep breath to get it out while he still looked astonished: I've thrown a stone and broken someone's window down the street.

My father grabbed for his smelling-salts, but hay-fever attacked him before he could speak, and he sneezed explosively into a handkerchief jerked from his sleeve, turning, as always, the normal Atishoo into the Spanish expletive ¡Carajo! Do you mean, he said then like a mutter of thunder, you got out of the garden when I expressly forbade it? And on your birthday too? Yes, Father, I said, trying to stand my ground against the storm that must surely burst, with blue lightnings from his eyes, And now I must go to prison. He looked at me hard over the green bottle in his hand: Did anyone see you break the window? No Father, I said. Whose window was it? he asked. Mrs Bradlaw's, I told him.

At this Father half-rose from his chair: Mrs Bradlaw? Yes, Father, I said: as he stood completely up I thought the end had come, that he would beat me; though, as I've said, he had never done this before. But instead without a word he turned and bent, with a grunt because of the tight truss, towards a cabinet in the corner; this contained sticks of Edinburgh Rock, which were only given to me on special occasions, whilst a ginger one marked a gala day. I could not credit it was for this purpose that he now opened the doors, and thought he kept a cane in there: his shoulders were shaking, it seemed to me with rage; but his face, when he straightened up and turned it to me, was little more than normally stern, and the veins at his temples were not swollen, which was the danger-sign.

Now my boy, he said, you know it's very bad to throw stones, what made you do it? I wanted to see what it was like in prison, I told him. My father's mouth twitched under his moustache and he put a hand on his beard as though to hide it. Then he brought the other hand from behind his back and it was a stick of Rock which he held out to me. James, he said (for this is my first name, by which I was known, always, to my parents) James there are times when I dont pretend to understand you, but this is one of the times when I do. Go now and be a good boy, but dont say anything about this to your mother. But the police Father, I blurted. There won't be any police, he told me. Yes Father, thank you, I said and bolted for the door, which however I did not forget to close behind me. In the hall I examined the stick of Rock and found it to be ginger, which made this one of the times when I definitely failed to understand my father: however well, conversely, he may have understood me.

There was a sequel to this, though; for two days later curtains were drawn across Mrs Bradlaw's windows, including the one that I had broken, and that no glazier had come to mend; and the day after that she was dead. I quaked with remorse; for as I saw it some voodoo devilry had entered with the stone I'd flung: had cracked with the pane clean across her heart, which they said had stopped suddenly like a clock run down, as it might have been my own mother's. So in my mind I was worse than a murderer, and cowered in solitude and terror where I could not see, while the coffin, as it had to, passed in the hearse by our door; I expected any minute the Black Maria to call for me with handcuffs and prison, which in my folly I had dared, for life: since I knew I was too young to hang.

But as my father had promised, and sometimes seemed to reassure me by his expression, though he never spoke of the episode, there were no police; and, as gradually I forgot my guilt, the summer stretched ahead, with no iron bars but a golden mesh of days: sunshine on green fields and blue water; sunshine strained mellow through the cream-coloured blinds with which our every room was equipped: yet fierce enough to strike down, like any death ray, a middle-aged man in bathing dress on the Bournemouth beach; sunshine flashing off the conservatory glass as it had from the window of the old lonely woman whose light, I used to fear, I had finally put out.

Miss Crisp and the Hooded Terror

*　　*　　*

THE ONLY OTHER SEASON THAT I REALLY REMEMBER IN THAT house is Christmas, and this was traditionally celebrated, with a spangled tree and a snow man outside: for in those days, as many will remember, Christmases were really white. On the eve, my father always read to me from a small book preserved perhaps from his own childhood. He donned for these occasions—and this was the only day, once a year, when he was ever seen to wear them—a tasselled smoking-cap, a souvenir of his sojourn at Heidelberg, and a black velvet jacket that must also have dated back to student days, since it would not meet across his chest. He seemed to regard the season, in spite of the war, as uniformly teutonic; for the book was in German too and bore on its paper cover, which had been mended down the back with adhesive tape, a coloured picture of Father Christmas standing with his sackful of surprises in the snow; his sleigh was in the background, and the reindeer, I remember, were named Donner und Blitzen: but the translation was Father's own, pencilled between the lines of the Gothic script and he would always clear his throat twice before reading the first verse, which ran:

> Twas the Eve of St Nicholas,
> And all over the house,
> Nothing was stirring,
> Not even a mouse.

I do not remember when these readings stopped; it may have been after we travelled over to France: probably the book, and the raiment which accompanied it, got lost in transit.

But it was at Christmas the same year I was seven (or, as I'd have put it then, seven and a half) that Carol came home on leave. Her uniform became her, bringing out the buttercup curl of her hair and making her eyes blue lakes to drown in. As she stooped down to kiss me and those enormous orbs looked straight into mine, as I smelt the scent she now used and something sticky and perfumed also came off on my lips with the kiss, though I rubbed these after, I fell in love with her at once. I was old enough, however, to know—and regret—that we could never marry, and it may be because of this that blondes were to attract me so irresistibly as a boy: though giving place, by degrees, to brunettes in adult life.

My mother did not fail to observe, either, that Carol had on make-up, which she had the presence of mind to remove before greeting Father, still there was about her, even without artificial coloration, a heightened glow that made me follow her wherever she went, and transformed me from a teasing pest into an adoring slave. Carol had little time to notice the change in me, she was too busy recounting her recent experiences: Mother was the main recipient of these confidences, for they would not have done for Father, though I listened in, whenever I could, on the sly.

It seems Carol shared a hut, or wherever Waacs slept, with a Welsh girl called Morgan who was a bigamist: she drew marriage allowances from three husbands and was well-off, but then things went wrong. While she was on leave with one of them, another appeared who was supposed to be serving abroad, and at a moment when nothing but the truth would explain the situation. Instead of fighting, the two men went off, wisely, to get drunk together, after one had given Morgan a black eye; now they had cancelled their allowances, which their wife thought unfair: there was always the chance, too, that the third, remaining husband would get to hear.

At this point Carol saw me listening and turned me out of the room: I hung about outside in the hope of being allowed to say goodnight, and heard my sister remark casually, as Mother was about to emerge, Oh and Mumsy I forgot to tell you, I'm engaged. Mother stood for a moment transfixed with one hand on the light-switch; then she returned abruptly to the room, the door was closed again, and Maud took me off to my bath before I'd time to take in fully what I'd heard.

Next day there were sulks, my father's voice was raised in his study, where he was closeted with Carol, and it was not long before the name of the unofficial fiancé rang all over the house. This was Al Laperle: he was French-Canadian and at home had been a trapper; Carol told me of his adventures when she took me out walking in the town, and these were enthralling: he sounded better than Buffalo Bill, the very sort of brother-in-law any boy would like to have. My parents did not agree with me: Carol was threatened with lock-and-key when Laperle sent a telegram that he was on his way for a visit, but this extreme measure proved unnecessary, for another telegram arrived almost at once cancelling the appointment and giving news of a posting to the other end of England. Carol flung herself face down on her bed and violently repulsed my attempts to console her; the whole business became unbearably tense.

Hostilities were suspended on Christmas Day itself, when even in the trenches Tommy and Fritz were said to fraternise and to exchange cigarettes through the barbed wire, before preparing to kill one another again on the morrow; and so with us on Boxing Day a thunderous row broke out: it had been brewing all afternoon and finally burst just about my bedtime. I came upon Carol at bay in the corridor; in front of her stood my father barring the path with his huge shoulders humped: I dont know if she was about to leave the house, perhaps on her way to join Laperle, or what she may have said to make Father, for the first time, raise his hand to her; but before the blow could fall, Mother, appearing from nowhere, flung herself between with a cry of protest; I too set up a despairing wail, thus drawing attention to my presence on the scene.

Instantly I was scooped up by Father and none too gently bundled through the nearest door, which was then shut and locked in my face. The room was dark: groping, I could not find the switch; it was worse than being in the trunk. I beat and beat on the panels of the door: desperate, I even kicked, though this was practically a penal offence; but all sounds of strife in the passage outside had ceased and I might have been abandoned alive in my tomb, like that man in Poe's story which I had not yet read. It seemed an hour, but was probably less, before Maud came to release me, and then the sal volatile had to be uncorked; no one came up to say goodnight, and in my fitful dreams the Little Bit of Linoleum figured largely: for the last time, incidentally, in my life.

The following afternoon was the last of Carol's leave: we two went walking through a park shrouded white, with ground that crackled underfoot, my sister's nose was red with more than cold; and later she sat on a bench and sobbed, for perhaps the snow surrounding us put her in mind of those Canadian wastes which she might never see. I remember kissing over and over again the palm of her hand, which was slightly sticky and smelt of chocolate, and assuring her that I, at least, would love her always, until her fingers, numb with frost, had to be thrust back in the muff she carried, as she was wearing civvies. So, warm inside with our love and our loyalty (hers of course for Al), we returned to the house where my father waited grimly to give a final admonition. There was coldness saying good-bye because of this, and Carol's perfunctory kiss seemed to include me in her general disdain as, uniformed once again, she stepped with her kit into the cab from whose window she did not wave.

Now it was my turn to cry, and between my bitter sobs I came to hate the Canadian for spoiling her stay: had I been asked—as I was not—I would willingly have joined my parents in their campaign against my former hero. But as my tears dried with time and the snow man melted in the garden at a touch of the sun, so the situation righted itself. Al Laperle was drafted overseas: like Nana's sergeant he did not write; there was no occasion to send back the ring, since in the first instance he had given none, and my sister was so angered and distressed by the whole affair that, having been christened Caroline Mary, she changed her name temporarily to May.

My parents' relief at this outcome, naturally, was enormous; but their troubles were not yet over, for no sooner had Mother written Carol, or May, an adroitly worded letter of sympathy, than she was stricken down with gastritis and forced to take to her bed. The duties of Maud becoming more onerous as a result, I once more presented a problem: since the incipient stone in my bladder, a legend had grown up about my delicate health, and kindergarten was rejected as a solution; tutors, certainly, were talked about, but in the meantime it fell to my father to take me, first, as a companion on his morning walks, and secondly to the picture-houses that he'd begun to visit in the afternoons of late; and it was thus that I came to take an interest in the cinema: a circumstance which was to change the whole course of my later life— and not always, by any means, for the better.

The first film I ever went to was the Italian production of *Quo Vadis*, when it was shown at the Albert Hall in 1912 or thereabouts. People, on hearing this statement and reckoning up what they think is my age, often believe they have caught me out in an obvious lie; but it is the literal truth, though being a baby in arms and not long born at the time, I slept peacefully through the entire performance when expected by everyone to cry; in fact good as gold was how Mother described my conduct on that occasion: a form of words not used, however, at my christening, when I dropped my comforter in the font.

Nor was my behaviour so satisfactory next time I remember being taken to the pictures, soon after my seventh birthday. I started off in disgrace, not having had time to recover from the Charlie Chaplin which had been shown before the Big Picture, or as we call it now the First Feature, came on: this was a very serious film about the conflict of loyalties in wartime, at which my smothered explosions of mirth were out of place and I was told to hush. It was called *Civilisation*: a blond and handsome German fell in love, on neutral ground, with an English girl, brunette but equally beautiful; their troth was plighted and they were to marry, but the outbreak of war broke all that up; and finally came the moment when the German, now a submarine commander, had orders to sink the liner on which his fiancée was returning to England. There were agonised close-ups of indecision at this juncture, but duty to the Fatherland prevailed: the torpedo was fired and we followed its wake as the ship was struck and the girl struggled in the water, with her lover powerless to save her. But the German was overcome by remorse; and to atone for what he'd done, he pulled a lever which flooded the submarine, consigning all aboard to a watery grave, as the sub-title told us. This now seems to me hardly fair, since the crew had done nothing but carry out his orders, and they had not been engaged to the girl; but the audience was deeply moved, women were sobbing in the row behind us; and now an epilogue in Hell ensued: the Germans were shown thirsting in a pit of fire; only our hero, the erstwhile submarine commander, endured in silence, his arms stoically crossed while the flames flickered and devils danced delightedly with pitchforks on the rim of the crater.

Then suddenly the devils scampered away panic-stricken out of a path of light which flooded them from above, and the figure of Our Lord appeared, wearing a halo and stretching His hand compassionately out to the suffering souls. It may be, as they afterwards explained to me, that He had merely come to raise the commander to a heavenly plane where the forgiveness of the drowned fiancée awaited him; but to me the apparition meant one thing only: my time had come and I was to be judged for the murder of Mrs Bradlaw. My parents were unprepared for my reaction, since I had watched the devils with equanimity; and before they'd even time to call out, I had sprung from my seat and bolted incontinently up the aisle and out of the cinema, to be picked up later by a policeman who, disregarding my frenzied assertion that Jesus Christ was after me, hauled me off to the Station, from which I was later fetched by a relieved but irritable Father.

It was consequently with grave misgivings that he took me again to what had just begun to be called the movies: but he'd chosen a cowboy film, with an exciting serial to follow, and was not wrong in assuming that this programme would keep me riveted to my seat. The serial, called *Patria*, had not long started, and the synopsis made it easy to catch up: it featured Mrs Vernon Castle in the rôle not of a dancer but an aviatrix, and the scene was Mexico in the grip of civil war; but the character who particularly fired my imagination was the villain, a rebel general named Manuel Moralés, and played with suave ferocity by Mr Warner Oland. Soon I was speaking of him, not as Moralés but by his real name, for my father explained to me about actors and taught me to look at the cast which appeared at the beginning of each episode; and from then on I became a devotee, or in the current phrase a Fan.

Warner Oland appeared in many other serials, often opposite Pearl White, and in many different parts: I can see in my mind's eye now his drooping eyelid, the cruel twist of his thin moustache over the thick smiling lips; it was not until much later that they cast him as the sympathetic Chinese detective Charlie Chan: in those days he was always the villain. Once he vanished completely at the end of the film, dissolved into thin air by the invention of a mad scientist which he was endeavouring to convert to his own, naturally nefarious, uses; another time he fell into one of his own traps, it may have been a pit of snakes; this was when he was playing a sinister mandarin, and I particularly admired the manner in which he waved victims away to the torture: a characteristic gesture of his long-nailed hand, with only the index and little fingers extended—inimitable yet at once imitated by me; though my father drew the line at allowing me to grow my hair long, so that I could toss it back out of my eyes as my favourite actor did when his broke loose from its parting during a fight.

Then there were mystery men (who were only rarely revealed to be women): one dressed as a diver and having his hide-out in a transparent submarine; others dressed as airmen or motor-cyclists, their faces hidden behind leather helmets and mica goggles: masked, muffled, or clad from head to foot in furs; the most formidable being made entirely of steel, an automaton supposedly equipped with a human brain by a scientist (as usual insane), but turning out in the last episode to be operated from within by the criminal son of a criminal lawyer—this latter serial forming a vehicle for the technical skill of Houdini the Handcuff King. These monsters did not horrify me to the extent that the vision of Our Lord had done; I easily became inured to their appearances, since I soon learned that they were only one of the characters in disguise or— disappointingly—long-lost relative of the heroine who did not appear otherwise in the film, but was always at hand to rescue her from danger when the hero, perhaps through the machinations of the villain, was unable to perform this function himself. These, like the Phantom Rider, who rode a white horse in a black cloak and emerged from an Ali Baba's cave of inca treasure through an open-sesame door of rock, I took in my stride; and there was only one whom I couldnt take at all: the familiar spirit, or *kâ*, of a mummy from a desecrated Egyptian tomb, described on the sub-titles as a Strange Soulless Thing; for he had tusks, and I thought this a bit much. Whenever his skeletal, crooked hand, the back covered with a sparse growth of hair, each nail a talon, appeared as a foretaste of his full horror on the screen, I would start to shift about uneasily, and my father would then rise, saying briskly Time we had our tea, my boy, with a sigh of relief: for sitting through the serials must have been agony to him.

Besides the ones I've mentioned there were many other mystery men, there was the Clutching Hand, unfortunately before my time as a film-goer, and I must not miss out the most infamous of all: the Hooded Terror, a homicidal maniac so fearsome that a Bishop had tried to get the film featuring him banned altogether as unfit for public exhibition. This, another Pearl White serial called *The House of Hate*, was on show in the town, though at a cinema too far off our usual beat for a regular weekly visit; but I shall not soon forget the one episode I saw, which opened as I recall with the exterior of a house, so humped and menacing against a livid sky that it may well have been the one to which the title referred, and all in darkness save for a solitary light flashing a message in Morse from an upstairs window. The message must have been an S.O.S.; for in the room beyond, Miss White (the title did not have to explain) was in deadly peril. While she signalled desperately with her handlamp for help, the panels of the door were splintering under savage blows which we could not hear but which were echoed by the pianist thumping louder a tempestuous tune: as this music reached its climax black-gloved hands tore the wood away, and I closed my eyes at the final crash, opening them again too soon to face a lunatic glare through slits in the black cowl that gave the Hooded Terror his name: my nerve went as he came sidling and stooping forward, as it seemed, straight for me, and in another minute I might have fled, but just in time the title TO BE CONTINUED saved me as the bell might a boxer.

After this single encounter with the dread figure, I plagued my father no more to patronise the outlying cinema and contented myself to visit the ones we usually went to in Boscombe. The most important of these was called by us the Old Man's, though its manager, who had been in the police but more closely resembled a publican of a type obsolete today, must have been, I realise now, some years younger than my father at the time. Stout, red and smiling, with a convivial paunch: as a rule in shirtsleeves, waistcoat and watchchain, he catered chiefly for a youthful clientèle, showing serials twice a week, with Westerns and Keystone comedies to accompany them; under his benevolent eye, backed with the authority of his former profession, the small patrons more or less behaved themselves: that is to say they did not actually smash up the cinema, though there were outbreaks of stamping and whistling if the film, as happened frequently, broke down at a critical moment, and frantic warnings were shouted to the hero as whatever menace might be crept up behind him on the screen.

The din they kicked up at these times was torture to my father; and once he gave vent to his annoyance, tapping a particularly vociferous child on the shoulder and saying testily: What's the good of raising that row? They're not really there, they cant possibly hear you. The boy stared back with open mouth, in stupefaction and disbelief: obviously he thought my father, as he'd have phrased it, plain daft; and this theory was borne out by the fact that the hero did turn, as though he'd taken their advice, in the nick of time, and disarmed the villain who'd have done him else.

But the presiding genius of this place was less the Old Man himself than the pianist, Miss Crisp! As she took her seat in what must once have been the orchestra pit, a roar of welcome rose, of the sort usually reserved for Tom Mix or William S. Hart: and she would acknowledge, with a timid smile from under her close-fitting brown hat, the applause that greeted her appearance before settling down on the piano stool to strike up, as the lights went down, whatever music seemed appropriate to the picture about to be projected. The first day of the programme was not a good one to choose; for then Miss Crisp, not having seen the film before, would crane her head up at the screen to see, and who can blame her, what was going on: and her execution sometimes faltered in consequence; but on the whole she carried out a difficult and exacting task with—are these the right words?—verve and brio; certainly, though I never had the courage to speak to her—as many after the performance did—she had no more devoted admirer than I.

I've a quick ear for melody, and soon I was humming the tunes she played, especially those which announced the entrances of the villains or mystery men, for each of these had his own *leit-motif*: the one I recall most clearly, and I can hear it now, was named 'Remember Louvain' and had a picture of Louvain itself, in flames after enemy action, on the cover of the music which, having extracted the name from the Old Man in person, I now persuaded my mother to buy, so that I could hear its martial measure more often, and in our own home.

Our back drawing-room contained a piano; and Mother, by now recovered from her gastritis, though not yet allowed to leave the house, spent much time in there playing softly to herself. This room had hitherto been out of bounds to me, but now I was permitted to stand by and turn the sheets of music for her, when my father was out seeing one of the rare films to which children were not admitted. (Even with this provision, the choice of themes would seem more sophisticated than anything passed by censor nowadays, since the Adults Only I remember included *The Yoke*, with Theda Bara as an aunt seducing her own nephew, and *The Knife*, which depicted on the posters a turbaned Indian bending, with a gleaming blade in his hand, over a European woman on a couch: I was furious at not being taken, for I thought the subject was murder; though I now see it must have been abortion.)

But to return to 'Remember Louvain': there came a day when my mother was busy, the door of the back drawing-room left unlocked, and the temptation to knock out for myself that rousing tune proved too strong for me. I had never touched a piano before, my hands were then too small to strike an octave, nor of course could I read music but I had watched carefully the disposition of my mother's fingers on the keys and now, making an effort of memory and fumbling with many false notes at first, I managed to pick out stealthily something approximating to the desired air. As I grew in confidence and ceased to stumble, some instinct guiding me to the keys which brought forth the right sound, where I had struck only single notes to start with I began to put in chords, pressing the loud pedal down, so that the room rang with as close a pastiche of Miss Crisp as my limited technical experience could produce. Swaying to a sort of tribal rhythm on the piano-stool, elated and absorbed by the noise I was making, I failed to notice that the door had opened to reveal my mother standing on the threshold, struck into an attitude of astonishment as though by the black thunder I beat up from the bass. Behind her was Maud, looking in also aghast, and before I became fully aware that I had an audience, this was swelled by my father, just in from outdoors, who had hurried up without even removing his hat to see who, in his own words, was murdering the piano.

I expected the worst, but for once it did not come; instead, and to my vast surprise even my father appeared impressed by the impromptu recital: and thenceforward I was assigned the back drawing-room as a sort of studio to practise in, not only my painting but the piano; since a further door could be closed in the passage, thus sealing off the sound of my solo-concerts from the rest of the household. There was an attempt at one point to give me lessons, but I promptly routed the rather genteel spinster put in to teach me, and refused to read music, preferring to vamp out by trial and error the pieces that appealed to my ear: soon, besides 'Remember Louvain' and a similar composition called 'The Wind', I had added to my repertoire a very individual version of Rachmaninov's Prelude in C Sharp Minor, played by Miss Crisp to herald the appearance of a new mystery man, who was able, owing to pre-natal influence, to roar like a lion and had an iron foot, which however was detachable and did not prevent him from negotiating fire-escapes and the walls of buildings with the utmost celerity when pursued by the police.

During this musical interlude my collection of butterflies and moths suffered neglect, though drawing and painting still proceeded, as there were posters to be designed for the cinemas which in my mind I now owned. These changed their programmes twice weekly and were advertised on large slates which I hung in frames round the walls, lettered carefully in coloured chalks with the title of the film and the names of its stars, the times of showing being appended underneath, as an additional touch of realism. The programmes did not coincide by any means with those of the Boscombe and Bournemouth cinemas: as an exhibitor I was keenly competitive, and besides *The Picturegoer* and other kiné-weeklies, just beginning at that time to come out, genuine tradepapers had to be bought; so that, by learning advance news from their columns, I was able to scoop, so to speak, the local managers by announcing pictures before their release to the general public—and, in many cases, before their actual completion on the studio-floor.

It must not be thought, however, that these activities, though taking up a great deal of my time, kept me too busy to have any outside life: for besides the cinemas, which we still attended regularly in the afternoons, there were the morning walks with my father, undertaken daily summer or winter—except on days of torrential rain, when he sallied forth alone, sheltered by the ivory-handled umbrella that was a companion-piece to his stick and which, like it, had been the property of his father before him.

The walks began briskly: now that I was older there was no need for me to be dragged along by the hand, and I could skip freely at his side or run on ahead to look up the long steep hill which awaited us at the corner, winding upwards into the town. Then the pace slackened, for now the road-sweeper would be encountered, plying his broom at the kerb and ready for an interchange of political views or prophetic judgment on the course of the war. My father, a true democrat though not politically Left, would slow down as he drew level with the sweeper: if it were summer he would mop his forehead and neck during the discussion that followed; in winter he would hiss gently through his teeth like an ostler grooming an invisible horse, while the sweeper stamped in rhythm with the sound, beating his arms backwards and forwards about his middle to keep warm—the broom standing up meanwhile, whatever the season, on its own, like an interested third party about to venture at any moment an alternative opinion. During my entomological period, I had welcomed these talks, which were never less than ten minutes in duration, as they gave me an opportunity of searching the hedges nearby, for the Privet Hawk caterpillars which I never found; now I was impatient to press on, but my father declined to be hurried and would restrain sharply any attempt on my part to hasten the course of events. Then at last there'd be ceremonious leave-takings, which included always enquiries after the sweeper's wife and children, and wishes for their continued good health; the sweeper would reciprocate these sentiments in regard to our own family, and my father would rejoin me on the corner, with a final backward flourish of his stick.

Now the hill had to be embarked upon; halfway there was another halt: for Captain Forbes, toiling painfully up the slope ahead of us, would come in sight and heave-to alongside. Reminiscences of the sea would be exchanged, my father describing himself deprecatingly as a mere landlubber, though he had in fact sailed round the world in one of the ships owned by his father, and worked part of the time as one of the crew. Captain Forbes would politely demur, and by putting a question on troop movements overseas, redress the balance: the two men would then get into motion again, my father assuming a nautical gait in sympathy with that of the Captain, whose natural inclination to toll from side to side was exaggerated by the stroke he'd recently had. As they breasted the hill, breathing heavily and using their sticks as stags for leverage, I was allowed to out-distance them, providing I kept myself in view throughout; and I would await their arrival at the top, where the road curved round into the Southbourne shopping centre near a red-brick wall overgrown with dust-covered ivy.

This creeper had a special sentimental significance for me, and every morning I would pluck a leaf of it: for Ivy was the name of the girl whom I, like the heroes of those romantic dramas which until then I had thought effete, now worshipped from afar. She must have been all of eleven and tall for her age; her hair swung in plaits with bows on them down her back; and she wore the blue-and-white uniform of the girls' school situated halfway up the hill: so that on this climb twice a day as we passed, there was always the possibility that I might see her in the playground, or if not on the way down. I never spoke to her, and she was probably unaware of my existence; but in this way I got calf-love early out of my system, and when, later on in France, my contemporaries were proudly disporting themselves with mistresses old enough to be their mothers, I was going about, more fittingly, with girls of my own age.

My father and the Captain parted company at the point where I awaited them, and there were now two courses open to us: we could either turn left along Fisherman's Walk and round by the seafront; or, and this was more likely, straight on down towards the crossroads where, in the evenings as we returned from the cinema, the train made a long halt while the driver had his tea, brought to him in a covered basket by what he no doubt called his better half: a procedure which by the delay it caused in getting home infuriated my father, himself in urgent need of refreshment. On the corner by the crossroads was a large public-house in a gravel space curtained off by posts with chains across them; and on these chains I used to sit and swing to and fro while my father had what can only have been a glass of beer inside; for, as I've already said, he scarcely drank, though known as a three-bottle man in his day. Then, emerging with his thirst quenched, Home James! he'd cry heartily, and I'd be allowed to run all the way down the hill: sliding of course to a standstill halfway down to see if Ivy could be glimpsed anywhere about the grounds of her school.

Those were the mornings: this progress was repeated once again after lunch, minus the road-sweeper and Captain Forbes, and a tram would be taken down into Boscombe from the hill-top. Opposite me in this vehicle sat invariably a girl of about Ivy's height and age, though wearing a different school uniform she naturally reminded me of the hopelessness of my love, the more so since her feet, in their black shiny sensible shoes, were planted firmly on the floor of the tram, whereas mine dangled absurdly short over the edge of the seat. This emphasis on the gulf of the years firmly fixed, as they say, between Ivy and myself, would either make me grind my teeth in fury at not being grown-up, or pray fervently that, when adult status were reached at last, my legs would not only touch the ground, but stretch halfway across the aisle when I was seated: a prayer which in the fullness of time has been more than answered.

Then came the picture-house, not yet called a palace though ice-cream or Devonshire teas were served on trays during the performance; and Ivy would merge in my mind with whichever hard-done-by heroine suffered with glycerine tears upon the screen.

Thus I came to notice the female stars whom I'd hitherto taken for granted: a couple that especially captivated me—and in a short time superseded Ivy altogether, being even older and less attainable—were Gloria Swanson and Wanda Hawley, whose latest pictures I cut from the photogravure supplement of *The Picturegoer* and framed, to sigh over, among the posters and slates upon the wall. I used to fancy myself engaged, or even married, to them (and who can doubt that others, older, did the same?); unable finally to plump for dark or fair, my choice wavered between: and the one most in favour at the moment would take the place of honour upon the piano, while I played for her alone whatever romantic theme of an only girl I'd picked up from Miss Crisp or, more probably, the full orchestra (complete with an Italian conductor) that one of the bigger cinemas in Bournemouth boasted.

It was not long, however, before these emotions became translated once more into terms of flesh and blood: a new little girl had appeared in the neighbourhood, and no sooner did I see her, through the glass of the conservatory, tripping past one morning on her way to the Dame school down the road, than my affections were transferred to her *en bloc*; it was the *coup de foudre*, as the French say and Weidmann the mass murderer called the special shot that killed his victims stone dead: struck, as it might have been, by love's lightning or a bullet in the nape, I fell figuratively, and would have done literally, at her feet had I dared. Not knowing what she was really called, because of her hair bleached almost white by sun and seeming silk in texture like the big blue bow she wore in it to match her cornflower eyes, I christened her Wanda; she was nearer my own age than her namesake or Ivy, and therefore approachable: but how? I could have told my mother, who would probably have called on her parents and asked her round to tea, but this was scarcely in keeping with the romantic tradition I favoured, and nothing but a dramatic rescue would satisfy my sense of fitness in this direction.

Rescue, however, from what? It was true, I discovered in some way I forget, that twice a week she went to dancing class, and alone at that: an item of information that irked me, since I was still not allowed, officially, to leave the grounds on my own, and certainly not to roam, unescorted, the streets round about; nor was it likely that these were beset with the sort of perils from which I could snatch my darling in the approved manner. She seemed never to notice me as each day I watched her pass: my own shyness separating us in addition to the sheet of glass that lay between, so that I could not stare directly; and it was then that I began for the first time to take stock of my appearance, to ask myself did I look the gallant figure that I longed, in her eyes, to appear.

The mirror answered an emphatic no: I've always had an eye for the worst points of my own reflection, and as I see now the grooved lines and the grey in the hair, so what I saw then was a cissy: pale, narrow shouldered, the head too big for the body, the legs too skinny by half. This was not what it took to make a hero: in vain I tried to square my jaw like Tom Mix, to frown determinedly like Bill Hart, but I'd no chin to speak of, and what I had was round; as for frowning, how could one without eyebrows? The way I was dressed also began to disgust me: I demanded the big floppy grey flannel hats then in vogue among boys and was curtly refused; when, to seem more dashing, I turned up on one side the brim of the small round felt I was compelled to wear instead, and pulled this aslant on my head, I was told to put it straight and the brim down properly; nor was my hair cut in the regulation fringe across the forehead: worse still, it had a tendency to wave.

Determined that daring should triumph over these physical drawbacks, I took to scaling the back-garden wall and straddling atop of it, screened by a flowering tree from sight of the house: my intention being to drop down into the road when Wanda passed in transit to the dancing class; and, placing myself firmly in her path, by some urbane opening strike up an acquaintance; but somehow when the moment came and she appeared in the intersection of the street beyond, my nerve always failed, and I would stay astride, hot-faced with a sudden fear the sight of me would make her laugh.

Then came an afternoon when the chance I'd waited for so long was dropped, as they say, into my lap: as the spider with Nana, it seemed to me, an age ago, for scarcely had Wanda turned the corner out of sight than I heard a scream—shrill, unmistakably feminine—though on a smaller scale, naturally, than those shrieks that had rung through the nursery at the time of the arachnoid invasion. It could not be doubted that there was danger; and, prepared to defend Wanda with, if it had to be, my life, I leaped down from my perch, sped on up the road, and round the corner in my turn. What I saw made me halt, when I should have rushed in regardless as Doug Fairbanks would; nor would Jack Holt have been so backward; for there stood Wanda against a wall in tears, at her feet lay the satchel that no doubt contained her dancing shoes, and swaggering in front o' her were three boys of the type called rough, or even common, as their clothes proclaimed and the way that one now drew his sleeve across his nose, sneering like those villains whom he, too, had surely seen.

This one, the biggest and obviously the leader, then caught sight of me, calling out: What chew lookin for, hay? At the sound of his voice, hoarse in a way I'd never heard before, and at the contempt which it and his look contained, all my fighting spirit fled; as he came slouching forward, my knees, I'm now no longer ashamed to say, began to knock together, and next moment a shove in the chest sent me flying back into the wall. Bugger off, the leader said, you cissy bastard. And with these words, which no villain on sub-title ever used, and this must have been the first time I heard bad language, he lashed out at my bare knees with the switch he carried, doubtless whittled from some hedge. At this I loosed a piercing yell, not only at the pain, though that was sharp enough, but in panic at the blood I saw spurt out: shock and outrage also played their part, for no one had hit me in this way before.

With a grin the leader aimed another blow: Cry-baby cissy bastard, he said as the henchmen gathered round to watch the fun. Wanda, seizing her chance of escape, snatched up the satchel and ran at top speed, still sobbing, down the road, without a backward glance to see the fate I suffered: though, blinded with the hot salt that burst from my own eyes, I hardly knew she'd gone. Everything swam as the switch cut in a second time, I screamed and struck out wildly, anything to get away, my knuckles jarred on something solid, the henchmen flew aside; and suddenly, so much to my surprise I ceased to cry, I saw the leader sit down bang on his bottom in the dust.

In terror lest he rise and start again, I flung myself on top and smashed my fists down upon his face, inexpertly and not punching, but using them as hammers. I grabbed the switch from his hand and getting up belaboured him as he lay, both arms up to shield his head, bellowing the only word that fits the noise he made. Then I swung round on the henchmen, still in fear and not in fury, but they were already in flight; and when I turned again, the leader too had taken to his heels.

Was it then I learned that, if when cornered one hits out, opposition that seems impassable can smash like straw: and I dont mean fist-fighting? If so, it was a valuable lesson that has stood me in good stead since; but I remember that my sole concern at the time was how to explain, back at the house, the state I was in. Happily, despite the row we'd made, no one had come along to see, and I was able to climb back in, as well, without witnesses. My father was out at the time; he'd gone to a film about the white-slave traffic, at which my presence was neither requested nor desired, and I did what seemed the wisest thing: made a partial confession to my mother that I had climbed the wall and fallen off into the street. I think she was too relieved I'd cut knees and knuckles instead of a broken neck to do more than make me promise to be less foolhardy in the future. But with the sting of soap and water in the weals, as my knees were bathed and bandaged and a strip of sticking-plaster affixed to my fist, a sense of elation, which I had not felt whilst laying into the leader with the switch, inflated me to twice my size; and I made out to myself I had not done badly as a hero after all. Wanda of course should have stayed to thank me, but that would take place, I was sure, on the morrow; and the following morning I awaited her coming in the conservatory with what it would be understatement to describe as the liveliest anticipation.

She did not come, either that morning or the next; and when on the third day she was hauled quickly past by what was evidently a bad-tempered housemaid, and caught sight of me, plainly with recognition, through the glass, far from breaking away to greet me as her saviour, she turned her head aside as if in shame and increased, if that were possible, her pace, until she and her attendant were almost running. I was aghast with anger at this ingratitude: useless to argue that she had witnessed only my humiliation, and none of my ultimate triumph: she had spurned my love and I was now against her for good.

Thenceforward I saw myself as a hero no longer, but as Moralés, the man of blood and power: or any other villain bent on the persecution of a blonde. There was, for instance, that one in the serial at the cinema recently opened in Southbourne itself, played by William Pyke, who had operated the automaton in the Houdini film; he was always thinking up new ways of exterminating the heroine: baths of acid, magnetic beetles, petrifying powder; it was true that these methods always failed, when a bullet in the head, I often felt, would have been more successful; true also that his motive was not thwarted passion but a million dollars he'd inherit at her death; nonetheless, my ideas of revenge on Wanda ran on similar lines: the problem was how, in the event, to escape detection? William Pyke could transform himself, at a moment's notice, by the application of a dark stain on the skin, a kinky grey wig, and a set of projecting false teeth, from a handsome young man into a hideous creature known as the Mysterious Kaffir. I had not the means of assuming this elaborate disguise, nor could I even lay hands on the tail-coat and wide-brimmed Veld hat which was the costume that went with it.

A handkerchief tied round the lower half of the face, then: in default of the mask I was not allowed to buy? This might do at a pinch, but what about the housemaid, who now obviously had orders to accompany Wanda everywhere? An arrow, fired from over the wall, might dispose of her: I had, alas, no bow. Poisoned darts from a blowpipe were better: failing these, a stone from a catapult? This brought back memories of Mrs Bradlaw: I didnt want to risk the police again; but on the other hand Wanda must be dealt with soon, for my pride's sake alone: and kidnapping was the very least that would do. Sitting up on the wall, despite my promise to my mother, I'd watch for her to show up at the hour of the dancing class: the housemaid still presented an obstacle that seemed insuperable, and I was deep in new plans for her removal when one afternoon I met Elton.

He was a boy of about my own age, but with all the attributes which I so woefully lacked: he was sturdily built, his cheeks flushed with pink and white healthy patches, and from under the brim of his floppy grey hat a fringe of fair hair could be seen neatly combed across his forehead. I can't recall what actually started the argument; I think he called Hullo Sonny up to me as I sat astride the wall: I resented this patronising form of address from a contemporary and told him so, where-upon I was challenged to come down and fight. Fresh from my victory over what had seemed a much tougher proposition, I dropped into the road without more ado and leaped at Elton with whirling fists; next thing I knew I was down on my back without having landed a blow. Twice I got up and twice I was thrown: the third time with such a thump I was more than winded and Elton had to help me up. Jiu-jitsu, he explained, easy when you know how. Show you how to do it if you like.

I'd heard of jiu-jitsu, Warner Oland had been known to use it when impersonating a Chinaman, and I could see at once that it was a necessary part of a villain's equipment: an immediate demonstration was about to take place, but had to be postponed, as my father, who'd been doing some shopping, appeared unexpectedly round the bend of the road and bore heavily down upon us. First of all he wanted to know what I was doing out in the street, and secondly why I was covered with dust, had we been fighting? He made us shake hands, which by now we were quite ready to do; then to my surprise asked Elton to come and have tea one day soon: an invitation unprecedented in all my experience. Do the boy good to have a friend of his own age, I heard him tell my mother that evening. Fine manly-looking little fellow, too.

So Elton duly arrived at the house, wearing an Eton suit, and in the course of conversation it turned out he knew Wanda, they'd met at the dancing class, only her name was really Gladys: moreover her parents were moving shortly to Christchurch, where she'd be out of my reach, which meant that more than ever I had to work fast. Meanwhile there was jiu-jitsu to be learned, and we went out into the back garden for our first lesson. Now try and hit me, Elton said. Go on. Try. I obeyed, he slipped the blow, caught my wrist, and jerked me over his shoulder so that I somersaulted into the grass: with, this time, inconsiderable impact. Again, he said; I got up, same outcome; now you do it to me,

Elton said, flicking a fist at my face. I in my turn ducked, grabbed his arm, and hauled him over my back; as he'd told me, it was astonishingly easy: the only trouble being that Elton landed too heavily on the point of his shoulder and broke his collarbone—at the very moment, too, when my father had come to an upstairs window to overlook our play.

The immediate results of this misadventure are too painful to dwell upon, though less painful than they were for Elton: he was carried away groaning on a stretcher; I was confined to an attic under lock and key; and in the evening Mr and Mrs Elton arrived for an extremely stormy interview, during which I acquired, my own parents agreeing, a reputation as an unmitigated young thug. An earlier incident, when I had thrown sand in the eyes of another boy who had annoyed me on the beach, was recalled in confirmation of this; and all visits to the cinema were cancelled for the next few weeks, as Father blamed my brutality and violence on ideas assimilated from what he called those confounded serials. Consequently I never found out what happened to the Kaffir, as this particular film came to an end while I was confined to the house. Nor had I any opportunity of getting my own back on Wanda, whom I refused even in my mind to call Gladys, and whom I held in some way responsible for my downfall, since the back garden was placed temporarily out of bounds, and she no longer passed by the conservatory in the mornings. I was forced to conclude that she had gone—which I afterwards found to be correct—and like many another, and for by no means the last time in my life, I sought to forget my frustration and my sorrow by throwing myself with renewed energy into what, even then, I called my work.

Bigger and better programmes, sensational double-bills, were chalked up on my slates, for the trade-papers, at least, had not been stopped; and, starved of actual film-going, I was compelled to write, or rather to draw, my own: sketching each shot to a page, with the captions printed underneath; thus anticipating a mode later introduced in the early German films, for I refused to spare a separate sheet for sub-titles: paper being, then and now, one of the few things I am economical about. The piano also came in for much punishment at this time, the piece I chose to play in memory of Wanda being Chopin's Funeral March, though whether from wishful thinking or in mourning for what might have been, I cant after all these years remember.

Meanwhile my lack of formal education was once more worrying my parents, though their reasons now for not sending me to school were no longer because they believed I was too delicate to withstand the régime, but because they feared I might burn down or blow up the establishment, having first broken the collarbones of all the pupils. I could read and write: had, indeed, read more than most boys of my age; I could add up, subtract and multiply, though not divide; but my father considered in any case that knowledge of the three Rs alone was insufficient. Private tutors, again put forward as the ideal answer, proved, like nannies previously, hard to obtain; most young men of the right type and qualifications were serving in one or other of the Forces; and the only example who presented himself for inspection smelt so strongly of alcohol and was in other ways so obviously unsuitable that he got no further than the threshold of the house. A governess was out of the question, as the ruthless treatment I'd meted out to the unfortunate woman who'd tried to teach me music showed that a strong masculine hand was required to keep me in order.

My father now took on this task himself, and every morning I reported to his study where at last, during the geography lesson, he let me spin the globe of the world. This was the lesson I liked best, since my father would sometimes digress from routine methods of instruction to speak from personal experience of the countries on the revolving atlas: earthquakes and a revolution in Cuba; grizzly bears and a blizzard in Canada, where for a short time he had been in the Mounted Police; a storm off the Cape of Good Hope and a show-boat on the Mississippi River. His tales of the life he'd lived in London as a young man, though there were many details of this which were not then fit for my ears, seemed to me no less exotic than the albatross dying on the deck, the Chinese bank-tellers in Singapore counting stacks of silver dollars with unerring accuracy, or the Kelly Brothers, Australian bushrangers who were eventually roasted to death in their own protective armour, made, like that of another famous fraternity, from household utensils: though in the Kellys' case these were doubt-less melted down. I had never consciously seen London, though born in one of its suburbs, and I imagined it like the cover of the *Strand* magazine only wrapped in a thick fog which lifted from time to time to reveal brief glimpses of hansom-cabs, suffragettes, and people in Edwardian dress drinking ceaseless champagne: Oscar Wilde or Jack the Ripper might emerge at any moment, or perhaps my favourite character, the Tichbourne Claimant, whom years after his release from prison my father had met personally in a French pension, where despite everything he still insisted on being addressed as Sir Roger.

Once my father had got really started on his recollections, time passed quickly for us both, and with luck I would escape the history lesson which, though interesting also, I liked less because I could never remember the dates required of me. I would therefore lure him towards the Tichbourne case whenever possible: this could sometimes be done through the Claimant's connection with Australia, which brought the affair within the scope of geography; and after that the description of the trial (which he had attended daily, while the special Bonds sold in Court, a sort of legalised lottery, fluctuated in value according to the evidence) would more than cover the time allotted to my studies, besides being absorbing in its own right. My father would act all the parts: he was especially good as the Prosecuting Counsel, playing cat and mouse with the claimant in the box: Would it surprise you to know, Sir Roger—as some damaging fact was suavely produced to discomfit his wretched opponent, for whom a blustering tone and a Cockney accent were always used. Then suddenly he would break off, it might be in mid-sentence: his eyes would pull focus from far away on to the dial of the watch, this made of gun-metal and not the one he used outdoors, which lay on the desk before him; he would start as if stung, and with a muttered God bless my soul, dismiss me for the day.

At this time his desk would be covered, not only with Napoleonic notes, but with letters from his two sisters, bordered always in heavy black and bearing foreign stamps, for one lived in Havana and the other in Marseille. The funereal notepaper was due most likely to a bereavement in some distant branch of the family with which these aunts, unlike my father, kept up correspondence assiduously, though they themselves had quarrelled bitterly years before and continued the feud today: never writing to one another directly but using my father as a buffer-state, a position which he occupied none too willingly.

There were estates in Cuba over which a controversy was now raging: also a house, actually not far from Bournemouth, but too big for any of us to live in, that was up for sale, both sisters claiming the lion's share of the proceeds. Aunt Enid threatened to come over from Cuba in person to settle matters; my father was intent on staving off this visit, since we were stricken by the servant problem: Cook having left and Maud taken over under my mother's expert tuition, which made for better meals but far too much work for Mother to cope with; a daily woman came in to help, but my brother was due at last for his long-delayed leave (to my parents' satisfaction he had meanwhile been commissioned and had sent a snapshot of himself standing with a brother-officer in front of the Sphinx). On top of this, there was a move to demobilise Carol, who'd had a violent brush with the authorities (the arrest of her friend Morgan for bigamy may have had something to do with this). Anyway my father foresaw them all arriving at the same time, and an army of retainers would be needed to attend to my aunt alone, to say nothing of sleeping accommodation. He wrote frantically back and forth to no avail, for a cablegram arrived abruptly announcing that Aunt Enid was already on the high seas.

Trouble, Father muttered gloomily when he received this news; we're in for it, mark my words. That woman's a stormy petrel if ever there was one. He was not far wrong: for though her arrival did not coincide after all with that of either my brother or sister, the visit brought about a family tumult of such violence that the war, it seemed to me then, gave up attempting to compete: since shortly afterwards a general armistice was declared.

The Brown Man

*   *   *

AND NOW MY AUNT WAS UPON US. A DESCENT WOULD BE THE only way to describe her arrival: for though she had not actually flown over, as she swept into our hall, with a long peacock-blue silk travelling cloak trailing behind in the wind of her passage, calling out greetings and commands concerning the disposal of her luggage in a high-pitched penetrating drawl, attended by a French maid with clattering high heels, she gave a definite feeling of having swooped down from the skies. I had visualised her wearing a mantilla and wielding a fan, as in the portraits of my grandmother that I'd seen: instead she had her hair up in tight red curls which the maid renewed with heated tongs every morning, and nothing could have been less Spanish than her clothes, which was not surprising since, as I did not know then, they came from Paris. In her youth she had been a suffragette, had chained herself to railings and gone to prison, so she claimed, for the cause (though the family had bailed her out almost at once); and though extremely beautiful then and still handsome now, she had never married. This, my father said (a remark I was not intended to overhear), was because no man worthy of the name would allow himself to be bossed about in the way she expected; and masterful was undoubtedly the word for her manner, nor can she ever have been easy to get along with.

The moment she entered the house it was turned immediately upside down; she rapped out orders to the maid in French with a French accent, she acknowledged us in English with an accent unfamiliar to me which I thought at first was Cuban, but soon realised was American; she took small notice of me when I was led forward to be introduced, being evidently a believer in the theory that little boys should be seen and not heard: a conviction which she was later to voice aloud. To my consternation, having demanded what she called A Little Den of Her Own, she was allotted the back drawing-room for the duration of her visit: her reaction, on being confronted with my slates and posters, with the photographs of film stars and the evidence of my painting, was instantaneous: All this'll have to be cleared out. What is it anyway? My mother embarked on an embarrassed explanation, during which Aunt Enid scarcely concealed her amusement; and turning a brief glance on me, she said: Well isnt he just quaint. Then she motioned to her maid, and the slates were already being lifted from the walls when I was led away to be got ready for tea.

It was not until the end of this meal, after she had commented with displeasure upon the scarcity of butter at our table and been reminded by my father that there was a war on, that she again addressed me directly; then, lighting a gold-tipped cigarette and leaning across with what was meant to be a gracious smile, but which terrified me by its gleaming suggestion that I was to be eaten instead of butter, she asked: And what are you going to be when you're grown up, my little man? Unable to take my eyes off the cigarette, for I had never seen a woman smoke before, except dance-hall girls and gun-molls in movies; overawed yet resentful at her tone, I was silent; and she continued: A soldier? An engine-driver? Answer your Aunt Enid, my father told me heavily.

It was now, for the first time (but not the last), that I put my foot in it during her stay. I should explain first that, since my recent behaviour had been irreproachable, cinema-going had once again been sanctioned, but was restricted to the small picture-house near the top of the hill in Southbourne, where until the ban I had followed the career of the Mysterious Kaffir. Now, however, a new serial called The Woman in Grey had started in place of the other: the woman of the title had the scar of a bite on the back of her hand hidden from sight by a jewelled plaque, and believed to have been inflicted, in her death-struggles, by an old lady for whose murder she had served a long term of imprisonment. Needless to say she was not guilty, and it was with her efforts to uncover the truth, and also a hoard of precious stones concealed in a grandfather clock, that the story was concerned. Opposing her was the real murderer, introduced on the sub-titles as J. DE HAVILLAND HUNTER, AN ADVENT-URER, a debonair young man dressed usually in white ducks, for he originally appeared from some tropical country, and armed with a sword-stick with which he used ruthlessly to run through all who stood in his path: excepting our heroine, for whom, like the Kaffir before him, he devised more diabolical and complicated deaths which were defeated by their very ingenuity, when the sword-stick would have served.

The influence which this character came to exercise over me exceeded by far that of any villain I'd yet encountered, and for all I know it may be for this reason that I carry to this day a malacca cane of the type affected by Hunter, although without a sword inside; so that when my aunt asked me this leading question over the tea-table, and my father insisted on an answer, only one profession appeared desirable: An adventurer, Aunt Enid, I said stoutly. There was a stunned silence: my aunt's glittering smile slowly faded, the smoke from her cigarette curled up in front of a face frozen and incredulous; my mother sat bolt upright with the tea-pot suspended in her hand; then, breaking the rigidity of this waxwork tableau, my father sneezed convulsively ¡Carajo! into his handkerchief, and snatching up his smelling-bottle: James, he thundered, leave the room instantly.

I obeyed, though failing to understand what all the fuss was about: to me the word Adventurer at that time and for some years after seemed to sum up everything any self-respecting boy could possibly want out of life; though I learned to keep this opinion to myself, for I found it led to unpopularity if publicly expressed, especially with adults: indeed, I remember becoming furiously indignant myself when, in 1937, a girl to whom I'd once been engaged accused me of having achieved my erstwhile ambition, which only goes to show, does it not, how one's ideas change with the passage of time.

In the course of the next few days I often asked my mother how much longer Aunt Enid was going to stay, and while she always replied that to ask such a question was most inhospitable, I'd an idea that she too hoped for an early departure, for my aunt was not, to say the least of it, an accommodating guest. Moreover, the French maid gave herself the airs of a princess in disguise, and when preparing in the kitchen some American patent food which Aunt Enid could not do without, got both in the way and on the nerves of Maud and the daily woman, Mrs Bagge.

Meanwhile I was confined to my former nursery upstairs, now much too small for me to do more than sleep in. It was impossible to paint in such conditions and my cinemas had to close pending repairs; nor was I able to play the piano, since this instrument was sequestrated in the back drawing-room, where I could not venture without my aunt's permission: which showed no signs, so far, of being granted. There she would retire, for a smoke she said, after breakfast, and re-emerge, another gold-tipped cigarette waggling between her lips, to besiege my father in his study with family business about eleven, so that our morning walks were temporarily discontinued and I was left with no companionship at all save that of the woodlice in the conservatory: and to play even there was frowned upon, since my aunt said she liked to see little boys with clean hands at all times of day, not only at meals.

At table Aunt Enid talked family: her views on other relatives were uncharitable even by my father's elastic standards in this respect, and he was frequently driven to disagree, thereby finding himself, *malgré lui*, on the side of some distant connection whom in fact he cordially detested. But my aunt's especial venom was reserved for her sister in Marseille, who according to her was a Machiavellian schemer by nature, a malicious intriguer by choice, artful as a wagon-load of monkeys: the female of the species indeed. She would cite as an example of her sister's cunning a visit which Aunt Jane had once paid to cousins in Canada: these were Presbyterians and said family prayers at some unearthly hour of the morning, whereas Aunt Jane like all of us was a Catholic and had not since convent days attended anything earlier than eleven o'clock Mass, if that. Coming down half-awake, therefore, to an unheated chapel in the bitter Canadian cold, she found she was expected to read the Bible and, what's more, to know her place in it: promptly and with great presence of mind, she dropped the book at the feet of a kindly cousin, who handed it back to her open at the appropriate verse, thus saving, for the time being, her bacon. Again, while staying away as a child, she had broken wind at breakfast (Aunt Enid used a Spanish word for this, but I guessed her meaning); naturally her hosts were too polite to take notice, and continued to eat quietly, but Aunt Jane, pointing out of the window at some cattle in a far-away pasture, exclaimed indignantly, Oh the naughty cow. These proofs of her quick-wittedness privately delighted me; and I hoped she would get the better of Aunt Enid in the financial complications then afoot, though I believe it would not have been to the advantage of our particular branch had she done so.

Then they'd all start to talk business, these discussions took place always in Spanish, and during them Aunt Enid would rise from the table and pace the floor restlessly: even my mother would occasionally chime in, though my aunt's attitude to her remained condescending to a degree. There were papers to be signed, some of these were in

Spanish too: a transfer of shares as far as I could understand; and this was the main reason for her visit, though the House bulked largely, also, in her mind. Once we drove out, in a limousine hired by my aunt, to look at it, though I was made to wait outside with the chauffeur while they entered through a gate in the high surrounding wall; and it was the same car that took us to visit an Abbey in the neighbourhood, on the day when I was supposed to have finally disgraced myself in the eyes of my aunt. What I did wrong was never quite clear to me: I expressed disappointment, it's true, that the monk who acted as guide was not got up with a black cowl over his face like the Hooded Terror; I also called attention to the circular piece cut out of the long refectory table, deducing, in a voice perhaps too loud, that the reason for this was to accommodate, in olden days, the stomach of the presiding Abbot, who would otherwise have been unable to sit down in comfort: a theory borne out, as I did not fail to indicate, by a painting on the wall which showed the monks tucking with relish into a well-stocked table. I cannot deny that these remarks were not well received, but it was in the car coming back that the really terrible thing occurred: perhaps I was sick; anyhow my aunt then and there, as she stated more than once, washed her hands of me for all time.

From that day onward I took my meals upstairs, and practically the only place where I remained persona grata was in the kitchen, where I sought insidiously, in the manner attributed to my Aunt Jane, to encourage a revolt against the French maid. I rather fancied myself in the rôle of agent provocateur, following once again the example of J. De Havilland Hunter, who was by no means averse to creating disruption in the ranks of his enemies by setting one against the other. Also I enjoyed the company of Mrs Bagge: a fanatical film fan, always prepared to abandon mop and pail for a nice little chat, over a cup of tea, about the serials she'd seen. It was Mrs Bagge who enlightened me as to the real identity of the Hooded Terror, but in such a way that it has still remained an enigma throughout the years: Oh im, she sniffed contemptuously, e was just er idiot brother, when they took is ood off. What can she have meant? That the Terror was a brother of Pearl White's in the film, outwardly normal but in secret a homicidal lunatic: using the word idiot in the sense that Nurse used it? Or that he was a brother posing merely as a congenital idiot whilst in reality dangerously insane? Small wonder in either case that the Bishop had done his best to have the film suppressed; but the question continues to perplex me from time to time: and if any reader of these pages should happen to know the answer, it would be an act of kindness to communicate with me care of the publishers and so reduce by one the number of things I shall never know.

My liking for Mrs Bagge was reciprocated, also she shared my distaste for the maid and was more than ready to lead a rebellion: the difficulty was to inflame Maud, a pacifist by nature, to the necessary pitch. Before this result could be brought about, however, the enemy position fell of its own weight; for early one morning I was awakened by voices of such volume that, since sound ascends, they penetrated even to the top floor where I had my quarters. Half curious, half scared, for I was not sure that with her smoking Aunt Enid had not set the house alight, I jumped out of bed and in my night clothes ran downstairs to a vantage point from which I could overlook the hall: obviously the place this row was rising from.

Sure enough, there stood my father, framed on the threshold of his study, and pointing with a gesture whose meaning was unmistakable towards the outer door of the house; while Aunt Enid, drawn up to her full height, which though considerable was not equal to that of her brother, despite his heavy stoop, was fighting a losing battle to shout down, in the same language, the flood of evidently vituperative Spanish that poured from him. I danced, literally, with glee as unseen by the protagonists I peered over those banisters down which I was forbidden to slide: my only regret being that, as on the day of Nana's dismissal, I was unable to understand what was said, and I made up my mind to learn languages in preparation for any such occasion in the future: though it did not look as if there would be another involving Aunt Enid, for the scene down in the hall, from tone and attitude alone, bore every sign of an irreconcilable quarrel. Regretfully I was now obliged to withdraw, for my aunt suddenly stalked forward, rigid as a poker (and equally incandescent) with rage; as she started to climb the staircase, my father followed her to the foot of it and seemed almost to shake his fist, though I could not swear to this: the gesture was made as I turned to run silently up to my room, and I was in too big a hurry to make certain, for in another moment Aunt Enid would assuredly have seen me.

I was able, however (as I had not been with Nana), to observe her departure from my window, which over-looked the road; it took place in the hired limousine, maid and all, and was not, since there was more packing to be done, effected as speedily as that of Nurse: though quickly enough to constitute a complete rout. But it was not for several days that I managed, by roundabout methods, to discover the cause of the eruption. It seems that Aunt Enid, entering my father's study early, before he himself had come downstairs, had found lying on his desk a letter from Aunt Jane, delivered the day before: this she had opened and read, and while she was still gasping with indignation at the attacks on her that it contained, Father had entered and caught her with the letter in her hand. Far from being abashed, she proceeded to forbid him further correspondence with what she called That Woman (and may be worse) in Spanish. Father, losing control completely, retorted that he would do as he pleased in his own house, in which, as his junior by several years, she remained on sufferance only: and one's imagination can supply the rest.

It was not until she had gone, unfortunately, that he remembered the final papers concerning the share-transfer had not been signed: this entailed an almost endless interchange of letters with bankers, attorneys and trustees, many of them on the other side of what Aunt Enid might have called the mill-pond. Meanwhile our fortunes were temporarily in a bad way, as he was having trouble over the bomb-damage claim which he had registered in respect of our house at Ramsgate, and all this caused him to plunge heavily on the horses in an endeavour to bridge the financial gap, across which the repercussions of his row with Aunt Enid echoed hollowly for many a year.

But of these things I at that time knew nothing and cared less: I was too busy re-installing myself in the back drawing-room; and while in various parts of the world, not excluding Scotland, members of our scattered clan rallied to the defence of one or another party in the family schism, or sniped as lone guerrillas at all and sundry from outposts of their own, the imaginary doors of my cinemas, re-painted and decorated, were flung open, to the tune of a triumphal march, in gala premières attended, in one case at least, by Royalty.

Soon after, as I've already told, the war came to an end. There were banner headlines in the newspapers, the streets were strung with bunting, and the houses round about (with one exception: our own) hung out huge flags, which their occupants must have been saving up, for just such another celebration, ever since the relief of Mafeking. I was very upset that our home should be the only one left undecorated, for like most children I wanted passionately to conform (hence my desire for fringes and floppy grey hats), and it was no fault of mine that

I remained invariably in some way different and out of the movement: a position to which I have by now become resigned and even, at times, considered a matter for self-congratulation.

But in this instance my father paid no attention to my pleas: he refused brusquely and point-blank to buy any flags, saying he'd no money to waste on such nonsense.

He did, however, get me a small Union Jack to wave when I accompanied him downtown on the night of what was called Peace Day, an occasion antedating, as I recall, the official armistice celebrations. My mother remained at home: very wisely, since the streets were black with a dense crowd, apparently gone berserk in an excess of relief and brief brotherly love; we were deafened by singing, cheering and the whirr of rattles, together with roars of DOWN WITH KAISER BILL, for the crowd, sportsmanship notwithstanding, did not yet extend its good-fellowship to the vanquished foe, and this would have been too much to expect. Finally I was torn from my father's side and almost trampled to death underfoot, losing my flag into the bargain, before he was again able to catch sight of me in the mêlée and effect a rescue by reason of his bulk and weight and, I regret to say, the use of his stick.

As regards daily life, the cessation of hostilities made little difference to me personally, except that it seemed sugar-rationing was relaxed soon afterwards, though I may be wrong there; at any rate saccharine tablets went out of circulation, and I no longer used to shout SUGAR —DAVENPORT! over my porridge: a cry of protest against the Food Minister which I had learned from my sister at a time when supplies were particularly short, and continued to raise long after, for all I know, the Ministry may have changed hands.

And now Carol herself, or May as she had become since Al Laperle went out of her life (though I will continue calling her by her former name, to avoid confusion), came home, definitely demobilised. I had not, of course, forgotten my protestations of undying love on the park bench, and had indeed looked forward longingly to this reunion; but somehow, in the realisation, it was a slight disappointment, as meetings too often rehearsed in the mind sometimes are; besides which, Ivy and Wanda had come in between since we parted, and we were both a little burnt-out with the emotions that for each of us by now had become extinct. Then, too, her army service had changed her; she now felt she had earned her independence, used a modicum of make-up (or as Mother expressed it, Paint) openly, wore her hair bobbed and fluffed out at the sides, and lit cigarettes after meals, like Aunt Enid, without apology. All this excited no outward disapproval from our parents, who had decided, as once I heard them say, to give the girl her head.

In her room she played records on the phonograph she had brought with her: I was sometimes allowed to go up and listen; and thus I became familiar with jazz, called ragtime then: not the nostalgic dreamy rhythm with a dying fall to which I was afterwards to dance, but a cheerful jangling series of tunes—'Tickling the Ivories', 'Samoa Samoa', 'Oh Johnny oh Johnny how you can love'—which were immediately reproduced by me on the piano downstairs. While the phonograph wheezed and scratched—though its faulty recording seemed to me magic—Carol would practise steps, whirling and sliding in the arms of an invisible partner. She frequently complained that we never gave dances, Father replied that he could not afford to entertain, and his one restriction was that she should not go alone to those given publicly in the town. When your brother comes home, he'd say, will be time enough my dear, and Carol would retort witheringly When! For new complications connected with post-war army-office routine had again put back my brother's leave, as he was now on the staff in Cairo: snap-shots of the pyramids arrived but no Willie; Carol unburdened her loneliness in long desperate letters to which he replied by postcards in French, and still he did not come.

It was Carol who now took me on my morning walks and to the pictures; together we saw the last of Hunter who, to my great disap-pointment, died of fright: not at all the fate which, as a prospective adventurer, I envisaged for myself. Just as he had uncovered the hoard and was gloating over the heap of jewels a pet monkey belonging to the aunt he'd murdered sprang on him in the dark; and the touch of its cold fingers, we were told by the titles, froze him, with their suggestion of the dead woman come back from the grave, to everlasting ice: though until then he'd showed no signs of suffering from a weak heart. Despite this incongruous end, I remained nonetheless loyal to his memory, and spent much time in searching, without success, the shelves of the libraries visited daily with my sister for the book of the film, which was by C.N. and A.M. Williamson. (I was not to find a copy until 1943, when I came across one by chance in a military hospital near Birmingham; it bore but a distant resemblance to the serial I'd seen: Hunter was there after a fashion, but under the name Haines-Havilland and having the outward appearance of a saint in a stained-glass window in contrast to the satanic beauty of the figure in the film; nor was there any swordstick.)

What I found in Boscombe, however, was a number of books by Arthur B. Reeve, the adaptor of the screenplay, also of the one containing the Kaffir (from a book, if I mistake not, by the same authors). He had in fact done the scripts of most of the serials I'd followed, and this was the first time I realised, as most people still have not, that a film must be written before it can be seen. Reeve immediately became my favourite author, putting in the shade even the Tarzan and Martian series that were appearing at the time, and I took to reading again with a vengeance: *The Exploits and Triumph of Elaine*, *The Silent Bullet*, *The Poisoned Pen*, are titles I remember; also a volume of short stories called simply *An Adventuress*, which I read avidly, thinking to find in it the lineaments of my female counterpart in the future, and which I re-read many years later as *The Panama Plot*. Under the influence of these novels, which featured Craig Kennedy the scientific detective, I redoubled my output as a scenarist and filled whole exercise books with shots, as a serial ran to so many pages (a fight alone taking up twenty or thirty) that to find a single one thick enough to contain the full eighteen episodes was impossible, though it was my dream (unfulfilled) to have such a book specially made.

Carol began to take an interest in my films, and one of them in particular, called 'The Gilded Lily', a title I had found in a trade-paper and used as a basis for my original screenplay, as some authors are said to choose their titles first and build a story around them: though I myself have rarely if ever done this during my adult career. The Gilded Lily in my version was the name of a nightclub and also what its patrons called the girl who acted as attraction there; the villain was the proprietor, and the story did not greatly differ from those films now featuring Miss Jane Russell; though I do not claim priority of invention: there must have been many similar even then for me to crib from. But there was one twist which I added out of my own head, and it was this that nearly landed me in bad trouble.

I had noticed, in pictures of this type, that the heroine was always in danger of being Ruined. I did not know the meaning of this phrase, which was sometimes described, alternatively, as a Fate Worse than Death: but the heroine always contrived to escape it, by the same good fortune that enabled her to give Death itself the slip. I determined to be different: my heroine was to succumb; I was uncertain what picture should be drawn in this connection, but after much thought contented myself with one of the proprietor half-strangling the Gilded Lily, for I'd a suspicion there had to be some kind of struggle first; and this I followed with a page left blank except for the brief announcement that Ruination had taken place.

My sister, reading this, was highly amused; and thinking he would take it in the same spirit, showed the script to my father. He was not amused: in fact the reverse; I came in for a lecture almost as severe and incomprehensible to me as that which I received later, at school, from Monsieur l'Abbé when, being used to mispronounce in French the word camp, I spelt it accordingly in an essay; and but for Carol's intervention on my behalf, all cinemas would once again have been out of bounds. Despite this, I believed that she had acted with deliberate malice; and, when I spoke to her at all, addressed her as 'Jordan': as who should say Judas, for Jordan was the name of the traitor in the current serial at the Old Man's, where the part of the hero was played by Jack Dempsey.

Carol was upset by this attitude, which she considered undeserved, and finally won me over by buying me as a present a magnificent black velvet mask, which covered the entire face without actually being a hood, and had an ornamental fringe hanging down from the chin. All my resentment melted at sight of this, when the box containing it was opened to tempt me, and there was a tearful reconciliation: after which our relationship became almost as idyllic as it had been the previous Christmas; though the mask, for obvious reasons, had to be buried in its box in the garden, and assumed only when we were alone together in Carol's bedroom. Very often, during this phase, we used, after the pictures, to have tea at Bobby's, the big department store in Bournemouth itself, and afterwards wander in the gardens overlooking the sea, where there were clumps of torch-lilies, or red-hot pokers: a flower which obsessed me to the extent that I once in later years fell in love with a girl because she wore a frock of the same flame colour, though my passion for the red-hot pokers proved on the whole more lasting.

It was here that we first became aware of the Brown Man. On this initial occasion he followed us for quite a distance before we could shake him off; and he was frequently to be seen, during the days that followed, lurking outside Bobby's itself, waiting without a doubt for us to emerge, when he would saunter quietly along a pace or two behind, puffing at his pipe, a light cane crooked over his arm, and apparently unconcerned with us; so that, since no proof existed that he was taking anything but a constitutional stroll, he could not be given in charge as Carol once or twice threatened in a loud voice to do: though not addressing herself directly to him. His nickname was not derived from any notable swarthiness: he was in point of fact rather pale; it referred rather to the colour of his suits which, whatever their material, were always some shade of brown, mostly dark, and worn as a rule with a check cap pulled rakishly over one eye, at an angle I secretly admired. He was of medium height and indeterminate age, though as he seemed to have grey hair at the one visible side of his head we both decided he was old, that is we put him at about forty; and we might never have noticed him at all, but for his one conspicuous feature: his eyes were hidden by spectacles with black lenses, which in winter seemed out of place and, to us, highly sinister.

It was these glasses that made my sister sure he was a German spy, though he could not have looked more British: the pipe he smoked was a briar and not a Meerschaum with a lid on it; but Carol had a nose for them, she insisted, adding: Remember Schwob. Perhaps, I said, he's an accomplice of Schwob's, come to exact a terrible revenge. This was not a comforting theory, Carol was by no means sure that it was inaccurate, and now we fairly shot along whenever the Brown Man, with the black circles in his pale face that made him seem sightless, appeared unexpectedly, as though from ambush, among the red-hot pokers or, as happened once or twice, in a crowded street: his own pace, however, never quickened, and we soon left him behind.

At first he seemed restricted to Bournemouth, but one day he showed up in Boscombe and then in Southbourne, where shortly we began to see him all the time. He's found out where we live, I told Carol, he's preparing to attack. She thought so too, and this seemed to call for Father's intervention, as in the case of the Old Civvy. The moment chosen to put it to him was at table, when the dessert had been served and he was usually in a receptive mood, but father had not forgotten Mr Foxe either: I suppose, he said, this man will turn out to be our landlord, like last time.

Oh Father, Carol said, how could he be? Well, Father said, I've never seen our present landlord, so I cant tell. But I'm not taking any chances on it. Do you mean you're not going to do anything? Carol asked with rising indignation. Father looked at her over the plate of bananas on which he'd begun to sprinkle salt instead of sugar, for he claimed it brought out the flavour. My dear girl, he said, if you are old enough to paint your face and walk around puffing at a cigarette, you are old enough to deal with men who follow you about the streets. As you suppose, I shall do nothing. Besides, I'm perfectly sure your Brown Man is quite harmless. He's a German spy, Carol shouted. Then he must be out of employment, poor fellow, my father said mildly. The war is over, if you remember. He began to eat his bananas, there was plainly no more to be said, and that afternoon the Brown Man penetrated to the tea-room at Bobby's and sat at a table not far from ours, but with his head turned away, though we were sure he watched us.

In face of this sly surveillance, and the fact that the Brown Man was next seen upon our very hill, Carol was more than ever impatient for our brother's homecoming, since I was too small to protect her when the attack finally materialised; and when a letter came giving a definite date for his return she sobbed with relief; alas, it was cancelled at once from GHQ Cairo by cable; then one evening there was a knock at the door and it was Willie at last; the cable had been sent in error: typical of the army, as my father already knew and I in my turn was to find out twenty years later, and to call by another name than confusion.

My brother, I have mentioned before, had shown, from his earliest years, a vocation for the priesthood. As a child, instead of building forts and barracks with his bricks, he had constructed from them a cathedral complete with altar: tin soldiers, carefully wrapped in coloured foil of appropriate hues to represent the various vestments, were transformed into priests and acolytes; and he used, with the help of these properties, to enact the ritual of the Mass daily and with the utmost reverence, down to the last detail. This preoccupation did not escape the good fathers at the Catholic school in Paris to which he was sent when small; and since his academic record both at home and abroad showed him subsequently to be a boy of unexampled brilliance, a great future was predicted for him by those who knew. Even my father, though the reverse of overjoyed, bowed to the inevitable, especially after Willie was publicly blessed in church by Cardinal Bourne and there seemed little doubt that, D.V. as my aunt Jane used to write in her letters, he would become, himself, at least a Monsignor in whatever time it took.

Then a number of things went amiss: first of all his gift for mimicry, which he shared with the rest of the family (and which was frequently mistaken, as with all of us, for an ability to act by people not themselves in the profession) got him into hot water with the authorities at his college. Egged on by a fellow student jealous of his popularity, he had in boyish high spirits (for though devout he was never a prig) taken off, to the delight of an assembled gathering, the salient characteristics of some of his teachers, not knowing that this rival had arranged for those parodied to be stationed outside within earshot.

This incident earned him an undeserved reputation for frivolity, and while still under a cloud of disapproval he had been caught in a tea-shop with two local ladies of easy virtue, whom with burning zeal he was attempting to reform. His intentions could not have been more blameless and the tarts were actually in tears at his eloquence, about to forswear sin straightaway: nonetheless he was not yet ordained, and despite all his protestations it was decided that he hadnt a vocation after all.

My brother, pardonably bitter, turned his back on the church, and for a time went about getting drunk in a black cloak lined with crimson silk—but somehow he was not really cut out for a roisterer, and the next thing he took up was Socialism, resisting firmly my father's efforts to thrust him into a bank with which we had family connections. The declaration of war found him addressing a meeting of workers in the East End, and he enlisted almost at once but, to our parents' distress, in the ranks: where he proved enormously popular, was promoted against his will to Corporal, drafted overseas (where he was twice mentioned in despatches) and thence to the Middle East, ending up in Egypt as a commissioned officer and connected with, as I said, the staff.

Now he was back in Blighty, awaiting orders to proceed for demobilisation at a depot in Woolwich, where my sister had been stationed, and uncertain what career to follow after that: only one thing he was sure about, and that was his forthcoming marriage. It was not the first time he had been engaged: between the black cloak and the early socialist days he'd bought a ring for the daughter of his landlady in some seaside town where he had digs. The disturbance this betrothal brought about exceeded that which had shaken us at the advent of Al Laperle, but my mother finally succeeded where threats and reasoning alike had failed. Visiting the town on what in the more recent war we called a recce, she arranged a tennis match with Dolly, guessing that the girl would be a bad loser; she had no doubt as to the outcome, having been a tournament player in her youth, and she was right on both counts: in the mixed doubles that followed, Dolly, though partnered by my brother himself, suffered an ignominious defeat, and ended by throwing her racquet on the ground and bursting into tears. Love was not proof against this show of bad sportsmanship, especially since it was accompanied by an accusation of foul play on Mother's part; and though Dolly came out of the affair in pocket by the price of the ring, which had not been cheap, my father was spared the embarrassment this wedding would have caused him: for, though no snob, he was not politically advanced enough to welcome a daughter-in-law whose mother dropped her aitches and was, moreover, out for what she could get.

None of these drawbacks attended the present fiancée, who was called Margaret and whom Willie had met in France while she was serving as a VAD; before that she had been a mistress at a most exclusive school for girls, and her photograph, in a cabinet frame, stood on the dressing table in his bedroom. I used to glance covertly at the large eyes and long lily neck in the intervals of watching my brother shave, for I was allowed, most mornings, to take him up the can of hot water which he required for this purpose.

My brother used an open razor, leaning his head with its black widow's peak of hair sideways and close to the mirror, for he was short-sighted; his cheeks shone blue as the blade scraped the lather away, with that glabrous bloom I have since observed on the faces of certain priests, Monsieur l'Abbé among them: and more than a trace of Jesuitical severity was stamped even now upon his features in repose, though this vanished when he smiled. I had never seen anyone shave before—my father of course was bearded, nor would I have been admitted whilst he was performing his toilet—and the whole process fascinated me: the flick and sweep of the cut-throat steel which never drew blood, the stropping of the blade in readiness for the morrow, the astringent lotion dabbed on after. There was a moment equally absorbing, when he drew on the brown supple boots which came up below the knee and were worn with knife-creased khaki breeches. The boots, the Sam Browne belt, and also the buttons and brasses of his tunic and greatcoat were polished personally by my brother (for he had brought no batman) until they shone, in the case of the leather, almost purple and you could see your reflection in miniature in the crested brass. The only regret I had (one not shared by my brother) was that, as a subaltern, he no longer had to wear puttees; during his first leaves, when he was a private, I'd enjoyed seeing him wind these expertly, without creases, round his legs: though I was to be thankful later that this practice had died out before my own enlistment. The boots, however, more than made up for the puttees' absence; then, when he'd adjusted his belt, the rimless monocle—a relic from the days of his roistering with which he used sometimes to give his startling impersonation of a Prussian officer—would be screwed into its socket, where it remained immovable, without a cord; his cigarette lighter was flourished at an Abdulla Egyptian in a short amber holder, and he was ready to come down to another day.

He had the gift of charming people which was never to be mine; Maud and Mrs Bagge were enslaved at once, and even our new cook, inclined to be temperamental, made no demur when he instructed her in the preparation of some Oriental dish, which was not a success because he turned out to have forgotten its principal ingredient; while to Carol of course he was almost a god. In the way she clung to his arm and looked up to him literally when they walked out together, for she was small by comparison, and because of the courtesy with which he treated her, unlike the brusque camaraderie other young men showed their sisters, strangers saw romance and smiled; many times they were congratulated by officious persons on their engagement, a joke they never failed to enjoy and even came to angle for. The Brown Man was never encountered nowadays during these walks, and Carol prided herself that he'd been scared off for good.

My mother held to every moment of his stay, as treasures to be hoarded in memory against the time when, inevitably (and it might be soon) she would lose him to Margaret; and while my father disagreed with him over politics, there were masculine jokes to be shared: stories of service life which the rest of us were not told but which produced bellows of laughter from behind the doors of the study, out of which Father would emerge frequently wiping tears of merriment from his eyes. Nor was I neglected; for Willie, who knew all about pictures, devised new advertisements for my cinemas, which now showed foreign programmes as well, distributed by Pathé Frères: their trademark was a cockerel, whose coloured plumage, under my brother's tuition, now permanently adorned my slates. We were also to collaborate on a serial called The Hatchet Man, about tong-war in Limehouse but with a prologue set in China itself: I remember this first episode was to be called The Mysterious Sampan.

Then, too, I occasionally made a third on his outings with Carol, and one of these I have never forgotten. We came all three, on a sunless day, to a wood where the trees were so thick the sky, already leaden, was almost shut out overhead and our footsteps, in this un-natural twilight, were hushed by the deep carpet of loam on which we walked. Even the cheerful voice of my brother, whose nerves were not weak, sank gradually to a murmur as we emerged in a glade or clearing where every word spoken loudly echoed out from trunk to trunk of the trees that ringed it round, and which seemed the place for a trap to be sprung, as the waiting stillness should have warned us.

Standing motionless we watched a squirrel, startlingly red-brown, hop across the open space with its bushy tail upright, a nut clasped between its paws, and disappear up a tree into a hollow where it doubtless had its nest. My brother pointed with the cane he carried across the glade to where a spike of purple foxgloves grew, on the far side of a lake of mud that lay with moss and lichen in between. I had never seen such flowers before: so exotically sinister, with a snake's fascination, did they seem that I broke into a cry at the sight of them and started forward at a run; but my brother called in a voice of command HALT, and as the echo circled and died away he walked towards that mud, beckoning us to follow where I had halted dead. I remember to this day the turn it gave me, and worse to Carol, when he stabbed downwards with the ferrule of his stick and the mud sucked it avidly in, without a sound, and so quickly the cane vanished altogether before he'd time to pull it back, whilst he himself almost overbalanced into what we now saw, and he'd suspected, was more than mud or even marsh: must indeed have been a stretch of quicksand.

Instantly, as though the failure of this snare, of which the foxgloves were the lure, had angered the creatures, all unseen, who'd kept silent to see us sink, a clamour broke out around: squirrels chattered, birds squawked and harshly screamed from the branches of the trees—and as we hurried away without looking back, leaving the cane behind as toll, I could have sworn I heard an owl hoot twice.

This episode I recall not only because of its hint of the uncanny, which has remained with me till now, but because it marked a temporary break in my brother's stay; for that same night a telegram summoned him to Woolwich: and when he came back he was different, as you shall hear.

No sooner had he gone than the Brown Man reappeared in the streets of Southbourne; he followed us down Fisherman's Walk and, a thing he'd never dared before, sat behind us in the cinema, disturbing by his presence our concentration on the screen. We took walks, to avoid him, in the countryside beyond our house: at the end of the road was a wooded hill which one afternoon we climbed, only to see a brown suit skulking in the gorse bushes at the top. At last, after he'd trailed us for about a mile, Carol decided to turn and launch the first attack: I could not help feeling that the edge of a quarry was not a good place to make this stand, but she was much too angry to draw back now.

The Brown Man came in sight: seeing her thus at bay, he stopped to light his pipe and perhaps to think things over; but Carol marched straight up, she didnt give him time. Look here, she fairly shouted into his face, into the blank black glitter of his glasses, if you dont stop following me about this minute, I'll call the police and have you arrested, you damned dirty German spy: hissing this last so close she blew out his lighted match.

The Brown Man seemed not in the least disconcerted; he removed the pipe politely from his mouth before speaking: not in thick gutturals but quietly, in a pleasant cultured voice and perfect English. He said, How clever of you to know I was German. I flatter myself as a rule it's not immediately apparent.

Now, I thought with dread, now it's coming; of course some of them could pass for British, it was in all the books, and when found out they always killed to cover up. No need for time-fuses or magnetic beetles: I saw a gap in the palings behind Carol, and how easy it would be to send her over, down into the chalky cleft where now in winter the fritillaries did not flutter. I prepared forthwith to make a bolt for it, wondering how fast the Brown Man could run, for I'd be a witness and I didnt fancy sharing the same fate. My sister seemed unaware of her danger, even now he'd admitted his nationality: she'd taken this so long for granted it never occurred to her she might be wrong and went raging on regardless: The last German spy I caught was shot, so you'd better be off quick!

Who shot him? the Brown Man asked; That very dashing young officer of yours? He's not my young officer, Carol shouted, That's my brother, and if he was here he would kill you, so there! Then he'd be hanged for murder, the Brown Man said composedly, leaning on his cane. As to my being a spy, he went on, I'm sorry to say you're wrong, in fact I've not long been invalided out of the Service—touching his black glasses as though in explanation—so I'm afraid, he wound up, you wont be able to have me shot just yet.

He had spoken throughout with the utmost gravity, and not even the shadow of a smile, but I'd an idea his eyes were amused behind the dark lenses; and I stayed my flight, since it was now obvious there was to be no murder: that the Brown Man, as Father had foretold, was harmless after all. Carol too had realised her error: she'd gone gradually pinker and pinker until her face was finally aflame, for she feared the man might be permanently blind; but he must have read her mind on this score, for he said: Oh no, I can see. In fact they say I may be able to go about without these glasses soon; and doffing his cap he delivered, unwittingly, the final blow: By the way, may I formally introduce myself, now that we've spoken? My name, he said, is Brown.

This last coincidence was too much for Carol, already uncertain which way to look, and all she could find to mutter was, Are you really a German, or just pulling my leg? Of course not, it's the truth, the Brown Man told her. That is, my father was German, he's naturalised now, I was born and brought up here and my mother was British, but our name used to be spelt B-R-A-U-N; then turning to me and smiling for the first time, he asked: And what is your name, old man? Rather pompously I gave him this in full, and he made me a solemn bow. And yours, he said to Carol, if I may ask? May, answered Carol, whose blush showed no sign of abating. A pretty name, smiled Mr Brown; It sounds a note of hope. What else do you do besides catching spies?

It will be seen from these exchanges that he had what we'd now call a lot of personality under his quiet exterior, also that my sister was no match for him; before the afternoon ended and we walked back together down the hill, all misunderstandings and antagonisms had been ironed out, and we'd learned a great deal about him. His father, now retired, had been German master at a big public school nearby; and though technically British for twenty-five years, his son had come in for a fair amount of suspicion at the outbreak of war: the account of this increased Carol's contrition and made her more than ever anxious to make amends. He had tried to join the Air Force but it would have none of him; as a dual national he was also suspect to the Army and Navy; finally the only branch that seemed open was a sort of Bomb Disposal Squad, dangerous work for which it was difficult to get volunteers: he had duly joined but at last a bomb went off too close and without injuring him otherwise had affected the optic nerve in a way that made the black glasses obligatory for the time being.

We left him at the bottom of the hill: it turned out after all this that he lived in the avenue adjacent to ours, and though no definite appointment was made for the future it was tacitly agreed we should meet again round about. We did, the very next day, and for many after since that; soon we referred to him as Rudolf: in view of his patronymic our old nickname would have sounded impolite, if not actually insulting, while Mr Brown seemed too formal. His real christian name was Cuthbert, which even he realised was impossible, as Carol told him to his face, and he accepted his re-christening with equanimity: the reason for this particular choice slips my memory, unless it were somehow connected with a visit paid by Carol to the current film version of *The Prisoner of Zenda*; anyhow Rudolf he definitely became. My sister now began to find the grey hair at his temples distinguished, for there were many precedents in the work of Ethel M. Dell, and to speculate both about his age and how he would look without his glasses; then came the time when these were taken off, and with them it seemed to us he shed several years: it was also decided by Carol that he had nice eyes. By then she was going out with him alone in the afternoons; he took her to tea-dances at the Winter Garden and taught her to skate; soon my father got to know.

What's all this, he said, about your meeting that man who used to follow you about? I remember not so long ago you were asking me to warn him off. Carol answered evasively, and this caught the attention of my mother, who began to register anxiety. I came in, myself, for a good deal of close questioning during this period, for when they went on country walks I acted as chaperon; though (as I did not let on to Mother) I was always sent to play in the next field once we got far enough out: while looking in her lakes of eyes, I suppose, all his past life flashed before him as they kissed. My father was in favour of direct action, of the sort he'd previously refused to take, but Mother advised against: Do nothing until Willie comes back, she said. He's the only one who can handle this.

When my brother returned, this time definitely on discharge leave, it was put to him by our parents; at first he refused to interfere, remembering how he had resented their objections to Dolly, but Father reminded him that after all in that affair they had acted for the best: otherwise he would now be married and unable to espouse Margaret. So in the end he went to Carol and remonstrated: my sister, and this was the measure of her attachment for Rudolf, became mutinous, saying (not without justice) that he couldnt possibly talk without ever having met the man. I happened to come in as Willie had got to the point of asking Look here Sis all I want to know is, are you in love with this chap or not? I was immediately ordered out, but not before I heard Carol reply, and at this she burst into tears, Oh Willie I dont know, I simply dont know.

Soon after, a meeting was arranged between my brother and Rudolf; he came back saying he could find nothing wrong with the fellow; Father sighed and stroked his beard; he closed one eye in meditation as he sniffed at his bottle of salts, which was often in use at this difficult time; finally he said Right, better ask him over to tea and we'll have a look at him.

The invitation was extended and accepted; Carol, who much to the annoyance of all in the kitchen had now begun attempting to cook, prepared a special dish of potato cakes which I was forbidden to sample lest I get indigestion; and Rudolf, wearing his best brown suit, presented himself, quietly self-possessed, for the ordeal. My father bade him welcome with the heartiness usually reserved for the visits, luckily rare, of his mother-in-law: it was also the manner he used to adopt towards Mrs Bradlaw, and I knew it to be a sure sign of his dislike. Carol was not taken in either, and showed marks of apprehension, though there was no open clash, nor did Father, as she feared might happen, greet his guest in German or give his name its teutonic pro-nunciation: a brief reference to his student days in Heidelberg was as far as he went in this direction. The meal indeed proceeded entirely without incident and with every appearance of outward enjoyment, even when Carol's potato cakes were brought to the table; it was not until afterwards, when my sister returned from seeing Rudolf to the gate with her lip-rouge smudged, as Father did not fail to observe, that the dissension started.

Nice feller, extremely civil, my father began with deceptive mildness; and since even he could find little fault with Rudolf's birth, education or manners, nor, without further knowledge, cast doubt upon the integrity of his character, it came down in the last analysis to a question of age, starting with a preliminary allusion to May and December and ending with a direct He's much too old for you, my dear. He's only thirty-eight, said Carol, her back up instantly as Father's eyebrows also rose: Only? That's nearly twenty years between you. You forget Father, retorted Carol, you were thirty-four when you married Mother, and she was eighteen, why is it so different for us? You surely, Father rumbled, dont intend to marry him? A man who picked you up in the street? What other chance have I got of meeting anyone? Carol cried jumping to her feet, Nobody ever comes to the house, I haven't even another girl for a friend, what am I supposed to do? You can make friends, Father told her, providing they're not bigamists like that woman you met in the army, and have young men too that are nearer your own age. But I must say I think this association with Brown should cease.

But here my mother unexpectedly took a hand. She had liked Rudolf, he had made her laugh, also he was personable and polite, which was more than one could say for most of the younger generation: marriage of course was another matter, but who had mentioned such a prospect except Father himself? An older man might be just the steadying influence Carol needed, in any case thirty-eight was not altogether antediluvian when all was said and done.

Father, finding himself outnumbered, for I too would have thrown in with Rudolf had I been asked to vote, now abandoned his position and tried a flanking attack: what did Brown intend to do in life, to earn a living? At his age a man should be firmly established, at any rate have a job. When was he going to get one? Or perhaps he'd private means: if so how much? Here he'd struck a weak point in the opposing stronghold; for Rudolf, as even I knew, was far from rich: he had held in the past a succession of highly temporary posts such as one sees quoted, in biographical notes on the backs of book-jackets, as having been occupied by writers before they began to write; but Rudolf was not likely to become a writer, and though he had farmed sheep in Australia and once, when particularly hard pressed been a barman in Paris, at the moment he'd no prospects at all in view. My father, at once perceiving this, pressed home his advantage: Oh what does it matter, Carol burst out, as you say I'm not to marry him? Besides, she added bitterly, he hasnt asked me yet. YET! Father took her up in the loudest voice he'd used that evening, and at this they all went off into French; Maud was also summoned to take me up to bed.

Rudolf's mother being dead, a return invitation for all of us to have tea at his house arrived next day from Professor Braun who, it seemed from his signature, had not troubled to anglicise his name. My father declined politely, making some specious excuse and in German: in fact he never did meet Rudolf's father, though my brother did, since he commented on the old man's heavy teutonic accent, and Mother must have done later; I saw the Professor only once myself, and that for me was enough.

One day I was to accompany Carol and Rudolf on an excursion to Christchurch, but we'd barely started out when they found some essential article, I forget what, had been left behind at Rudolf's house; while they went back to fetch it, I was told to wait at the foot of the hill associated in my mind with Ivy and the morning appearances of Captain Forbes; but after what seemed an age I decided to investigate on my own. The sun was shining, so that I didnt notice the clouds piling up as I walked along to the next avenue, where Rudolf lived, and looked up it to see if they were in sight. Here too there was a hill, a shorter one, which went in a curve like a black hump against the sky: itself suddenly become pitch-black, though rays of sun still forked fanwise downwards from it. Obviously a storm was about to break, I'd no wish to be caught in the rain; and, braving the savage threat of trouble the hump of the hill and the thunderous sky seemed to promise me over the crest, I went up at a run towards where I knew the Braun house to be.

My head was bent, for I feared to look at those bulging black clouds above, then suddenly a growl of thunder made me glance up and there, outlined against the fitful sunshine, as though it had dropped bat-like from the terrible sky itself, a figure faced me more fearful than any mystery man I had ever seen in serial form on the screen: seeming, as it might be, the epitome of them all. It was hunched with the head thrust forward, a bushy black beard hid the lower half of the face, black glasses the eyes; a shovel hat, like a priest's but with a higher crown, was pulled down low on the head and a black cloak with sleeves like wings wrapped the whole shape around. As I gazed aghast, the sun went out altogether, the figure shuffled forward; and, the spell of horror breaking with its implacable advance, I gave a wild shriek and plunged back down the hill, cannoning, in my headlong flight round the next corner, into Rudolf and Carol, who had come down a different way and were alarmed by my absence at the appointed place.

As you'll have already guessed, my ogre was, not G.K. Chesterton disguised in a false beard, but the Herr Doktor Braun himself; my description of him was greeted with peals of laughter, only cut short by the rain that now poured down: and the need to find shelter happily prevented Rudolf from introducing me to his father and thus demonstrating that, as he said, the old boy would not hurt a fly. Despite this reassurance, however, it was days before I could forget the impact of that encounter, though at nights, I'm glad to say, it did not haunt me: I rid myself finally of this lingering fear by embarking on an entirely original film-serial in which the mystery man, called by me the Phantom Personage, was modelled outwardly upon the figure of Professor Braun.

Thus I learned, for the first time, when I was eight years old, how the terrors of daily life could be used with profit, and thereby triumphed over, as raw material for the work that, much later on, was to be my living.

The Days of the Comet

*　　*　　*

MEANWHILE—MORE WORRY FOR MY PARENTS—A MARKED
change in my brother had become apparent since his return from the
depot in Woolwich. Always slightly solitary by nature, he began to
exhibit once again the tendency to be by himself which the enforced
gregariousness of service life appeared at first to have permanently
overcome. I was no longer admitted to his bedroom in the mornings,
and though he did sometimes accompany Carol and Rudolf across the
meadows or to the skating-rink, he now seemed to prefer long walks
alone: perhaps he drank a little, too; at this time, certainly there was
often a smell about him not that of tobacco or shaving lotion, which
was reminiscent, to me, of the late Mrs Bradlaw. He still wore uniform,
since he could no longer get into the suits that had belonged to him
before his enlistment, and new ones were now being made for him; but
though boots, belt and brasses shone as smartly as ever and his monocle
was always in place, there was less swagger in the tilt of his chin and
the angle of his cap: less of the quality which had caused Rudolf to call
him dashing.

My father began to fear that he had contracted a venereal disease, and
at last put the question as heartily as he could over a bottle of whisky
got in specially for the occasion; but while the answer he received was
thoroughly reassuring, the two deep clefts that had recently drawn my
brother's brows together below his widow's peak did not disappear,
and my father then began to speak about the future, supposing that
this might conceivably be what worried his son. On his arrival from
Egypt, my brother had been undecided what to do after his discharge:
in Cairo he had made friends with a wealthy young man, who had been
in the photograph beside him with the Sphinx as background and

79

whose money derived from a brand of milk chocolate often devoured by Carol. This comrade-in-arms was due shortly for demobilisation and had offered my brother a well-paid post in the family business, but the appointment for some reason involved his becoming a Mason, and here the influence of the seminary proved too strong for him to agree offhand, though he never, nowadays, went to Mass and had completely severed any Catholic ties. Much depended on his fiancée's return from France: there was a plan, already half decided upon, to open a school together on communal lines, for she also was a Socialist and my brother had the academic training and qualifications necessary for a scholastic career. The legacy left to him in trust at our grandmother's death (an inheritance to be shared also by my sister and myself, when we should attain our respective majorities), plus his army gratuity and what Margaret had, should more than cover the initial expenses of this project: my father now expressed his willingness to contribute as much as he could, and suggested that as a stop-gap meantime, and to keep his hand in, Willie should take on a job as my tutor.

My morning lessons had been neglected during the visit from Aunt Enid, and again for the first part of my brother's stay; and though my father tried to fit them in whenever possible, to have me off his hands for a while would be a great relief, as the influx of War Office translations had not decreased with the end of the war, nor had correspondence concerning the family feud (Aunt Jane being especially assiduous in this connection), and work on the biography of Bonaparte had been brought to a temporary standstill in consequence. My brother agreed, even with enthusiasm, to enrol me as his first pupil, the whisky glasses were raised in a toast, and for the first time since he came back from Woolwich, Willie told a story about his former quartermaster-sergeant, an NCO famous for his uncompromising attitude towards Brass Hats, and what had happened when a visiting general attempted to inspect the Company stores. In short it seemed the shadow had lifted, that he was getting back to his old form; while, at the prospect of having him to myself for a whole two hours each day, I of course could hardly wait for the new routine to begin, which it did on the very next morning.

For the life of me I cannot remember much about the lessons them-selves, except that my brother was tirelessly patient in his method of teaching, so that even history, despite my disinclination for dates, became palatable, and my vicarious knowledge of foreign parts was greatly added to by his vivid re-creation of the places visited during his service: these now came alive where before they'd been mere names on the face of the spinning globe, for this tuition took place in the study, given over to us while my father climbed the hill, doubtless, with Captain Forbes on his morning walk.

But once again my education was to be interrupted, and in a way I was not to forget. A buff envelope stamped OHMS lay on the mat one morning: my brother was to report forthwith for a final Medical Board to be held at a hospital not far away. He did not return until after we'd all retired, but even I, in my eyrie at the top of the house, heard him come in, his footsteps stumbling on the stairs and the slam of the bedroom door, when ordinarily he was so quiet: next morning he was not up until late, his breakfast tray remained untouched, and I had been waiting in the study, before he appeared, for some considerable time.

What could I know of hangovers then, but now, from hard experience, I see how the sunlight made his head swim and the room flicker, as if through that heat-haze rising from the desert sands he'd often described to me, so that he at once pulled down the blind: I realise, too, how the tidings of the day before leapt out at him on awaking, as these things do, with the irrational thirst and the sick sense of shame. Yes, thirty-two years after I can find excuse enough for what followed; I daresay, too, I was inattentive that day and, in his condition, a trial; but then it seemed like an act of God or the end of the world. The first thing I knew was his voice raised harshly, which I'd never heard before: next moment my head seemed to explode with the impact of his palm, I truly saw stars, then the hard floor hit my back and hip; I was too stunned by more than the blow to make a sound, I could not believe at first he'd done it: dazed and with my whole head, inside, a peal of bells, I lay there and watched, as a camera placed low-angle on the set, my brother lunge to his feet and stride from the room slamming the door.

I know now that he encountered my father outside in the hall, and what passed between them; but then I was only concerned, picking myself painfully up, with the horror, the injustice, and above all the bewilderment, of this: the first betrayal of trust I had ever known; for he had been kind to me always and now came the slap, which in my confusion it seemed my very admiration for him had earned. So, much of what I came, later, to expect from life early left its mark, with the span of his hand imprinted, all five fingers, on my swelling cheek: so shocking that I could not cry.

My brother had developed TB. That was what he'd feared since the result of his medical in Woolwich, they had confirmed it at the hospital, and he now told our parents: my father, in the hall after I had been slapped, being the first to whom this news was broken. Copies of the specialist's report and of the X-ray photographs were produced: the disease had not taken hold as yet, it was just a spot on the lung, and hope of a cure in six months was held out following an immediate course of treatment in a military sanatorium outside Bournemouth.

Both our parents were for sending Willie to Switzerland instead, and straightaway, but he himself was not in favour, saying that the specialist he'd seen, though now holding army rank, had a Harley Street reputation as one of the leading men in his profession, and had assured him, as officer commanding the hospital in question, of personal care and supervision. When the signature of this physician was deciphered, he proved to have been at school with my father: a letter was written off to him at once, and since the reply repeated in the most cordial terms the assurances already given to my brother, and named a date early in the following week for his entry to the sanatorium, even Mother withdrew her opposition; and anxiety, naturally acute at first, was considerably lessened on all sides.

Margaret was now wired for; my brother of course feared the result of the disclosure on their relationship, but he need not have worried. When she arrived, very tall and, as I remember, all in white, with fair hair braided round a Madonna-like head, her first proposal, before even looking at the documents in the case, was that they should be married at once by special licence, and hang the consequences. Willie would not hear of this, the doctors also advised against such a course, as it might have the effect of retarding the speedy recovery they all predicted, but it was agreed, and with my parents' blessing, that the wedding should take place as soon as he was given a clean bill of health. Both Mother and Father approved highly of Margaret, and even Carol liked her, though my father frequently drew an unfavourable comparison between my brother's taste and her own in selecting Rudolf. As for me I watched her every move with awe, for she seemed a personification of the fairy queen in pantomime, whose traditional likeness she did resemble to a great degree, though without magic wand or crown of stars.

Before this, in fact on the very same day it happened, my brother had apologised for striking me. The apology was accompanied by the surreptitious gift of a pistol which fired caps, such as I'd often longed for but was not allowed to possess; both apology and pistol were accepted, though secretly and for some time I nursed resentment, contrary to what I'd been taught; it had been too great a shock for me to forgive so easily, and while I managed this later, I was never quite at ease with him after that day: always watching warily for another outbreak, once slapped more than twice shy. Then too I had been told he was ill, yet he was not in bed and showed no outward sign of sickness as I knew it: in fact he looked very healthy, nor had the blow I'd received borne any mark of diminishing physical vigour. It was all too puzzling for me, at that age, to take in, and though I buried the pistol in the same box that contained the mask given me by Carol, I felt no emotion of loss or anxiety when the time came for him to move into the sanatorium: in any case we could visit him there and he was allowed out once a week.

On these days he always came over to lunch, Margaret was invited also, and they would occasionally make up a foursome with Carol and Rudolf for some expedition in the town, though such arrangements were not officially recognised inside our home. Rudolf had now grown a small toothbrush moustache, which had come out blond and which he kept carefully clipped, but despite this he was no nearer obtaining lucrative employment, though he often answered advertisements and it was hoped that, as the school had been definitely agreed upon as a future for my brother and his bride, the milk-chocolate man might do something for Rudolf instead. On the other hand the arrival of this legendary figure was being constantly delayed by the seeming reluctance of the army to release him from his term of enlistment.

By this time it was spring, Carol had known Rudolf for over six months, and my father, whose concern about her had been in abeyance during the first phase of my brother's illness, became active, once again, in his disapproval; for the affair did not appear, as he had hoped and half expected, to have blown itself out: a meteorological metaphor only too appropriate in view of the emotional storm that was shortly to break over our house.

For as the days grew longer my sister stayed out later and later; she demanded a latch-key; Father refused; Carol found a window she could climb into: after she had done this twice, he went round at night personally securing all methods of entry, so that she was obliged to ring for admittance, when he would confront her at the door watch in hand, as though timing the result of a race. Then at last came the day, or rather the night, when she did not come home at all; we were sure she'd been kidnapped or the victim of an accident, and Father, dressed already in funereal black and grasping his stick, was about to go for the police, when through the side panels of stained glass which flanked the hall floor, my sister was sighted coming up the path outside.

It was the end; for during the resultant row, to defend herself from the accusation of having behaved, at the least, like a hussy (since Mother restrained my father from using a stronger word), Carol came out with her bombshell: that she and Rudolf were married, and had been, secretly, for over a week; at this announcement even Mother gave a horrified gasp of *Caroline*! while my father refused flatly to believe his ears. Ask Willie then, Carol told him, he was there as a witness, and Margaret too. Willie? Father repeated dumbfounded, D'you mean that Willie was a party to this, this scandalous, he choked; Yes he was Carol shouted and it's not scandalous, we were legally married by a registrar and there's nothing you can do about it. Ah but there you're wrong, Father said recovering, You're under age, you cannot marry without our consent, I can have the marriage annulled immediately. But you wont, Carol retorted, because I've already spent the night with him, remember.

My father drew a deep breath: Very well, he said, in that case you had better go upstairs and do your packing, for I'm sure you must be anxious to rejoin your bridegroom as soon as possible. Lambden, Mother protested, Kindly refrain from interfering, Father told her. You have done enough harm already, you and Willie, by encouraging this most unsuitable union; and turning back to Carol: A wife's place, he said with the utmost suavity, is by her husband's side, and I would not like my daughter to be slow in assuming her new responsibilities. You will oblige me, therefore, by leaving this house within an hour at the latest. Dont worry, Carol told him, I was going anyway, and she slammed out. But Lambden, Mother remonstrated, where will she go? My father raised his eyebrows: Why, to her husband of course, he said. Mr Cuthbert Brown, or as I believe you call him, Rudolf.

When my father wished someone to leave his house, their departure was not long delayed, as Nana, Nurse and Aunt Enid had already found. Carol was no exception to this rule, and well within the prescribed hour she was down in the hall with what hand-luggage she had, and Maud had been sent out to find a cab. But my father had not quite done with her yet: suddenly he reappeared on the threshold of his study. One thing more, he said, and Carol looked up: since it's probable that in the future I shall be expected to contribute to your support, and unless I'm mistaken, to that of your husband, may I ask what you propose to do with yourselves now?

We'd neither of us ever accept a penny of yours, Carol told him, but if you must know, we are going to Canada. Father opened his blue eyes wide: To seek your former fiancé, Monsieur Laperle? Or perhaps your husband imagines the Klondike gold-rush is still in progress? I can assure you that it has been over for many years: your Uncle Reggie was frozen to death there in 1896. Stiff as a board, I remember, was the way they put it at the time.

These were the last words he ever spoke to his daughter. Like all of us, he may have expected her to return, if not for good, at any rate for an attempt at reconciliation before she sailed for Canada, but she did not; and I only saw her once more myself: when Mother took me to say good-bye outside the Braun house, where she and Rudolf were then staying, to the inconvenience, I believe, of the Professor, on whom the marriage had also been sprung suddenly and whose disapproval, while not equal to that of my father, was not slight, for he had to pay both their passages to the land of opportunity.

My father developed a headache almost directly after he had spoken of the manner of Uncle Reggie's death, and kept to his study seeing almost no one, even for meals. For a long time he would not forgive Willie for the part he had played at the wedding, and only consented to do so after the intercession of Margaret on his behalf; but we saw less of my brother for a while in any case, since he had entered a more rigorous phase of his treatment at the sanatorium, where he was forced to stay in bed.

For me the period that followed was one of acute loneliness and boredom, too many things reminded me of Carol, especially the gilt-edged postcards she had painted in the Japanese manner then all the rage: a gold moon and the outline of a pagoda on a black ground were the main ingredients favoured by this school of art, with perhaps the impression of a fan unfurled or a junk sailing down a silvery river; and when later on, in the shop windows of Marseille, I came across a preponderance of these, they were still capable of giving me a lively pang. I was too depressed to devise programmes for my picture-houses; my serial had stuck at Episode Seven; since my mother was fully occupied in ministering to my father's headache, there was no one to take me to the cinema, and while the headache lasted I was naturally forbidden to play the piano, even with the two doors closed in between; there again, when the ban was finally lifted, the melodies of the moment were all too evocative. (I was to hear them again, in a film called *The Story of Irene and Vernon Castle*; another war had broken out by then and my first story had at last been accepted for publication: but the sadness, the sense of loss, those tunes brought back even after twenty years overshadowed, though not for long, in the dark of the cinema, the elation I felt at that inconsiderable—but to me, at the time, tremendous— triumph.)

Only one bright spot enlivened the dullness of those days after my sister's departure, and that was the visit paid to us, quite suddenly, that summer by my Uncle Bertie.

You may recall that it was to this relative I was always compared by my mother when I had done something to excite her disapproval: the breaking of Elton's collarbone was the last time I'd heard his name mentioned as a prototype; but much earlier in my life I had been compared to him in a connection more favourable to both of us, for I had been able, when a very small boy, to identify correctly the make of any motor-car at whatever distance the vehicle might be, as my sight when little was almost telescopic, though this cannot be said of it now. Since Uncle Bertie was an extremely skilful engineer besides being a black sheep, it was hoped that I might have inherited some of his genius in the first direction, but later my interest in all things mechanical rapidly declined and was never revived: although I retained enough knowledge to recognise as a Daimler the high-backed automobile in which he came to call upon us.

Uncle Bertie arrived, as usual, unannounced except for the high harsh scream of a motor-horn many times repeated in the road outside our gates. I happened to be upstairs in my room at the time, and rushing to the window saw the Daimler drawn up at the kerb with its hood down: a muffled figure of indeterminate sex crouched, wrapped round with rugs, in the back, and a man in a blazer and straw boater waved gaily up at the house from the driving seat, in the intervals of sounding his klaxon. This was my first conscious sight of him, for though he had once driven over to Ramsgate when I was a baby l was of course too young to remember. The muffled shape accompanying him, when the tartan rugs were unwrapped from around her, turned out to be my maternal grandmother, with whom he lived and who was regarded by my father with the greatest detestation, though he had a correspondingly great affection for Uncle Bertie himself. It was owing to the mutual antipathy between Father and Grandma Emily, as she was always called, that they visited us so rarely, to the regret of my mother, who not unnaturally did not share her husband's dislike of her parent. Every time they met, my father would make an heroic effort to overcome this, as on the present occasion: the strain of which was reflected in the fixed brightness of his smile while his voice, pitched a tone louder than usual, held the spurious and rather ferocious geniality with which he had greeted Rudolf and, in the more distant past, Mrs Bradlaw. But Grandma Emily was not deluded, nor did she make any reciprocal attempt to disguise her own feelings: her opening remark, as I recall, prefaced with the eerie cackle that had been in her youth a gay ironical laugh, was: Why, Lambden, you're looking old.

My father was not a man who prided himself on eternal youth but, coming from such a quarter, the sally made him gulp for a second, though he was too polite to return the compliment. For it could not be denied that Grandma Emily herself was old, although not as old as she later became. She, who had once been the Belle of Bangalore and had sucked the poison from the jackal's bite, had lost with age all traces of her legendary beauty, nor had time imposed its seal of peace and dignity, as it is popularly supposed to, on the mummified mask which was revealed when the motoring veil was removed, and in which the eyes flickered darkly with a monkey's cunning and malice. Her personality and appearance, the faint musty smell, as of something embalmed, that emanated from her as out of courtesy I steeled myself to peck her cheek, together with the cold touch of her crooked hand on mine, all actively repelled me, but my uncle I took to on sight: his slow, twisted smile made an accomplice of me at once, as it did with most, in whatever designs the intimate conspiratorial murmur of his voice seemed to promise one an equal part.

From what I had managed to overhear of him, the stories of his violence, his arrogance and feats of physical strength, I'd imagined an enormous man, bigger perhaps than my father if that could be, or like Elmo Lincoln on the films. Instead, even to my eight-year-old eyes, he was plainly not tall, and seemed in fact almost frail: he spoke, as I say, softly and rather sadly, without the foreign accent I expected, since he'd been born in France and lived so much abroad; nor could I find, in his sallow oblong face and sleepy stare, any sign of the demoniacal temper attributed to him and which I was supposed to share. I was too young then to appraise the length of his arms, at the end of which his powerful hands hung down, blunt and square, the first and second fingers of each stained mahogany almost to the knuckle with the nicotine from his incessant cigarettes, so that he appeared at a casual glance to be wearing fingerstalls on them; nor was I yet to see the heavy lids fly open on his eyes dilated hot in anger: I must say immediately that these outbursts, which I was afterward to witness, were never in the whole time I knew him directed at me. We liked each other from the start and always, no matter what he was said to have done later: although I cannot pretend to understand or explain his motives.

At the time I am writing of now, he was the only grown-up I'd ever met for whom I felt affection and admiration untinged with awe: even with my brother, especially since the day he struck me, there had always been some constraint, but with Uncle Bertie there was none. He took a keen interest in all my pastimes, nodded approvingly at my ambition to be an adventurer (which, now that I come to think of it, must have struck a responsive chord), and told me the stories of two films I had not been allowed to see: in one of them Bill Hart, as Blue Blazes Rawden, tore out the throat of an enemy with his teeth; in the other, Hobart Bosworth revenged himself on a brutal Prussian officer, who had been responsible for his wife's death, by skinning and stuffing him, and hanging him on a hook behind a door: You see, Uncle Bertie said with relish, in private life he'd been a taxidermist.

With my father, too, as always, Uncle Bertie was a great success; he knew jockeys, talked racing, and gave him tips, at least two of which came up during the three days he and Grandma Emily stayed with us; and though Mother watched him warily in case, he did not, as had happened in the past, attempt to borrow money or interest Father in any of the schemes he had on hand: though he talked freely of these, one of which involved a formula for making artificial diamonds and appeared to me wonderfully romantic. During the war he had not served, to our knowledge, in any of the armed forces, but he had travelled about extensively and was understood to have rendered the Government, in an unspecified civilian capacity and owing to his gift for languages, some service which had earned him a decoration; it was not until long afterwards that we learned he had been, all the time, a British agent: in other words a spy. Now he was shortly on his way to the South of France, where he had business and might settle for a time, taking my grandmother with him; he proposed that we should pack up and go too, my father protested with a chuckle that he was getting too old to be uprooted at a moment's notice, but nonetheless a seed of unrest had been sown in his mind, which later bore fruit in our journey to Marseille: for it was Uncle Bertie's special power to influence people in this way, very often against their own better judgment.

On the last day of their visit (they were to drive back home to Brighton that night) Uncle Bertie took me out for what he called a spin, just the two of us, in the car. The previous afternoon we had driven over to see Willie, of whom he was very fond, in the sanatorium; but that was a sedate family affair, very different from this excursion à deux, as my uncle put it, on which it was generally agreed I should do more or less what I liked. We set off; asked what sweets I preferred, I had chosen sherbet tablets, and sucked these contentedly as I sat beside my uncle in the driving seat while the telegraph poles sang past. Uncle Bertie made purposely for hilly country, since I enjoyed the sensation of chugging in low gear up a gradient then plunging steeply, and at speed, down the other side: better than a switchback railway; as we straightened out, the sun struck up sparks from flints embedded in the long blue road ahead, and flashed off windscreens of cars heading from the opposite direction so that they seemed to signal to us as they came: my ears still hummed, like the wires overhead, with the rush of the wind and the shriek of the klaxon, as we sat, later, having tea on a terrace overlooking a lake of swans. I longed to wait there until sunset, to see the pink glow, that the sky already foretold, turn those white birds into flamingos; but here my uncle regretfully shook his head, for there was his own homeward journey, and the age of my grandmother, to be considered: so with a last sorrowful glance at the lake and the swans (still, so far, unroseate) I climbed into the car and we started back for Southbourne.

Now for some nice hills, my uncle said cheerfully; but for some reason, it may have been the ices I had just eaten, I found them less fun this time: as with a shout of Whoops we dived, my stomach dropped also; saliva gathered in my mouth and I could feel myself going green: at last we came to one which going up had seemed almost vertical, like scaling the side of a cliff, you can imagine the descent, and as we reached the bottom, all the sherbet I'd swallowed fizzed up sparkling like a dose of salts in my throat and nostrils; at my desperate signals, for I could not speak, Uncle Bertie gauging the situation at a glance pulled over to the hedge and stood by sympathetically while, in his expressive phrase, I rendered all unto Caesar.

When I had done gasping and foaming (luckily my clothes were unspotted for at the critical moment Uncle Bertie had held my head down) I was so ashamed I could hardly look him in the face, but he speedily set me at ease: Nothing to worry about dear boy, Do you good in fact, cleanse the bosom of much perilous stuff: and he went on to say I should read Shakespeare. The drive back was resumed while he told me about his pet leech: previously, and this was how he came to adopt it, the leech had been employed by a French doctor for cupping my grandmother during a grave illness, Uncle Bertie had become fond of it during the time it was applied to her, and since it had played a large part in saving her life, he felt it should be preserved. Now it lived in a bottle, raw meat was provided daily to supply the blood needed for its sustenance, and he described how, when the meat was sucked dry, it would let go and fall gorged to the bottom of the bottle, where it lay until no longer replete and ready for the next meal: otherwise, to make it loose hold when once anchored to a prey, the best method was to sprinkle salt on it, as with ticks on dogs.

The recital of the leech's habits lasted us until we got to the house, where we found them all at tea and a tense atmosphere prevailing, for Grandma Emily had just expressed her unqualified approval of the independent spirit shown by Carol in cutting adrift from the family circle, all Uncle Bertie's tact was required to calm down my fuming father and remove her from the scene, on the plea of urgent packing to be done, and within an hour they had driven off: but not before Uncle Bertie had bestowed on me a farewell gift.

When asked by him earlier what sort of present I wanted most at the moment, I had replied a boomerang, since one of these had been used by the villain in a current serial as a means of decreasing the number of people he did not like, and I felt that one was always handy to have about the house; my uncle was unable to provide this, Australia being one of the few countries he had never visited, but he had done the next best thing by buying a magnificent new catapult, which he pressed into my hand at parting, while Mother was tucking the rugs round Grandma Emily, together with a box containing bird-shot, to use as ammunition, and the advice that I conceal my possession of both these from my parents. Seeing at once the wisdom of this I slipped the catapult, rolled up small, into my pocket, stuffing a handkerchief on top of the box to prevent the pellets from betraying their presence by rattling; and not until that evening, when I was safely alone in the back garden, did I take out my new acquisition, load it with the appropriate charge, and start looking round for something to shoot at.

Not long ago I happened to see, among the nature notes in a national newspaper, a short piece curtly entitled, if I remember correctly, SPEEDS OF BATS. I read it with interest because of its relevance to the incident I am about to recount, which, in the light of the information it contained, seems scarcely credible: still, the reader will have to take my word for it. For, fired at random into the air at the bats that flickered and glided in the dusk overhead, one of my pellets struck home and a winged furry shape, stayed stone dead in its course, dropped out of the sky without a squeak and lay limp and pathetically small not far from my feet. My career as a naturalist had not included the study of bats, so I've no way of knowing what particular species I brought down, except that it was unlikely on the face of it to have been the Hoary Bat of North America, credited in the paragraph I've mentioned with a speed of 90 miles per hour. it might have been the Common Pipistrelle, the Serotine for all I know, or even Natterer's Bat: its smallness seems to debar it definitely from being the Greater Horseshoe Bat, and in the matter of size the Lesser Horseshoe sounds much more probable, though this is credited with a speed of 25 miles per hour as against the 15 m.p.h. of its larger and presumably heavier cousin.

Anyhow there it was, still warm as I picked it up: despite the speeds they are said to fly at, killed by a random pellet on the wing. At first I was elated by what I did not realise then was a remarkable feat, or stroke of chance, but when I examined closely the corpse of the victim more like a mouse and frailer than I'd expected, the membranes of the wings almost transparent, I was seized with a sudden sense of guilt, for at that age I was soft-hearted as any killer on the screen, and at the full realisation that I had stilled its flight and taken life (for the fur on this mammal was different from the fuzz on the wings of moths I had clapped with no compunction into the killing bottle in my entomo-logical days, besides it had no beauty), I began to blubber, and like any murderer with a sentimental streak ran into the house to confess and receive absolution for my crime.

My abrupt appearance on the threshold of the drawing-room, bat in hand and streaming tears of remorse, disturbed my father in the midst of a detailed though uncomplimentary analysis of Grandma Emily's character: to the relief, no doubt, of my mother, who sprang up and came towards me with concern when she saw the state I was in. To her anxious enquiries I mutely shook my head, holding the dead bat out for inspection; my father, who had seen bigger ones in Havana, was not impressed. Yes yes I see, it's a bat, he said impatiently, but what are you crying for. I killed it, I managed to blurt out between sobs; Nonsense boy, Father boomed, how could you kill a bat, what with? At this question, and the flash of suspicion that entered his eyes as he asked it, I saw my error: more than murder was out, and breaking from my mother's arms I turned, too late, to flee; Father's heavy hand on my shoulder already held me back. Not so fast my lad, he said. Let's see what you've got in that pocket.

That of course was the end of the catapult. Yet again I was deprived of a source of amusement, Uncle Bertie received the censure of my mother for putting this engine of destruction into my hands (only by now he was in France and too far away to care) and I mooned about the house at a loose end once more: there was nothing to read, no new book by Arthur B. Reeve on the library shelves, and the works of Shakespeare, recommended to me by my uncle on the day I'd been sick, were shut away in Father's study as unsuitable for children.

It must have been about then that the Comet first appeared in the sky. Before this there had been a lot in the papers about sun-spots, which had caused me vague uneasiness, but the Comet was much more serious, for many predicted it meant the end of the world itself. Also sun-spots were not visible except from an observatory and through an astronomer's telescope, whereas the Comet could be seen with the naked eye, I saw it myself every day: it did not seem to move though we were told how all this time it was in reality rushing through space towards our planet, with which it had, on the best authority, every chance of colliding. From the newspapers' point of view this was better than sun-spots, it rapidly became front-page news: soon there were diagrams showing the course of the Comet's trajectory, and how we stood directly in the path of its progress; leading scientists and astronomers contributed a daily symposium of conflicting views, all of which I read with growing anxiety: I looked up Comets in the encyclopædia and trembled to see this portent of doom grow larger day by day, from a feathery stain lightly brushed in on the blue, as it might be the aftermath of sky-writing, to what was now curved up there, the shape of the boomerang I no longer desired, or a query-mark to which I dreaded the answer, in the otherwise cloudless summer sky. I was not alone in my terror: churches began to be packed all over the country, and not only on Sundays, as they had not been since the worst moments of the war; preachers from the pulpit delivered hell-fire sermons on the day of judgment and exhorted the people to repent while there was time; even cinema audiences were affected, and panic almost broke out when a Swedish film on the prevailing theme, entitled *The Flaming Sword*, was shown in Southbourne. I saw this myself and could scarcely keep my seat for fear as the comet on the screen seemed to hurtle right down at us in a trail of fire: as a motorist might, faced with a head-on crash, I shut my eyes tight at the moment of collision which, in this version, destroyed all on the face of the earth save one man and a woman, who were left at the end, after floods and pestilence had taken their toll, to build, according to the translated caption, a new world among the ruins.

This conclusion, though sounding, as my sister's name had to Rudolf, a note of hope, afforded me no comfort, for I was not conceited enough to imagine I should be singled out for preservation; and when we emerged from the foyer, confronting us with its dread question was the authentic Comet which, originally pale pink, had now begun to glow red, as if in anger, at night when, waiting until the household was asleep, I would creep out of bed to gaze shivering up at it from the window of my room. What seemed to me most unfair—and the sense of resentment almost, at times, overrode my fear of the final catastrophe: the crumbling stone, the tidal waves, the earth reft open—was that this should happen before I'd had time to grow up and enjoy the golden future which I believed, then, would otherwise have been in store for me. I would shake my fist at Fate—it could not be God, since He would never be so cruel—for decreeing this disaster, worse than the confiscation of the catapult, for that I had brought partly upon myself, whereas I had done nothing to deserve eternity so soon. Or perhaps I had: the recollection of Mrs Bradlaw and the murdered bat would leap into my mind, driving me to utter despair, for there seemed no defence I could offer when their shades rose to accuse me before the judgment seat.

In the kitchen, Maud and Mrs Bagge were not sanguine either, in fact so dire were their forebodings that I kept out of there altogether; my parents on the other hand did not seem the least bit perturbed, Father even laughed at the Comet, and derided it in conversation with the road-sweeper (himself inclined to a pessimistic view) as though daring the menace that hung above us like a Damoclean blade, and shaped, now, not unlike a scimitar: on a morning too, when the head-lines asked ANNIHILATION? in the biggest and blackest type bang across every breakfast table. He had begun, as though the end of mankind were not threatened within a matter of days, to talk after all of going abroad; he was in correspondence with Uncle Bertie in Nice and Aunt Jane in Marseille; but the thought of travel was no escape to me. What would be the use, the Comet would follow, be there wherever we went, for I knew that it was the same sky over all countries, though a few years before the realisation of this, which I now accepted as a matter of course, had come as a surprise I could hardly credit.

And then one morning, just when the papers were announcing a definite date for the fearful Day, I awoke to find the Comet had vanished out of the sky. The night before it had blazed more luridly than ever, I could have sworn I saw it move: now it was gone without trace. I rubbed my eyes, which I could not at first believe, but there was no doubt about its disappearance; a professor afterwards gave some scientific explanation of how in its orbit it had come to bypass the Earth, but I was too overjoyed to bother, for once, with reasons. The world, because it was not to end just yet, seemed to me a new and glorious place, the sunlight warmer and stronger, the air sweeter to breathe, as those who've escaped death for the time being always say; and to celebrate my reprieve, despite the memories of my sister it conjured up, that afternoon I disinterred the box which housed the mask, the pistol, and the caps it fired, which, because the box was made of lead, had remained undamaged by being buried in the earth where but for a miracle I myself, with millions of others, might have lain. By a chance I then thought lucky, but the reverse later on, my parents had gone out together for the day; perhaps they too were celebrating the disappearance of the Comet, though I doubt it; anyway I was left alone, and it seemed a heaven sent opportunity to slip on the mask and, loaded pistol in hand, climb to the top of the wall, which I dont believe I'd done since the day I first met Elton. Sitting astride, I glanced from left to right through the slits in my mask: the street was asleep in the mid-afternoon sun, shadowed by trees along the pavements where no one walked, but, who knew what excitements and adventures lay just around the corner where the big chestnut branched? I fired my pistol gleefully into the air, as I'd seen bandits on the screen sometimes do, and next moment I had dropped cat-like, in a manner learnt from watching Hunter himself, to the other side. My face was sticky with sweat behind the black stuffy velvet, the fringe tickled my chin, but the privilege of wearing the mask at all more than made up for these discomforts; the weight of the pistol-butt in my hand was also gratifying, and as I ran crouching forward I fired off a few more caps to advertise my approach, for I was in no mood for stealthiness: this was a marauding attack, intended to spread terror on all sides.

The results were all that I could have wished; for as I rounded the corner, re-loading my gun, there, stricken to a standstill in front of me, clutching a school satchel under her arm, stood a girl roughly my own age, who might have been Wanda but wasnt: if anything blonder and with eyes a bigger blue, wide open as they were with consternation and horror at the sight of mine gleaming through the diamond-shaped holes in the mask; so, doubtless, I must have looked when the Herr Doktor loomed up before me on the hill.

At first I could barely believe my good fortune, for here was prey undreamt of; the black fringe hid my grin of triumph as, like the Hooded Terror on Pearl White, I advanced crabwise upon her, taking careful aim with a fresh cap; no acid baths for me but a bullet in the brain: I meant to make sure. Alas, like many another mystery man, I took too long to savour my triumph; and before I fully realised what was going on, the girl had whirled with a scream and taken to her heels, the long blonde hair, streaming out like a pennant behind her, adding to the impression she gave of actual flight, and perhaps this is what people mean when they talk of fear lending wings.

I gave chase to the music of Rachmaninov, unheard except by me, firing off my pistol frantically, but my shots must have all gone wide: for the girl, still screaming and with a good start, ran on ahead and dived suddenly down a lane leading off the street, on to which the back gardens of adjoining houses abutted. I turned the corner full-tilt in pursuit, pistol at the ready; then stopped for a moment disconcerted, for what faced me was a seething mass of small girls, all carrying the same kind of satchel and wearing what I now could see was a sort of uniform. They had emerged from a gate at the end of the lane, beyond which was a board bearing the word SCHOOL, and I recognised then that this was the establishment once patronised by Wanda herself, though seeing it from the back I had not realised at once where I was heading.

No villain in my film-going experience had ever attacked a Dame school before: it was before the days of extensive kidnapping; but plainly I could not draw back, so I bore down on the pupils, struck silent at my approach, covering them with the pistol: behind the mask my face was deeply flushed though this they could not see. My particular prey had pushed her way in deeply hoping to find cover in the crowd, but I could see the betraying glint of her golden hair from where she crouched. Feeling a little like one raiding a harem, but without speaking, in the time-honoured Western tradition, I jerked my gun-barrel motioning those in the way to move aside. They obeyed, falling back, the broken reeds, to reveal the blondie who shot up with a piercing shriek and tried to scramble backwards through the gate, but those behind blocked her path; and, too intent on my implacable advance to notice anything else, I was almost within point-blank range, my pistol was already levelled (and this time I would not miss) when a voice spoke in a tone of command, from out of the air it seemed, spoiling my aim. Put that pistol down at once, it said, you nasty little boy.

The hammer fell, the blondie flinched as the cap cracked, sharply as that sudden voice: I looked up to see the squat shape of what was evidently a woman, since it wore a skirt and was clad in wool, waddling towards me on short swollen legs from the outskirts of the crowd. The face was square and the colour of putty, all the features squashed up and foreshortened as if pressurised; the eyes bulged out from behind enormous black-rimmed spectacles, Gig-lamps as they called them then, and the mouth was only visible when it cracked open across the face to speak. I have only once seen a specimen as uncompromisingly hideous and unpleasant, and that was the manageress of a hotel I stayed at during the recent war, also a detestable woman: on reflection they may easily have been the same, toads are ageless we are told, and there was much of the batrachian in the physical make-up of both.

The pupils broke out in a hubbub when they saw her, the blondie ran to hide behind, but with a lifted palm the toad-schoolmistress silenced them at once: Girls, she called out, go inside immediately, all of you. They obeyed in a scamper, leaving me isolated in the lane opposite their mentor, but once inside the gate they stayed huddled there to watch as the toad came forward and I backed away.

Who are you? she said, How dare you come here frightening my girls. Do you realise I could call the police for this? I continued to give ground, keeping my pistol pointed as she clappered on, though it was unloaded now and I couldnt spare the time to insert a fresh cap. Come along now, she ordered, take that thing off your face and give me your name and address at once. Your parents shall be informed of your behaviour, that I promise you.

I knew better than to unmask, she was not getting my name and address either, and the only course open seemed to be flight, unless I wished to suffer the consequences, which I could tell from her tone would not be light; accordingly, as she made a sudden dart with the obvious intention of detaining me forcibly, I turned and beat it down the lane without more ado: a few catcalls from the girls followed and the toad's voice commanded me to come back, but I arrived at our house otherwise unpursued and, as I thought, unrecognised. My first action was to rip off the mask, which to tell the truth I was thankful to shed, since I could hardly breathe in it by this time and the elastic cut into the skin above my ears; my next was to re-bury it and the pistol in their box: there was no earthly reason now why anyone should learn of my escapade, and I settled down to planning a nasty surprise in the future for that blonde who had decoyed me into the trap.

Judge of my astonishment, therefore, when as I was playing the Funeral March in the back drawing-room that evening, I heard first a thunderous knocking at the front door and then the voice of the toad-woman upraised in the hall, plainly audible even above that of my father, who seemed to be expostulating with her. I could not believe it possible, and have never discovered to this day how she found out my address: I thumped louder and louder on the piano to drown in my own ears the sound of those voices, though I feared the music I'd chosen might prove only too appropriate, and I had long since lost my curiosity about prison. Then, after what seemed to be prolonged and even violent argument, the voices ceased, the front door slammed causing an earthquake tremor, and the footsteps of my father, heavy with judgment to come, were heard approaching the room where by now I had ceased to play.

This time it was worse than the occasion of Elton's collarbone: not only was Uncle Bertie invoked by my mother and cinema-going cancelled, but script-writing came under the ban as well: posters and slates were removed from the walls and the film trade-papers stopped; even the piano was shut and locked until further notice. As for the mask and pistol, they were dug up and destroyed forthwith; it had particularly enraged my father, who hated telling unnecessary lies, that he'd had to give me an alibi, for the woman meant business and magistrates, the birch and houses of correction had been mentioned; even now her suspicions were not allayed, but in face of my father's assurance that I, his son, had remained in the house, under his eye, for the whole afternoon, there was little she could do except threaten more drastic action, i.e. the immediate summoning of a constable, should I ever cross her path again.

As a result of all this Father was more than ever determined to leave England; a French Catholic school, he said, would soon knock the Devil out of me, remembering the one that he'd attended when small; then, too, about this time he won a tremendous sum of money on a horse, I dont know exactly how much but it was a really record win, and this, as the transfer of shares was also concluded by now, enabled him to settle something on my brother and his fiancée against the time, rapidly approaching now, when they would be married. For Willie's cure was almost complete, the specialist said he could soon be discharged without danger; he was once more up and about and the milk-chocolate man had at last arrived in the town.

Everything seemed propitious for a move; a letter had even come from Carol announcing her safe landing in Canada (this was addressed to my mother, though the ones asking for money, which came later, were addressed to Father instead) and, since Willie and Margaret would also be setting up a separate establishment shortly, there seemed no reason for keeping on a large house for just the three of us to live in, especially as our lease had expired and was awaiting renewal.

A letter was therefore despatched to Aunt Jane, asking her to find us temporary accommodation in Marseille, passports were applied for and issued, the big black trunk corded up for the journey; and when one day, it was going on for winter, we were seen off for Southampton at the station, I was too excited at the prospect of all that awaited me on French soil to feel sorrow, even at leaving Maud who had looked after me so faithfully for years: impatient already to be on the water. As our train began to pull out I waved good-bye without a tear, not only to my brother and Margaret on the platform, but to Miss Crisp and the Old Man by the arcade, to Captain Forbes upon the hill and Mrs Bradlaw in her grave: to the house which I came, much later, to look upon as home, and which I was not to see again for another thirty years.

Looking back, it is not surprising that with the passage of time I should recall that house so clearly when other places I've lived in since have faded in memory: for there I first made acquaintance with the few interests, both work and play, that were to absorb me throughout my adult life: reading and writing, painting (at one time) and the piano, the cinema and the composition of screenplays; even, in a rudimentary form, with that game for two players called love, in which, in after years, I was always to be the ultimate loser.

During the war I began to dream of the house at night, and the scene was always afternoon: the garden seen through the French windows of the drawing-room I used to occupy; sunlight drenching down but with a black sky above, presaging storm, as over the hill-top where I saw Professor Braun. Why, I've often wondered, and a psychiatrist would doubtless know, this note of menace when my days there had on the whole been happier than any since? I can find no answer, but the dream recurred so often, as though to call me back, that being in the vicinity last year I returned to see if the house still held some message I could now decode.

There were trolley-buses, these days, instead of trams, and the driver did not stop for tea as, leaving the arcade briefly glimpsed behind, we passed that pub with the chains across it on which I used to swing, but the exterior of this was unchanged, unlike me: so was the hill when we got to it, though the buses now ran down the slope that was not so steep as I had thought. The house was very different, however, and but for its corner site I might not have known it: for the façade now was of some grim grey stucco instead of the gay brick I remembered, the conservatory seemed half its size, and a tree had been planted which prevented one from seeing into the back garden over that wall I had so often climbed; besides it was unoccupied and up for sale.

I was not alone on this return journey, the wife of my oldest friend bar one had made the pilgrimage also: we'd left her husband playing in the cricket match which was the reason for our trip, and Lydia now began to worry lest their small son, left in the meantime unattended, had got up to mischief in our absence. There was some cause for her misgivings, since the boy, who called me—his godfather—Uncle Julian, was about the age I had been when I lived in that house and was known as James: earlier that afternoon we had heard him give another child a highly documentary account of his birth in China when in fact he'd been born in Bognor Regis, and it was not impossible that he had succumbed to some of the temptations to which, as an eight-year-old, I had not myself been immune.

So, after a final glance up the other hill, where Rudolf had lived and I had seen his father standing (but trees in bloom hid with greenery the black hump of the hill and the sky overhead was cloudless as in the days of the Comet), we boarded a bus bound for the cricket field and the whisky at club-prices I looked forward to at the conclusion of the match, leaving those scenes of my boyhood behind for the last time: nor have I ever dreamt of them again.

Monsieur Félix

*   *   *

MY FIRST SIGHT OF FRANCE WAS OF A CLOAKED MAN HOLDING AN enormous key. It had been a good crossing, no one was sick, and, too excited to sleep, I was up on deck early with my father, himself so pleased at being aboard ship again, and at the idea of landing in France once more, that he developed no headache either then or during the subsequent journey, despite all the French trains, many of them hideously uncomfortable, that we were to travel in. So we two, and I for the first time, watched the sun rise, apparently out of the steel-grey sea: a sullen red ball seen through a mist to begin with, rather like the illustrations in a book purporting to represent life on another planet; then as the rays it shot out dispelled the mist, injecting the sea with cobalt, the white buildings of Le Havre, and the gigantic gaily-coloured posters pasted to their sides, gradually took shape, coming finally into focus with the sun on them, like a slow dissolve on the screen, as the ship we were on steamed into the harbour and the cloaked figure with his symbolical key welcomed us rather forbiddingly from the shore. He was the subject of one of the posters and advertised not as I thought some super-serial but, Mother told me, translating the letters above and below him that I couldn't read, a detective agency: even more satisfactory, since I had not imagined such concerns existed outside films or books.

Another poster that excited me showed a man with long hair and beard like Rasputin strangling a girl not dissimilar from the one I'd persecuted at the toad-woman's school, only older: this did advertise a serial and not a rival agency; the film was French and called *L'Orphéline*; later I was to see some episodes of it, though not the initial one heralded on the hoarding; also, by the time I caught up with it, the villain had trimmed his beard to a neat naval point.

The next thing I remember is breaking the journey in a cathedral town which had been badly strafed during the war: I know its name began with R (Rheims? Rouen?) and that it had a famous clock which, damaged by the shelling, now chimed cracked, as I have reason to know; for the hotel we put up at must have been directly below the clock itself, judging by the loudness of those cracked chimes that, striking not only the hour but each separate quarter, kept me awake and fretful all night, so that next day I slept soundly, in the train, until whatever stage of our trip came after. This may have been Paris, certainly we arrived there by night for I remember the lights spinning and whirling past as we drove through the streets of the capital in a taxi on what seemed to me the wrong side of the road, and the names, spelt out in electric bulbs, of the super-cinemas that we had not time to visit; and it was then I noticed that each big production and distribution firm had its own special theatre, GAUMONT, OMNIA-PATHÉ etc, as they had not at that time in Britain; I determined to set up a similar company of my own as soon as I could, for my parents had promised that, if I were a good boy, my slates, chalks and scripts would be restored to me on reaching our final destination, Marseille, which we did the very next evening.

There were a lot of beggars in Marseille, there was a dwarf with a hump on his back and a hare-lip, who apparently lived in the Cathédral de Notre Dame and used to pounce on passers-by from its doorway, pursuing them for some way down the street with curses if he failed to receive a donation. Farther along, a blind woman was stationed, holding a child, also blind, in her arms. The dwarf always stopped short when he reached her territory; so you were safe from him if you got as far as that. The blind woman never cursed or demanded and her appeal was purely mute. Perhaps she was dumb as well.

After her there was a fairly beggarless stretch of pavement; then came two men in rags, both legless, between the Dames de France and the Galeries Lafayette. One sat in a sort of box on wheels, exposing the stump of a shoulder like yellow wax, where his arm had seemingly been hacked off with a hatchet. The second man had no box but was propped up on the sidewalk itself and had only sores to exhibit, less interesting than the stump and more repulsive to look at. I always turned my head away when I came to him.

Past his pitch was the Cannebière, where beggars were discouraged and their place taken by men in check suits selling toy animals on elastic, which bobbed and squeaked round your feet as you walked along, or else imitation dogs which barked in your face when a rubber bulb concealed under the fur was pressed. The noise on the corner occupied by these touts was like that of a miniature menagerie; sometimes real puppies were brought out for sale in a basket, but not often.

Beggars started again in the rue du Paradis, which, with a paradox that at that age I did not appreciate, led down to the Bourse. The rue du Paradis was swarming with beggars who accosted everyone: going up it was like running the gauntlet. The most spectacular of all was a man without legs or arms and with his tongue cut out: his mouth was by some means held permanently open so that one could see this had been done. There was a notice pinned on him which proclaimed him to be also deaf, and underneath was written in block capitals BLESSÉ DE GUERRE.

The beggars fascinated me: they were the first I'd ever seen, as strange and glamorous as the newspaper kiosks hung with lurid posters, the foreign speech and food, the brioches and croissants dipped in coffee, the sirops, the sucres d'orge.

Later I got used to them as I did to the paper-money, the spurting sulphur matches, and the *Continental Daily Mail*; but there was still plenty in Marseille to interest a child; the man in the next room at the hotel beat his wife every night and you could hear it going on through the wall; a female shark, harpooned off the shore, gave birth to little sharks in her death-agony on the quay.

I became accustomed early to sitting on the terraces of cafés, with my parents on either side of me; but instead of drinking vieux marc or pernod, as I was to drink later, I drank sirops of grenadine or orgeat. This was in the morning. Round about midday my father would look at his watch. He'd snap open the top and the time shown on the dial always seemed to surprise him. For a while he'd sigh to himself, stroking his beard; then, leaving my mother and me sitting before our sirops on the café terrace, he would lumber off towards a place called the American Bar. This place was not, apparently, American; but the barman had lived for so long in the States that he refused, categorically, to speak French to the customers. However, my father had lived in the States too, so doubtless he understood what was said to him.

Then one day my father became ill. Nothing serious: just an attack of his normal vertigo. My mother stayed behind at the hotel to look after him, and during this period I was allowed out on my own, provided with a sum of money sufficient for me to buy sweets or go to the cinema. I dispensed a portion of this, naturally, to the beggars, in order to see their peculiarities at closer quarters: only the dwarf was exempt, as I considered him too nimble and vociferous to merit remuneration. Then came the cinemas: I hunted round for serials. There were several showing, but being unable to read French I didnt know what the titles meant and had to rely on the posters outside the cinemas to tell me what the films were about. I chose one which depicted a man having his eyes gouged out, but this proved unrewarding; the stills outside the Kursaal looked interesting, but they wouldnt let me in because I wasnt an adult: the film was *The Cabinet of Doctor Caligari*. Another thing, all the comedians had been provided with esoteric French nicknames; it was difficult to identify them: Harold Lloyd became Lui, Clyde Cook Dudule, Chaplin Charlot, and so on. When I did run a favourite actor to earth I couldnt understand the sub-titles when my mother was not there to translate them to me, and I soon became forced to read French in self-defence. Soon I was speaking it, too, and reasonably well.

Armed with this knowledge of the language I started to explore the town. I strayed off the main streets and up the steep cobbled alleyways that twisted behind them. I know now that this must have been the brothel quarter, through which no man, let alone a foreigner, may pass at night without having his hat snatched or a slop-pail emptied over him, at the very least; but by day and as a child I passed through unscathed. In any case, in the daytime the alleyways were untenanted, strung with washing and the gutters running with bright red blood, presumably from the abattoirs higher up, unless this blood came indeed from the slit throats of foreigners murdered at night in the brothels for their money.

Beyond the abattoirs were streets of rather dull small shops; these at first attracted me, by reason of their strange smells of cheese and stockfish, but I soon exhausted their possibilities.

It was winter and the sun set early over the Vieux Port. By 4.30 it was already getting dark. I had orders to be in by nightfall. I watched the sun setting in fierce unfamiliar colours over the sea, outlining in crimson and orange the masts and funnels of ships which I had never before seen so close; then I made my way back to the hotel to my parents and the man who beat his wife next door: with increasing regularity as the weather got colder.

The weather got colder and my father got better; soon I was able to go for walks with my mother in the afternoons again. It was during one of these walks that something happened which put the beggars and cinemas, as a source of entertainment, completely out of my head. In other words, I met Monsieur Félix.

We were walking across the Plaine one afternoon, quickly, because there was a mistral blowing. In summer the mistral blows hot and contains dust; in winter it seems to contain particles of ice. On the wide open space of the Plaine it slashed at us from all sides, and we were hurrying to keep warm. Then we noticed a crowd of children dancing about in excitement, apparently oblivious of the icy wind. They were grouped around a sort of palisade erected at one end of the Plaine, and we approached out of curiosity, to see what intrigued them.

Directly I saw, I became, myself, enthralled. I had once seen a Punch-and-Judy show at the seaside and had remained unimpressed. But this was entirely different. On the stage of the puppet theatre surrounded by the palisade, a tremendous drama was being enacted. One of the characters was the Devil. The other was a smaller puppet, wearing a pigtail and evidently the hero: his name, according to the encouraging shouts of the children, seemed to be Guignol.

An argument, presumably theological, was in progress, but it was impossible to get the gist of it from outside because the wind blew the words away. The argument reached a climax and the Devil advanced to claim his victim. Guignol backed away, unprepared for Hell. He stooped beneath the stage and came up clasping in his arms a stick. With this he set about beating up the Devil, cheered on by the children, both those outside and inside the palisade. I cheered myself, forgetting the cold and the wind. When, eventually, the Devil was laid out limp and a hoarse voice announced the séance terminée, I pleaded with my mother to attend the next performance, which was entitled Le Voleur.

We paid fifty centimes each, this time, to go inside the palisade. We sat on wooden benches and the high palings kept the wind off, though occasionally a gust of it shook the theatre itself, tall and painted blue, with red curtains on each side of the stage. The performance started and a Miser appeared. He wore a dressing-gown and a night-cap. We saw him gloating over a bag of gold. He hid this under a floorboard and went off to bed. Then the Thief emerged from his hiding-place. He was very large and in face a cross between Don Quixote and D'Artagnan. In order, no doubt, to inspire confidence, he was more richly dressed than any puppet I had seen so far. He wore a crimson satin cloak and had a sword buckled on at his side. This he drew to murder the Miser when disturbed just as he was about to dig up the bag of gold. But he in turn was disturbed by Guignol, the miser's servant, coming in from his night out. The Thief persuaded Guignol to come in with him on the crime and share the loot. Together they hid the body of the Miser, but later a quarrel developed over the gold. Guignol's voice was a perpetual characteristic squeak; that used for the Thief was smooth and suave. Both the voices rose and violence was resorted to: the Thief's sword against Guignol's stick. Guignol won, and beat the Thief to death. He hid the body with that of the miser and the bag of gold. But the Gendarme, an old enemy of Guignol's, arrived on the scene to make investigations and speedily uncovered the bodies. The Gendarme was even bigger than the Thief. His face was enormous, bearded and crowned by a tricorne hat with a cockade in front. Towering over Guignol, he arrested him in the name of the republic.

The Judge arrived to try the case, in white wig and black gown. He condemned Guignol to death on the spot. There was no jury, and soon the guillotine was dragged on to the stage, en bloc, by the Gendarme and the Executioner. It seemed Guignol was for it this time, but no: his stick appeared by magic in his arms and he proceeded to murder all the representatives of the law, guillotining personally the Judge and the Executioner after he had stunned them with the stick.

One would have expected this drama of greed and mass murder to conclude, somehow, on a moral note; instead it concluded, oddly, with a pæan in praise of drink. A boozing pal of Guignol's staggered in with a bottle nose painted bright scarlet and, swaying in each other's arms, they sang a song which went something like this:

> Au Cabaret,
> Au Cabaret,
> Nous allons au Cabaret.
> Au Cabaret,
> Au Cabaret,
> C'est là où je m'en vais.

When the song was over they reeled off to the tavern with the bag of gold, and the séance was again terminée. Enchanted by the antics of the puppets, I had not realised that they were manipulated by any human agency, although I had noticed they were not on strings. But now a door in the side of the theatre opened and a man came out.

He was short and thick-set, with a round head too big for his body and rough black hair. He had a meridional face, scowling, dark and sullen. Despite the cold, his shirt was open at the neck and he wore a thin shabby blue suit: no overcoat. He did not smile, although the children greeted him joyfully with cries of Comment ça va, Monsieur Félix? Ça gaze? Ça grouille? Ça barde? etc, to all of which Monsieur Félix responded simply by grunting Huh!

Then he passed round the hat: a procedure known for some reason as La Quête. While he was passing it round he did not speak to any of the children except to say Merci rather menacingly, and before a donation was received: not after. My mother and I dropped in fifty centimes each, which sent our entrance fee up to a franc apiece, and Monsieur Félix glanced at us with surprise and a slight expression of contempt. I think he took us for suckers: everyone else had given him coppers. Then he coughed and went away into the theatre again with the hat. Another play started: this time Guignol was at sea, shanghaied by the machinations of a wicked uncle, played by the same actor who had previously been the miser, but differently dressed. We saw three more plays all told, then it got dark and we had to go. Each play concluded with the drinking song and was followed by the Quête; I could talk of nothing but Guignol all the way back to the hotel.

Where the deuce have you been all this time? my father demanded querulously; I want my tea.

That night in my room I rigged up an impromptu performance of Guignol, played out on a table de nuit between a hammer and a pair of pincers. The hammer, as Guignol, won easily over the pincers, representing the Devil. The couple in the next room remained completely silent for the whole of the evening, supposing from the noise that a row even more serious than their own was in progress, or perhaps even that murder was taking place.

But this didnt really satisfy me, and in the morning I set out with my mother to buy real Guignols. It was not easy; the first day we only found two: a very small edition of Guignol himself, and the Devil. Unfortunately the Devil was made of plaster, and his head split open at the first whack from Guignol's stick. I burst into tears; but next day we found a wooden Devil in the Galeries Lafayette, and not only the Devil, but the Gendarme and the Judge as well.

The Galeries Lafayette sold only the heads and hands; that is all these puppets consist of, apart from their clothes. The head has a hole in through the neck, up which you put your finger, with two more fingers in the sleeves to make the hands and arms move. The hand of the manipulator is hidden by the dress of the puppet, which should be long and come down over the wrist.

Later I acquired the Thief, the Boozing Pal, the Miser, and other characters; my mother made appropriate clothes for all of them: the Gendarme and the Thief were especially magnificent. During all this time I attended, naturally, every performance of Monsieur Félix; I got to know the whole repertoire and even had most of the dialogue off by heart. One of my favourites was Guignol in the jungle. The jungle was in Pondicherry, where Guignol had got sent for some misdeed. He slept in the forest and was attacked by several savage animals, including a spider, which was lowered from the roof by a thread on to Guignol's recumbent form.

This was one play I could never reproduce, because I could not control the animals, or even the spider, satisfactorily. I had no theatre, either; the theatres on sale in the shops were all too small for me, as I was growing fast, and a full-sized one was of course out of the question. So I contented myself with playing with my Guignols on a table, all alone and without an audience, occasionally incorporating some of my own dialogue in the script. I forgot all about the beggars and seldom went to the cinema.

Playing with those damned dolls all day long, my father said. One thing, it's teaching the boy French.

One day I nerved myself and went along to the Guignol Theatre with the Gendarme and the Thief, my show-pieces, one on each hand. When Monsieur Félix came round with the Quête, I shook them at him and made them bow in his face. Monsieur Félix recoiled. A look of disgust caused him to purse his lips and narrow his eyes. Afraid that I had offended him, I lowered the puppets shamefacedly. Monsieur Félix said nothing. He passed on, coughing and rattling the hatful of coppers under the noses of the audience.

I had gone scarlet; and directly the séance was terminated for the afternoon I tried to escape as quickly as possible. But a voice called me back. I turned and saw Monsieur Félix leaning against the door of his theatre lighting a cigarette. I went towards him, my knees knocking together. I expected a good round telling-off for daring to bring my amateur Guignols anywhere near his performance. Instead Monsieur Félix said: Ça t'interesse, hein, le Guignol?

Oui, Monsieur Félix,
Tu viens ici tous les jours.
Oui, Monsieur Félix.
T'es étranger? D'ou ça?
D'Angleterre, Monsieur Félix.
Et en Angleterre, est-ce qu on joue du Guignol?
Non, Monsieur Félix.

Monsieur Félix nodded to himself. Then he puffed out a cloud of smoke and became convulsed in a fit of coughing. The veins on his temples swelled and he put a hand to his throat as though something too large for him to swallow had lodged there. His cigarette flew from between his lips with the force of his cough, and fell at his feet. He stamped on it, then opened the door of the theatre and beckoned me to follow him inside.

I was overwhelmed. I didnt know what to say. There I stood surrounded by the puppets, some hanging on hooks, some lying flat on shelves inside the dark box-like interior. I was amazed at their size: I'd had no idea they were so big. Even Guignol, whom I'd imagined to be small, was twice the size of anything I possessed. I asked Monsieur Félix where one could buy some as large as that. He shrugged his shoulders. À Paris, he said.

Then he explained to me how to split the end of the stick so that it made sufficient noise when blows were struck, without causing the paint to flake from the faces of the victims. Ripolin, or enamel paint, should be used for the faces, as this did not flake easily, and only needed another coat on top when the puppets began to look a bit battered. He explained all this in pigeon French, as I was a foreigner, and in a hoarse voice quite unlike the voices he used for the various characters on the stage. Then his voice failed altogether and another fit of coughing came on, even more sudden and violent than the previous one. His face went purple and he caught at his throat again. I was alarmed; I thought he was going to choke to death then and there.

Vous êtes malade, Monsieur Félix? I asked him, Je vais chercher le médecin? But mention of the doctor seemed to aggravate, if anything, Monsieur Félix's condition. He waved his arms furiously and came forward as though about to drive me by main force out of the theatre. Not knowing what I had done to annoy him I ducked quickly out through the door and fled.

Next day Monsieur Félix ignored me; it was difficult to believe we had ever spoken. He did not seem ill, but he coughed and was as brusque and surly as ever. I didnt dare approach him, of course, but I took his advice religiously: split the stick and bought pots of Ripolin; soon the faces of my Guignols shone with new health and vigour, which did not crack, however much I belaboured them.

Monsieur Félix was painting his puppets too. One afternoon they were all drying in the sun outside his theatre, lying in rows on a table inside the palisade. Looking through the palings I could see them, and Monsieur Félix was there as well. He called me over to the gate.

Fermé aujourd'hui, he said. Faut qu'ils séchent, jerking his thumb at the puppets. C'est le printemps, he added, as though in explanation. It was true. I'd been so preoccupied with my Guignols that I'd hardly noticed the springtime. I stared astounded at the pale green leaves the plane trees had started to sprout.

Tu veux entrer? Monsieur Félix said, holding open the gate for me. I stood in awe looking down at the newly-painted puppets on the table. Faut pas toucher, Monsieur Félix warned me.

I asked him when they would be ready. Some had been stripped of their clothes and were now merely heads standing on end. One of these was the Gendarme's, square and bald on top, without his cockaded hat. Monsieur Félix said: Deux jours, trois jours, puis on recommence. He coughed a little and sighed. Then suddenly he said: Allons, fiche-moi la paix, toi. J'ai pas l'temps d'bavarder ici toute la journée, j'ai un tas d'choses à faire. Va ton chemin. Ouste!

He opened the gate and almost pushed me through it, shouting after me as I stumbled away: Et ne viens plus m'emmerder avec tes questions, hein!

That was the second and last time I ever spoke to him. The weather abruptly became very hot: too hot to suit my father, who developed an attack of nettlerash and sat about in his pyjamas scratching himself. In summer North Africa comes very close to Marseille. In winter it retreats, but now it was very near indeed. The sky was a dark sultry blue and clouds of hot dust blew across the Plaine: one might easily have been in the desert.

My father decided to take a villa outside the town, where it was supposed to be cooler. So I saw Monsieur Félix more rarely, and had to content myself with making up plays of my own for my puppets to perform.

Then, on the fourteenth of July, my mother took me down to the town for a special treat: a gala performance of Guignol by night. I hardly recognised the theatre when we got there. The stage was lit up, there were fairy lanterns and tinsel decorations, and the theatre itself had been repainted red. Monsieur Félix was not there: I recognised that at once from the voices of the actors. The puppets were different too; many of my old favourites were missing from the cast and new characters had been introduced, many of whom had legs which dangled over the front of the stage. I disapproved strongly of all these changes and when the substitute puppet-master came round for the Quête, I asked him what had happened to Monsieur Félix.

The new man was bearded and old. He looked at me through red-rimmed eyes and said: Il est malade à l'hôpital. I said I hoped he would soon be better. The old man nodded and shuffled off. The performance continued, but it was not the same: even the drinking song seemed to lack something of its old vigour and sparkle. It's not as good without Monsieur Félix, all the children said.

It was a fortnight before I went down to the town again; by now, I thought, Monsieur Félix would surely be out of hospital. But he wasnt: the old man was standing by the gate of the palisade, inside which attendance seemed poor. I asked him how Monsieur Félix was, if he had any news,

Félix? the old man said; Félix est mort. I stared at him, unbelieving, so he added: C'était un cancer. Ici. He tapped his throat and spat: the spittle rolled itself up instantly into a ball of dust at his feet. Then I knew that Monsieur Félix was really dead. I turned and started to run at top speed across the Plaine and away from the theatre, towards the tram-lines and home.

Uncle Max

*　　　*　　　*

PART OF THE FOREGOING WAS ORIGINALLY CONCEIVED AS A
separate story; and therefore, though it gives a true enough description
of that time, it naturally leaves out everything irrelevant to its subject,
i.e. my relationship with the puppet-master, whose death, by the way,
I did not hear of in reality until a year afterwards, when we rented a
villa at Endoûme, a suburb in the country outside Marseille, after a
sojourn in Paris and a brief return to England, which was to be my last
for ten years.

One of the things the story leaves out, for instance, is all reference
to my Aunt Jane.

She was the one who had quarrelled with Aunt Enid and had
purposely dropped the Bible when staying with our Canadian cousins:
in her youth she'd had an ambition to sing in grand opera and was
trained in Milan by the best teachers; big things were expected of her,
an alternative career being offered as a concert-pianist; but instead, and
to everyone's surprise, she made a runaway marriage with a French
cavalry officer and from that day onward never sang or played again:
certainly I never heard her do so. (Once, however, when I was present,
my father happened to mention this and Aunt Jane for some reason
denied everything, saying instead that she had wanted to be an architect:
my father never cared to be contradicted or for his memory to be called
into question, and I well remember the frightful row that ensued.)

Aunt Jane's husband though technically French came from the part of
Alsace-Lorraine where they have German names, so on her marriage
she became Madame Schwartz, a circumstance which led to terrible
confusion both during and after the war, for the French do not readily
forgive an invasion of their soil and my aunt, who identified herself

111

completely with her adopted country, lost all control when mistaken for a Boche: the more so since Uncle Max, while fighting with conspicuous gallantry for France, had been taken prisoner and sent to a camp comparable in reputation to Dachau or Belsen in the more recent conflict. He had later managed to escape, however; and now, since they had retired him with a pension from the army, ran a business connected with hair-dye, a special process invented and patented by himself: but his experiences in prison, though he never talked about them, had nevertheless left their mark, as I will shortly relate.

Uncle Max was stocky and dapper, with a shining bald flushed forehead at which he frequently mopped. Typically Gallic in appearance, though without the big spade-shaped beard worn by many of his countrymen in those days, his partner in the hair-dye business among them; instead he wore a black moustache, not of the type introduced by his namesake Max Linder, but curling fiercely upward and waxed at the ends: his carriage had a certain cockiness born of years in the saddle, for though the cavalry was even then becoming mechanised and in the war he had, I believe commanded a tank company, his early service had undoubtedly been passed in an equestrian posture, and when he bowed stiffly and brought his heels together with a click one still expected to hear the jingle of spurs. It was possible even now to see how handsome he had looked when younger in his képi and horizon blue and how Aunt Jane, hitherto contemptuous of suitors, had come to be swept off her feet; and while nowadays he dressed soberly in a businessman's dark suits and overcoats, there remained the appeal of his eyes, like his wife's rather protuberant, but dog-brown in colour and with a pleading quality that she had not been able to resist.

They were now permanently domiciled in Marseille, Uncle Max had his office there and the laboratory was in the basement of the house where they lived: a building which delighted me by having an outer door that opened by itself; you pushed a button under the name Schwartz, Aunt Jane in the basement or the apartment upstairs pressed in response a device which automatically drew the bolts in the hall, and after several clicks and buzzes in the lock, the door swung wide, which seemed to me magical and was certainly for that time extremely modern.

In other ways too Aunt Jane was progressive: she had the first typewriter I had ever seen and used it moreover with tolerable accuracy, though when later she stayed with us at Endoûme my father used to compare the noise it made with a horse kicking a loose-box to bits. She was a tall woman, more stately and less dynamic than Aunt Enid, but with something of the same grenadier's stride; her crêpe-de-chine coats and cloaks trailed out behind her too as she swept along the streets; she was hung with jewelled chains and each of her large white pianist's hands, much given to emphatic and dramatic gestures, was decorated on every finger with heavy rings, disparagingly referred to by my father as knuckle-dusters, though many of them had been inherited from his mother's collection. In face also Aunt Jane bore a slight resemblance to the sister she so disliked, but her features were less aquiline and more fleshy, the eyes bolder, bluer and more prominent. Her hair on the other hand still seemed naturally auburn and there was no indication that she made personal use of the product manufactured by her husband and, on occasion, by herself, since the formula was known to her also and I have often seen her in the laboratory bottling the mixture and affixing labels to the flasks: when engaged in this task she always wore a Japanese kimono instead of a smock, and these were the only occasions I ever saw her wearing bright colours, though her appearance was at all times extremely smart or, as she would have said, mondaine. For, as I've indicated earlier, she considered herself wholly a Frenchwoman, and like a highbrow book reviewer used a French word in preference to an English one any time: her accent however—unlike, in most cases, those of the reviewers—would not have disgraced the Comédie Française and at one point, when the family had offended her by opposing her marriage to Uncle Max, she had sworn a vow never to speak English again, which on this visit my father forced her to break; for though at home he had often spoken French with my mother for practice, he suddenly, now that he was abroad, became intensely British, assumed in public the air of a retired naval commodore, and refused any conversation with his sister unless it were conducted in the language of their birth.

Then, also, all talks with me had to be in English at first, though as I've said before, I did not take long to learn French. With Uncle Max communication proved difficult at first: apparently he had spoken English quite well once but Aunt Jane had discouraged his use of it after their marriage; years had passed since then plus the prison camp, and now he had forgotten everything except How-do-you-do and Good-bye. An arrangement was finally arrived at by which we each chattered on in our own tongue when out together alone, supplementing with signs when special urgency required the use of them: sometimes it would give Uncle Max great pleasure to recall a phrase from his English-speaking past, as when he wanted to buy me some cakes and, pointing at a confectioner's window, brought out with triumph and a good British pronunciation the word Dessert: remembering doubtless some occasion when he had dined at an English house, it might have been my grandmother's.

Their marriage had turned out childless, this was their one regret, and perhaps in consequence they were both endlessly kind and thoughtful to me: for example, when we first arrived I developed a bad bout of diarrhœa, it may have been due to the difference in diet, my father dosed me with chlorodyne but this did not stem the flow; Uncle Max, much troubled, disappeared out and returned with an elaborate canister of some special powdered chocolate which when drunk, he assured us, would do the trick besides being more palatable than ordinary medicine, and he was right both times. Then at Christmas they clubbed together to buy me a tremendous wooden box of the most expensive pastels, such as many an artist would have envied me: this gift was attributed to Santa Claus, but I no longer believed in him and knew it came from them. Aunt Jane also, knowing that I was repelled by the grey shiny paper, with a red ruled margin down the left-hand side, in most French exercise books, put herself out to find me very thick ones, with no red line but cream laid paper like vellum, bound in moleskin and gold-blocked round the edges, for my film-scripts: all this in addition to the constant presents of pocket-money she showered on me, never less than ten francs whenever I saw her, and not less than fifty on high-days and holidays, to say nothing of the boxes of marrons glacés, the chocolates and stone jars of quince jelly, for which I had at that time a not easily satisfied passion.

They cannot have been rich, the pension of a retired army officer is not munificent anywhere, still less in France, and most of Aunt Jane's money had long ago been swallowed up by the business, which was not bringing in large returns: moreover they did not live frugally and the rent of their apartment on a fashionable boulevard can hardly have been small; yet with all the worries they must have had then, no expense was spared to bring me added happiness, so much so that even my parents, not mean themselves in that respect, were moved to protest that I would become hopelessly spoiled.

But it is for more than money or presents that I am grateful now: it is above all for the tireless patience with which Aunt Jane listened to the descriptions of books and films that had thrilled me at that time, and the outpouring of plots I was beginning at this period to concoct for myself: my parents not unreasonably sighed or became overtly impatient when I commenced these recitals, Aunt Jane never; and though years later we quarrelled and drew finally apart, I shall always remember, among many kindnesses, how she listened then so gravely, as one adult to another, with no sign of the boredom she must have felt, thus helping to build up the sense of self-importance so necessary, it seems, if life is to be coped with at all, but always lacking in me by nature: though never more than at the age of nine.

Now I must tell about Uncle Max; for unbeknown to any of us, even my aunt, all was not well with him.

The first intimation I had of anything wrong was when, coming back to our hotel one afternoon from a visit to the cinema, I heard him declaiming in what was evidently the most furious indignation from behind the closed door of Father's bedroom: my mother in the outer suite said quickly, as I moved towards the sound of voices, Dont disturb them now dear, they are busy.

A soothing rumble from my father followed, Uncle Max's harangue subsided for a moment then broke out with renewed vigour; I could distinguish only one word repeated over and over, and this seemed to be somebody's name: but Mother, when asked who S. Crow was, replied that it was not a person at all but a French word spelt e-s-c-r-o-c. Just then the door flew open and my uncle rushed out crimson in the face and mopping his forehead, followed by my father in pyjamas sniffing at his bottle of salts, for he was recovering at the time from an attack of vertigo; with no more than a curt bow to Mother and ignoring me completely for the first time since I had known him, Uncle Max snatched his velour hat from a chair and cramming it on almost ran from the room, banging the door behind him.

What on earth is the matter with Max? Mother asked in astonishment, for as a rule his manners were so punctilious: for answer my father beckoned her into the bedroom, closing the door between us, and I was left to conjecture why my uncle had seemed so flurried and unlike himself. I looked up *escroc* in the dictionary and found it meant swindler: but who had he been calling that—it could hardly have been my father. When after a long interval my parents reappeared it was with expressions of concern: brushing aside my questions they continued their conversation in French, and I began to wonder if Uncle Max had perhaps been drunk; for I knew all about drunkenness after seeing, not only a film called *The Danger Mark* in which Helen Ferguson worked her way up from eau-de-cologne on lumps of sugar to bottles of brandy emptied at a sitting in secret, but two French serials about dipsomania now running in Marseille: *La Pocharde* and *L'Assonimoir*; in the latter a workman had just fallen from a ladder, with grievous consequences to himself, through being blind drunk on the job: and I knew moreover, and not only from the evasive manner in which the sub-titles of the serials had been translated to me, that grown-ups always made a mystery of it when one of their number was under the influence of liquor; on the other hand Uncle Max so far as I knew did not drink, apart from a glass of wine at mealtimes: and he had certainly not touched alcohol, though we were sitting together on a café terrace, when the next incident occurred a few days later.

Uncle Max had already once or twice that afternoon exhibited signs of strain: less voluble than usual during the walk we'd taken, he had glanced behind him several times with a frown as though expecting to be followed, and now as we sat with sirops before us his gaze kept straying with some uneasiness towards a man reading *Le Petit Marseillais* at the next table. Finally this individual, doubtless feeling eyes upon him, put down his paper and turned in our direction: at his casual scrutiny Uncle Max's mouth fell open in alarm; he sprang up instantly, flinging some paper money on the table, and motioning me to follow made his way at a rapid trot down the Cannebière. I ran behind, protesting in English that we had barely touched our glasses and I was thirsty; but Uncle Max paid no attention: in the lurid red light diffused from the foyer of the Kursaal Cinema, reflected downwards from the looped letters over its entrance, that seem in recollection to have been neon-lit, his face under the velour hat brim showed fiery and streaming with sweat, his eyes rolled in what could only have been a panic fear; and putting a painful grip round my wrist he dragged me along with him in his by now almost headlong flight, so that passers-by turned to stare.

At the corner he slowed down, and still keeping hold of me, looked back cautiously the way we'd come, but there was no sign of the man from the café and for the moment he seemed reassured. Then, as we were halfway up the rue du Paradis, his fingers on my arm tightened again, this time at sight of a man who, emerging from a shop, had fallen into step behind us. Once more Uncle Max became galvanised, we shot up a side-street and found ourselves transported in a second to a region of ironmongery and shawled women laundering sheets on cobblestones. All the time my uncle was panting out muttered exclamations and exhortations, it may have been for me to hurry, and not until we reached the hotel by this circuitous route did his pace slacken: by that time it was dark; and though no footsteps sounded in pursuit, Uncle Max, mopping his forehead below a street lamp, stopped to make sure: now he delivered a long impassioned speech of which I understood only one word, repeated as often as *escroc* had been in the address to my father, but this time it was Pradier. I knew that to be the name of his partner in business, whom I had never seen, and perhaps, I thought as he left me abruptly at the hotel door, without coming up as he usually did, perhaps the man in the café had been Monsieur Pradier, whom for some reason my uncle had not wished to encounter at that particular time: but then there was the other man, totally dissimilar in appearance, whom he had feared was following us, and they could not both have been Pradier.

Did either of these men have a beard? my father asked, when I told him of the incident. No Father, I answered. Not a big black square beard? Father insisted, touching his own as an example of what he meant, though it was neither black nor square: No Father, I told him. Then neither of them was Pradier, Father said, and he took several sniffs at his smelling bottle in quick succession: a sure sign of grave anxiety.

And anxious he was indeed, for though prepared to believe, with reservations, Uncle Max's initial statement that Pradier was swindling him out of a share in the profits, he could not credit a subsequent assertion that the partner employed agents to follow him about the streets, with a view to obtaining the formula for the hair dye which, according to Uncle Max, he wished to convert to his own uses, like Warner Oland with the death-ray: nor that Pradier had attempted to poison or in other ways to murder him.

So the day I've just described proved to be the last time I ever saw Uncle Max, for I was not there on the morning he called, flourishing a service revolver and proposing to settle accounts with his partner once and for all; my father, failing to dissuade him from such a course, felt obliged to telephone Pradier, who in turn informed the police: Uncle Max, arrested outside the office with the pistol in his pocket, put up such a violent resistance they had to strap him down, and consequent examination by specialists confirmed what Father had feared: that he was hopelessly and even dangerously insane; a course of injections given him at the prison camp, for experimental purposes, was believed to be the cause of this sudden mental disintegration.

All this, of course, I have pieced together from fragments overheard and imperfectly understood at the time: it was not for years after that I learned the truth, and even then in a more roundabout way than I have told it here. I remember a visit from Aunt Jane, her eyes obviously swollen from weeping, it must have been the day when, despite all her protests, he was certified and committed to the asylum: I was told, first, that he had gone away for a rest-cure, and then, much later, that he was dead, and indeed the heavy crêpe assumed, thenceforward, by my aunt lent colour to this story: though in fact he lingered on for years, growing progressively worse, until at last he had to be placed in a padded cell and my aunt was no longer allowed to visit him.

Poor Uncle Max. I often wish I could have spoken French then, I might have been able, somehow, to help, though I suppose it was too late; already the shadows were massing around him and there must have been indications, unnoticed by me at that age but visible to others, that the poison was working in his blood and the paranoia with its sly insinuation in his brain: though Aunt Jane maintained to the end, at the risk of a slander suit, that without the machinations of Pradier (real enough up to a point, as events proved) his sanity might still have been preserved.

It must have been before this, since I recall no note of sadness on that occasion—moreover Aunt Jane was there though not, for some reason, her husband—that Uncle Bertie drove over from Nice to Marseille and took us all out to lunch. I do not remember, however, the presence of my grandmother at the restaurant we went to: this was famous for the local dish bouillabaisse (though I was not allowed to partake of it personally) and was enclosed on two sides by thick bluish glass, giving the impression of being, itself, an aquarium; I think they may have had a tank of tropical fish there too, unless I am confusing it with the Réserve somewhere else.

Asti Spumanti was served to drink, and Uncle Bertie in his most festive mood insisted that I should be allowed to sample it, since I had been forced to make do with chicken instead of the famous fish-stew; my father shrugged with a touch of coldness, but submitted to his host: later, recovering his good humour, he told a story which drew cries of protest from the ladies towards its conclusion but convulsed

Uncle Bertie and myself. Years ago, he said, he had been invited to dinner by a noted epicure who, having developed dyspepsia, was no longer able to indulge, himself, in the delights of the table; the meal served to his guests, however, was more than up to the standard of his gastronomic days, and all were enjoying themselves when they noticed one peculiarity: the host was not eating. As each dish, soup, fish, entrée etc was brought to the table, his share of it was put not on a plate but emptied into a large glass bowl in front of him: the same with his wine-glass as vintage succeeded vintage; the guests being well bred made no comment and continued to eat; then came the dessert—in Father's version the name of every dish was rolled sonorously out but I cant remember them—anyway this was some kind of flaming bombe, and the bowl too flared up as the host's portion was added to it, toasting the sliver of cheese that followed, but the conflagration was soon extinguished by brandy, port and coffee: the host waited until cigars had been passed around and were well alight, then pushing the bowl to the centre of the table so all could examine through the glass that hotchpotch of foodstuffs floating in a gruesome cocktail, he said: Allow me, gentlemen, to present you with the contents of your stomachs, fortunately invisible otherwise, since you are not transparent.

At the thought of these men, my father among them, and how they must have looked, though now I find it much less funny and even cruel, then I fairly yelled, with mirth so immoderate the whole restaurant turned round, while Father darted a look at my empty glass direct enough to be traced by that dotted line customary in the cartoons of the day. Bertie, he said, no more please, he's had enough; but too late: the Asti had already gushed from the bottle tilted by my uncle, himself shaking with laughter so that some spilled on the cloth. I grabbed the refilled glass and drank, gulping the sweet froth for fear it might be snatched away: Father with a groan turned his eyes up to the ceiling; and it must have been soon after this I found myself on my feet making a speech. I can see now their faces turned towards me: the encouragement of Uncle Bertie's grin, the embarrassment of all the rest; but not even Father's baleful glare could stop me, though I dont know what I said. It was the first time I'd been drunk, and I could not understand why the walls of glass seemed to expand and contract, those faces to rise and fall, as if we were in a lift while I babbled on: I had not been ill on the boat coming over, but now the marine suggestion of a tank enclosing us, outside which the sea itself could be seen, induced a sudden nausea; a rising hiccup stemmed my flood of words, and I fell abruptly silent, swallowing a taste of salt, while the room seemed poised for a plunge as steep as those hills, also associated with my uncle, down which we'd dived in the car, only now it was into the hollow of a wave. Father, whose eyes had not left me, though Mother's were fixed on her plate, did not misinterpret my expression; Bertie, he said, I decline to deal with this, you had better take charge: and then I was in a tiled place under the experienced care of my uncle, who said (as the aerated bubbles burst scalding from my mouth and nose, worse by far than sherbet) History repeats itself dear boy, and went on once more to mention Caesar.

The sequel was that I had to be put to bed promptly; and though too young then for a hangover, I felt a new sympathy, as a result of this experience, with the protagonists of the dipsomaniac serials next time these staggered across the screen. Uncle Bertie made a quick getaway in his car before he could receive the full weight of Mother's disapproval for having got me drunk: before he went, however, he promised, bending over my sick bed, that when I visited him in Nice he would show me his leech, for he had arranged earlier that we should all come over soon, plus Willie and Margaret, who were to spend their honeymoon in the South of France after the wedding, due to take place any moment now.

It never, alas, took place at all. For one morning a cablegram arrived: BILLY PASSED PEACEFULLY AWAY IN HIS SLEEP LAST NIGHT DEEPEST SYMPATHY LETTER FOLLOWS MARGARET. Afterwards, in her letter, calling him Billy as she always had, Margaret told how, having said goodnight to the ward-sister, my brother had turned quietly over on his side to sleep; he was to have been discharged, with a clean bill of health, in the morning; instead he never woke, a blood-clot, which had existed unknown to the doctors, having burst in his brain: as they'd call it now, thrombosis.

But it is my reactions at the time I must set down, that I have never told before: for when I put my head on that table where the cable lay as the door behind my parents slammed and Mother sobbed with Father's arm around her in the other room; in the dark which my hands, squeezed over eyeballs, made, I too waited for the tears which by convention should have flowed; but all that came to mind, instead of sorrow, was the slap he once had dealt me, the shock of his fingers on my cheek remembered, so that now, as then, I could not cry, even when I knew he'd gone: unmourned by me, a splendid stranger still.

And as though, from being forced, the tear-ducts from that moment froze, crying has always been, for me, a rare and painful process since.

So, at my brother's death, there's the truth of how I felt; for in a book like this, facts may be out of focus through the haze of time: chronology, for all I care, skew-wiff; but feelings, unfalsified, must go down here for any who may wish to read: the bad with whatever good may be.

Paris and the Cinder Path

*　　　*　　　*

I SPENT MY TENTH BIRTHDAY IN BED WITH PLEURISY, AND IN PARIS. For it was to the capital that we moved in the summer of that year, and not, as I stated in the story Monsieur Félix, to a villa outside Marseille, which we left in point of fact soon after I came across the puppet-master giving his Guignols their spring coat of paint upon the Plaine. The cause of our departure was a disagreement which my father had with Aunt Jane over her conduct of business affairs; for, of the two tragedies that had struck in such quick succession at our family, the madness of Uncle Max brought more complications in its train than the death of my brother.

In the latter case Margaret arranged everything, we did not go over for the funeral since my mother being prostrate with grief was in no condition to travel: became in fact so ill that I see now it must have been her change of life; doctors had at one moment shaken their heads seriously, and I can still recall the terrible shock I had when, returning from a walk one day with my father, I saw a funeral cortège approaching us from the direction of the hotel, a plumed black hearse with a procession of mourners, and I cried out in consternation, making sure it must be Mother's. But bit by bit she got better, meanwhile my brother was buried, and Margaret wrote that she meant to carry on alone with the school, as this would have been his wish, then went on to say that of course she would never marry now, which quite certainly would not have been his wish; and while I hope that later on her resolve in this direction faltered, for she deserved happiness and fulfilment, I cannot say either way for certain since, though a correspondence was kept up for some time, we drifted apart in the end, as people will.

Uncle Max's forced retirement was another matter: there was the hair-dye business to be looked after, and it seems clear that, though the swindling and attempts at murder were beyond doubt delusive, my uncle's suspicions of Pradier were justified to some extent; for no sooner was Max certified than the bearded partner, who had obviously been intriguing for some time behind the scenes, openly attempted to gain full control of the concern, by trying (a) to have the Schwartzes' share in it wound up, and (b) to buy the hair-dye formula from Aunt Jane for a sum which she found, in the French phrase, derisory, and refused with peals of angry mirth, intimating that she would carry on in her husband's place and demanding at the same time a full statement of accounts to date. Pradier for the moment was stumped, for without the formula, now her sole property, the process could not be manufactured at all. His next move was to instigate a complicated wrangle over letters-patent, and my father was called in at this juncture to negotiate with the solicitors on both sides. He disapproved of those acting for his sister, deeming them too old-fashioned to outmanœuvre the more astute and modern firm employed by Pradier: they had, however, been chosen by Uncle Max and in Aunt Jane's opinion he would not have wished her to change; Father retorted that he would not have wished for ruin either, and argument on this point led at last to an open quarrel, during which my aunt declared she could do without his help, finally referring to this as unwarranted interference: hence we found ourselves, in the summer of what must have been 1922, at an apartment in Montparnasse, not far from the boulevard Raspail and built, to our sorrow, above the premises of a sawmill.

On the corner of the street where we lived was a café with tin tables outside and a zinc counter, supposed to have been the meeting-place of Lenin and Trotsky during their days of exile but now no longer frequented by revolutionaries of any nation, judging by the appearance of the present customers, though I liked to think these were in disguise; and the apartment itself belonged to an Irish poet, who held a post as curator of a museum in Paris and had returned for a holiday to his homeland. We leased the apartment for the summer from his wife, and I never saw the poet himself, though his son, whom I did meet, was about my age, having moreover the same christian name, and we were soon on the best of terms. I remember being heartbroken for fully a week, since he was the first friend I ever had, when he finally left for Ireland to join his father; I remember too that while experimenting with the hot and cold water system we through inadvertence allowed the bath to overflow and flood the flat: an accident for which he insisted on taking an equal share of blame, though it was in fact my fault.

Things in life have a habit of coming my way when I no longer need them, few wishes of mine have failed to be granted in this fashion: and now that I was able to attend at any time those super-cinemas at which I'd looked so longingly when we passed through Paris for the first time, I cannot remember visiting them once; for by then of course my ruling passion was the Guignol Theatre. I had at first mistaken the Théâtre du Grand Guignol for a special centre of this, at which life-sized puppets perhaps formed the cast; Father put me right here, and proposed instead an expedition to the Champs Elysées, where we found two rival puppet-shows in progress, both attended by an enthusiastic clientèle of both sexes, with the Arc de Triomphe as a background.

These Parisian theatres differed from the performances of Monsieur Félix in that the Guignol himself was not the protagonist: this rôle instead was filled by his son Grandgalet, a very small puppet with a bald pink baby face, while Guignol took a back seat as a sometimes stern and respectable parent, who had given up, rather like my own father, the drinking song and the cabaret altogether. This change may have been instituted because Grandgalet's age was nearer to that of his public and therefore allowed of mass-identification, on the same principle that prompts writers' of boys stories to involve in the action youngsters whose physical endurance and prowess, like those of Grandgalet, are out of all proportion to their age.

We often went to the Champs Elysées: there was also a local theatre in the Luxembourg Gardens, rather dank and ill-attended, whose small repertoire of plays soon became over-familiar and spurred me on to greater efforts in creating my own, which I now composed instead of film-scripts and performed for my own benefit (Grandgalet having been added to my repertory company), with my mother as an occasional guest whenever I could get her to attend. At this time, so obsessed was I with the Guignols, I had almost ceased to read, and I am grateful to the attack of pleurisy which came on just before my birthday for bringing to my notice a small shelf of books, left behind by the poet's family in my bedroom, and hitherto shunned by me as being more than likely the sort of stuff that adults read, though I realised after they must have belonged to my namesake, the son. For when the worst of the pleurisy subsided (more acutely painful at first than the bladder trouble I'd experienced before, but uncomplicated by pneumonia like the attack I suffered twenty years later, in the army) as I looked around for something to help pass the long hours of convalescence, for it was impossible to perform Guignol sitting up in bed, two titles on this shelf caught my attention, *The Adventures of Jimmie Dale*, and *Through the Wall* by Cleveland Moffett.

I am not sure now which of these two books enthralled me more: the exploits of Frank L. Packard's amateur cracksman and that beautiful enigma Marie La Salle, The Tocsin, who spurred him on to action, or those of the French detective Coquelin and his gallant collie-dog, murdered, alas, by the shadowy left-handed figure whom he pursued; perhaps I liked the latter best, since the pursuit took place in Paris, and across avenues known to me: Coquelin and the master-criminal fought, using jiu-jitsu, on a corner of the Champs Elysées, and I had visited the cathedral in whose vast gloom the candle-seller of the book sat troubled by her hallucinations of an intangible past; moreover I had seen for myself the gargoyles profiled against the blood-red sky similar to that under which the story opens with its portent of murder yet to come.

So, sunk deep in the atmosphere of these tales, which I have never since forgotten, while the sawmill on its annual holiday was mercifully silent below, I was hardly conscious of the summer that I could not share staining with sun the glass of the window facing my bed and declining day by day: until, by the time I was well again, it was autumn, and my father had already booked our passage for England.

The town in which we stayed on our return was not Bournemouth, for that contained too many memories which Mother would have found unbearable; but it too was at the seaside and had an arcade, though on a smaller scale than the one at Boscombe and there were fewer cinemas: in fact, as I remember, in those days only two.

It was a winter town: that is to say winter is the season with which I principally associate it, as Bournemouth with summer. Winter of course meant cosiness then: muffins and crumpets for tea, and cold hands, stripped of woollen gloves, being held out to thaw at a blazing fire; I remember being 'wrapped up warm': thick jerseys and scarves and mufflers thrown thrice round my neck with the ends hanging down behind; I chafed at this coddling, though there's no doubt that the care they gave me then stored up the stamina I required later, when I was to walk the streets of that very town feeling the wet pavement through the soles of shoes worn thin: or those of London only last year, in winter and without an overcoat through the lack of funds, the literary life being what it is and the film world worse.

We lived about two miles out, in a bungalow taken furnished, around and behind us were railway carriages converted for residential purposes, and at the end of our road a sandy beach sloped down to the sea. Next door there was a small boy named Alec, a year or two younger than I and therefore treated by me with aloof condescension when, as sometimes happened, he peered over the wall separating our respective lawns: he was in any case not very stimulating and spent much of his time whistling and singing a repetitive tune, the refrain of which, I remember, went:

> Not a cent,
> Not a cent,
> An' me clothes is only lent,

and then, after a few indistinguishable lines, 'That Coal-black Mammy o' Mine'.

Over the way, however, in a house built high on, as it were, stilts, the front door of which was reached by a ladder, lived a little girl my own age, called Mabs, much more interesting than Alec, whom I had first picked up on the cinder path, bordered on one side by a thicket of brambles and on the other by waste land over which rooks cawed circling, that formed between a short district and the town. My father used to walk me back, for exercise, across the path after our excursions to the cinema; there was a shop just at the entrance of it, built oddly askew and small like a gnome's dwelling, so that Father had to bend almost double when he went in to buy me sweets, a bag of which he'd press into my hand before allowing me to run on ahead towards home, while he with his stick stumped behind, his breath blowing out visibly on the air which was always cold, though never to freezing point.

Outdistancing him in this way one afternoon, I saw in front of me a small girl in russet brown, the gold of whose hair revived my dormant criminal instincts: though unprovided this time with mask or gun I bore down on her instantly from behind in a manner that to anyone else of her age might appear most menacing, but which Mabs did not seem even to notice; for when, hearing my footsteps, she turned, it was with a smile and a welcoming Hullo.

In Mabs's company it was impossible to be other than friendly, her smile disarmed at once the feeling of what even then must have been sex-antagonism, with which I had initially approached her; and when we found we lived opposite to one another I used frequently to climb the ladder to the house on stilts and ask her very charming widowed mother if she might come over to tea. Permission was always granted, and to the end of our stay there Mabs and I never, so far as I can recall, had a falling-out.

She was like Wanda or that other, whose name I never knew, who had lured me into the hands of the toad-schoolmistress, but with none of the superciliousness or affectation of superiority: there were the blue eyes, the blonde hair in soft curls done up on top with a bow, the physical equipment of a fairy princess in miniature; but while those other two seemed by the airs they put on already conscious of the power that, growing up into beauties, they would later wield, and to be spoilt by it in advance, Mabs, though plainly endowed by nature to enjoy the same advantages, remained utterly unwarped, and was in any case incapable of being anything but natural in every way.

I cant remember what we talked about: I used, I know, sometimes to give a performance of Guignol in her honour, which she cannot really have enjoyed since the dialogue was in French; our relationship was not, despite her beauty, romantic: we certainly never kissed as we played on the lawn or walked along the sands with the tide way out, and though I may have entertained the idea of marrying her when we grew up, I don't remember formulating an actual proposal. No, to me now what we said and did remains blank, except for the very happy and unclouded memory that I keep of her; she had an aptitude, peculiar in a child of ten, for spreading her own tranquillity about; and at the risk of seeming sentimental, I like to think that she, though now a woman happily married, I hope, and middle-aged (as I am myself) might read this tribute that I pay her: for she brought peace, as no member of her sex has since, to what was, even in those days when I knew her, a very restless mind.

My father too was restless about this time. He had thought to settle for a while in France, the quarrel with Aunt Jane had upset him, then of course the death of my brother had been a stunning blow: he'd looked forward, as my mother had also, to grandchildren about him in his old age; now the family had crumbled and there was only me left. The question of my education bobbed up again: there were endless wrangles about this, for Father, though he liked Mabs, viewed our association on the whole with disfavour, saying that it wasn't good for me to have a girl all day long as sole companion, if we weren't careful I'd turn into one myself, and a public school would soon correct all that.

The prospect of public school terrified me, for though Father now conventionally referred to his sojourn at one of these as the happiest days of his life, I had not forgotten the story of how his front teeth were broken by a cricket ball bowled at him by a sadistic prefect, who strapped the boys as Aunt Sallies to the wicket, nor of how his chilblains had been stamped on in the rugger scrum. Mother, however, refused to allow me to be sent away, and anyway I was too young; Father then proposed prep-school for a start, there was one nearby where the boys wore green caps, and the argument was still going on when a letter arrived from my sister containing momentous news.

Carol and my father had become reconciled after Willie's death and now wrote to one another regularly; she and Rudolf seemed to have settled down happily enough, though Father still shook his head at the thought of their future, complicated as this now was, we learned from her letter, by an addition to the family. The birth of the baby, a boy christened Logan, delighted my parents nevertheless, though Toronto was too far away to permit of a reunion just yet; Mother became at once employed at knitting socks and bootees of an appropriate powder-blue, and even I felt proud at my new importance as an uncle, which seemed to place me on par with my own uncle Bertie.

I remember a journey we made to London about that time, when I first saw the scarlet buses and was allowed to ride on the upper deck of one, in those days open to the sky: the purpose of this visit was partly the bomb-damage claim, still unsettled, and there were also lawyers and trustees to be seen about the transference of money from my sister's inheritance to Canada; for though she was not yet of age, Rudolf had, so far, been able to find only temporary employment in a government office and the arrival of my nephew necessitated urgent financial aid.

This trip to London was also of importance because of a purchase I made at Victoria Station on the way back, but for which I might never really have embarked on a literary career, though it's possible the seeds of this were there from the start. Peering at the station bookstall for something to read on the journey, and disregarding my father's suggestion of *The Wide World*, for that was supposed to contain fact and I preferred fiction, I saw a quarto-sized periodical with a pink cover, bearing, I think, a picture of one man being knocked out by another with what, I learned from the text, was called a Right Cross: I passed over my twopence and that issue of *The Boy's Magazine* accompanied me to the train.

Until now, though Carol had at one time subscribed to a weekly called *The School Friend*, in which Billy Bunter's sister Bessie figured prominently, I had avoided *The Gem* and *Magnet* etc, as the setting of the stories recalled too poignantly the sort of place in which I might shortly find myself; but that day marked the beginning of a new phase, and in the end of the Guignols, for the magazine I bought contained the first instalment of a serial called 'Top o' the League' by John Hunter, who rapidly replaced Arthur B. Reeve as my favourite author. The story was ostensibly concerned with football, a sport that did not interest me, and the efforts, eventually successful, of a provincial team to acquire first-division status and also win the Cup, but there was a sub-plot revolving round a Spanish treasure-galleon shipwrecked in a sunken cave, and the man-eating octopus that lived on board it: and an adventurer named Stacey Augustus Twentyman, who coveted the gold, and ultimately fell a victim to this cephalopod, but not before he had tried every conceivable method of removing the obstructive footballer-hero from the scene of action, on one occasion lashing him to the stack of a factory chimney when this was about to be detonated from below. (I don't remember how, in any case, a rescue was effected.)

Twentyman was an American, the forerunner of the gangster sagas that I later enjoyed: in the illustrations he wore a panama hat irrespective of the season, a cigar protruded invariably from his thin-lipped mouth, from the corner of which crepitated, at almost every sentence, a stream of what were not then called wisecracks, and an automatic pistol was packed in his hip pocket; soon my speech became peppered with transatlantic slang, and I regretted that panamas of the type he wore were not obtainable in England, also that I was still too young to smoke.

'Top o' the League' came finally to an end and was succeeded by another serial from the same pen (as the editor would have put it) entitled 'The Luck of the Leather'; by that time I was buying other periodicals of the same type: *The Champion* and its companion-paper *Pluck*; each of these features every week what was described as a 'Book-Length 12,000 Word Novel Complete in this Issue', and while my own publishers nowadays might not regard this as a truthful definition of the length prescribed for separate printing, one must admit it was a good value for twopence, especially since several serials were included also. Among these were 'The Quest of the Golden Web' by Eric W.

Townsend: giant spiders in Patagonia and a sinister silk-merchant, who was hung up in a cage for vultures to peck at by a rival competitor for the valuable strands which the spiders wove, and 'Splash Page Sensation Hunter' by Gwyn Evans, creator also of 'Danger Dane the Cyclone Sleuth': Page was star crime reporter of the *Daily Radio*, and I avidly followed his adventures in pursuit of a murderer's wax image, which had walked, one day, out of Mme Tussaud's to commence a new career of crime.

It was largely owing to these authors that I first recognised the existence of style, i.e. I became able to distinguish the differences in their manner of writing and choice of subject-manner: Eric W. Townsend for instance was an arachnophile (the giant spiders reappeared later in another story, 'The Lure of Ophir') and he chose Biblical christian names for his characters (Habakkuk Home, Judas Bleak etc); Gwyn Evans specialised in the bizarre (human flies, vanishing omnibuses, and a criminal who lived behind a bead curtain and had the face of a new-born baby); while John Hunter's style was the most individual of all, whether he wrote about sport or the lamasaries of Tibet.

There were, too, countless other serials about football, in which the heroes always played centre-forward; they were sometimes written by famous footballers themselves: at least theirs were the names appended below the titles of the stories, though with my new knowledge of style I could sometimes recognise from the text the work of other writers, and it was from reading these that I developed an interest in the game itself and was soon able to follow a highly technical account of a match without having been on a football field as either participant or spectator. I began to plague my father to take me to a see the local eleven play; he was glad to find me becoming a supporter of so manly a sport and together we watched many a match; for a while, in fact for the whole of the season, I became a fervent fan; though on the other hand nobody has ever been able to interest me in cricket: indeed my friend C.K. Jaeger, himself a local cricketer of renown, often states truthfully that I am unable to tell one end of a bat from the other, which he considers a disgrace but I do not.

Another feature of the periodicals I favoured was The Editor's Chat. This was principally devoted to advance news of the material due to appear in future columns of the paper, the style was lyrical in praise of the contributions to come, and in the top left-hand corner was a drawing of the Editor himself, represented as a remarkably youthful-looking figure, sitting at a desk covered with correspondence from his readers. A prize was offered for the best letter, and I once competed for this myself: perhaps the neatness and legibility of my block letters caught the attention of the staff, anyway I received as a reward a copy of Jules Verne's *Clipper of the Clouds*, which I had already read in the original French, though it would have seemed ungrateful and even pompous to write and tell the Editor so.

There was also the Editor's Secret. This had been coyly hinted at for some weeks in the space reserved for his Chat, and as the time grew nearer for it to be revealed I, in common no doubt with other readers, was worked up into a fever of excited speculation; then at last the secret was out: *The Champion* and *Pluck* were to have a third companion-paper called *The Rocket* (on sale next week Price 2d). I jumped for joy at the news, it also solved two mysteries at one stroke, since I had been pondering for the last fortnight the meaning of the posters, plastered up all over town, which announced in large type THE ROCKET IS COMING: now I sighed with relief, for I had half-feared the advent of another comet.

The Rocket was duly obtainable on the promised date and was well worth the price advertised, for the first number not only contained a new serial by John Hunter, 'Wolves of Doom' (which featured another gunman, Stahl, of the Twentyman pattern though more sympathetic than his prototype), but also the adventures of a new character called Dr Sinister, despite his name an amateur detective, who lived in Egypt and exclaimed Bismillah! at moments of annoyance, much as Father said ¡Carajo! when he sneezed. Dr Sinister's main opponent styled himself the Phantom Cracksman, and remained not only unknown but unseen, for he operated from a helicopter, hovering at too great a height for one to get at him; and his activities caused the doctor to exclaim Bismillah! only too often, especially when, at the end of each episode, he broadcast a mocking message through a stentorphone before his helicopter took wing until the following week.

This was the year when Tut-ankh-Amen's Tomb was discovered, when Gerald Lee Bevan was front-page news (as Uncle Bertie was to be later, though for a different reason); wireless was beginning to come into its own: there was talk of crystal-sets and 2LO, while BEAVER was called after people with beards as they walked along the streets (though I do not remember anyone addressing my father in this manner). But, lost in the private world created by boys' papers and in the process, painfully, of creating my own, for I had just begun to write stories in imitation of those that drugged me, I remained deaf and blind to these manifestations of the period: only the excavation of the Pharaoh's tomb penetrated to me, for the Valley of the Kings was the topical setting for a new serial, announced in the Editor's Chat, and besides my father had been friendly, in his younger days, with the leader of the expedition.

Without knowing it, however, the last moments of peace were drawing near: life, like a cheerful bustling bully, was soon to break up the solitude of my childhood that Mabs was the only one to share, and this enchanted state was never again to be recovered by me save in the exercise of that precarious profession to which I was, even then, serving a stumbling apprenticeship: and I don't mean adventurer.

Suddenly I was shocked awake by my parents, in the rude way that grown-ups have: Aunt Jane, forced to communicate with my father over the sale of the house near Bournemouth, had gradually come round to apologising for her harsh words in the past and, the sale having at last been effected, now proposed that we share a villa with her at Endoûme, as she was giving up the apartment which held for her too many painful souvenirs; Father, increasingly restive in the past few months, jumped at this excuse for quitting once more his native land, and in a trice, it seemed to me, we were all packed, passports stamped, and passages once more booked for Marseille.

I was, to use a French construction, desolated: according to the dictionary definition this aptly described my feelings, which were indeed 'barren, dreary; forlorn, disconsolate and wretched' at the thought of leaving Mabs and also that it might prove impossible to obtain my favourite magazines across the Channel. Even the certainty of escaping a public-school education did not compensate for these losses: besides, now that I took an interest in football, the idea of playing-fields no longer held such terror in store.

It was useless, however, to argue: pleading and tears, difficultly shed, proved to be of no avail; an education of a very different type, both scholastic and psychological, awaited me upon the other shore, not long after we embarked on what turned out to be a rough crossing, and this time via Boulogne, leaving, as I thought, the winter town behind for ever.

For how, not having second sight, could I know I was to walk the cinder path again, as a young man, not with Mabs but with my first, real, agonising (I had almost written only) love, and later with the one

I was to marry; that I was to suffer poverty there, and hunger, and afterwards, for a brief spell, triumph; that I would make it—this town—the background for one of my books and return there again and yet again, as a murderer is said to be drawn, by some irresistible attraction, back to the scene of his crime.

London 1952

THE RITES
OF SPRING

Monsieur L'Abbé: A Memoir

*   *   *

I CAN SEE HIM PLAINLY AFTER THIRTY YEARS, MONSIEUR L'ABBÉ: a sturdy man of middle height, with a stern, plump, clerical face, shining slightly blue about the jowls. He came of peasant stock and had the strength of a bull: in winter, when the water-tank in the grounds froze into a solid block of ice and the earth itself gave out, under our boots, a ring like iron, he felled trees and chopped them into logs for the stove himself, wielding his axe with the precision of a professional wood-cutter, the skirts of his black soutane tucked neatly up around his waist as he skipped nimbly to and fro.

There were no other masters at the school: personal tuition and supervision, it said in the prospectus, and Monsieur l'Abbé was a man of his word. He taught all subjects personally, correcting the exercise books but adding up the marks on separate sheets of paper to be sent home monthly to the parents: the results were never shown to us, lest the sins of pride or, more likely, despair be occasioned thereby. The Abbé even conducted the drawing lesson, though it is doubtful whether he himself could sketch; in the intervals of these tasks, he ministered to our spiritual needs, prepared pupils for their first communion, said Mass in the chapel, and wrote thundering sermons which he preached, on alternate Sundays, in the local church.

He had enormous vitality and an explosive temper that burst out suddenly in shouts of Chameau and Bon Sang (the only expletive he indulged in); once he knocked me clean off the form with an open-handed buffet on the side of the head. Punishments, however, were administered in cold blood and always in the same manner: the offending pupil stood facing the Abbé roughly in the attitude of attention, one hand extended, the fingertips bunched together. On these the Abbé then brought down a special ruler whose end was split, to afford greater pain. To flinch earned one another couple of strokes: stoicism was the order of the day, tears absolutely out of the question. The ruler made a terrifying swish through the air as it descended, and the agony was intense; one's hand trembled for hours afterwards (it was always the left hand, since the right was required to write out the lines in Latin which were awarded as an additional punishment).

In the case of Dallo, who was left-handed, the process was reversed: he was a backward scholar and came in for it a good deal. Whenever the Abbé happened to leave the classroom, he used to conjugate irregular verbs aloud, at the top of his voice, je vais, tu vas, il va, nous allons, vous allez, ils vont, as an aid to memory, his eyes rolled up in an agony of apprehension, as though he were about to fall in a fit. (Thus I was to hear, seventeen years later, recruits in an army depot mugging up the Bren Gun period, repeating over and over in monotonous rhythm, the barrel-nut-retainer-plunger, the gas-cylinder-locking-bar.) This habit of Dallo's annoyed us: it disturbed our own concentration. As soon as he banged his book shut and started to bawl out his version of the lesson, we turned with one accord and threw things at him: it was for heaving an india-rubber at his head and hitting the Abbé, as he entered unexpectedly, instead, that I got knocked off the form.

The school, called the Chalet, was the first I ever attended: built on a plateau, the grounds overlooking a bay, it was not nearly so bad as the one my father had inspected earlier, on deciding that, like my brother before me, I was to receive a Catholic and continental education. This initial establishment was run by a Curé at Grasse, where the perfumes come from. It was perched on a precipice and to reach it my father toiled up a goat track, in the teeth of a terrible wind. Although it was barely autumn, a chill blast already coursed along the long unheated corridor where a group of cowed small boys crouched, blue with cold and blowing on their fingers, while a grim housekeeper, dressed all in black, like a character in a horror-film, stood by, ladling thin soup into cracked china bowls. No, my father thought, this would not do: though I had become difficult lately, and boarding-school seemed an obvious means of getting me out of the way, he felt it hardly fair to condemn me to this hell of ice.

The Chalet by comparison seemed almost cheerful; and, having handed me over to the Abbé's care, he made off with as buoyant a stride as his limp would allow, a load lifted from his mind. My mother had not been allowed to accompany him, lest she cry under the stress of parting and her tears disgrace me in the eyes of my future schoolfellows: already, as I knew without looking up, watching critically from the windows of the classroom overhead. My father had been a new boy once himself, and fully recognised the importance of avoiding an invidious start.

I watched him go, standing on the gravel drive by the side of the house: before passing through the gate, not unlike that of a levelcrossing, which opened on to the main road beyond, he turned and, with a flourish of his stick, called back one word, which sounded to me like Valley. Combined with the slam of the gate, the Latin farewell had a final sound: though ignorant of its meaning then, I was to become only too familiar with this in the weeks that followed, as my father must have known; and I realised, as the high hedges hid his broad, stooping shoulders from sight, that henceforward, for the first time (though not by any means the last) I was left alone to make my way as best I could.

There were at this time, the beginning of term, only two other pupils: Dallo and Delinon; a perspective of empty desks stretched ahead down the classroom, which was on the first-floor front, enclosed on two sides by a wall of glass like a conservatory: appropriately enough, since it was indeed an educational forcing-house for the tender plants that we, as backward scholars, were.

Voici donc vos camarades, the Abbé announced, introducing me as Jacques, the nearest French equivalent to my first name James, by which I was always called at home; he at once put me on my honour to speak nothing but French: an unnecessary precaution, as neither of the other boys knew a single word of English apart from Yes and No, though the Abbé hoped to correct this deficiency on their part in the fullness of time. I on the other hand spoke fluent French, but with an accent and vocabulary acquired in the Midi and not at all to the Abbé's taste; I was immediately forbidden to say Écoute voir and causer instead of parler: it was only concierges, he informed me severely, who did that. Then, too, since the greater part of juvenile conversation consists in telling one's interlocutor to shut up, I'd taken pains to collect a variety of synonyms in this connection: La ferme, Boucle-la, Ta boîte, bébé, etc; these, and other colloquialisms picked up in the public gardens of Nice (La barbe! Pige-moi ça! Piqué, Cinglé, Chiche, Ballot, Dégueulasse, Débiner and Frangin), together with a ditty beginning Le bon roi

Dagobert, a mis sa culotte a l'envers, were also put on the Index of prohibited words and phrases.

Nor did my conduct in other ways meet with the Abbé's approval. I had in those days a temper almost as explosive as his own, and was given to drawing my clasp-knife and flinging it, open, at the backs of retreating boys who had in some manner offended me: I never hit them, but the Abbé nonetheless impounded the knife and also the pistol that fired packets of cordite, which I had brought along as a protection against possible bullying; while fights and any form of horse-play (called by the Abbé jeux de mains) were discouraged altogether: the penalty being at least five strokes of the ruler, plus confinement in class during the hours normally set aside for recreation.

All this, of course, came later: at first the knife was unclasped solely for the purpose of whittling sticks and the pistol remained in its hiding-place at the bottom of my private play-box, for I saw at once that I'd nothing to fear from either Dallo or Delinon in the matter of physical or moral persecution, and the defensive swagger which I assumed in greeting them was soon abandoned in view of their obvious desire to make me welcome. Both were boys about my age, between eleven and twelve years old, not overburdened with brains, as their presence chez Monsieur l'Abbé indicated: for he enjoyed a formidable, and fully deserved, reputation as a crammer, extending to regions far beyond that coast.

At first sight Dallo was easily the more attractive, with a flushed rosy face, tousled fair curls, and an appealing urchin grin: even his name, Honoré, had a frank and open sound confirmed by his candid eyes; but as the son of a rich hotel-keeper in an Alpine resort, fashionable during the season for winter sports, he had been given his head at home, and the attributes of his charm concealed a talent for intrigue, a basic sulkiness and spite which were not slow in coming to the surface, as I was shortly to learn. Delinon, by nature simple, affectionate and unselfish to a degree, was ill-served by his appearance: enormously fat, bursting out of clothes too tight for him, he combined the characteristics of Billy Bunter and the Michelin tyre-man; his shining pneumatic cheeks, puffed humorously up to the size of balloons, and the myopic eyes magnified by powerful spectacles, made it difficult to regard him, initially, as other than a figure of fun.

Dallo in the manner of his kind set out to captivate me at once; and, during the long weekend we'd been given to get acquainted in, as, wearing the black overalls and studded boots that (except on Sundays) were the uniform of school and leisure hours alike, we roamed the grounds, exploring the thickets of trees and bamboo that bordered the gravel paths, peering into the reservoir or water tank at the bottom of which frog-spawn was said to exist, and finally watching, from the flat green stretch of sward at the foot of the plateau, a train puffing with its plume of smoke along the railway line that bisected the countryside below, while the curve of the Bay, its waters still October-blue, lay beyond, we drew closer, the two of us, together, and Delinon dropped behind.

So thirty years later I try to evoke again, in clichés as above, the feeling of that brief alliance, my first plunge into friendship: for the hackneyed phrase seems, to a child, heaven-sent to clothe the thoughts which otherwise there'd be no words for; and, as I stood beside Dallo, seeing what might have been the whole wide world spread out beneath for the evening sun to set upon, a spurious poetry doubtless gilded, like that sun's last glow, the emotions going on inside; though the declining light seemed symbolically inappropriate at the start of such an idyll, instead of being, as it proved, an omen.

Our relationship lasted less than a week. We swore eternal loyalty, crouched in a clump of bamboos during a game of hide-and-seek, while Delinon in a vain search for us jog-trotted, wheezing, by; as the crunch of heavy boots and the hopeless gasp of his difficult breath receded, we broke into convulsive giggles, as lovers in their exclusive joy mock cruelly at those not linked, like they, by bonds from which no freedom is desired: though for how long a time, depends. We had secret passwords and a sign; conspiratorial glances were exchanged whenever school routine prevented speech: in class, at table, behind the Abbé's back and, regrettably, at prayers. In the dormitory we'd bagged beds next each other; and under cover of Delinon's resounding snores (moonlight blue beyond the open windows, splashed white across linoleum floor) we whispered excitedly our plans for the coming day that we could hardly wait for, though sleep would claim us in mid-sentence. (This seems the place to emphasise that there was no suggestion of what some might call 'unnatural' in all this; our ignorance of sex bordered on the idiotic, and besides none of us, so far, had reached the age of puberty.)

Then the long weekend was over; Monday tolled ahead like a foreboding bell; we gulped down bowls of café au lait for breakfast and assembled hastily in the classroom for instruction. And oddly enough it was here: at the pitchpine desks, among the unfamiliar smells of chalk and slate and india-rubber, where every morning Monsieur l'Abbé, entering in silence, with abrupt severity, would summon us to order by three sharp taps of an ebony ruler upon the blackboard, as the conductor of an orchestra, rapping on the music-stand, calls for his audience's attention; here, with the map of France and the larger one of the world itself (this called a *mappemonde*) covering the panelled walls which faced those of glass encircling us upon the left, that my disillusionment with Dallo began.

When, earlier in this record, I included myself in the category of backward scholars, I meant simply that, for reasons which I've stated elsewhere, I had not been to school at all, let alone in France. Of course I was not illiterate; my father had managed to instil into me—although I hadn't inherited his mathematical ability—a certain amount of arithmetic; from him, also, I had gained a working knowledge of geography and, from reading, a mass of miscellaneous information, not all of which could be considered commendable: but, apart from the salient facts about Napoleon and the outcome of various wars (these viewed, moreover, from a strictly British standpoint), I was almost totally ignorant of French history and even more of French grammar, though not by any means unwilling to learn. The Abbé, with a tact and patience that in those early days seemed endless, encouraged my efforts, and soon I knew all about Vercingétorix, Charlemagne, and the Vase de Soissons: also the indicative and imperative forms of verbs like être and avoir; the feminine gender of various nouns, such as louve and cantatrice; the plural of words ending in ou; and whether or not to aspirate the aitches in hérisson, héritage, héros, and héroine, respectively.

It was then that the extreme unreceptivity of Dallo forced itself upon my attention. His behaviour in class began to affect my nerves: the loud somnambulant shout, already alluded to, with which he committed his lessons to memory or, even worse, the rapid adenoidal mutter stressed by kicking out a rhythmic tattoo on the side of his desk, as though he sought, by this emphasis, to drive the words, like nails into the solid wood his skull seemed made of. I had not failed to notice that he was fond of his own way, but nor was I averse to getting mine, and when any clash of wills occurred I'd won, hitherto, hands down. Now, out of school, he'd become moody and capricious, apt to fly out in shrill malice at the slightest provocation, or sulk in silence until the end of our break, when another display of crass stupidity in the form-room would follow.

Though not, even now, insistent on high intellectual standards in those few people I am fond of, still less at the age that I was then, I felt a let-down nonetheless: Dallo, it could no longer be denied, was a dunce; and during a row in which he caught me on the raw I stated this unpalatable truth in the harshest of terms; Dallo retaliated by a piercing fishwife's shriek, which wouldn't have disgraced the *vieille commère* he called me, with such venom that I thought he spat. That, to use the idiom of today, was the end of a beautiful friendship: only the sudden appearance of the Abbé—who luckily had not overheard our quarrel —prevented me from dealing out, in the manner I'd been taught at Nice, a series of swift hard slaps back and forth across Dallo's face, much as gangsters discipline their henchmen in the films that hadn't then been made.

Balked of this intention I swung off in a fury towards the Chalet; evening prep lay ahead; an hour of absolute silence broken only by the crackle of wood catching alight in the big stove and the industrious scratching of our pens; over us presided the Abbé, a breviary open before him, raking one hand, while he read, through the sparse hair upon his scalp, then lowering the fingers to his nostrils for a stealthy abstracted sniff, a habit which, quite unconscious in his case, would have earned any pupil who indulged in it a severe reproof: the principle summed up by the Service phrase 'Don't do as I do, do as I tell you' being common to all systems of rule by coercion. Hunched at my desk, as the stove began to glow red, giving out with the heat its attendant odour of black-lead polish, I too smouldered inside, not looking up even to glare at Dallo in difficulties with his exercise across the room, but resolutely determined to reject his apology when, as I confidently expected, he sought me out later in an attempt at reconciliation.

Instead, Dallo did nothing of the sort, but switched his allegiance at once to Delinon, so that I found myself in turn the odd man out, and a period of acute jealous misery in store. I reacted to this by instituting a ruthless persecution of Dallo, shouting Cancre! after him whenever the Abbé was not within hearing: the ugly French 'dunce', with its aural suggestion of cankerous growth or incurable disease; out came the gun from its hiding-place, and the cordite bombs it fired, aimed from an upstairs window, exploded around him as he emerged from the house, putting him off his lessons so completely that he got caned in class; when he retaliated with a water-pistol fired in my face from ambush, I further shook his nerve by hurling the clasp-knife at him as he dodged away among the trees; unfortunately the Abbé observed this incident and I suffered corporal punishment, by means of the ruler, for the first time in consequence: my one satisfaction being that Dallo was also awarded three strokes on the hand, since my clothes were still soaking wet from the deluge he'd directed at me. The good-hearted Delinon was distressed by these manifestations of internecine strife, and characteristically offered to mediate; but unrepentant in spite of having had to write out the seven deadly sins twenty times with the hand that had not been caned, I spurned his peace proposals and drove him away in dejection with scornful yells of Va te faire dégonfler, gros bouffi! Forbidden by the Abbé to shout Cancre in future at my comrades, I substituted the word's second meaning, Crustacé, a crab: and this seemed specially designed to get under Dallo's shell, for the second time it was applied to him he actually flew at me with clawing hands, and got tipped into a bed of thistles (which were sometimes served up to us as a vegetable) during the scuffle that ensued.

But, despite these minor triumphs, it was not a time I like to look back upon, or would care to live through again: its only value consisting in the fact that it prepared me for many periods of unpopularity with which I had similarly to cope in the years that were to come. The general unpleasantness was aggravated also, round about then, by a sudden attack of toothache, which resulted in weekly visits to the dentist, always on Thursday afternoons, our half-holiday, to make matters worse.

The dentist appointed by Monsieur l'Abbé was an elderly man with a grey walrus moustache, extremely short-sighted, his limited vision further obscured by a pair of smoked spectacles: his surgery overlooked a built-in area and the single narrow window was of a type from which arrows might have been aimed, in mediæval times, at an invader; consequently, the mistakes which he made with the drill were many, and I had to be strapped hand and foot in the chair with a clamp around my neck before he could start his excavations at all, owing to the violence of my reactions when his stuttering instrument of torture slipped, as it frequently did, off the ivory on to an exposed nerve. There was a thing like a boat-hook which he employed occasionally, murmuring, when he approached me with it, Courage, courage, as though he were the executioner entering the cell of an assassin about to be guillotined; but we always came back to his first love, the drill: perhaps he had only recently acquired this, and regarded it in the light of a new toy; for he even hollowed out, I feel certain, cavities in teeth where none existed before, and filled these with lumps of a leaden mixture which fell out quite soon in adult life, leaving large gaps surrounded by jagged shells, with nerves underneath that had not been killed.

On the opposite side of the square where his premises were situated, a rival surgery had recently started up: this one advertising American Dentistry, only just beginning to become known in France at that date; and sometimes I believe my dentist identified me, by reason of my nationality, with this competitor, since to his way of thinking American and English would amount to the same: certainly he spent much time in denouncing, during our weekly sessions, the idea of cocaine injections as a dangerous notion apt to further the practice of drug-taking among the patients, and originated, no doubt, by perfidious Albion as a part of a scheme to obtain world domination in the future. He himself was strictly conservative in his professional opinions, and disapproved even of administering gas: so far as I was concerned, all extractions (luckily few, because of his preference for the drill and the lead stoppings) were performed without it, for his anæsthetist was suffering from some illness during the whole period of my visits to him, and he was unwilling or unable to operate the nitrous oxide apparatus in person.

In view of all this, it is not surprising that my private conception of Hell (though Monsieur l'Abbé would have considered this unorthodox) took the form of a gigantic dentist's chair, with Satan himself in charge of the drill; and when, not so long ago, I read an American thriller in which the detective-hero imagined himself under treatment in such conditions on awaking with a hangover, I wondered whether the author had been subjected in youth to experiences not dissimilar from my own, before the introduction of the painless dentistry for which his country is justly celebrated, and which was regarded so unfavourably by the purblind old fool who attended me.

Faced, at the present time, with circumstances of such all-round wretchedness, I might either get drunk or write a book; but in those days I abhorred the taste of alcohol: moreover, none was obtainable, and my literary aspirations, though already formulated, were insufficiently advanced to provide an escape from the sphere of reality. I was forced, therefore, to seek relief in what might be considered, at the age of eleven, an unexpected direction: i.e. my studies.

Calligraphy was the first pursuit that engaged my attention: hitherto I'd regarded this as a bore, refusing to copy out pot-hooks at home, and evolving, for my own purposes, a peculiar system of small block capitals, designed to resemble the print of a book, and executed always with a soft lead pencil. Now of course I was obliged to use pen-and-ink and to make some attempt at forming cursive characters. The style of handwriting in vogue at this school was a fine slanting oblique script: sometimes known in France, I believe, as *l'écriture bâtarde*; though not to the Abbé, who called it, instead, *l'écriture penchée*. This was completely beyond me at first, particularly as I held my pen in a manner all my own, which caused the Abbé to exclaim in horror at its apparent awkwardness: the pen was poked at an angle through a loosely clenched hand, supported by the membraneous curve between thumb and forefinger, the thumb hooked round the holder and tucked underneath the index, with the middle finger pressing it down near the nib. The Abbé instantly taught me a more normal position, by which the nib was guided by fingers and thumb forming a rough oval: though this is the method commonly used by nine persons out of every ten, it resulted in my getting writer's cramp if adopted for any length of time; the pages of my exercise books were covered with unsightly blots, the surface rubbed thin and rough by constant erasures; I was publicly taken to task and saw, with mortification, that Dallo, whose handwriting would have disgraced a child of six, was grinning gleefully in the background. Determined that he should not score off me again, I began to take more trouble with my penmanship, increasingly so since the Abbé (perhaps with this end in view, for he was in many ways an able psychologist) had confiscated my old, ink-stained exercise book, and had allotted me instead a new cahier, much superior in quality and thickness to those we were usually handed out, with smooth cream-woven paper inside, on which the ink (violet in hue) did not blur and run as it did on the grey fibrous sheets provided for us as a rule.

To spoil such a surface would have been more than a shame, and I traced with care the broad upward stroke of the majuscules, then their thinning downward curve: curling, as was required of me, the scrolled flourish of each capital letter and linking it to its successors at the prescribed slant; for this purpose I even bought, out of the pocket-money my parents sent me each week, special narrow-pointed steel nibs, which I changed regularly and polished clean of clogging acids after each exercise: as I ceased, with practice, to suffer from cramp, my speed increased proportionately, and not long after I received the Abbé's congratulations, standing in triumph on the very spot to which I had been summoned for his condemnation a few weeks before. (Alas, all to no avail, as things turned out. For at the Collège in the town nearby, where I was later sent, another calligraphic style prevailed, and everything had to be unlearned; now my handwriting resembles neither to any extent, and I have reverted to my original way of holding a pen which, though still appearing awkward, seems to serve me well enough and is much more comfortable: an important factor, considering the amount of writing I have, nowadays, to do.)

We had a separate cahier devoted to each subject on the school curriculum, and the special one given me by the Abbé was that devoted to Composition and Essays: the care which I devoted to the script in which these were set down soon extended to the material itself; with my nascent literary leanings I began to find the construction of sentences and the development of a theme fascinating in themselves; a knowledge of grammar, however, was essential to any accomplishment in this sphere, and it follows, therefore, that in these branches of study also I was soon top of the class.

The Abbé did not inform me of this fact, for too much appreciation, he felt—and not without reason—might result in my developing a swelled head; but my father had been sent reports of my progress, and the letters he now began to write me (in French, of course, at the Abbé's urgent request) contained the first praise I'd ever received from that stern, inscrutable man, for he was even more sparing of commendation than the Abbé himself. My mathematical standard, unfortunately, was still below par (where, indeed, it remains today) and Father's letters concluded invariably with exhortations to greater application in this field, and the final salutation Vale, no longer an enigma to me, as by this time I was learning Latin.

To have earned his approbation on any terms, however, put new heart into me: a brighter outlook altogether seemed about to succeed the bleak eclipse through which I'd passed; though this could not be said of the weather, for the first months of winter (always the worst in this particular region) burst suddenly upon us: a wet banshee wind flung squalls of rain against the classroom windows; beyond the rattling panes an aquarium world swam suspended, drowning in liquid blue twilight whatever the time of day, while the surgery was now so dark on my visits that the dentist had to operate with an incandescent lamp strapped to his forehead, giving him the air of a cyclops or perhaps a coal-miner about to descend into the pit. Happily the worst of the drilling was now over, the fillings were being fixed, and I was able to enjoy my meals once more; for the food at the Chalet, unlike that provided at my father's public school and despite the occasional thistles, was extremely good, especially on the days when we had jugged hare, since Philomène, the matron and housekeeper, came from a village near Perpignan, where this dish is a speciality, and was a magnificent cook at any time.

Philomène had feared, on my arrival, that being English I might not like the fare, and was relieved to find her anxiety unjustified: though at first I'd found it very odd, having soup sometimes for breakfast and red wine and water with my lunch; sparrow pie also made its appearance occasionally and I am by no means sure we did not eat rook; these had formed no part of my staple diet at home, nor for that matter had artichokes in oil, stuffed cabbage, or salsify: and certainly not leeks, which I now consumed with relish, preferring them by far to thistles, which may have been disloyal, since I am not Welsh and the latter are our national emblem. Philomène was pleased, now, to see my appetite returning, for in the darkest days I'd often sought sanctuary in the big stone-flagged kitchen where she sat after supper, occupied even then with some household task, for her day's work was never done: though she was seldom too busy to listen to our problems or to comfort us with her tired, compassionate smile, when the Abbé, if approached on other than religions difficulties, might have been impatient.

It was Philomène who was ultimately responsible for the comradeship that grew up between Delinon and myself: this came about when the rainy season ended, leaving great pools of water undrained upon the gravel paths, to be icily congealed by the rigid frost that took its place, crystallising the trees and adding a new word, *engelure*, to my French vocabulary with the chilblains that itched upon our fingertips and swelled painfully the lobes of our ears. For with this frozen spell a batch of new boys arrived at the school: the first of them was Vergniette, who drove up, clad in a fur-collared overcoat, in a Rolls-Royce with a liveried chauffeur at the wheel and his parents, both wrapped in coats made entirely of fur, sitting at the back; he was followed by Euan Douglas, like myself a Scot, who donned Highland dress on Sundays, when his kilt and sporran struck the others agape with wonder, for they could not see why he should choose to wear a skirt with a fur pouch in front; later still came the intransigent Magagnos, whom I will tell about in another place.

Dallo of course immediately abandoned Delinon, seeing new victims for his charm; I personally found Vergniette a little too advanced (so much so that he was afterwards expelled), and Euan a trifle too naïf for my taste: another obstacle in his case being that he spoke only elementary French; and while the Abbé was prepared to relax, in this instance, his ban on speaking English (indeed he had often to call upon me as interpreter), I could not readily understand the Scots accent and half the time had no idea what Euan was attempting to say.

So, promoted and encouraged by Philomène, the association with Delinon began, and I was to find him a loyal and devoted friend until the end of my stay at the Chalet: which should have taught me—though of course it didn't—that appearances may be deceptive and beauty but skin-deep. Our relationship was, it's true, lived on a less ecstatic plane than any which involved Dallo, but on the other hand it provided a foretaste of what male companionship, based on mutual esteem and a degree of affection, would come to mean in adult life, without being a substitute for the love-affair which I was emotionally (though not yet physically) developed enough obscurely to desire.

Delinon's dearest ambition was to become a priest, and the example of his sincere piety and the purity of his faith had an important influence on my own spiritual development, though naturally the Abbé had been far from idle in attempting to inspire me with a proper sense of religious zeal. He'd been horrified at first to discover how much my Catholic education had been neglected: I had never been to Confession, nor made my First Communion; why, I hardly knew my Catechism, and until I had this off by heart I couldn't be confirmed: a rite which, also, had never been performed upon my person. Secretly I dreaded this prospect, since part of the ceremony entailed the slapping of the candidate's face by a bishop, and I imagined a full-armed smack like that dealt out to me on one occasion by the Abbé, which had caused my head to ring for hours after.

Perhaps, in his anxiety to accelerate the progress of my instruction, the Abbé laid an overemphasis on the consequences of transgression and the force of divine retribution: too little upon God's mercy; then, too, the sermons he preached, invariably on eschatological themes, had instilled into me a panic fear: I could see that in my sinful state I was destined without a doubt for the Devil's dental chair, and, like my own dentist, Satan would never countenance the use of local anæsthetics. I prayed fervently for forgiveness, but with little hope, since I'd formed (how could I help it?) a mental image of the Almighty compounded of my father and Monsieur l'Abbé himself: neither of them persons whose hearts were easily softened once their ire had been aroused to the full. Intercession by Our Lady was my only chance, but I clutched my rosary as a drowning man is said to grasp at straws: for how often had my own mother's compassion prevailed over Father's wrath when she pleaded with him to remit a punishment?

There was one more test I could apply: on my way to the dentist, just before entering the town, the road was spanned by a metal railway bridge, across which, about the time of my weekly appointment, an express was scheduled to pass; and I always hurried to stand beneath as the whistle in the distance heralded its approaching roar: for I made out to myself that the reverberant clangour of the wheels overhead must sound not unlike the Voice of God; and, half deafened by its iron thunder, I tried to distinguish some softer underlying echo, a promise that perhaps pardon might be granted: but always without success; and I went despairingly on towards the torture that, in the ill-lit surgery, awaited: bad enough, especially in its early stages, but the merest twinge to what I would endure when the Devil worked the drill.

It was largely due to Delinon, in whom of course I'd confided all these terrors, that I had my first glimpse of how the miracle of forgiveness might be worked through love; I gave up to a great extent my persecution of Dallo and tried to purge my heart of hate and malice: during this period Philomène feared that I was sickening for something, and even the Abbé glanced at me once or twice with a shadow of concern. As the day marked down for my first confession drew near, however, I felt a renewal of dread: despite Delinon's earnest reassurances I knew there was still too much upon my conscience for any possibility of redemption.

The day came: it must have been in spring, for the sun lit strongly from without the figure of Our Lord on the stained-glass window facing which I knelt to make the Act of Contrition. His hand was raised in benediction, but this, I thought in misery, could not be meant for me, and I struck myself so hard upon the chest while avowing my faults that my breast-bone was bruised and ached for weeks to come. Then, rising with a shiver, I entered that darkened box which, I feared, might prove the coffin of my eternal hopes: where behind the grille another priest, not Monsieur l'Abbé, waited to hear the recital of my sins. But the Saviour's blessing in rainbow glass was, after all, a sign; and in a very different mood I left the church, to wander, with a lightness of heart that I had never known before, through the golden fume of sunshine rising in clouds above the town; across the square; towards the bridge, telling myself (as how many times since then) that I would never, never, sin again.

A goods train hooted and clanked, lighter than the express, across the bridge as, absolved and pure, I ran in gratitude to stand below its arch: because of the lesser weight upon those rails above, the reflection of the sound was more gentle than the usual strident echo, and it seemed to me that God had supplemented the absolution I'd received already with an added murmur of indulgence. Or was this, instead, a muffled warning for the future: since, within a year, on the embankment that rose above this very spot, among those bramble-bushes not as yet in flower, I was to feel, with a girl's face bent laughing close to mine, the first uneasy stirrings of the flesh.

The Gondolier of Death

*   *   *

ALL THIS HAPPENED THIRTY YEARS AGO, WHEN I WAS ELEVEN: a pupil at a Catholic private school in the South of France.

Magagnos, who afterwards became known as the Gondolier of Death, was older than most of us at the time of his arrival: about thirteen I should imagine. In other ways he was different too. To begin with, he was a day-boy and spent weekends with an aunt in the town nearby, whereas we were boarders and not allowed to see parents or relatives except when school broke up. Then again he was a Protestant, and that set him altogether apart: for even I, though a foreigner and of Scottish parentage to boot, was a Catholic like all the rest.

Magagnos was not only conscious of his isolation; he seemed actively to enjoy it, so far as we could tell, for he was not given to expressing emotion of any kind, still less enjoyment; some gesture signifying indifference or unwillingness to venture an opinion was the most one got out of him: a limp turn of the wrist, an equivocal shrug, or a side-long twitch of the tough flexible lips that was almost a sneer. He was tall for his age, raw-boned and sinewy, with big knobby wrists that swiftly outgrew his sleeves, and the skin of his face had a leathery look: it might easily have been treated with tannic acid and mineral salts, then exposed to the sun; there were deep cracks in the surface, especially where the corners of his mouth curved downward, that lent colour to this theory. His eyes as a rule were sombre and fixed in a brooding melancholy, but if he were startled out of whatever reverie he was sunk in, they rolled with sudden wildness, like those of an unbroken horse, which come to think of it he rather resembled, both by reason of his intractable nature and the roughly equine shape of his skull.

152

Philomène, who acted as matron, cook and housekeeper at the school, had summed him up as farouche when he first appeared on the scene; but she had added, with a compassionate shake of the head: 'Pauvre garçon', which wouldn't have pleased Magagnos at all had he heard it, for pity was the last thing he asked for or expected from anyone. Philomène felt sorry for him because he was an orphan, and also because she too came from Provence, though not from Nîmes, the Protestant stronghold, where their Temple is and Magagnos was born.

When he was a small boy and his parents were still alive, Magagnos had spoken Provençal with them at home: yet another unusual point; then after their death an uncle in Paris had adopted him, which accounted for the inflexions he now spoke with. Whenever I hear English people say admiringly, of some friend's linguistic prowess, 'Why, he speaks French just like a Parisian!' I always think of Magagnos and the tireless efforts which Monsieur l'Abbé made to eradicate from his speech (though without success) the very accent they regard as so enviable a possession.

He was the Abbé's only failure. Before the Parisian uncle lost patience at last and transferred him, for the time being, to the aunt in Antibes, three schools had already despaired of teaching him anything and he had run away from a fourth; when asked by the Abbé, on his very first day, which of these he had liked the best, he summarised his attitude at once by replying, without the suspicion of a smile, 'L'école buisson-nière': in other words, playing truant. Any attempt to correct the accent and locutions he had acquired during his stay in the capital, or to alter his behaviour in general, came to nothing. In class he was neither stupid nor overtly impertinent, but simply set up a passive resistance to learning anything that didn't interest him, which included almost all subjects in the school curriculum.

It may have been that in his case Monsieur l'Abbé lacked the spiritual authority which he wielded over us: we felt, without actually being told so, that disobedience to him meant incurring the wrath of God Himself, whereas Magagnos as a Protestant did not hold any such belief. In the first open clash that came, he emerged an easy victor, by refusing politely but point-blank to be caned on the hand, in the approved manner, as a punishment for some misdeed: 'Ah ça, m'sieu, faut m'escuser. C'est la tante, quoi-ça n'lui reviendra pas qu'on m'corrige d'cette façon.' The aunt, a small grey mousy woman plainly under the nephew's thumb, did not look capable of much objection; and for a moment we fully expected the Abbé to sweep like a black thunder-cloud down the classroom and exact the penalty without more ado: Magagnos too may have anticipated something of the sort; for, though he stood firm, his eyes rolled alarmingly and he started to jerk his head from side to side, more than ever like a stallion about to kick its loose-box to bits; and—wisely, in my opinion—the Abbé did not insist, substituting a formidable *impot* in lieu of the proposed caning.

Then came the matter of Magagnos's hair. This was black and he wore it long, *à l'embusqué* as the French say: combed straight back from the forehead and swept into a single curve at the nape of the neck, a fashion popularised, I think, by the late Harry Pilcer. Though other-wise careless of his appearance, Magagnos took great pride in his hair, particularly in its length; the Abbé, however, preferred to see short hair around him, and since several of us offended his sense of fitness in this respect, he suddenly decided to have all our heads shaved. Again Magagnos asked firmly to be let off, again his aunt's possible dis-pleasure was invoked as an excuse, and again he won the day: the Abbé in consequence had to abandon his plan, fearing a mutiny should Magagnos be the only boy spared the barber's clippers, though his habit of passing a comb through his hair in class was forbidden forthwith as a reprisal.

From this moment on Monsieur l'Abbé came to regard Magagnos as the cross he had to bear; but his professional reputation was at stake, and gritting his teeth he threw himself with redoubled vigour into the task of transforming this obdurate pupil into a credit to the school, though we could have told him he was wasting his time: a conclusion shared by Magagnos himself to the fullest degree.

It could not be said that we ourselves, at this period, had much liking for Magagnos. We admired him, naturally, for his show of inde-pendence: for this same reason, we respected him, but he was not really one of us. Intolerance of other religious creeds had no place in our teaching, but nonetheless, because of his difference in this respect, there was much of our life which he could not share, and besides, he for his part certainly showed no sign of wishing to become intimate or to earn our affection. If he had a Christian name, we did not know it; even the Abbé called him, contrary to his usual custom, Magagnos *tout court*; even his ambition in life, what he wanted to become when grown up, was unknown to us; nor did he join in the discussions on this burning topic which were held so frequently in our hours of leisure.

He took part in our games, but only when invited to, and then with a hint of condescension, as an adult might: except for quieter pastimes such as croquet, which he would have none of, pronouncing them fit only for girls. When we indulged in these, he would sit down on a tree stump and read a paper-covered book. Or rather study it, for he often stared at the same page for minutes on end, moving his lips silently as though memorising a lesson, while the cleft which existed already between his brows became more and more deeply marked.

The book was printed in a language unfamiliar to us, and apart from the information that this was Provençal, Magagnos left our curiosity unsatisfied until the day of the charity matinée. I don't quite remember what this function was in aid of, but evidently something to which all Christians could contribute—irrespective of schisms in dogma, for the audience seemed composed of Catholics and Protestants in equal measure; the whole school was invited; and Magagnos's aunt played some organisational rôle: though not Monsieur l'Abbé, who, like his pupils, was present purely as a guest. The Christmas season was almost upon us, I distinctly recall a lighted crêche in one corner of the hall where the matinée took place, and this may have been the feast which we were celebrating.

Anyhow, the curtain went up at last, disclosing, to our astonishment, the figure of Magagnos facing us from the stage, dressed as a peasant and plainly about to do a turn. A new Magagnos, quite unselfconscious: smiling, carefree and gay. We gasped, almost forgetting to applaud. Without further parley Magagnos broke into a comic song. He strutted up and down as he sang, and I remember nothing of the song except that it was a wryly humorous chronicle of misfortune, and that each stanza ended with the refrain: ''Cré nom d'une soupe a l'oignon.' The first time Magagnos brought out this audacity, he delivered the words ''Cré nom!' with tremendous force and a slight pause to follow, rolling one eye towards the Abbé, who, as expected, shot straight up in his seat, believing that an actual oath was about to be uttered; then Magagnos, with a sudden impish grin, completed the phrase, to the accompaniment of a delighted roar from the audience, in which even the Abbé was obliged eventually to join. It was an unqualified triumph for Magagnos, who now called upon the Abbé to lead the chorus: an invitation to which, being basically a sportsman, he responded with a will; as for us we were hoarse and croaking by the time the curtain finally came down. In between Magagnos had to take three encores; the Abbé led a cheer for him when he made his bow at the end; the palms of our hands were sore from applauding, and we scarcely took account of the subsequent turns in our eagerness for Magagnos to appear again.

This, the first part of the programme, was in French, but the pièce de résistance, the play that came after the entr'acte, was entirely in Provençal, except for the title, *Le Gondolier de la Mort*, from which Magagnos was to derive his nickname, since it was he who enacted the title rôle. One might have expected a rather different sort of subject in these surroundings and on such an occasion: a morality or nativity play, perhaps; instead, this was a full-blooded melodrama, set in Venice at the time of the Renaissance; and though we could not, of course, follow the dialogue, the action was of a nature that aroused our interest from the start.

In the shadowy corners of a marble palace, conspirators planned to assassinate a Prince, using as their agent a beautiful woman named Guilia. Then two friends swaggered in. Esperanzo, in a resplendent uniform, was plainly a Captain of the Guard: Andréa (Magagnos), in doublet and hose, was perhaps a student, and certainly of noble blood. We watched them drink a toast to undying comradeship out of Venetian glass goblets. Then the woman came between them. Andréa, the intellectual, saw at once what she was up to, but Esperanzo, more susceptible and obviously an ass, was soon her devoted slave, while the plotters, from places of concealment, looked on with satisfaction and prepared for the big push. Andréa was in their way and Guilia enlisted the services of Esperanzo to lure him into a trap. But Esperanzo, coming to suddenly at the realisation of his unwitting treachery, broke from her arms and drew a sword as the conspirators closed in, receiving, as he flung himself between, the deadly thrust meant for his friend.

At this the plotters fled; Andréa, kneeling beside Esperanzo's body, unsheathed a dagger and swore on it to avenge his death. This was a long soliloquy and may have been in blank verse; we didn't understand a word, but Magagnos delivered it magnificently. Then the Palace Guards came piling in. Misunderstanding Andréa's position by the slain corpse of their commander, and believing his stained blade to be the murder weapon (for the oath had been sworn in blood), they brought him before the Prince, who, on this circumstantial evidence, banished him from the realm.

Years had evidently passed between this and the next act, but the conspirators were still at it: now they glided up in a gondola, cloaked and masked, for a meeting on the edge of a canal. And in the background, privy to their councils, it seemed, was Andréa: plainly recognisable to us, despite his domino and the addition of a false beard, though not, apparently, to them. When Guilia entered, however, he stepped into the shadow; she now appeared to have exercised her wiles on the Prince himself, for very soon after he arrived unattended, clearly for the purpose of an assignation. We expected Andréa to give some warning of impending attack, but he did not: resenting, perhaps, the false accusation of his friend's murder, and feeling that the Prince, in consequence, deserved all he got—which proved to be a knife in the back; Andréa's eyes even gleamed slightly, with satisfaction, through the slits of his mask as the Prince's cousin, chief of the plotters and the actual murderer of Esperanzo, struck his kinsman down.

The following scene was a wedding feast, to celebrate the nuptials of Guilia and the homicidal cousin; there was much carousing, in which Andréa did not share: in fact he was not present at all, though we were meant to feel the menace of his absence; then the bridal pair prepared to embark, alone together, on their honeymoon trip: bound, presumably, for the palace, where the usurper would now take up residence. They stepped into the waiting gondola, we caught a glimpse of them reclining at ease in the cabin amidships; the conspirators waved good-bye and staggered singing off the stage, which abruptly darkened: then as the gondola started to slide away from the shore and the song of the conspirators faded, a single spotlight threw into relief the figure of Andréa, his malefic face and vengeful eyes revealed now without either mask or beard, slowly plying the oar at the stern—the Gondolier of Death.

Even today, when at the age of over forty I recall it, this curtain seems to me by no means ineffective: imagine, then, its impact on us at the time. We talked of nothing else for days: our enthusiasm for the play in general, and Magagnos's performance in particular, survived even the discovery that Guilia, so sinfully beautiful upon the stage, was in fact extremely ill-favoured when wig and make-up were removed, and a boy into the bargain.

As for Magagnos, he'd become the hero of the hour: a daily incarnation of the deadly Gondolier, his presence among us was a constant reminder of his thespian triumphs. To these we paid incessant tribute, calling him Andréa, re-enacting scenes from the play (though not in Provençal), and chanting as a *leit-motif*, whenever he appeared, the song of the onion soup: its refrain became, indeed, our favourite oath, since the Abbé could not very well forbid the use of it. And Magagnos seemed to take as much pleasure in his sudden popularity as he had derived previously from remaining aloof. His isolation and indifference broke down under the assault of our friendship. He smiled frequently and sometimes laughed. He discussed freely with us the choice of a future career: we were all in favour of his becoming a professional actor, but he, surprisingly, was less enthusiastic. He didn't want to tie himself down to anything before he'd had a look at the world first.

Then term ended, and soon after we returned from the Christmas holidays things began to be different. Without our knowing it, a reign of terror was in store, and we were to look back at the period before and after the charity matinée as one does, longingly, at the last days of peace. Already the harbinger of the new régime was in our midst, but even the shrewdest of us failed to recognise the lineaments of evil behind the bland, rather foolish mask and gold-rimmed spectacles of Lecoq, the latest addition to our ranks.

Lecoq came from Paris, though his accent was less marred than that of Magagnos; he was nearly seventeen, the oldest boy we'd ever had at the school, and was scheduled for a special cramming course, due to his complete inability to pass any form of examination. He excused this to us by implying, with a wink, that convivial and amorous pastimes had interrupted too often the pursuit of his studies at the lycée: 'Ah, là-bas au Bahut, c'est que j'ai fait un petit peu la noce, autrement, vous savez…' To uphold his reputation as a gay dog, he spent much time pomading his hair and every morning shaved off with great flourishes, and a cut-throat razor, the scanty blond fluff that grew on his chin; he was a snappy dresser and adjusted at a rakish angle his smart soft felt hat before venturing out of doors, where the rest of us went bareheaded.

The hat was removed only at times when Angéline happened to pass by, perhaps on her return from market, in the grounds. Angéline was Philomène's daughter, and helped with the work of the house; she was a girl whose sweet nature and simple charm were hard to resist; even Magagnos, who disapproved of women in general, was completely captivated and would, like the rest, do anything for her: whereas he had sternly resisted the earlier efforts of Philomène to mother him. Even we, at our age, were aware that Angéline was exceptionally good-looking, and Lecoq's consciousness in this direction was more highly developed than ours; at sight of her, his hat would be doffed in a wide sweep while he bowed low, holding it to his chest: Angéline's damask flush always heightened at this clownish gallantry and she hurried on with a faint shy smile, pulling tighter under her chin the purple shawl that bound up her black glossy hair. On these occasions we thought that Lecoq was being even sillier than usual, for we never believed him to be other than an ass, while exhibiting, outwardly, the measure of deference due to an elder; it was not until the arrival, shortly afterwards, of Maillet that Lecoq's latent potentialities were revealed: and, with them, the danger we stood in.

Maillet was even older than Lecoq, he had already passed his seventeenth birthday; the same reason was responsible for his attendance at the Abbé's classes, and the excuse offered in his case for abjectly low educational standards was a congenital deafness of the left ear. In point of fact he was abnormally dull-witted, so slow in the uptake at any branch of study that we began by feeling sorry for him, though our pity was soon replaced by sentiments of a very different character.

Owing to his limited mental level he had been placed, at previous schools, in forms with much younger boys, but he had turned this to advantage, and simultaneously avenged his humiliation, by subjecting them to a tyrannical rule. He was loosely and clumsily built, with a small square hammer-shaped head, flat on top and shorn at the sides. As this swayed to and fro on the long reptilian neck it was attached to, peering about through narrow near-set eyes in search of prey, it gave him the aspect of some pea-brained saurian of primæval times: the sort that stands upright; there was something sluggish and viscous in his movements, as though he dragged himself around through a lake of lava-mud. The skin of his hands was always rough and reddened, and he used constantly to crack the knuckles, sometimes producing, as a particular mark of satisfaction, a series of sharp reports by pulling at the joints of his fingers one by one: we heard this sound more and more often as his power over us increased apace.

Craftily enough, he had disguised the opening moves of his campaign as a game: this consisted of playing at Christian slaves, and was an old favourite with us, though as organised by Maillet it included many unfamiliar features which we could well have done without. The introduction of the Emperor Nero as a member of the cast was the one we chiefly objected to: Maillet had allotted to himself this meaty part, while his contemporary Lecoq, with whom he'd quickly formed a firm alliance, was assigned the position of Consul-General. We, needless to say, were the Christian slaves, and Nero personally declared the grounds open as an arena for us to be hunted down, tortured and sacrificed in. Any refusal to participate in this so-called game resulted in punitive measures more stringent by far than those laid down in the ordinary rules: Lecoq grew particularly adept at devising painful forfeits; and as we cowered in our hiding places listening for the enemy's approach, the distant echo of his loud senseless laugh struck more panic into us than even the cric-crac of Maillet's knuckles as he came past with his clumsy purposeful tread.

Luckily, lions were not easy to obtain, otherwise it might have gone hard with us indeed: Maillet was often heard to deplore their scarcity and to console himself by adding that the Abbé would not, anyway, have allowed them in the grounds. Of course the Abbé, himself, had no idea of what went on; the schoolboy code, alike the world over, would not permit us to sneak, and it was no real comfort to know that we were martyrs for the Faith or that the Christian ethic would eventually win out; the triumph was too far off to avail us against Nero's persecution.

Then Magagnos, the Gondolier of Death, took a hand. As he was senior to the rest of us, and also more resourceful, we'd appointed him a People's Tribune, to champion our cause before the Emperor and Consul. He took his duties seriously, like a good shop steward; and, though Maillet and Lecoq did not in any way desist from their efforts to make our lives hell, they made a pretence of hearing his complaints and, perhaps out of prudence, inflicted no actual tortures upon his person. But when he stood gauntly up and in the name of the People demanded that the game be abolished altogether, Nero's imperial anger broke loose. Magagnos fought furiously and bravely, but both the tyrants were older, bigger and stronger: besides most of the time the Consul-General was kneeling on his chest. We did endeavour to rescue him, but our collective spirit was sadly cowed; and as a retribution Nero decreed a massacre in the arena, in which Magagnos came off worst of anyone, most of the clothes being torn nearly from his back.

Afterwards he had to endure a stern admonition from the Abbé for getting himself in such a state; during this, his face wore an expression identical with the one he'd assumed, as Andréa, when kneeling beside Esperanzo's body, and we knew that he was silently swearing revenge on our tormentors. But what shape would his vengeance ultimately take? That he would strike in his own time none of us doubted: but when, and how soon? To our eager question, Magagnos merely replied with the dark prophecy: 'Attendez-voir! J'suis débrouillard, moi. On les aura tous deux, les vaches, vous en faites pas pour ça.' Then he went home, and after supper we settled down for the evening. It was the only time when we could be sure of some peace; the Abbé was preparing a sermon in his study; Lecoq and Maillet were competing for a sign of Angéline's approval in the kitchen, helping her prepare tomorrow's vegetables or holding the wool for her knitting: only the quiet presence of her mother prevented their reward (or so they told themselves) from amounting to more than a smile.

Such a brief respite: for directly the clock struck our bedtime the terror began again. To overcome any sense of inferiority that Maillet or Lecoq might have acquired in the past, the Abbé had made each one a dormitory prefect, and the unpleasantness which this entailed, from our point of view, may readily be imagined, though it varied in degree according to the frequency of Angéline's smiles on any given evening. Then in the mornings now we had to fetch their hot shaving water and stand by them holding it ready in mugs while the sacred rite was performed, making ourselves late for breakfast, so that every day began with a reprimand from the Abbé as a result.

We looked to Magagnos for a sign that all this would soon be brought to an end, but the sign we received was not the one which, at nights, we rather unsuitably prayed for. After he'd slouched about, brooding and preoccupied, hardly speaking to us for a couple of days, we suddenly came upon him, during the after-lunch break, in earnest conversation with Maillet and Lecoq: we could scarcely believe our eyes, but even as we gaped, dumbfounded, at this unforeseen tableau, all three burst into convulsions of laughter, Maillet cracked his knuckles and all of his finger-joints in quick succession, and Lecoq began to slap Magagnos with great heartiness and enthusiasm on the back. Before the day was out our worst suspicions were abundantly confirmed: instead of avenging us, the Gondolier of Death had gone over to the enemy.

That afternoon the tyrants declared a truce and left us alone for once, but we took no chances and, hidden in a thicket of bamboos, heard with mortification and a sinking sense of betrayal a familiar refrain ringing out from the clearing where Maillet and Lecoq lounged on marble benches, holding their court. Magagnos—and this seemed to us the last straw—was singing, for Nero's edification, the song of the onion soup. It was a Command Performance. As a reward he was officially appointed Court Jester, and took no active part in the perse- cution of the Christians which was duly renewed next day. He had no time, anyway: he was too busy fetching and carrying for the bullies, obeying their imperious bidding, ministering to their every need. It made us sick to see him toady, and we turned ostentatiously aside, spitting in disgust upon the ground whenever he came near.

The first time we did this, he stopped short and stared at us with what, oddly enough, seemed to be surprise; then, twitching his lips side-long, and lifting one shoulder in the ambiguous shrug character- istic of him before his rise to popularity, he passed on without a word: his destination evidently the back door, where Angéline no doubt awaited him. Our spies reported that he carried messages to her from Maillet or Lecoq, or it might be both: these were written and sealed up in envelopes, but whether she replied in kind or any actual meetings took place, apart from the evening sessions at which her mother acted as chaperone, we'd no means of knowing. Magagnos was often seen whispering to her urgently at all times of day in the kitchen-porch; Angéline's eyes were cast down while she fingered the gold crucifix at her throat: she made no audible answer and it was impossible to deduce anything from her demeanour or to guess what all the secrecy was about. We were soon to know, however; for our release from bondage came earlier than we dreamed: unexpectedly our prayers had been answered and the Neronian Age was drawing rapidly to a close.

One evening after school, an uproar arose from the Emperor's amphitheatre, so violent and sudden that we started out of our hiding places in panic at the possibility that Maillet had, perhaps, imported lions after all. We were not, this time, in sight of the clearing and could only hear the savage crescendo of sound that arose from it; as though muted by a sourdine, this initial swell abruptly decreased diminuendo, the confused animal snarls reminiscent of a menagerie, which had so alarmed us, subsiding into easily recognisable echoes of physical combat: arduous breath exhaled in gasps, stamp and slither of scuffling feet, fists thumping dull on flesh, the ivory kiss of bone meeting bone.

All caution thrown aside, we doubled in the direction of the amphi- theatre; I for one hoped that Magagnos was getting the good beating-up which in my opinion he deserved for his treachery to our cause (though I was to be heartily ashamed of this wish before the end of the evening) and in any case it remained unfulfilled: for Magagnos was not involved in the fight at all. The contestants, as even in our wildest imaginings we could not have prophesied, were Maillet and Lecoq themselves. Between the two marble benches which had, only a short while ago, served them as thrones, they were having it out hand to hand: though not toe to toe, since Maillet's erratic taurine lunges, and the tempestuous, ill-timed swings of his long lumpy arms, at the ends of which his fists whirled like Indian clubs, rendered any attempt at in-fighting both impracticable and unwise from his opponent's point of view. Luckily for Lecoq, most of the blows aimed at him went wide of their target; for even in this, his chosen sphere of violence, Maillet exhibited the striking ineptitude so typical of him: whenever one of his punches failed to land, the impetus behind it carried him blindly on off-balance, and more than once brought him to his knees; Lecoq had no knowledge of ringcraft either, but he was cooler and more nimble on his feet, while Maillet had lost all control in a blind red-hot yammering rage: he was too short-winded now to emit the bestial growls which had originally attracted our attention.

Considered by the standards of professional pugilism, or even by those of the street-corner, this fight might have seemed puerile: any bar-room brawler would have pronounced it a sorry affair or lousy scrap; but the pleasure we derived from watching sprang from entirely different sources. A revolution had come about, a turning of the tables: we, the erstwhile slaves, now occupied the amphitheatre; they, our former masters (for all of us knew that, after this, they could never rule again) fought each other in the arena; we cheered and jeered and groaned ironically, turning down our thumbs as Nero used to do, at the sight of our deposed Emperor's blood spurting from split lips and a long cut on the Consul-General's cheek laid open.

Lecoq's hat and spectacles had been knocked off early on; the glitter of gold rims, caught out of the corner of my eye, drew my attention for a moment from the fight; nearby, the glasses lay, by a miracle, unbroken: not far away, had rolled the hat; I was just in time to see the heel of a boot, unnoticed by other spectators, descend with deliberation upon the spectacles, splintering the lenses to powder and ruining the rims for evermore; then the crown of the hat was lifted, soaring, by the boot, in a goal-kick that scored among the laurels on our left.

And the boot itself belonged to Magagnos, whom I hadn't noticed until now. He did not return my glance but, having treated Lecoq's accessories in the way I've just described, stepped back and leaned, arms folded, against the bole of a tree, his lips just faintly curled, a gleam of anticipatory joy in his eyes as he bent these, once again, upon the fight: though he now wore neither domino nor beard affixed with spirit-gum, his attitude was the one that he'd adopted in the play when, as the Gondolier of Death, he rowed the conspirators to the canal's edge, and, posing as one of them, had bided his time in the background, listening meanwhile to the disclosure of all their plans.

And then I realised how cruelly we'd misjudged him. Of course he'd not betrayed us: hence his surprise when, at sight of him, we spat. He thought we'd recognise the technique that he had employed upon the stage to sabotage, from within, the régime he was supposed to serve. This was his doing: these writhing figures entwined in hatred on the turf (they'd abandoned boxing for all-in); I knew it now; Angéline had been the bait; he'd engineered the quarrel, playing them one against the other till the rivalry burst out in this (Maillet had Lecoq down at last; was pulling his head back by pomaded hair). So Magagnos had worked to free us single-handed; he'd succeeded; the oppression was at an end, the tyrants overthrown: and instead of trusting him, we'd spat.

A sudden yell of alarm from the boys made me jump; a black wind swept past, a rush of retributive air, scattering us in its passage to right and left: the skirts of the Abbé's cassock went swishing by, billowing out as he straddled above the fight. The back of his neck was bulging red with anger; no verbal explosion came as for small misdeeds: this dead silence was the danger sign. Maillet and Lecoq were torn from each other like limpets from a rock and held apart, one in each of his hairy powerful peasant's hands. He shook them to and fro, his eyes and lips protruding, possibly not trusting himself to speak.

And then Lecoq made his mistake. He may have been taken by surprise or, without his glasses, could not perhaps see who held him. He may have thought it was Maillet. But, whatever his reason, he braced himself against the grip and raised his fist to strike out at the Abbé. A gasp went up from all of us; only Magagnos, leaning back against his tree, made no movement and no sound. There was the sharp crack of a weighty palm on flesh: Lecoq's head rocked upon his shoulders; another slap and it rolled the other way. The hand he'd raised dropped slowly to his side and he sat down stunned upon the turf.

Before we could take in properly what we'd seen, the slap rang out again: twice more and twice as heavily, it seemed to us. The Abbé had not only boxed Lecoq's ears but Maillet's, into the bargain; and, though he did not know it then, justice had been done for us at last.

Maillet stood still for a moment, both hands clutching the sides of his small square head, his face gradually crumpling and flushing crimson, before his mouth fell open on a long-drawn wail of distress and he burst incontinently into tears. I glanced over my shoulder, wondering how Magagnos would react to this sight, which he had done so much to bring about, but he'd already turned away and was slowly slouching, his hands in his pockets, back towards the house.

The Bird Man

*   *   *

for Margot Walmsley

NOBODY SEEMED TO KNOW HOW OLD GIAOUSÉ WAS, AND HIS surname too had long been forgotten; but for at least thirty years he'd lived in the abandoned windmill whose broken sails could be seen over the hillcrest above the village nine miles from Nice, alone except for the birds that were his pride and joy, and—unwillingly—his livelihood.

The windmill, overgrown with moss outside, had a heavy oaken door, hanging askew on its hinges and never completely closed. Inside, it consisted of one large high-ceilinged room, furnished with home-made table and chair, a charcoal brazier and a candle stuck in a bottle. Long dark cylinders of smoked sausage and strips of stockfish hung from the rafters overhead: on the stone floor below them was the mattress on which Giaousé stretched himself by day and slept by night. To enter the windmill, which few people—except myself at the age of thirteen—were allowed to do, was like coming into an aviary. The air was vibrant with bird-song, twittering cooing, and the flutter of wings; for the birds were allowed to fly freely about the room, entering their cages only when Giaousé bade them do so at bedtime: except for those not fully trained, which hopped about behind bars until they'd learnt better.

The walls were lined completely with cages in a double row, as other rooms might be with bookshelves; some, housing very special birds, were hung higher up, on nails. One of these contained a blue jay, whose harsh scream struck an occasional discord in the general symphony. There had once been a parrot; but this had somehow learnt to talk, and Giaousé got rid of it at once; besides, he feared it might spread

166

psittacosis, at that time the cause of a public scare. On the whole he disapproved of big birds. Once he had seen ostriches, and spoke of them with awe, but still they were too big. Most of his birds were small, long-tailed, and gaily coloured: parakeets, budgerigars or lovebirds, and others more exotic which I was never able to identify; though there were a good few canaries too, and even a nightingale (never allowed out of its cage in any circumstances).

When Giaousé took them outdoors for an airing or went down into the village to make his few weekly purchases, the birds clung to him with their claws, perched on his shoulders, and pecked affectionately at his cheeks: there were always some beaks and bright beady eyes peeping out of the many pockets of his patched corduroy coat. He was a tall, loosely-built, stooping man with a long body, long arms and short legs, one of which dragged a little, and he carried a thick thorny stick with a crutch-like handle and an iron spike for ferrule, that was always propped up, at home, behind the windmill door. His face and hair were a rough uniform grey and he held his head slightly to one side, the mouth crinkled as a rule in an oddly gentle smile. His age was impossible to compute: though it was known that, like all of us, he had once been young.

In those days, like most of the other villagers, he'd been employed at the Ramenta, the giant incinerator into which all the refuse from the cities along the Côte was shovelled by a huge mechanical scoop that worked backwards and forwards like a see-saw. Heaped around with rubbish, it was isolated from human habitation on a hill beyond the river that flowed between it and our village, along whose further bank the workers bicycled home late in the evening, blanched with dust, cinders and ash. The Ramenta never slept. A lurid pall of smoke shrouded it by day, and at night long tongues of orange flame flickered up from the sullen furnace glow.

It was this furnace that was supposed to have swallowed Giaousé's rival, with whom he'd been on night-shift after they had fought with knives, during a fête the evening before, over Giaousé's very captivating young wife. There was no proof, but after all the rival was never seen again; and Giaousé not only lost his job but also the wife, who fled to her parents in Nice and refused to return despite her husband's most agonised pleading. After this, Giaousé disappeared from the village—some said, into the Foreign Legion, which might account for his having seen ostriches—and only came back many years later, so changed that few recognised him, to set up house with his birds in the windmill.

The windmill stood on the edge of a wood, where family men had been accustomed to go, every Sunday, for la chasse, dressed like game-keepers and with formidable-looking shotguns under their arms. All day long they'd creep stealthily about, using the technique employed elsewhere for stalking a tiger; some crouched for hours in ambush until a bird happened to alight within point-blank range. Giaousé had put a stop to these practices, so violently that the hunters were driven altogether from the wood and had thereafter to wait until the birds, at twilight, were settling down to roost in the trees lining the main road, when they would loose off both barrels at random into the foliage: the result often being sparrow or starling pie for supper next day.

Another menace to birds in general, and Giaousé's aviary in parti-cular, were the wild cats that infested the wood at the time of his arrival. No one could say where they'd initially come from, but they had multiplied considerably over the years and also grown, with each successive generation, in size, audacity and strength. At first they'd made a mass attack on the windmill, but were beaten off with only a few feathered casualties, for which Giaousé made them pay in more than kind. He even cooked his victims over the brazier and ate them with relish. He also took to hunting them through the wood, and the cats, in order to live, were forced to make sorties into the village itself, where many people kept chickens. They scarcely dared to venture near the windmill, and Giaousé and his birds were soon left to live together in peace; though when obliged to leave home on business, he always persuaded Monsieur Bontemps, the garde-champêtre, to keep an eye on his place by promising him a bottle of calvados when he got back.

Giaousé hated selling any of his birds; but, driven by necessity, about three times a year he would trudge along the road to Nice, the cages slung on poles across his shoulders (as onion-men carry their wares) and take up a pitch on the Promenade des Anglais, where he did a roaring trade with the tourists, his air of great sadness whenever he made a sale being part of his attraction. Then, after a couple of days, he would return, carrying the empty cages and rocking, reeling, roaring drunk, on the outer platform of a tramcar: at such times the old story about him was remembered, and people kept well out of his way. But Giaousé never hurt anyone. Perhaps because he'd none of his own, he seemed especially fond of children, and would sometimes pull a rather crumpled bird from his pocket and bestow it on some kid who'd taken his fancy. All the same, no child from the village was encouraged on his hill; and I was certainly the only one who was ever invited into the windmill.

The solitary, the strange and the withdrawn always fascinated me as a boy; perhaps I recognised in them a foretoken of my future self; and possibly because Giaousé sensed this and also because, being English, I was like himself a stranger, he liked to have me call on him. He didn't talk much—certainly not, as I'd hoped, about the Legion—and when he spoke it was invariably in French: never in Niçardé, the local patois, though by now I'd picked up enough to carry on a conversation.

These visits continued even after the vendetta boiled up between Giaousé and the Mattone brothers: more furtively, however; for I was a member of the Main Noire (or Mané Noiré, as they called it), a secret organisation controlled by the Mattones, whose forebears had more than likely belonged to the parent branch; and all loyal Blackhanders were formally forbidden to consort with the Bird Man.

The vendetta began when Etienne, the younger Mattone, aged twelve, trespassing in the wood one day, shot and killed, with a powerful homemade catapult, an owl that Giaousé was very fond of, and that in some obscure way told him the time. Giaousé caught Etienne bending over the body, and beat him severely.

The Mattone father was dead. Louis, at fourteen, was the head of the house, and it was up to him to avenge the insult to his kin. Every blow, he decreed, must be paid for in blood; and his resolve was redoubled when he got beaten by Giaousé himself for teaching the other boys to make the sign of protection against the Evil Eye whenever the Bird Man passed. Louis knew that the time for one of Giaousé's visits to Nice was approaching, and he thought up a terrible plan.

The wild cats had recently launched a series of raids on the village; and the Mattones, having laid snares for them, had secured three. These were now confined, snarling, spitting and scratching, in boxes at the back of our most secret meeting place. Next, Louis detailed a party to steal a pile of empty flour-sacks and a large wheelbarrow from the yard behind Panzani's store. By the time Giaousé left on his journey, this had been done; and next day every cat in the village disappeared: the Mattones' among them, to disarm suspicion. Louis then outlined his scheme: the full horror of which was scheduled for the night of Giaousé's return. Monsieur Bontemps was to be lured away by the news of a fake burglary; the writhing sacks which now surrounded us were to be conveyed up the hill in the wheelbarrow, and the whole lot—plus the boxes containing the three wild cats—was to be introduced among the birds in the windmill, as a surprise to greet Giaousé's homecoming.

Despite the stringent oath of allegiance that I'd sworn, this was too much for me to take; and I made a sudden bolt for it, determined to warn Monsieur Bontemps before it was too late, but the Mattones caught up with me outside and we all sprawled headlong in the dust. I'd probably have been lynched, had my father not happened along the street at that moment; and when we reached home, refusing to listen to my explanations, he immediately confined me to my room as a penalty for fighting.

It was late at night before I managed to escape; and as I stumbled up the hillside in the moonlight, I knew by the sounds coming from inside the windmill that I'd not made it in time. Several feline shapes shot screeching past the crooked, open door and vanished in the dark; Giaousé lunged abortively after them with his stick, then turned to thrash about inside the room. Creeping up to the window, I saw broken, twisted scraps of metal, strips of torn sacking, a floor ankle-deep in feathers; even the stockfish and smoked sausages had been pulled down, and a cat was now attempting to drag them through the doorway; another was swinging—while Giaousé struck at it—from the cage containing the nightingale: the blue jay had, of course, gone long ago.

Then all the cats were gone too, and Giaousé stood alone in the middle of the floor. The stick clattered from his hand: he turned his head from side to side, glaring dazedly around at the shattered empty cages and the evidence of carnage. A faint, subdued twittering came from above him, and he glanced up quickly. High on the rafters, under the roof, a few birds who'd managed to fly out of harm's way now clung and feebly fluttered.

Giaousé called hoarsely to them in Niçardé: forgetting, in his agitation, to use the special sound-language that they understood. I prepared to beat a retreat: there was no way I could help, nor was it a good moment for any boy to be found lurking near the windmill. The last I saw of Giaousé, he was staring upwards and stretching out his hands imploringly, as he might once have done towards his wife; but the birds were too terrified to take note of his appeal.

A Visit to the Villa Edouard Sept

*   *   *

MY FATHER, A CONTEMPORARY OF OSCAR WILDE, WAS ACTUALLY better acquainted with his brother, the journalist Willie Wilde; on the other hand, Robert Ross (though not a relative of ours) was a frequent visitor at my grandmother's house and had given her a copy, flatteringly inscribed, of a book entitled *Masques and Phases*, which later passed into my possession, while his elder brother Alec was a close friend of Father's and may even have been at school with him, though I am not certain of this.

'But Oscar?' I would persist: for, ever since I had read *The Picture of Dorian Grey* a year before, at the age of seventeen, I'd taken a passionate interest in everything pertaining to its author, about whom I planned, one day, to write a novel called *Paradox*; 'You must have known Oscar too?'

'Oscar Wilde,' my father said, 'was his own worst enemy, poor fellow' —it was a description which, in his view, could equally apply to me— 'Great charm when he chose to use it, of course, but arrogant, incurably arrogant...' Here my father, never conspicuous, himself, for abject humility, still less when young, shook his head reproachfully and sighed. 'Everybody shouting "Author"—and he'd come out in front of the curtain smoking a cigarette. Gold-tipped, too, like one of those things you smoke. Couldn't expect the public to like that, but damned if Wilde didn't seem to take a deliberate pride in antagonising everybody. I remember, for example, the first time I met him...'

This initial encounter had taken place in a London club with literary and theatrical associations, where my father was entertaining a visiting French comedian, known as Marius, to dinner. The meal was halfway through when Oscar Wilde entered the dining-room. ('Great big hulking man, six feet two and seventeen stone at least'—my father was some inches taller and more than a stone heavier—'effeminate? Far from it. He'd hands like a butcher. Affected, yes. Very overbearing manner. Damson velvet dinner coat wouldn't swear he wasn't wearing a frilled shirt as well.') Wilde recognised Marius and came over to greet him with great cordiality. Pulling up a chair without invitation, he sat down at the table as if unaware of my father's presence, and at once initiated a conversation in fluent French; Marius made several embarrassed attempts to interrupt the flow and introduce his host, but in face of Father's evident annoyance and Wilde's determination to ignore these tentative overtures, he soon desisted and pecked at the food on his plate, answering Oscar only in monosyllables. In defiance of the club regulations, Wilde lit a gold-tipped cigarette and continued his monologue; Father, swallowing his anger, tried to concentrate on the next course; Marius, by now completely silent, had given up eating altogether.

At last, as the savoury was served, Wilde turned to my father with a start of apology, and addressing him in English: 'I do hope you'll forgive me, sir, and you too, my dear Marius—the pleasure of seeing you again must be my excuse—it is really unpardonable to intrude at your table and to speak a language perhaps unfamiliar to your friend...'

Father interrupted, speaking for the first time and with his suavest smile: 'Ne vous gênez pas, monsieur Wilde, je vous en prie. J'ai fait mes études en France, et j'ai pu, par conséquent, suivre votre discours sans trop difficulté,' and in English: 'If I may be allowed to say so, Sir, you speak French very well—for an Irishman'.

But whatever personal distaste for Wilde he may have felt, and whatever verbal skirmishes they may have had, my father had nevertheless registered a violent protest when, after the sentence, Oscar's plays were presented in London without acknowledgement to the author, and had incurred much unpopularity by arguing that figures more prominent in the social register should also have stood trial if homosexuality were indeed to be treated as a criminal offence (a measure to which he declared himself rigorously opposed): this led to the suggestion, from a man named Cope-Frazer, that my father was himself, in the current phrase, 'addicted to unnatural practices'. Father, having recently got married, was not unreasonably annoyed; he replied by first throwing Cope-Frazer through the glass of a French window and then bringing a suit against him for slander: despite a counter threat of proceedings for assault, the case was settled out of court in my father's favour, after which no further allegations of this sort were made, though Father continued for long afterwards to defend Wilde in public whenever discussion arose.

'What about Frank Harris?' I asked.

'The *Fortnightly Review* man? Not above a bit of blackmail now and again, when it suited him—or so they used to say. Only knew him by sight myself, so I've no right to talk. Used to live here in Nice, too ... he and your Uncle Bertie were as thick as ...' Just in time he bit back a smile which might have been only to apt in both cases: 'Well, intimate anyway. Better ask Bertie if you want to know anything about Harris.'

'I'm lunching with him tomorrow.'

'Are you now? Funny, I thought he was in Algiers.'

'Not Uncle Bertie, Father—Frank Harris.'

The effect of this deliberately casual statement was all I could have wished: 'Lunching with Harris? Don't mean to say he's still alive? Why he must be older than I am.' At the age of seventy-two, my father had come to believe that if not actually immortal, he was destined at any rate to survive all other members of his generation: it disturbed him to find that any of these still existed contemporaneously.

'He's not only alive, but still in Nice,' I said; 'Working on a Life of Shaw. I haven't met him yet, but apparently he may help to get my novel printed.'

'But surely,' my father said, 'Harris no longer has a magazine or any other means of publication at his disposal?'

'No, but he might arrange it somehow.'

'God bless my soul. Well, be sure you don't give him any money.'

The friend responsible for my invitation to luncheon at the Villa Edouard Sept, in Cimiez, a suburb in the hills overlooking Nice, where Frank Harris lived during the last years of his life, was called Amberly. He was in his middle thirties, an explorer and archæologist of private means, who, while of conspicuously English origin, had become, in some manner not easy to elucidate, a Belgian marquis, though he never made use of this title. Amberly had known Frank Harris for many years, and once showed me a volume of his short stories, with an affectionate inscription in a coloured frontispiece depicting a large young man bathing naked, with his back turned, in a rock-pool, for which Amberly, some time before, had posed as a model.

Amberly had often urged me, as an admirer of Oscar Wilde, to meet Harris, who, as he pointed out, 'was, after all, practically our last link with the Great Man'; there was also the chance that he might find a publisher for the novel that I'd just written: and though, at eighteen, I was apt to scorn the idea that an author should attempt to succeed by any means other than the exercise of literary talent, an actual possibility—however remote—of getting one's work published was not of course to be neglected.

As I set out with Amberly, one torrid noonday in June 1930, for lunch at Harris's home, I was assailed, however, in the open taxi by the nervous tremor inseparable, in those days, from the prospect of any social occasion among strangers; I braced myself to meet the onslaught of welcome; felt, already, the bones of my hand grate together in Harris's iron grip; my ears rang in advance with the rich, deep, booming voice that I'd read about so often in memoirs of the Eighteen-Nineties but never actually heard.

What, I wondered, would be the best way to behave? It must be remembered that this was to be my first meeting with a real author: that Harris had, moreover, the reputation of being a formidable and even forbidding personality; this was the man, I called with a sinking stomach, who had talked Moore and Meredith to a standstill: to whom even Wilde had listened, on occasion, in respectful silence. A policy of modest self-effacment seemed the wisest to adopt in his presence: on the other hand Harris might then dismiss me with contempt as a mediocrity, and wonder—perhaps aloud—why the hell I had been brought to see him; if, however, I attempted to assert myself and talked too much, he might consider me a presumptuous young man who needed taking down a peg or two. Suppose he proved to be in one of his ferocious, bullying moods: drowning the conversation with salvoes of scornful mirth, picking on me as a ready-made butt for sallies of sardonic wit? One might, of course, appease him by a flattering evaluation of his own work; I'd been told that nine authors out of every ten were susceptible to such an approach (an estimate which later experience abundantly confirmed), and to this purpose I had re-read, the previous night, two volumes of stories, *The Bomb*, and the *Life of Oscar Wilde*; I began now to make a hurried mental précis of those portions of the autobiography —mainly of a pornographic nature—which I'd managed to assimilate, years before, at my uncle's hotel, on an afternoon when he was out.

My clothes, too, presented in additional source of worry; Harris might, for all I knew, be wearing cowboy chaps and a ten-gallon hat: in any case he was certain to regard me as a ridiculous fop. The white mess-jacket and clove carnation, even the crêpe-de-chine shirt might pass muster: but why, for Heaven's sake, had I chosen to gird my white drill trousers with a crimson sash instead of an ordinary belt, and why co-respondent shoes? The sash, it's true, could not be seen unless I removed my jacket; the shoes would, with luck, be hidden below the table, and my gold-topped malacca cane could be given up swiftly to a servant before the host had a chance to see it.

I turned towards Amberly—dressed, I noticed, much less obtrusively in a dark blue blazer and white flannels—and was about to ask his opinion on these sartorial questions, when he forestalled me by saying: 'Now, about Harris. You know he was very sick last year—had hiccups for over a week, something to do with his stomach, they all thought he'd peg out but in the end he foiled them once again—and then of course he's been short of cash lately, though his new book ought to remedy that: he's pushing on with it all he can, but it seems GBS is being bloody difficult about the whole affair; I wish to God he'd die, don't you? So you see Frank's got a lot to try him at the moment, and I hope you won't take offence if he seems a bit abrupt at first: take my word for it, his bark's much worse than his bite and, after all, you're not the easiest person in the world to get on with, yourself—God knows what you'll be like at his age.'

I listened to this homily with increasing dismay. 'Just one more thing, dear boy,' Amberly went on. 'Frank's getting on in years now, of course, but he's always been pretty outspoken whatever company he's in, so you mustn't be shocked at anything he says—his language is still picturesque at times, to put it mildly.'

I choked, too furious to answer at first; the idea that I, at my age, with more than twelve months of Côte d'Azur café-society behind me, could be shocked at all, let alone by strong language, was intolerable: what did Amberly take me for, all of a sudden? 'Really!' I began, but our taxi had pulled up short and the driver had already jerked open the door for us to alight: it was plainly impossible to initiate a quarrel at this stage; nonetheless, as I followed Amberly towards what was evidently the Villa Edouard Sept, my annoyance was still so acute that I can remember nothing of my surroundings until confronted by a swarthy *majordome* in a striped waistcoat, who stood back smiling from an inner doorway, one hand out-stretched to take my stick.

A confused impression of marble busts on pedestals remains with me, but these may have been in the hall outside; Amberly had already passed the butler and his voice was raised heartily in the room beyond; long and low-ceilinged, with French windows open wide: so cool and dark after the meridian glare that I peered about dimsightedly; I'd not been wearing sun-glasses in the cab and now green bilious blots swam before my eyes: an iridescent dazzle out of which emerged, chimerically, the figure of my host.

A first glimpse of Frank Harris, at any time of his life, seems invariably to afford the beholder some surprise, according to the period-reminiscences in which he has so often figured, and I proved no exception to the general rule; this unexpected quality in his appearance may have been exaggerated by his advancing years at the time I met him: yet, though he must have been seventy-five, his face, while craggy and lividly mottled, especially about the curve of the nose, was no more ravaged than seemed consistent with his state of health and the pace at which he'd lived; the centre-parted hair, still fairly thick, plastered down low on his temples with the effect of a wig or a villain in melodrama, and the equally transpontine moustaches with their ascendant curve, showed little sign of grey; on the other hand, these may quite likely have been dyed: age itself was apparent mainly in the moist and vitreous stare, the broad shoulders shrunk in a forward stoop, the rapid shuffling step with which he moved.

All these things I had been led to anticipate; nevertheless the general ensemble, plus his lack of height, took me aback: I'd been told he was not tall, but had not imagined him to be so short; no one, moreover, had prepared me for the final shock, which was reserved for when he spoke. Instead of the resonant bass, the rumbling minatory bellow I had expected, his voice was now a muffled whisper wheezing in his larynx: a sound so eerily unforseen that for a second I was too disconcerted to answer his greeting or to take the knobbly hand extended to me.

When rehearsing this moment in the car, I had decided upon the firmest handshake I could manage as a defensive measure against Frank Harris's fabled strength, even though my fingers be ground to powder in the process; now Harris gave a start and examined his hand in surprise as I released it with a mutter of apology; he seemed, however, to be baffled rather than annoyed, for, having cocked up his head to scrutinise me more closely, he emitted the echo of a rasping chuckle.

'Bertie,' he seemed to say; and then, more audibly: 'Aren't-you-Bertie's nephew?'

'Yes, sir.'

'Ha! Strongest man—in the hands—I ever knew, except myself when younger, of course... And how is he, the rascal? Abroad again, eh—more of his schemes I suppose! Listen to me boy...' He leaned forward confidentially; the breath whistled in his throat: 'They used to talk about me, but Bertie...' He made a sweeping gesture with his hand, implying that any competition was out of the question: 'Biggest rascal unhung!'

The thought of my uncle's iniquity—and his skill in cheating, so far, the hangman's rope caused Harris to bring one hand down hard on his thigh and to become convulsed with a spasm of strangled mirth, which merged almost at once into an explosive fit of coughing: his face flushed purple, his eyes, already protuberant, seemed about to burst from their sockets; alarmed, I moved towards him and was waved irritably back; I glanced around for help and realised we were alone in the room: Amberly was out of earshot on the verandah, engaged in greeting our hostess; I became aware, also, that I was still clutching the parcel containing the MS of my first novel, which Amberly had insisted I should bring along, and there seemed nowhere handy to put it down. By this time, Harris had partly recovered, and when he had withdrawn from the folds of a large bandanna and was able to speak again, his voice seemed, paradoxically, stronger for the paroxysm through which he'd passed.

'Blasted bronchitis,' he wheezed. 'Won't even let a man bloody well laugh. Bah! Look here, me boy!' He reeled off rapidly, fixing me with a glaucous eye: 'Phlebitis, neuralgia, rheumatism, bronchial asthma,' an impressive pause, to let this list of ailments sink in before the punch-line: 'Ulcers. Here—in the belly! How's that, eh? But I'll beat 'em yet, you wait and see, the bloody lot,' and sharply, before I could express my faith in his eventual victory over his infirmaries: 'Oxford?'

I shook my head, just managing to follow his swift transition from ulcers to education: 'No. Over here, in France.'

'Good boy! Splendid! Educated on the Continent meself—and in the States, of course. Much the best way. These English universities...' He made again the convulsive gesture that had previously served to demonstrate my Uncle Bertie's unique position in the sphere of unpunished villainy: 'Effete!' He glared up, suddenly caught sight of majordome, who had hurried in at the close of the coughing fit, and banished him—before I could hand over my parcel of MS—with terse command: 'Drinks!'

With Harris's hand on my elbow, I was now led on to the verandah and presented to his wife as Bertie's nephew; an illusory physical resemblance was commented on, with comparison rather in my favour and 'taller, of course' from Harris; Mrs Harris, herself of a fair height and handsome, with burnished hair, aged about forty to my eighteen year old eyes, relieved me at last of the MS, elicited my actual surname —which had become confused with that of my maternal uncle—and introduced me by it to a rather dim English couple (possibly neighbours invited for reasons of reciprocal hospitality), and to a man tanned the colour of chocolate, whom Harris said, with his gusty whistling laugh, was 'a fellow-Scotch man', though he spoke English in a manner scarcely compatible with a countryman of Burns: I soon discovered he was a Hungarian named Kalnay, who had written a book about Jews under the pseudonym of Jim McKay.

'McKay's not merely a writer,' Harris told me. 'He's something much more important.' He drew a deep breath and hissed with extraordinary venom: 'A publisher!' But his animosity seemed directed at this profession in general rather than its present representative, for he simultaneously clapped Mr Kalnay upon the shoulder: 'And President of the International Writers' League! Do you belong to the International Writers' League, Ross? No? Well, we'll have to make you a member—right, McKay? This young man has written a book,' he continued, pointing at me: to my horror I felt a deep flush overspreading my face, and threw a baleful glance at Amberly, who smiled imperturbably back: 'But we'll talk about that later, see what we can do.' Harris picked up a glass and drained it at a gulp: 'Now for some lunch.'

The verandah ran the whole length of the villa and was, I think, roofed-in: or else an awning was placed over the long table at which we ate, for I cannot remember any encroachment of the sun until well towards the end of the meal.

I sat with my back to the view and on the right hand of Harris himself: an arrangement for which Amberly was perhaps responsible, as his conspiratorial glances down the table, from a similar position next to the hostess (with Mr Kalnay opposite and the dim English distributed along the centre), seemed to confirm. My annoyance with him evaporated in face of this kindness and goodwill. I hoped, however, that the subject of my book would not again be brought up, since I believed quite rightly that no good could come out of rushing anything: even membership of the International Writers' League.

Meanwhile I began to put my original plan into action and talk to Harris about his own work; since his involuntary *sotto voce* precluded him from taking part in any general conversation, I had him more or less to myself, and lost no time in asking after the book in progress, as this seemed the most promising gambit: how was it getting on? Would it soon be finished? Amberly had told me that Bernard Shaw…

Harris laid down his knife and fork. 'Don't talk to me about Bernard bloody Shaw,' he said in a voice that sudden fury, luckily, made more stifled than ever: fortunately, again, the sight of the butler bringing the wine at this point diverted his attention elsewhere and seemed to quench his wrath. Though the food was excellent, I cannot recall any dish we ate: the memory of this wine, however—and not only because of its providential appearance—remains with me to this day; it was golden in colour and called Camp Romain; soon the whole table was united in its praise: Amberly showing himself especially eager to discover the secret of its origin. This, Harris refused to divulge: an incongruously coy smile puckered his lips as he pointed to the picture of the Roman camp on the label (a litre bottle in an ice-bucket had been placed before each guest) and his vague gesture towards the surrounding hills implied that it was home-grown, or that a private vineyard was concealed among the Roman ruins which—apart from Frank Harris's selection of this locality as his home—were Cimiez's main claim to fame.

This extremely pleasant and potent vintage had not only the immediate effect of mellowing Harris and causing all signs of irascibility, thenceforward, to disappear, but of removing my remaining inhibitions: reckless of further snubs, I plunged on, taking *My Life and Loves* as the next topic; Harris looked up from his plate in consternation: 'How d'you get a hold of that? You surely can't have bought the set?'

'My Uncle Bertie has one.'

'Yes, I know, gave it him myself, but he ought never to have lent it to you. Pure filth—not fit to be in the hands of any decent person…' He called croakingly up the table to his wife: 'Isn't it, my dear? Pure filth?'

'What's that my dear?'

'My autobiography, of course. Pure filth!'

'Well, not all of it, Frank,' his wife said soothingly; the faces of the English couple were fixed in feeble apprehensive smiles: they obviously hoped this subject would soon be changed. 'The parts about the Wild West…' Mrs Harris continued; 'Ah, yes—those,' wheezed her husband and, turning back to me: 'The rest's just dirt, that's all. I'd give my right arm not to have written that first volume—the pornographic stuff, I mean.'

'Why did you then?' The question slipped out before I could prevent it; I stopped aghast: but Harris seemed unaware of my impertinence: his blurred eyes became focused abstractly on the distant horizon.

'Money,' he answered simply, and pouring himself another glass of wine: 'I needed money. You can't understand what that means, me boy—hope you never do.' It was a hope, alas, unrealised. Harris continued histrionically: 'And did I make any? No! That book did me more harm than the pox—banned everywhere, threats of prosecution, pirated in the States: nothing but trouble came of it all round. I deserved what I got! "Whatsoever a man shall sow, that also shall he reap"... a bloody black harvest, me boy. Never, however much you are tempted...' He gulped at the Camp Romain, which seemed to have a restorative effect on his voice: 'Never prostitute the gifts you were given at birth. For an artist'—the characteristic peremptory sweep of his broad blunt hand—'it's fatal! Ruin for sure. And I'll tell you something else. When you become a literary figure—and trying to look modest won't help to make you one—if you happen to get hard up,' he glared portentously: 'Never borrow any money! Nobody in the literary ramp'll put up with a borrower! Even if you pay 'em back,' he screwed up his eyes as if in pain at the thought of contingency; 'Even then, the seeds of mistrust are sown. Word gets about; feller's always after a touch; they'll turn their backs, editors won't look at your work, everyone's against you once they smell you're broke. Mark my words—I'm speaking from experience!'

This wise and truthful precept seemed inapplicable at the time (though it came back to me years after, when—having been forced by economic necessity to disregard it—I was passing through a period identical with that so trenchantly described by Harris): besides, I was impatiently waiting to question him about Oscar Wilde. Here, however, I drew a blank ('It's all there, in my book'), with exception of a brief and pungent comment on the character of Lord Alfred Douglas, which was certainly not in his book, and which Mrs Harris was called upon to confirm from the head of the table.

The smiles of the English couple became more constrained than ever at this; the mousy wife almost spilled her glass, whereupon Mr Kalnay, gallantly springing to his feet, sought to create a diversion by asking Mrs Harris for permission to remove his jacket. To my dismay, not only was this granted, but Amberly and even the dim English husband proceeded to follow Kalnay's example. 'What about you, Mr Maclaren-Ross?' Mrs Harris cried; 'I'm sure you must be very hot!' There seemed no way out: I looked desperately at my host, but he nodded too, excusing himself from doing likewise by reason of his malady; slowly I stood up and unbuttoned my mess-jacket, and the crimson sash was manifestly revealed.

My worst expectations were realised: Harris's attention was caught immediately by the flash of colour; with bottle and glass suspended in hand, he blinked and peered across the table at the sash, at the crêpe-de-chine shirt: a dawning suspicion gathered like a cloud behind his glassy eyes.

'Are you a sodomite?' he shot out suddenly.

'I beg your pardon?' I stammered, seeing out of the corner of my eye Mr Kalnay suddenly pause with some witticism balanced, it seemed, on his bunched fingertips, and lean forward in his chair to listen.

'Are you a bugger?' This time it came loud enough for all to hear: Mrs Harris called 'Frank!' sharply down the table.

Harris turned slightly in his seat: 'It's all right, my dear,' he said testily; 'I'm just asking Ross a civil question—nothing to be alarmed about ... Not offended, are you, me boy—don't mind me asking, eh?'

'No,' I said. 'No, not at all.'

'And you're not a sodomite, now are you?'

'As a matter of fact, no.'

'You see, Nellie,' Harris called triumphantly up to his wife. 'He isn't one at all, what'd I tell you? And now,' glancing for approval at his guests, 'let's all have something more to drink!'

But the English couple, in every sense, had had enough: they were getting up to leave: 'Extraordinary thing,' Harris said, blowing out an audible breath of relief when they'd departed; 'Anybody'd think I'd done something to offend 'em ... Well, well—people have no manners nowadays. Now then, boy,' turning to me, 'We must hear all about this book of yours. What kind of book is it? A novel? Poetry? Or what?'

There's not much more to tell. Before we left, and after another bottle apiece of Camp Romain, plus some cognac, had been drunk, Harris had promised to read every word of my novel and to find a publisher for it; Kalnay might do, of course; we'd have to see. Meanwhile I was to come and lunch without fail on Monday week, when he'd have a full plan of campaign outlined for me.

I went home walking, as they say, on air: though luckily in view of the sequel, I made no mention to my father of Harris's promise or my buoyant hopes. But on the Monday morning, just as I was dressing to go out, a packet arrived by messenger containing my MS—in its original parcel which, I could tell, had never been opened—and a letter from Harris saying, quite politely, that owing to his state of health and the fact that he'd promised to deliver the biography of Shaw by a certain date, and was obliged therefore to work on it at redoubled speed, he would be unable to help me find a publisher for my book— which, however, he had greatly enjoyed.

This letter, which I tore into little pieces and thrust forthwith into the kitchen stove (an act I now regret), made, needless to say, no mention of the invitation to lunch; the rest of my mail that morning consisted of a postcard from Amberly announcing that he'd been compelled to return to London on urgent family business and would not be in Nice again until the following season.

I saw Frank Harris only once more: about six months later, hunched up over an apéritif at a table outside the Casino de la Méditerranée. His wife was with him; she caught sight of me and smiled, plucking at her husband's sleeve to attract his attention: Harris swivelled round in his chair and stared glassily about in search of a familiar face, but before his gaze could light on me, I had bowed frigidly—to Mrs Harris—and passed on.

Not long after, I heard that he had died, having first completed his life of Shaw; but I felt no emotion and never read the book: to me, for many years, the name of Frank Harris stood for treachery, hum-bug and—worst of all—humiliation: I wanted to put him wholly out of my mind. Now, as a middle-aged man, I can view the situation from a different angle: more than understand the stringent force that drove him on, leaving no leisure to help others or concentrate on anything save the task in hand; but at eighteen I had not yet felt the pressure of poverty or the annual erosions of time; sickness and anxiety sapping the body; the buzz of fatigue in the brain.

MEMOIRS
OF THE FORTIES

A quoi bon raconter une histoire qui ne porte pas en elle le poids inimitable du vrai? A quoi bon des mémoires imaginaires, de fausses anecdotes, des phrases qui se trompent de bouche, des souvenirs pittoresques?...Tout cela ne rend pas commode le travail de se souvenir et de matérialiser des fantômes. A ce jeu dangereux, à se retourner vers le passé qui flambe, on risque d'être changé en statue de sel, c'est-à-dire en statue de larmes.

Jean Cocteau
Portraits-souvenirs

AUTHOR'S NOTE

I am a professional writer as opposed to being a professional literary man, and those seeking scandal or inside accounts of literary politics, in which I have never taken part, would do well to look for them elsewhere.

At the same time, since writing is my business, I have come in contact with many people engaged in various branches of literary and artistic activity, and it has been my concern to portray them accurately in these pages.

I have an extremely good memory, and almost total recall where the actual material of conversations is concerned; my grasp of chronology, however, is much less exact, I cannot always remember dates, and it may well be that such and such a conversation did not take place on precisely the occasion where I have situated it. But that it took place on another, similar occasion, the reader has my word.

I have also attempted never to fall into the trap open to all writers of memoirs—i.e. to falsify an incident in the interest of making it a better story—for my further views on this, see the section entitled 'The Ham'.[1]

The book excluding prologue and epilogue covers roughly the years between 1940–49; and except for the early chapters, these recollections are not presented in strict chronological sequence—my method being to follow a train of events to its conclusion, or a person episodically through the length of our acquaintance, even if this meant moving into the Fifties—a decade I could well have done without.

J.M.-R.
London 1964

---

1 This section was never completed.

PROLOGUE

Meeting a Publisher

*   *   *

ACROSS THE CLASSROOM STRETCHED A BANNER BEARING THE firm's motto:

'IT ALL DEPENDS ON YOU!'

In some branches, it was said, the pupils after graduation were required to sing every morning a paraphrase of the once-popular song called that, but none of us had graduated yet. In fact we were still on the first day of the course, though this was now drawing to a close.

On the dais beneath the banner our instructor, spectacled, dapper, and dressed like something in the City, was completing his lecture on the Three Types of Dirt.

'And, most insidious enemy of all, Dangerous Destructive Germ-laden Grit,' he said (the two other types were dust and fluff, which included clinging litter). 'Tomorrow morning when we are again assembled, I will explain the Science of Positive Agitation, which may be summed up by our slogan It Beats as It Sweeps as It Cleans, and which is the only satisfactory method of combating all three types of dirt. Thank you gentlemen. Tomorrow at 9 a.m. please,' and soon I was clattering downstairs with other members of what an American author would undoubtedly describe as the Class of '38.

I was there because I had answered an advertisement which began INTELLIGENT MEN WANTED, and found out too late that it meant learning to sell vacuum cleaners. The firm, however, paid an advance of £2–10s and the fare to London, find your own digs, so I'd enrolled at the training school.

Outside it was April in Regent Street. I emerged from a building where a car park now stands instead. Next door was a coffee house with wheels turning in the window where sandwiches of hot ham on rye could then be obtained by those able to afford them, unlike myself. Diagonally on my right was Broadcasting House where I was later to have a promising but currently unproductive interview with the Assistant Director of Drama, at that time Moray McLaren. The clock in its tower said 6 p.m., and I flagged a taxi which I could not afford either, so as to be in time for my interview with Mr Jonathan Cape.

I had high hopes of this meeting, for Mr Cape had replied personally concerning the short stories which I'd sent him, asking me to call at the office when I was next in London; and on the telephone that morning, when I explained that I was unable for business reasons to reach him before six in the evening, he had agreed to spare me half an hour, after which he was due to attend a publishers' cocktail party.

Almost immediately my taxi stopped, chugging in a stream of traffic by the lights at the corner of Mortimer and Great Portland Streets— the meter ticked money and minutes away, and I feared Mr Cape would give me up as a bad job. I was unaware that we had halted right outside the public house called the George, where I was to spend much time when writing for the BBC in the 1950s, and that by walking in there I stood a much better chance of being signed up to write scripts by some radio producer than by having a hundred interviews at executive level.

My ignorance in those days was staggering. I had not been at Oxford or Cambridge, had no useful connections, and failed completely to realise that all one had to do at this period, according to the auto-biographical pieces which various writers published later, was to ask at the office of a literary weekly for books to review, or simply to hang around Bloomsbury bookshops or Fleet Street pubs until engaged in conversation by some influential type. I believed that one had actually to produce something before being received anywhere of consequence.

I had in fact been received by Norman Collins, then deputy chair-man of Victor Gollancz Ltd, but only after submitting a novel which was too far out for his firm and probably no good at that, though he thought the dialogue showed promise. This was three years before, in 1935, so Jonathan Cape would not be my very first publisher.

I went to see Norman Collins on the day Italy declared war on Abyssinia, and newspaper placards announcing this event stood on every corner as I picked my way through mud, slime and cabbage stalks in Covent Garden. Collins, pleasant, pipe-smoking, and only a few years my senior, though he'd already been novel critic for the *News Chronicle* and was the author of a critical work called *The Facts of Fiction*, greeted me jovially with his feet up on the desk, and we talked about our respective enthusiasms, Arnold Bennett and Evelyn Waugh, above the rattle of typewriters, separated by only a flimsy matchboard partition from other offices beyond.

Very soon after, Collins's own second novel *The Three Friends* appeared and began to establish him as a potential bestseller. I too embarked on a second novel as he had urged me. In the middle of it I developed mumps and I well remember his ribald letters about the possible consequences of this disease if contracted in adult life, though luckily in my case no such complications supervened. After three weeks in bed reading Thomas Wolfe, my legs would hardly support me across the room, but nonetheless I despatched to Henrietta Street my novel which could not have been less like Thomas Wolfe. Though today it might have been accepted as a Black Comedy, there was no label to tie on it then and back it came. Norman Collins held out some hope of getting it done if the ending were altered to one less macabre, I haughtily refused this compromise, and twenty years later I was the first script-writer he employed when his Independent Television Company was launched, though I didn't last long at that either.

The taxi drew up at 30 Bedford Square, after circling for a while the wrong side, and the door swung open at my touch as I'd been told to expect. But it also closed behind me with a hollow boom and a decisive click, the catch must have somehow fallen, and to my dismay I could not get it open again. The staff had evidently left, there was no time to be lost, and again as directed I sped up the stairs in search of Mr Cape.

He rose tall from behind a big broad desk in a large high-ceilinged room the beauty of which was perceptible even to one in my flustered state. White-haired with a strong square face arranged in kindly folds like an elderly American judge, the sort who on the screen tries to administer justice despite the corrupt encroachment of industrial civilisation, and wearing a judge's square-cut sober black. Bookshelves round the walls framed him like a film-set, with a long window back-centre beyond.

He spoke slowly and at first in formal measured phrases, but without the kind of accent such a judge would have had: he was in reality very English. The unhurried atmosphere of comfort surrounding him calmed me down at once, though his opening sentence was not exactly what I had hoped for.

'I'm not going to publish these stories I'm afraid,' he said, patting the green springback binder containing them which lay before him on the desk. 'To begin with there aren't enough to make a collection. As I daresay you know a prejudice exists in the trade against books under 70,000 words in length, and this applies especially to first volumes of short stories by young writers not yet established by publication of a novel.'

'I've written two novels, sir,' I said quickly as he paused. 'Unpublished and I wouldn't waste your time submitting them. But suppose I were to write more stories, to make up the length? I don't know if you've read any of these yourself…'

But Mr Cape had. It so happened they arrived as he was about to leave for the country, and the pale green linen-faced paper I'd typed them on had caught his attention. The colour green was restful for his eyes. So he took the stories home for the weekend and there he had read them all. On such extraordinarily slender chances, I was to learn, much in the literary world depended.

'Have you had many opinions on these?'

'Only one,' I said. 'The features editor of the local paper, on the South Coast where I live, promised to interest one of the directors at Chapman and Hall if he thought the stories were any good.'

'And did he?'

'He did not, sir.'

'What were his comments?'

'There was a whole page of them, none flattering, and headed "PLOTS —WEAK". He's a Fellow of the Royal Zoological Society too. Signs his articles FRZS.'

Mr Cape chuckled. 'Happily you've got a sense of humour.'

'I've been led to believe the contrary,' I said. 'I can laugh at myself all right, but I don't like anybody else doing so, therefore according to my friends I haven't a sense of humour.'

'Not bad at all,' Mr Cape chuckled again. 'We might use some quote like that on the blurb of your book.'

'So there's going to be a book after all?' I asked eagerly: the case was apparently to be re-opened.

'We mustn't be in too much of a hurry,' Mr Cape admonished gently, and not until six years later did my first book appear under the Cape colophon—on the blurb was the bit about my having no sense of humour, and this was used by reviewers as a stick to beat me with ever after.

The book itself was certainly a collection of stories, but not those over which the publisher now bent his head, turning the green pages again as if re-examining the testimony of some key witness which might cause judgment to be reversed. I forced upon my face the dead-pan expression befitting a defendant determined to behave with dignity whatever the verdict; but as he closed the green folder and sat back for the summing up, the late afternoon sunlight framed in the long window behind him swam out of focus—isolated words only penetrated a sudden hush inside my head.

I heard 'Talent', 'Achievement', even 'Professional', though this proved to refer to the actual typing of the MSS. Sight and sound came rushing back. The sunlight steadied, shining it seems to me now on spring-green leaves, though at this remove of time I cannot be certain. It seems unlikely that trees could be seen from this side of the house.

Mr Cape was smiling paternally—the case had gone after all in my favour, or sentence was at any rate suspended, 'Have you tried the weeklies or magazines at all?' he was asking.

'Wouldn't the bad language be too much of a barrier?' I said. 'The FRZS was shocked to the core.'

'Luckily I seldom go to the Zoo,' Mr Cape smiled. 'I've no objection to language myself, used properly for purposes of realism. There are only two words I have to draw the line at, and those are Fuck and Cunt.'

'Shit?' I said hopefully.

'We've had shit in several times, that's no trouble, but Fuck and Cunt they just won't print, though young men are always trying. How old are you by the way?'

'I'll be twenty-six in July.'

Mr Cape slowly nodded, as at some further extenuating evidence. 'And, forgive me asking, have you any private means?'

'If I have,' I said, 'they're kept private even from me.'

'But you've got a job?'

'I'm at a sort of Technical Training College,' I replied, careful not to let on precisely what technique I was learning.

'Then stick to whatever it is,' Mr Cape advised me. 'For the time being anyway. Because I warn you there's no money to be made out of short stories. Authors can't readily be made to understand that. Take Liam O'Flaherty for instance.'

'One of my favourite writers.'

'Oh, magnificent I grant you. But he simply will not realise that all his books don't earn a fortune. Those tales about birds and animals, best things he's done, what did they bring in? He used to call round the Accounts Department wanting ten pounds cash, and if it wasn't immediately forthcoming he'd tap his raincoat pocket and say "I've got a gun in here". The accountants usually forked out, not that there were any royalties due.' He chuckled again, and from then on his speech became more informal and relaxed—the judge, once down from the dais, was a citizen of the world.

'Doesn't O'Flaherty tell that story himself?' I said. 'Only in his version he places a bomb on the publisher's desk.'

'Well he never put a bomb on mine, though I've frequently been threatened with the pistol. Don't suppose he had one on him at all if I'd called his bluff, or if he had he wouldn't have used it. He's really a very nice fellow O'Flaherty. Who are your other favourite writers?'

Many of these were published by Jonathan Cape, and we spoke of Arthur Calder-Marshall, who had done successfully in some of his work what I was trying to do—namely to create a completely English equivalent to the American vernacular used by such writers as Hemingway, Cain and O'Hara, concentrating in my case mainly on the middle and lower-middle classes, an area cornered so far by V.S. Pritchett and Patrick Hamilton. We spoke of H.E. Bates, in those days working along similar lines, Ralph Bates, whose volume *Rainbow Fish* included a great short novel 'Dead End of the Sky', and the strange *Novel on Yellow Paper* by Stevie Smith, which had brought me out in a rash of annoyance when Mr Cape published it two years before.

'Ah yes, Stevie. She used to work for me you know.' The chuckle had become a chortle now. 'I can see why you wouldn't like her stuff, all the same a clever girl you must admit.'

'Hanging by a sisal twist over the darkening void,' I quoted, 'lit by an electric blue flash: that's where the souls of smarties go?'

'You've left some out but still it's stuck in your memory,' Mr Cape said. 'The trouble is, she's intensely feminine and you, well frankly you're not. It'd never do for you to meet, you'd fight like cat and dog,' but many years later, when I'd re-read *Novel on Yellow Paper* and formed an opinion diametrically opposed to the one that I held then, I did meet Stevie Smith in the saloon bar of that very George outside which my cab got hung up on the way to Mr Cape, and we didn't fight like cat and dog. Quite the reverse. I quoted to her, this time in full, her own passage about the souls of smarties and the sisal twist, also what Mr Cape had said, and we agreed that for once he had been wrong. I found Miss Smith charming and delightful, and she was kind enough to say she wished she'd known me when I was young.

But that day in the office I said: 'An ultra-feminine Saroyan is a gruesome thought, God wot,' which brought us round to Faulkner, whom Mr Cape had also known.

'In fact I published him, over in the States. Our New York branch did *Sanctuary*, though Chatto and Windus brought it out over here because they'd a contract as his British publishers. Faulkner wrote it while he was working as a night-watchman, and when I'd read the typescript I said to him: "This is all very well, but I'd like to know more about Popeye's background, where he came from and so on, also why he's impotent like this". And Faulkner said: "Why it's all there in the first chapter, all about his parents and childhood". Well I looked back through the first chapter but damned if I could find anything like that except that Popeye was scared of birds, so then Faulkner himself had a look. "By God," he said, "If I haven't forgotten to write it after all!"'

The telephone at Mr Cape's elbow interrupted, and he said: 'Yes, speaking. Oh, I'm afraid I will be late. Delayed at the office, sorry. Later on, perhaps,' and cradling the phone: 'only the cocktail party people ringing up'.

I made hastily to rise but he waved me down. 'They'll have to wait. Besides, I'm getting too old to enjoy parties nowadays. What was I saying now?'

'Faulkner had left out the part about Popeye's childhood. It comes at the end actually.'

'I'm getting to that. He went off back to his watchman's shack and over a jug of corn liquor got out the missing chapter. But by that time the book was being printed, and we couldn't fit it in at the beginning, so Faulkner said: "Let's put it in last and the hell with them". So that's how the book comes to be constructed like that. Faulkner was most apologetic about it, couldn't think how it had come to slip his mind. Charming, quiet chap. Exquisite Southern manners. Only one foot, lost the other flying with the RFC. I've good reason to remember him, I had terrible dysentery all through that trip to the States. Thought it was ordinary diarrhoea at first, due to the change of diet, but no it was dysentery right enough. Made everything so awkward, having to run and relieve one's bowels in the middle of board meetings you know.'

'Most embarrassing sir,' I said, as he got up from his chair. 'I'm sorry to have kept you for so long.'

'It's been a pleasure,' Mr Cape said, handing my green springback folder across the desk. 'Oh and you'd better have this too': a new novel in its packet, *Serenade* by James M. Cain. 'An interesting experiment, the narrator's an opera singer but Cain makes him tell the story like a sailor off the boat. It's not out yet, and this may be your last chance of getting a copy before some prurient fool takes exception to the subject and the ban goes up.' However, I mustn't spoil it for you,' and though I protested he insisted on coming all the way downstairs to operate the complicated lock on the outer door, otherwise I might still be there.

Jonathan Cape has been dead for some time now, but I have never forgotten the white head and charcoal black suit, the tall spare figure standing on his doorstep in Bedford Square, one hand raised to wave good-bye and point the way to where I could best catch my bus. It was the only time we ever met, and though there was friction with his firm in after-years, I'd no quarrel with Mr Cape himself, nor was he to blame.

That evening I remember he said, apropos of what I can't recall, 'I will never publish a detective thriller unless it's as good as Dashiell Hammett's *Maltese Falcon*,' and as we shook hands by the door: 'When you've got enough stories together, address them to me personally, and if I'm away on business at the time, I'll arrange for William Plomer, who's one of our readers, to make a report pending my return, if that's all right for you?'

I walked away, as the saying goes, on air; but getting off the bus I was suddenly taken short. It may have been Mr Cape talking about his attack of dysentery that brought it on or simply just excitement. My digs in St George's Square were several streets away, but Victoria Station stood close at hand.

On one wall of the cubicle I entered a member of the BUF had scrawled: 'NO LOUSY JEWS OR COMMUNISTS ALLOWED IN HERE'. On the other, a sensualist had more carefully inscribed: 'THE SIGHT OF SCHOOLGIRLS KNEES IS HORNY'. On the third wall, above the lavatory bowl, a metal box exhorted me to 'BUY A SANI-SEAT! YOUR PROTECTION AGAINST INFECTION. INSERT ONE PENNY.'

One cannot be too careful, especially with Fascists about. Before sitting down between the perverted and the politically conscious, I dropped a penny in the Sani-Seat slot.

---

1   Mr Cape was unduly pessimistic here. *Serenade*, a study in crypto-homosexuality, was never banned — indeed it was afterwards made into a sort of Hollywood musical, with all the queerness omitted and Mario Lanza in the leading rôle.

Excursion in Greeneland

*   *   *

ONE DAY IN 1956 I WAS WALKING HOME WITH A FRIEND WHO LIVED off Clapham Common when pointing to a gutted ruin with a façade of blackened brick he said: 'That used to be a Queen Anne house before the blitz. Beautiful place I believe. It belonged to Graham Greene.'

'I know,' I said. 'I lunched there once. In 1938,' and my friend was suitably impressed.

It was noon and summer when I arrived at that house eighteen years before, aged twenty-six and carrying a copy of *Brighton Rock* wrapped in a *Daily Express* containing James Agate's review of the novel which had appeared that morning. I had not found the house easily since there are three tube-stations and three sides to the Common, Clapham Common North, Clapham Common South, and Clapham Common West, and I am incapable of telling which is which without the help of a compass. I did not carry a compass. I had moreover mislaid Graham Greene's letter which gave precise directions for getting to his house.

I would like to be able to describe the beauty of the exterior before it was blitzed, but at the time I was too busy mopping sweat from my face and then swishing dust from my shoes with the handkerchief to take anything in. The door came open suddenly and an elderly housekeeper glared at me in a manner with which, since I sold vacuum cleaners for a living, I had of late become only too familiar. But I had also learned to stand my ground in face of unspoken opposition.

'Could I see Mr Graham Greene please?'

She said: 'We don't want anything today, thank you.'

I said: 'He's expecting me to lunch.'

'Oh. Well why didn't you say so then. Come in.' We entered a hallway and the housekeeper, having pointed silently to a short flight of stairs, was obviously making off to her own quarters when I said: 'Perhaps you'll tell Mr Greene I'm here.'

'He's out. You'll have to wait. The drawing-room's up there. Can't be taking people up all those stairs at my age you know,' and she disappeared banging a door: an old family retainer and a character to boot, as befitted the household of a writer.

The drawing-room stood open at the top of the stairs: it was the house itself. Perhaps it was the kind called a Bijou house, I wouldn't know. Someone like Denton Welch would have been able to describe the interior and enumerate the articles of period furniture which I'm told it contained, but this bit is quite beyond me. The armchair I sat down in seemed like any other armchair, though rather low, and I saw immediately in a bookcase nearby the works of Joseph Conrad, which didn't come as a surprise.[1] Also Henry James. I'd have dearly liked a smoke, but the cigarettes I carried were Brazilian, the packet done up in a twist of yellow paper and picturesque to look at, but very pungent, and they didn't seem the right sort to be smoking in these rather fragile surroundings, also what would the housekeeper say if she caught me stinking out her drawing-room?

I stood up and my reflection in a looking-glass confronted me. Not to my mind that of a salesman, nor was I wearing the official uniform of raincoat and porkpie hat: nonetheless the housekeeper hadn't been deceived. She'd known by instinct that I was only a commercial of some kind masquerading as a luncheon guest. Suppose, despite the stairs, she suddenly came up demanding credentials?

I had written to Graham Greene asking permission to adapt his Entertainment *A Gun for Sale* as a radio play and he had replied cordially inviting me to lunch. I now searched my pockets frantically for his letter, while realising that I had left it on my dressing table at my digs. My digs were on the South Coast. The letter was on grey paper with envelope to match, in a small neat handwriting abounding in Greek Es.

I glanced round and as I did so Graham Greene himself appeared quite silently in the open doorway. I was startled because not even a creak on the stairs had announced his approach. Seeing me there gave him also a start, and he took a step back. He was wearing a brown suit

---

1   *The Secret Agent* turned out to be a favourite book of his, whose influence can be traced by comparing Conrad's Assistant Commissioner with Greene's in *It's a Battlefield*.

and large horn-rimmed spectacles, which he at once snatched off as if they had been his hat. He was not wearing a hat and this was the only time I saw him wearing spectacles. I had not expected him to be so tall.

'I hope you haven't been waiting long,' he said. He had a spontaneous pleasant smile. 'Nobody told me you were here. Would you like a cigarette? Something to drink?'

'Something cold if possible,' I said, accepting the cigarette avidly.

Greene said: 'We could go over to the local, if you won't find that a bore. They'll have ice there, and anyway I've forgotten to get in the beer.'

Each carrying a large jug, we set off for the pub which was on the other side of the Common and may have been the one afterwards featured in *The End of the Affair*. Greene took long lounging strides and his shoulders were well above mine as we walked across the grass. Though very lean he had high broad straight shoulders from which his jacket was loosely draped as if still on its hanger.

He said: 'I've just been asked to do a radio play myself, so I'm relying on you to show me how to write them.'

'I fear I'll not be much use. I've only written one so far and they wouldn't have that.' Then fearing that sounded too much like a total obscurity and failure, in fact the truth, I added: 'They did offer me a job on the strength of it though.'

'At the BBC?'

'Training to be a writer-producer, eventually.'

'Then obviously your play impressed them. Why wouldn't they take it?'

'Too sordid, was the general opinion.'

'Bloody fools. Well they can't say that about mine. It's to be about Benjamin Jowett, the Master of Balliol, you know.'

'Never explain never apologise?' I said, hoping I'd got it the right way round.

'That among other things,' Greene said. 'Are you going to take the BBC job?'

'When there's a vacancy. But I was warned I might have to wait a year.'

'What d'you do meantime? Besides writing radio plays I mean.'

'I sell vacuum cleaners,' I said.

Greene, almost on the threshold of the pub, halted abruptly and turned to take a good look at me. Unlike the housekeeper, it was clear that he'd not suspected this, 'Vacuum cleaners?' he said.

'Yes.'

'Are you doing it to get material?'

'No, I'm doing it because I wouldn't have any money otherwise.'

'But do you earn much as it is?'

'I don't do bad at the moment. Eight to ten quid a week.'

Greene said: 'Good for you,' plainly surprised, and we entered the pub, which I remember as a big empty barn-like place where he ordered two large scotches with ice while the beer jugs were being filled.

He said: 'I thought of signing on myself at one time. To write a book about it afterwards of course. I never knew one could actually sell the things.'

It would have taken too long and been too boring to explain the various rackets by which selling was really done, and I simply said: 'You wouldn't have enjoyed it much.'

He said: 'Well it doesn't matter now. Because you'll be writing your own book I expect?'

This honestly had not occurred to me. I hardly ever recognise material in my immediate situation or in any events which are still going on, nor would I ever choose any course of action deliberately in order to write about it. But this, I thought then, was the difference between amateur and professional, though that wouldn't be altogether my opinion today.

So I said: 'I expect I will. Sooner or later,' getting out my Brazilian cigarettes, and nine years in fact went by before I did publish a book on the subject.

Greene said: 'Oh splendid,' fumbling in the yellow pack with MENZALA on the green band around it. 'I'm off to Mexico shortly, so I must get used to smoking this type of tobacco.'

'They're rolled in real rice-paper,' I told him, but I noticed that he soon let his burn out tactfully in an ash tray on the bar.

'Mexico sounds exciting,' I said. 'To get copy for your work?' I was learning the language fast.

'A kind of travel book,' he said, the ice slid down the empty glasses and we were given the beer jugs, containing some sort of strong pale ale, to carry back across the Common.

'Not too heavy for you?' Greene asked anxiously as we halted midway to mop our faces in the noonday heat.

I said: 'It's childsplay compared to lugging one's dem-kit about.'

'Dem-kit?' Greene said, immediately alert at a technical expression he had not heard before.

'The suitcase containing the demonstration machine. It weighs a ton on its own.'

Greene said: 'One of your chaps who called at the house once carried the detachable parts of his cleaner in a golfbag. Rather enterprising of him I thought, and I suppose less heavy. I used it in a novel of mine.'

'*England Made Me*,' I nodded, and the Queen Anne façade came in sight not a bit too soon. The housekeeper was in the hall and Greene handed her the jugs of beer with instructions to keep it cool, which didn't please her at all.

In the upstairs drawing-room my advance copy of *Brighton Rock* was the first thing I caught sight of, which reminded me to thank him for having it sent to me.

'I brought along this review by Agate, though I expect you've already seen it,' I added, unconscious of the dreadful clanger I was dropping, for Agate compared the ending to that of Stevenson's *Ebb-Tide*, which I'd not then read but in which the villain's own vitriol explodes identically in his face.

Greene, however, merely asked: 'Do you know Agate's brother?'

'No. I don't know Agate himself either.'

'The brother's much less pompous. More amusing. He's rather ill at the moment though. In fact I've got to go and see how he is later on today.' He glanced at the review again and chuckled: 'The old boy of course has completely missed the point It's the theological aspect that's baffled him, I've never brought it in before.'

'The Boy being a Catholic and so on?'

He nodded. 'Half of them won't understand and those who do will hate it.'

'Perhaps the Catholic critics,' I began, but he said with every evidence of delight: 'They'll probably be the worst of all.'

'You are yourself a Catholic?' I asked: it must be remembered that much less was known about the author personally in those days, and I'd been unable to obtain so far the semi-autobiographical *Journey Without Maps*, which would have answered my question.

Greene said: 'Yes, I was converted in 1926.'

I said: 'I was baptised one in 1912,' which disconcerted him more than the vacuum cleaners. I suppose a salesman with literary ambitions was strange enough, but a cradle Catholic literary salesman bordered on the extravagant.

'In that case,' Greene said recovering, 'you must have enjoyed the bit in *Brighton Rock* with Sylvie in the Lancia.'

'I haven't got to anyone called Sylvie yet.'

'Oh well, you've that to come. Spicer's girl you see gets a sudden lech on the Boy, and she wants him to have a fuck in the back of a car.'

He shot me a piercing gunmetal glance to see my reaction to his use of the word, which itself was shot out like a bullet from the barrel of Raven's automatic: presumably as a Catholic I should have been shocked, but my face remained impassive.

'And does he fuck her?' I asked.

'No. You see when the girl asks him if he's got a French let ...' but at that moment his wife entered the room to announce that lunch was ready.

About the meal itself I remember nothing, except that the dining-room was rather dark; the blinds may have been drawn against the sun and it's possible that we had lemon pudding as a sweet. The house-keeper did not appear in person: heralded by shouts up a shaft, the dishes were borne from below by a dumb waiter and Greene himself went round pouring out the beer. Mrs Greene, handsome with black hair, was placid and sedate like a young Spanish matron, and even the repeated crash of the dumb waiter arriving at its destination in the serving hatch failed to shake her poise.

From time to time she left the table for brief periods. When she returned from each sortie her husband raised inquiring eyebrows and she nodded reassurance, but the last time she murmured something that I didn't catch; and when we rose from the table Greene said to me apologetically: 'It's an awful nuisance, but They are asking to see you I'm afraid. I wonder if you'd mind.'

'Why of course not,' I said mystified. 'I'd like to see Them very much.'

'I'm sorry but we'll get no peace otherwise,' he said, leading the way up another, darker flight of stairs; I could hear a strange twittering sound coming from behind the door in front of which he halted.

'By the way,' I asked slightly nervous, 'What are They?' imagining giant parrots or pet vultures brought from Africa, or even elderly female relatives not quite certifiable but confined nevertheless to their rooms.

'They are in here,' Greene said, opening the door for me to precede him, and I found myself facing a large railed cot raised off the floor to about the level of my chest. From behind the bars of this cage two small, extremely pretty blonde children peered out at me unblinking. They were perhaps aged four and five, and it's a sobering thought that they must be over thirty now.

'Well, come on,' Greene said from behind me, 'Say hullo politely.'

He was addressing the children actually, but I managed a ghastly smile and a subdued Hullo. The children did not reply. Without speaking they continued to stare intently through their bars. Then to my surprise, and perhaps that of their father, they started slowly to grin, and the youngest gave a sort of gurgle.

'He looks nice Daddy,' the elder one called out encouragingly, thus haunting me for weeks with shame, for few young men in their middle twenties are sold on looking nice and I was no exception.

'That'll do,' their father said. He explained to me: 'They insist on seeing everyone who comes to the house before They'll settle down,' and to the children: 'Shut up now and have your sleep.'

They both called out Good-bye as we left and giggles pursued us downstairs to the drawing-room where coffee and the rest of the beer awaited us on a tray: Mrs Greene had passed us on her way up to enforce Their afternoon rest.

'Lovely children,' I said, 'charming' in the hearty voice used by my father when he'd survived a social ordeal, and I was further relieved to see Greene had a brandy bottle in his hand.

He said: 'Who was it complained that not enough children get murdered in detective stories?' pouring me a large measure.

'A reviewer called Cyril Connolly,' I said. 'Thanks.'

'I expect you need it,' Greene said. 'There's that book of Philip MacDonald's of course, *Murder Gone Mad*, d'you know that one?'

'Plenty of kids get it there,' I agreed. 'A massacre of the innocents.'

Greene said: 'It was the old postmistress. With a swordstick disguised as an umbrella,' and over the coffee and brandy we discussed ruthlessness in the thriller, Greene's favourite example being from the initial *Four Just Men* by Edgar Wallace.

'D'you remember what they did to the Spanish priest who'd been guilty of Rape? When they condemned him to death he begged them to let him see a priest before the execution, and they showed him—a mirror!'

He had given full value to the capital 'R' in Rape and his eyes swivelled, glinting, towards me as when he'd told about Sylvie and the Boy. They had always an alert watchful quality, the eyeballs were slightly bloodshot, and one had a sense of tremendous energy and fun triumphing over inner fatigue.

I now had an opportunity to observe him more closely without staring, which I'd been brought up to believe was rude. He must have been thirty-four at the time, his lean face was un-lined then, but the skin was rough and little worn: though his cheeks were carefully shaven there was still a suggestion of stubble. He smiled a lot and the set of his mouth was amiable rather than severe as in the photographs. His lightish brown hair was parted at the side and brushed in a slight curl over a broad bumpy forehead. He sat forward in the low armchair with broad shoulders hunched up high and large knuckly hands hanging down with a cigarette fuming between the long fingers. I had offered him another Brazilian which, saying he'd been smoking far too much, he swiftly refused, then had stealthily taken one of his own. I don't know how he did manage out in Mexico.

We had passed on now to ruthlessness in films, how Hitchcock got away with it often despite the censorship and how Greene himself had tried and failed to slip a ruthless scene past British Lion while scripting for Korda in 1936. From there we arrived at Paramount's prospective film version of *A Gun for Sale* and who was to play the part of Raven: if made with an American star, then Bogart, Alan Baxter, or Greene's own personal choice Eduardo Ciannelli, the Trock Estrella in *Winterset*, about which we were both enthusiastic.

'Ciannelli lends distinction to any film,' I said.

'He does indeed.'

'No, no. I was quoting your own words. From a film article in *Night and Day*.'

'Oh, so you've read *Night and Day*.'

'Every issue.'

Night and Day had been an excellent sophisticated weekly magazine on *New Yorker* lines, edited by Greene and John Marks, the translator of Céline, and Greene had done the cinema criticism, which led to the magazine folding because some fool said that he'd libelled the child star Shirley Temple and there had been a case in court.

He said: 'I remember the article now. Wasn't it a review of *Marked Woman*, with Bogart and Bette Davis?' adding with relish: 'That was a pretty ruthless picture, where the henchman cuts the double-cross on Bette Davis's cheek.'

'Ciannelli was the Vice-Czar.'

'Lucky Luciano of course. Ninety-nine years in Sing-Sing.'

I said: 'You based your article on the resemblance between the city under gangster rule and the feudal system, Ciannelli being the latter-day equivalent of the Robber Baron.'

'I believe I did. Bogart as the crusading DA made the comparison actually, it was in the dialogue.'

'But you see,' I said, 'it wasn't.'

We had finished the coffee and the brandy and were now drinking up the remainder of the beer. It was, perhaps, not an awfully wise mixture and may have gone slightly to my head: the contradiction slipped out before I could bite it back.

'But surely,' Greene was saying, 'I remember perfectly. After one of his witnesses refused to talk, Bogart said: "It's feudal".'

'No I'm sorry. He didn't say that.' It was too late to stop now, and I continued gently: 'I went to the film just after reading your article and I was waiting for him to say it. But what he really said was "It's futel".'

'Futel? But what does it mean?'

'It's how Americans pronounce "futile".'

Greene stared at me for a moment then began to shake with laughter. The fact that he had based a whole careful piece of social criticism on a single misapprehended word seemed to fill him with genuine glee. I was relieved that he took it like that: many a writer not so well equipped with a sense of humour would have thought I was trying to score off him, which is the last thing I had in mind.

Now he began to tell me about the Shirley Temple libel case, which he evidently found less hilarious than his error about the feudal system, but accepted all the same with ironical detachment. Apparently he'd been abroad and incommunicado at the time, and returned to find the proceedings all wrapped up and judgment given against him, together with the censure of the judge.

'Two libel suits one after the other,' he said. 'There was a case about my Liberian book *Journey Without Maps* too and Heinemann's had to withdraw the whole edition, so that it seems to have been my unlucky year.'

'I've never been able to get *Journey Without Maps*,' I said after expressing my indignation: before this there had been the *Glastonbury Romance*/John Cowper Powys case and the *People in Cages*/Helon Ashton case, and as a prospective novelist I was naturally concerned. 'You don't happen to have a copy do you?' Greene began to shake his head. 'Just to borrow,' I added quickly. 'I wasn't asking you to give me one.'

'If I could of course I'd give you one,' he said. 'But honestly there's not a single copy in the house, they've all gone one way or another. I'm trying to get hold of the book myself.'

Frankly I didn't believe this, I believed that every author was well stocked up with copies of his own works; and it was not for many years, when I'd published several books myself, that I realised the fallacy of such an idea, more especially if the book in question has been officially withdrawn. But at the time I regretted having asked, and changed the subject swiftly to what I was really there for: namely the radio adaptation.

Greene said: 'Of course you'll have to clear it with Paramount, they bought the rights, including radio, before publication you see. That's just a formality though, they won't raise any objection. I'll drop the London office a line straightaway.'

'But first,' I said, 'there are some technical points, concerning the play itself, that I'd like to consult you about,' and he folded his fingers together to listen. Time and place, I explained, were easily conveyed by sound alone: Christmas carols being sung by the drunken reporters, newsboys shouting the threat of war and so on. 'But Raven's hare lip. The listeners can't see it, and characters would hardly comment on it to his face.'

Greene said: 'But they would behind his back. In the Corner House for instance, while he's waiting for Cholmondley to pay him for the murder. One waitress could say to another, "Ugh, he ain't arf an ugly bastard. That 'air lip of his makes me want to retch."'

'Excellent. Would "retch" be right for a girl of this sort, though?'

Greene said: '"Makes me want to vomit"?'

'How about "fair turns me stomach up"?'

'That's it.'

I said: 'Then another problem. How does Raven find out Cholmondley's going to Nottwich? Hanging about the station like he does in the book is visual stuff, so it'll have to be put over some other way.'

Greene said: 'Cholmondley could drop his railway ticket. In the Corner House again, when he takes out his wallet. Then Raven would also know which station he's leaving from.'

I said: '"Ought to be more careful dropping your ticket Mr Cholmondley. You don't want to pay the rail fare to Nottwich twice"?'

'Something like that, yes.'

These exchanges gave me an idea of the speed at which his trained mind worked: I would have taken days, perhaps weeks, to overcome such minor obstacles. Soon all the minor points had been thrashed out and we engaged in a discussion about the way in which Raven ought to speak.

'In the sort of voice some East End Jews have got,' was Greene's opinion. 'Not exactly a lisp, not quite guttural, in between the two.'

'But Raven isn't Jewish.'

'No, but he'd have a voice like that. Lots of Londoners do.' He told me that, when he worked for Korda, he had been taken round various clubs in the King's Cross area by a cameraman with underworld connections, and it was there that he had heard voices of the type he meant.

'In one place the regulars only drank milk. It was owned by a great fat homosexual known as the Giant Pander,' he spelt it out for me and laughed at the pun, 'but the customers weren't queer. Very tough looking, razor scars and all that, but quiet. Very quiet, I asked if the milk was laced with brandy or anything, but they said no. Straight milk. Made it much more sinister, I thought.'

'Is that where you got the idea of the Boy not drinking?' I asked, in an attempt to manœuvre him into talking of his own work, but he replied Perhaps, he hadn't really thought.

'D'you think you'll write any more Entertainments?' was my next question; for *Brighton Rock* was first published as one, as such despite the Catholic angle I considered it, and only much later did it become a Novel and later still a Modern Classic.

'I might,' Greene answered. 'Just one more. Based on an original idea I started to work on for Korda, only his outfit thought it would be too dangerous to film. About a Spanish Government agent who comes to London on a mission during the Civil War and finds that the war has followed him here.[1] I try to restrict myself to home ground if I can, English backgrounds, London whenever possible: I've always made that a rule.'

South America, Istanbul, Stockholm, the Gold Coast, and now Mexico went rapidly through my mind, I could hardly let this pass, but before I could speak Greene said: 'Oh I know, I've broken the rule several times. But all the same I think an English novelist should write about England, don't you?'

---

1 Later published as *The Confidential Agent*, 1939.

Presumably They had settled down at last upstairs, for Mrs Greene came in to join us, though not in the conversation. She sat in the armchair facing her husband, but turned sideways to him, with her legs tucked under her. She busied herself with head bent over some piece of needlework: embroidery, brocade, it may have been but not, I think, knitting.

I remember her speaking twice only: once was when we were talking about American short-story writers and Greene said: 'You liked Saroyan, didn't you darling?'

She looked puzzled and said: 'Saroyan?'

'You know, the Armenian.'

'Oh yes,' she said. 'The one who isn't Michael Arlen.'

The second time she spoke was to remind her husband that the time was half-past four. Greene glanced at his watch and sprang up with an exclamation. I rose also, saying: 'James Agate's brother?'

'Yes. I'll walk you to your bus.'

On the way up the High Street, past twopenny libraries and plate glass shops, he told me several anecdotes about the brother, but I remember none of them. The brandy, the beer and the heat had hit me as we left the house and I was struggling with a question in my muddled head. Would it be an imposition if I asked Greene to look at the short stories which I'd written?

There he stood, sympathetic and friendly, stooping slightly at my side, a soft wide-brimmed dented hat, like those worn by newspapermen in the movies, tilted to the back of his head. To neglect such an opportunity, of obtaining the opinion of a man whose work I so much admired, would be simply foolish and in a rather muzzy voice, as we waited by the bus stop, I made my halting request.

'Of course, I'd be glad to read them,' Greene said.

'Only difficulty, I'm going abroad tomorrow.'

'Mexico?'

'No, an assignment for *The Times*. But if you're not in a terrible hurry, you could send them on the day before I get back,' he gave me the date when he expected to return, 'and I'll let you know very quickly what I think.' My bus was approaching and I signalled it to stop. 'Good luck with the housewives meantime,' he called out as I climbed aboard.

'Prospects is what we cleaner-salesmen call them,' I told him. On the top deck I fell asleep and was woken by the conductor way past the stop; then in the train going back to the small South Coast town not far from Brighton itself, I realised I'd forgotten to ask Greene to sign my copy of *Brighton Rock*, which was the reason why I'd brought it with me.

The prospects kept me fully occupied during the following week, a love affair that had never properly begun was coming to an end, and on the day it ended I received a letter from the BBC expressing interest in my proposed version of *A Gun for Sale*: by the same post came a contract from Paramount Pictures several unpunctuated pages long which, deciphered, allowed me to retain any fees from the radio play in return for their right to use in the film anything they fancied from my adaptation.[1] I signed this contract and posted it back with the uneasy feeling that, not having read all the small print, I might somehow have signed away my soul: at the same time the MSS of my stories went registered to Greene at Clapham Common.

A reply came very quickly, as indeed he'd promised. With eagerness I tore open the small grey distinctive envelope, but realised from the first line and a glance at the signature that the letter was not from Greene at all, but from his wife. An extraordinary similarity in the handwriting, due perhaps to the fact that they were cousins, had misled me.

Her husband had returned the night before, Mrs Greene wrote, extremely over-tired by his trip, and she felt it her duty to prevent him from becoming completely exhausted by taking on more than was necessary. She was sure that he would have liked to read my stories but she was also sure that I would understand why this would not be possible. She was therefore returning the MSS under separate cover, and signed herself Sincerely Vivien Greene.

I still have the letter somewhere.

---

1 The Paramount film version, re-titled *This Gun for Hire*, scripted by
  W.R. Burnett and set in America, starring Alan Ladd, Veronica Lake and
  Laird Cregar, was shown over here in 1942 and contained nothing from
  my adaptation.

Up the BBC and Down the Labour

*   *   *

MORAY MCLAREN, THEN ASSISTANT DIRECTOR OF DRAMA AT THE BBC, wore a flowing Lavallière cravat and grey hair flowed back from his brow into a mane at the back like a musician or concert pianist. He was stockily built and sat squarely above his desk as if he'd been built out of it as an extension of the wood.

I faced him from a chair set slightly lower than the desk, as is customary in the monastic cells of BBC executives. This was my second interview with Moray McLaren, the previous one being some months before when he'd talked about a job they might have for me in the future.

'Graham Greene's novel *A Gun for Sale*,' he was saying, 'is concerned with the possibility of war, almost brought about by unscrupulous armament manufacturers for purposes of profit, but averted just in time.'

'I know,' I said. I'd just adapted the novel for radio, and the type-script lay before him on the desk.

'The book is fiction,' Moray McLaren told me, 'but the international situation in sober fact is extremely precarious at the moment.'

I knew that too, but didn't want to interrupt him again. He continued: 'Not quite the best time to broadcast a play on this subject, perhaps,' and smiled benevolently.

I said: 'Does that mean you're going to turn it down?'

He answered mildly: 'Turn it down? Oh dear me, we haven't got to that stage yet. No decision at all has been reached so far, you only sent it in a week ago. These things have to go through a lot of channels, various opinions must be obtained and so on, first.'

'But you personally have read the script?'

'I have glanced through it, seems to be a very competent adaptation, but of course it must go to the Readers for their report, then Val Gielgud

207

the Director of Drama will want to see it if the reports are favourable,' another benevolent smile, 'and if the international situation permits of a production, why then we'll be able to decide.'

'But all this will take time?'

'Quite a bit of time, I'm afraid. It's August you know. The summer holidays. The Readers, some of them are away.'

He smiled: 'You're very lucky, yourself, living at the seaside all the year round, you don't have to take a holiday.'

'No,' I said. 'I can't afford to, either.'

'But you still have a job?'

'If you can call it that.'

'Jobs,' Moray McLaren said. 'Just what I wanted to talk to you about. Have you thought any more about the one I mentioned to you last time you came? Training to be a writer-producer for radio, you know.'

'Yes,' I said. 'I've thought about it quite a lot. Are there any vacancies?'

'Alas no, rather a long waiting list just now, but I take it you'd be willing to accept if a vacancy occurred?'

'Yes.'

'Good!' he exclaimed beaming, and made a note on his desk pad. 'Now we have all your particulars, but there's just one question I didn't go into last time you were here. The question of marriage.'

'Marriage?' I said perplexed.

'Yes, I forgot to ask if you were married.'

'I am married.'

'And,' he coughed delicately, 'do you live with your wife?'

'I don't quite see what,' I began, but he soothingly interrupted: 'I'm sorry, I have to ask these questions, it's vital to know the answers I'm afraid.'

I said: 'Very well. I don't live with my wife.'

He said: 'Separated or divorced?'

I said: 'Separated. By mutual consent.'

He said: 'D'you think a reconciliation is likely?'

I said: 'No I don't,' and Moray McLaren made another note.

'And are you going to divorce?' he asked.

'I hadn't thought about it. Why?'

'Well you see, divorces are allowed in the Corporation if they're discreet, but a really resounding one, well Sir John wouldn't care for that at all.'

'Sir John.'

'The Director-General.'

'I'll bear that in mind then,' I said. 'Not too resounding a divorce, otherwise to have one is all right?'

'Perfectly,' he smiled, we stood up to shake hands and the difference in our heights was rectified.

'As for this adaptation,' he added, 'I fear its fate is as much in Mr Hitler's hands as ours,' and I travelled back by train to the small seaside town where I was so lucky to live, and where I was greeted on the station platform by my vacuum cleaner supervisor with news of the impending sack.

'Almighty Christ old man where you been all day. Up the BBC? Jesus you'll be down the Labour soon, you're getting your cards.'

'Who says?'

'New Branch Manager, that's who,' Soapy the supervisor said. 'He's been over after your blood, that woman at Arundel put the squeak in and you're for the bleeding jump.'

'The woman we sold the secondhand cleaner to?' Flogging second-hand machines to prospects as a sideline is accounted an unforgivable sin in the cleaner world: as Soapy was well aware, which was why he'd been careful to use me as a front.

'The Arundel woman was your idea,' I said. 'You took half the cash, why aren't you for the jump yourself?'

'Have a heart old man, you don't expect me to take the can back, Christ I got a wife and kids.'

'You'd flog them too if they'd fetch enough for a couple of pints,' I told him, buying a copy of the local rag at the station bookstall which was just about to close, and over a brandy in the buffet looked down the Salesmen Wanted.

Refrigerators and floor polishers (too heavy to hawk around unless you had a car); clothes-on-credit (distributing leaflets at ten bob a week: a cheap advertising stunt for a newly-opened store); canvassing for a national newspaper (commission only, though it said £3); then water softeners and that was all. I didn't fancy softeners: you had to go round asking housewives 'How's your water?' and I hadn't the nerve for that.

I'd not offered Soapy a drink, though he had hung around in hopes, but I bought a baby Guinness for the old London-Irish porter who'd served in several regiments and four campaigns and could remember when my father was still alive. This didn't require a tremendous effort since my father, a man not readily forgotten for his physical size alone, had died only two years before; but the porter could also remember having hydrocele as a young recruit: an experience which he was not at all unwilling to recount.

One morning at reveille he'd gone to get out of his bunk and had straightaway fallen flat upon the floor: the weight of serous fluid on his testicles would not allow him to stand upright.

'Matter o' gravity,' he said wiping brown froth from his Old Bill moustache. 'Pulls you down, upsets the balance d'you see, all that water on your balls, it has to be let out,' and he went on with relish to describe the operation they'd performed on him: 'But it didn't stop me having kids, they got to take the leader out for that,' which brought Hitler back to mind and he ended up by saying: 'Ah well, way things are going, you'll be in the army soon yourself, I've no doubt.'

Next morning, as Soapy had predicted, I was down the Labour Exchange with my cards, which had duly arrived with a curt letter of dismissal from the Brighton Branch. I hadn't enough stamps to draw the dole, so filled up an Unemployment Assistance form and sat down to await the arrival of the Means-Test Man, who took his time in coming.

The Means-Test Man looked round the ground floor back bedsitting-room to which I'd shifted, wrote down 'Rent: ten shillings,' then asked: 'Any private income?' I said 'None'.

He wrote down 'Now destitute', then said: 'Sign here, you'll be hearing in due course,' and three weeks went by without a thing.

Meanwhile Munich came, and it began to look as if the Irish porter had been right about me going in the army. Sandbagging, ARP practice and gas practice with box-like respirators were going on all round; recruiting posters pointed an accusing finger: 'YOUR COUNTRY EXPECTS YOU' and suddenly it was all too much like *A Gun for Sale* to be entirely comfortable.

I'd naturally given up all hope of the adaptation being accepted: September 1938 was certainly no time to broadcast a play about a war engineered by unscrupulous armament manufacturers for purposes of etcetera.

And yet the war, as in Greene's book, was averted just in time (for another year at any rate) and on the Friday following Chamberlain's return I was summoned to the Labour, outside which a chap in the dole queue had fallen in a faint from hunger; and the Head Clerk, wearing bi-focals, a butterfly collar and grey Homburg hat, counted silver coins on the counter in front of me, flinging them down contemptuously as if paying off Judas: except that instead of thirty pieces I got only seventeen.

The man who'd fainted had been propped by his mates against the kerb; on the wall above was painted: 'DO NOT LOITER IN THE STREET TO THE ANNOYANCE OF THE RESIDENTS', and the queue stretched halfway down, shouting advice to the group around the fallen man while the Head Clerk from inside was bawling: 'Silence out there, please!' The man bled quietly by the kerb.

To cap it all, it was Armistice Day and pretty smiling girls sold poppies by the cenotaph where a service was being held and a robed clergyman spoke of Peace: 'The crisis is over,' but for me it was just beginning, and at the doorway of the digs my landlady waited, hand out for the rent.

Like the Head Clerk at the Labour, the landlady wore even in the house a hat pulled down to her eyes, but hers was of greenish felt. She always wore an old stained black dress and carpet slippers, even when she went outdoors, which wasn't often. Mostly she crouched over a gas ring in her back kitchen cooking kippers, the whole house was permeated with their smell; and by dint of eating this fish all day long, her dark leathery skin had begun to take on the smoked complexion of a kipper.

For me no food was provided, there were no facilities for cooking in the room, and she didn't even make the bed: I came to dislike this landlady more than any I've had since, which is saying a great deal.

I did not find hunger a good discipline as Ernest Hemingway, then my great hero, did according to his posthumous memoir of early life in Paris; moreover ten Tenners[1] a day, which were the most I could afford, seemed an inadequate cigarette ration for a man who as a rule smoked fifty normal size.

Nevertheless I wrote a short story which comprised the landlady, the Head Clerk, the Means Test and the man who'd fainted in the dole queue on Armistice Day; I called this 'Peace in Our Time', which I considered a nice ironic touch.

Editors didn't agree: the typescript came back quicker than any I'd ever sent out, and in fact it was never printed anywhere until I included it in my second collection of stories, by which time (1945) it was deemed, no doubt rightly, as dated or old hat. Meantime, having kept fine as usual for the crisis, it poured down outside with rain.

---

1 A small extremely cheap cigarette, then much in favour with the unemployed.

Returning home one really dark cold wet November day, having spent the afternoon in the public library which was warmer than my room, I stepped on two letters evidently delivered by the last post and still lying on the mat, both of them for me.

One envelope had 'British Broadcasting Corporation' printed in the left-hand corner, and tearing it open I read unbelievingly: 'Gun for Sale, pleasure in accepting, proposed fee 30 guineas, Moray McLaren'; in the hall looking-glass, beside the seaweed barometer, I could see steam rising from the sudden heat that rushed up into my rain-soaked scalp.

The second envelope, addressed in the handwriting of my mother, then still alive but hard-up herself and unable to help me much, crackled to the touch: despite everything she'd enclosed £2 in cash for me to buy some shoes.

Those that I had on squelched with the water they'd absorbed through holes as, cramming both letters into my overcoat pocket, I returned at top speed to the high-street, where at that time a fairly good pair could be bought for eight-and-six. Then, well shod once more, with new dry socks, carrying parcels full of food and cigarettes, I made for the level crossing near which a friend of mine called Jaeger had his flat.

C.K. Jaeger was the same age as myself and also wrote, but unlike me he'd actually had two stories published in *The Standard* and worked on the scripts of feature films, but this was all some years ago and now he too was on the dole.

That evening I arrived just as he was hurling downstairs the son of his landlord who had called for the overdue rent and been rather unwisely rude to Jaeger's wife. The falling body knocked one of the food parcels from my hand, and retrieving it I climbed towards the first floor, where Jaeger, tall and rangy in kilt and sporran, leaned by the landing rail.

'I am not a man of violence but that insolent git made me see red,' he said as the landlord's son stumbled away into the rain. 'I'm seriously thinking of giving these people notice, damned if I'm not.'

He'd been educated in Edinburgh and looked every inch a Scottish laird, although actually of Danish origin and born in Bradford. A picture of the Angel Gabriel, dressed also as a Scot and about to blow the bagpipes instead of his horn, hung above the chimney-piece in the living-room, where an enormous fire blazed and Jaeger's wife stood clutching a scarlet screaming baby who in the sixties became secretary to a BBC-TV script editor.

I gave my news; Jaeger at once produced a flagon of the horrid patent wine which for financial reasons he was forced to drink; the fags were proffered, the food was eaten, the baby bedded down for the night; then Jaeger said: 'You know, Julian, Lydia and I were thinking of moving to a bungalow up the other end, I don't really think we ought to stay here after that fellow's atrocious behaviour tonight. Why don't you kick-in and share with us?' and when I agreed enthusiastically to this plan: 'Splendid, that's all settled then. Now let's have a butcher's at that BBC letter, see when you can expect the cheque.'

'Thirty guineas,' I said, tendering the letter which in my excitement at its arrival I'd had no time to read myself, except in snatches.

Jaeger said: 'On acceptance, according to Jonah Barrington. But shouldn't it be fifty guineas for a play this length? Is that not the sum Jonah Barrington mentioned in his column?'

Jonah Barrington was radio correspondent for the *Daily Express*, and any statement made by an *Express* contributor was believed implicitly by Jaeger, who refused to talk to anyone in the morning until he'd finished reading William Hickey. Jonah Barrington had indeed quoted 50 guineas as the sum paid for a full length radio play by the BBC, and in consequence a page from a radio play in progress protruded from Jaeger's portable typewriter on a side table.

'There's Graham Greene's share to be deducted in this case, though,' I said.

'Oh of course, it says so here.' Then Jaeger, frowning down at the letter, said: 'Hold on a bit. You get 30 all right, but payable in two halves: 15 when you sign the contract, 15 on production. There's no contract enclosed and it doesn't say when production's going to be,' and stroking with a thin smile his small golden moustache, he added: 'You've not forgotten Mr Kilham Roberts?'

I said: 'My God you don't suppose?' and Lydia Jaeger, entering from the nursery, cried out: 'Oh not all that again!'

The name of Denys Kilham Roberts, MA, Barrister-at-Law and Secretary of the Society of Authors, was engraved indeed on all our hearts. At that time he edited a paperback miscellany, the very first to appear, called *Penguin Parade*, to which I'd submitted a story that had been, to everyone's astonishment including mine, accepted for a future issue.

A fee of £4 was proposed by the editor and, nugatory though it seems today, would have made all the difference then, since I'd just recovered from a nasty go of 'flu and had a doctor's bill to pay as well as rent.

I asked if the cheque could be sent off by return: in reply came a letter from Mr Kilham Roberts' secretary saying that payment was not made on acceptance; on publication then, I queried hopefully, but the secretary answered that they did not precisely pay on publication either.

I wrote asking for a definite date on which I could expect to receive the money, and received instead the typescript of my story back, with a note regretting that I was not prepared to abide by *Penguin Parade's* rule regarding payment (they still did not say what this consisted of).

I was incensed, believing with Mr Edmund Wilson that 'a piece of writing should be paid for on the nail ... and once accepted, should be printed,' though I had not then read the eminent critic's admirable *Literary Worker's Polonius*, in which this precept is cited as one of the duties of Editor to Contributor.

No reply was forthcoming to my enquiry as to whether Mr Kilham Roberts in his rôle as Secretary to the Society of Authors would approve of his alter ego's editorial procedure, and I passed the correspondence to a local solicitor for legal action. The solicitor wrote one letter on my behalf, received a short answer stating simply that Mr Kilham Roberts was a qualified barrister, and dropped the case in terror and confusion.

My mother, though herself sick and in need of cash, paid both doctor and solicitor, I was back where I started with no story published, and Denys Kilham Roberts has since been awarded the OBE.

That was the *Penguin Parade* story, with which both the Jaegers were abundantly familiar; but despite this experience I'd yet to learn the snags surrounding payment of any literary fee, and payment in full most particularly.

We examined the relevant clipping from Jonah Barrington's column: payment on acceptance, yes, but there was nothing said about it being in two halves. Jaeger advised me not to argue the toss: 'Better write asking for the contract straightaway, only go canny, you don't want this lot sending back the bloody script as well,' and write off I did that very night.

As a matter of fact our fears in this case were unjustified: having signed the contract I did receive a cheque for half the fee, though after a certain time since cheques are prepared by accountants who are busy men. It's true that nowadays machines do most of the work, but they cannot affix signatures as well: this involves human agency, and I've known the business directors of a well-known literary weekly take longer to sign a cheque than I took to write the entire article for which they were paying.

But this 15 guineas from the BBC was the first money I'd ever earned by writing, my pride and pleasure in it mitigated only by not receiving the lot at one go. Moreover, regarding the date of production Moray McLaren simply couldn't say: with this particular subject great care had still to be exercised in choosing a suitable date for the broadcast, but no doubt this would be within the year.

I moved into the Jaeger's new bungalow at the other end of town, bidding good-bye without regret to the smell of kippers and the green-hatted landlady: nonetheless, in a roundabout way she was responsible for my meeting a most intriguing character, G.S. Marlowe.

In the mid-Thirties G.S. Marlowe had published a remarkable first novel called *I am Your Brother*. This has been out of print for many years, copies of it now fetching £2 or more apiece among book collectors, but at the time it had not only a critical success but got into the bestseller lists as well: very surprisingly, for Marlowe's staccato cinematic style was in direct contrast to that used by most bestsellers of the day. Also, since by the very nature of the story delusions were often fused with reality and vaudeville humour with scenes of Gothic nightmare, it was not always easy to tell what the novel was about or how many of the incidents happened outside the mind of the protagonist.

It was the physical appearance of my former landlady which reminded me of this work, for she strongly resembles the repulsive mother of the schizophrenic young composer, shuffling and snuffling about the Soho markets in search of offal on which to nourish her other, perhaps imaginary, son: a monster product of maybe artificial insemination, who lived in an attic above his brother's studio and had to be fed raw liver and fairy stories once a day.

Having re-read *I am Your Brother*, I was struck by what a sensational radio play it would make: the episodic structure of short sections, cross-fading as it were one the other, seemed already designed for the sound medium, and I wrote asking the author's permission to adapt. Besides, even in those days 15 guineas did not last for ever, and after the acceptance of *A Gun for Sale* I imagined a career as a radio writer was opening up before me, and for a brief period it did: but in 1958, not '38.

Gabriel Marlowe, as he signed himself, replied promptly. A long friendly letter full of pertinent suggestions—a dynamo fading up, for example, to convey to the listener when the hero's delusions were about to overtake him—and concluding with an invitation to call on him in London.

Marlowe's flat was in Kensington, a brisk good-looking girl whom he introduced as his secretary poured us glasses of scotch, heavy curtains shut out the dark rainy residential street, and the central heating was very comforting after the cold outside.

I had formed from reading Marlowe's work a mental picture of him as a short thin waspish man of middle-age, dark and slightly sinister perhaps, certainly sardonic: also it had not occurred to me that he would be anything but English. The off-beat quality of his books arose from an extremely individual attitude to life, rather than any foreign turn of phrase.

But Marlowe was definitely not English, and the exact opposite of what I'd imagined him to be like. He was not short, indeed when he stood up to greet me he seemed to fill the room, which was his study and admittedly not large. Marlowe, however, was very large. Nordic-looking, in his middle thirties, amiable, ambling, almost ursine in appearance. Like a big gentle blond bear, and he wore a light brown shaggy suit that fostered the resemblance. His eyes smiled short-sightedly behind shell-rimmed spectacles, his English was fluent, his voice soft and his accent heavy.

I never did find out where he came from. He could have been Scandinavian but somewhere round the Danube Basin was more likely, and I've heard all sorts of origin attributed to him, including Viennese. Despite his amiability there was something mysterious about him after all. Not sinister, as I'd expected: just mysterious. He really was a man of mystery.

The study being lit only by a desk lamp accentuated this ambiguous aura, its visible expression the lamplight halo behind his big blond smiling face as he told me about his career in Hollywood, where he'd written the script for the Freddie Bartholomew version of *David Copperfield*. There was no trace of American in his accent.

'Dickens,' he said, 'anticipated with his style the cinema. For example, *Bleak House*. The beginning, in the fog. There is no need to write a script, also Edwin Drood,' and one could see of course the Dickensian element in his own characters: the pawnbrokers, tailors, pavement artists and music-hall performers, revealed through their own elliptical speech.

Marlowe told me about his meeting with Greta Garbo then, crossing the Atlantic abruptly, how *I am Your Brother* had originated as a bedtime story which he used to tell in nightly instalments to the children of Sir Roderick and Lady Jones while staying as a guest at their country house. I wouldn't have said the subject was all that suitable for children myself, but presumably Lady Jones didn't disapprove, since it was she who encouraged him to write the novel, which was dedicated to her under her maiden name of Enid Bagnold.

Marlowe spoke warmly of *National Velvet*, the secretary came in to refill our glasses, and he cocked his head to listen, with one finger uplifted as one of his own characters might have done, to the rain dripping on the bushes outside the window.

He quoted: '"Such dank gardens cry aloud for a murder." Do you know this? Stevenson. *Cry Aloud For A Murder*, a wonderful title. But it's better in the suburbs. They have there laurel bushes and in the houses behind the bushes live murderers. Respectable little people, but with passions also. For love and for money. Like Crippen, Seddon, wonderful fellows. And all the time on the laurel bushes drips the rain.'

He slid open a drawer of his desk: 'I have written here about murder in the London suburbs,' taking out four typescripts clipped into manilla folders: 'Four novelettes to make a volume. But they will not be printed yet. My publishers say after the next novel only, otherwise they will not make money.'

His third book, *Their Little Lives*, had been a volume of stories and had not made money. *I am Your Brother* made money, his second novel about the pavement artist did not make so much, now the publishers were becoming cautious so the new suburban stories would have to wait. None of them was called *Cry Aloud For A Murder*, though I recall distinctly only one title, 'Dead Man's Money': perhaps the Stevenson quotation provided the overall title for the four. These were never published: later, when Marlowe disappeared, the stories apparently vanished with him. At all events neither his publishers nor his agents seemed to know what had become of them.

'Did you ever know a murderer?' Marlowe asked me, sliding the stories back into the drawer.

Yes, I told him, I had known a murderer though not well. A Russian con-man in the South of France who loved to dress up in uniform and pass himself off as a naval officer, who shot the woman who kept him six times through her bedroom door: imagining, as it proved erroneously, that she'd been unfaithful. He had escaped the guillotine and been sent instead to Devil's Island, since the murder was in a sense a crime passionel, though in my opinion he should have been certified insane.

'You will write about him one day,' Marlowe said; then asked, while the glasses were refilled once more, what I was writing now. He had clearly, on the evidence of his books, endured extreme poverty himself in early days, and showed great sympathy for my present plight, offering not only to read my stories but also to effect an introduction to Sir Hugh Walpole, whom he said would be able to help.

'We will arrange a little dinner party,' adding quickly: 'Informal,' a typical example of his tact, for he guessed quite rightly that I would have no evening clothes. Another example was shown when the secretary brought in my teddy bear coat from the airing cupboard where it had been put to dry. Marlowe helped me on with it himself and as he did so stroked the material admiringly: 'A magnificent coat. How I wish I had a coat like this myself,' thus sending me out into the cold and rain with the illusion that I owned one enviable possession at least.

This teddy bear coat at first caused much amusement among the other unemployed when I wore it to sign-on down the Labour, but then I became a sort of dole queue hero, having one day told the bullying Head Clerk to remove his hat while addressing me, since a notice on the wall said that the officials of the Exchange were but the servants of the public, and we were undoubtedly the public.

After this no one laughed even when I appeared in the teddy bear coat plus Wellington boots, because the continuous rain had caused floods up our end: at one time so bad that fishermen hired out boats for residents to do their shopping in.

The floods soon froze into sheets of solid ice as the full force of December struck, there was talk of skating and winter sport, but Jaeger had obtained a shedful of coal on credit and big fires crackled loudly in the grate by which I crouched to do my adaptation of *I am Your Brother*.

Jaeger too had fallen under the spell of this strange book; it strongly influenced his own first novel, *Angels on Horseback*, on which he was then engaged and which Routledge published in the winter of 1940. (A possession certainly envied was my copy of Marlowe's second novel *Pictures on the Pavement*, which he had inscribed and autographed for me in his enormous handwriting.)

Marlowe had also reported favourably on my stories and finally fixed the date for the Walpole dinner party, then came a last minute telegram:

Sir Hugh fallen sick; when he recovered it was to go for a spell abroad, so in fact we never met. Meanwhile Marlowe, who seemed to know everyone, promised he would get Arthur Bliss to compose the music for the radio play of *I am Your Brother*, which was now finished and awaiting decision at the BBC.

'We must be careful though with Bliss,' Marlowe told me. 'Or it will be music by Arthur Bliss, conducted by Arthur Bliss, script from a novel by Arthur Bliss, with Bliss also producing. He will take over everything including the rôle of the Brother if we don't watch out,' but as it turned out Arthur Bliss didn't even do the music, because the BBC decided not to broadcast *I am Your Brother* after all.

Val Gielgud, with whom the script had ended up, wrote me a letter saying that such a play would overstrain the resources of the Corporation, requiring not only a composer specially commissioned but the whole of the BBC symphony orchestra and chorus as well, besides being of unusual length and needing an enormous cast: the only way to produce it would be in serial form and this would not be possible either as the story was not suitable for a family audience (which didn't, apparently, include the children of Enid Bagnold). Gielgud hoped, however, that I would send to him personally any further radio plays of mine.

I continued notwithstanding to visit Gabriel Marlowe, who moved later on to a much bigger, very modern flat near Chelsea Barracks, in a new red-brick block rather resembling a barrack itself. Here, on an afternoon in Spring, I found him living in an Edgar Wallace-like opulence, surrounded by dictaphones, telephones and typewriters, with a brand new secretary even better looking than the last. Sunlight streamed in through the long window stretching across one wall, under which he sat in shirtsleeves at a huge desk covered with sheets of foolscap scrawled upon in his outsize script.

'Working overtime,' he told me. 'A play. Four acts, two complete but the other two,' he flung his arms wide: 'Confusion! I am going abroad next week, somewhere peaceful to finish this.'

'Where d'you think of going?'

Marlowe shrugged: 'It's not so easy now, with half Europe in the hands of Hitler, and I don't want to fall into them also because you see I'm Jewish. But I think I've found a place where the Nazis won't invade,' and at that moment the new secretary entered to announce that the laundry was at the door.

'Excellent,' Marlowe cried. 'Just in time, I am in great need of clean shirts, also socks. Compliment the laundry-man please on his so opportune arrival.'

'He says he won't leave the laundry, not until the bill is paid.'

'Bill paid? Ridiculous, tell him I will pay later at the shop.'

'He wants the money now.'

Marlowe sighed, fumbling among his papers until a wallet came to light, then from it extracted a one pound note which he extended with the weary gesture of one who meets, to keep the peace, some outrageous and extortionate demand.

But the secretary didn't take the note. 'He wants more than that,' she said. 'Or he'll take the laundry back.'

'This is despair,' Marlowe said throwing up his hands. 'I will go myself to reason with the man.'

He got up and ambled into the passage, voices were raised in argument outside, then the front door banged and Marlowe returned clasping to his chest a single shirt in a cellophane envelope.

'Only one. That's all that he would give. And no socks though I let him have the pound. The rest only when the bill is paid in full. Julian do you have such business with your shirts?'

I'd always taken it for granted that Marlowe was at least well off, and this scene had surprised me more than the news that he was Jewish, already astonishing in a man of such Nordic appearance; but I said: 'Where I live it's like this all the time.'

'Then how expect us to do our work?' Marlowe said chucking the shirt down among the foolscap sheets from which the secretary promptly snatched it up. 'How can a play be finished in such conditions. God be thanked, next week I'll be away from it all.'

I asked him again which country he had chosen for his temporary refuge.

'Norway,' he replied.

This was the spring of 1940, and naturally the last I saw of Gabriel Marlowe.

The place where the Nazis wouldn't invade was invaded, and Marlowe who had meant on returning to join the British army never returned, never published another book, was in due course written off as dead by all including his executors.

Yet was he dead? For a few years ago I was drinking champagne cider with a man who'd known Marlowe before the war, and claimed to have met him recently, alive and well, in some village the name of which I can't remember. This man had no idea he was supposed to have been lost in Norway, so asked no searching questions, and in the village inn they had together sunk a pint. Thus Marlowe contrived to enshroud himself in mystery right up to the end, if indeed it was his end.

But back to 1938 and the BBC.

Besides *I am Your Brother*, I adapted that winter yet another radio play, about a crooked astrologer, from a story by Anthony Skene[1] called *The Predicted Murder*. I re-titled this *The Stars Foretell* and despatched it to Val Gielgud personally, in accordance with his wish, but a secretary informed me that the Director of Drama was by this time in the USA and no decision could be reached until his return: date as yet unknown.

1938 became 1939 with still no news and creditors battering on the bungalow door, then a big BBC envelope arrived, containing a new transcript of *A Gun for Sale*, revised and lavishly cut by a young woman in the Script Department whose name I have forgotten. In her accompanying letter she hoped I would approve as she had, in her own words, 'tightened-up' the play considerably (as if it were some kind of scrotum), adding that the main thing was that Graham Greene himself had approved her version.

I replied sharply that my own approval didn't seem to matter all that much, and that to me the main thing was prompt production, since I urgently needed the remainder of the fee.

Moray McLaren then took over, explaining that the cutting and revision had taken some time, consequently the play had got behind in their schedules, already stocked with plays awaiting production, and no date for *A Gun for Sale* could be envisaged yet awhile.

Shortly afterwards Jonah Barrington wrote in his column that the BBC Drama Department was becoming desperate in its search for radio plays, prompt decisions and payment on acceptance would be made: fees of £25 and £50 according to length being once more held out as bait to authors willing to write for sound.

Jaeger, whose effort in this direction had just been returned after a lapse of two months with a simple rejection slip, showed me this item with relish, and I decided to write Barrington citing my own case in contradiction and putting him right on several points.

---

1 My meeting with this writer will be described elsewhere, and does not belong properly to these Memoirs.

The letter was sent, no reply came, but instead a few days later an incomprehensibly angry note from a firm of literary agents accusing me of divulging details to the public press of royalties paid to their client Graham Greene, in their opinion an unpardonable course of action.

I was completely in the dark; Jaeger, wearing his usual breakfast costume of black velvet jacket and black skull cap, and smoking the long-stemmed meerschaum pipe which was an accessory to this morning dress, declared himself equally mystified; then suddenly gave a sharp exclamation, and clapping the lid on his meerschaum, passed to me his copy of the *Daily Express*, open at Jonah Barrington's radio column.

In this Barrington complained that he had been deluged with letters in small handwriting and would future correspondents please address themselves not to him but to the department of the newspaper mentioned when the original item had been published.

It should now be explained that my handwriting is extremely small, neat and legible: in those days even smaller than it is now, age having taken its toll on my sight, and people seeing one of my MSS would frequently ask how it was done, to which the correct answer was, of course, 'With a pen.' To make my communication more personal, I had not typed my letter to Jonah Barrington, and the present complaint in his column was quite clearly related to it.

A search through back issues of the *Express* finally turned up, on a page where it had been overlooked, since none of us expected anything of the sort, a facsimile of the opening paragraphs of my letter, under the caption: 'CAN YOU WRITE SMALLER THAN THIS?'

The portion reproduced, dealing with my adaptation of *A Gun for Sale*, ended with a sentence explaining that the total fee was divided between Graham Greene and myself: the subsequent paragraph, revealing that only half had been paid and that I was unable to obtain the rest because no production date could be scheduled, was cut off short; a reference to my being on the dole, however, had been printed to the fore.

At that time a sort of stigma or shame attached in the public mind to people receiving Unemployment Assistance: certainly it had not yet become a matter for self-congratulation as now, when any number of bearded voluntary poverty beats from Soho and the Fulham Road boast loudly of spiving a livelihood from what they call The Lark. I imagined that this was really what had upset Greene and his agents, and wrote directly to him apologising for associating his name with someone on the dole, and furthermore explaining that my letter to

Barrington had been sent in the hope that he would in some way influence the BBC to pay the remainder of the fee, and having been marked 'Personal' in the first place, was plainly not intended for publication.

Greene replied curtly, on a postcard inscribed: 'Mr Graham Greene is in Mexico but will communicate with you on his return'. These words had been crossed out, and underneath he had written: 'Don't be a fool, of course I don't mind your being on the dole,' continuing that he did mind me making public the amount of his BBC royalties, and that no one would write letters to the papers if they didn't mean them to be published.

I realised that it would be useless to explain further; also I was rapidly losing patience with the whole business of *A Gun for Sale*, and indeed several years passed before I could bring myself to re-read what had once been a favourite book.

But repercussions from the Barrington letter had not yet died away. The holograph fragment in the *Express* cited my play *The Stars Foretell* as a contradiction of the prompt decisions promised by Barrington on the BBC's behalf, since the script had been with the Drama Department for I don't know how long; and I next found myself involved in correspondence with R.H. Naylor, the newspaper astrologer later remarkable for his prophecy that there would be no Second World War.

Mr Naylor, whose weekly horoscopes appeared under the heading 'WHAT THE STARS FORETELL', considered the title which I'd chosen to be an infringement of copyright: I was able to correct him on his assumption, but not before he had protested also to the BBC, and the upshot was that I was summoned to yet another interview at Broadcasting House.

Moray McLaren surveyed me sadly across the desk as a housemaster might a pupil who has let down the side.

'I appreciate your difficulties,' he said, 'but we have our own as well. Rules and regulations are not easily set aside nor exception made, but in this case and in view of the publicity it has received, a solution satisfactory to all parties might still be found.'

'That's heartening,' I said.

Moray McLaren exclaimed, as if struck by sudden inspiration: 'An early date. That's it! If your adaptation could be scheduled for broadcasting at an early date, that would be the solution to all our problems, would it not?'

'How early?' I asked.

Moray McLaren said: 'The schedules will have to be rearranged of course, but we'll see what can be done. The play might even be produced this year!'

He rubbed his hands, refreshed as Gabriel Marlowe would have put it, more than ever resembling in attire a musician or pianist of a slightly earlier period.

I asked: 'I suppose there wouldn't be any vacancies for training as a writer-producer yet?'

Moray McLaren replied: 'Well, in a view of the international situation we're cutting down on staff rather than increasing our personnel at present, but your name has not been overlooked, never fear.' Then glancing down at a note on his desk pad: 'Now there's the question of your other play, *The Stars Foretell*, and R.H. Naylor's claim that you've infringed his copyright.'

'That claim is nonsense, as you know.'

Moray McLaren nodded: 'We've already written to him on the subject.'

'And a decision on the script itself?'

'Actually,' Moray McLaren said with tremendous relief, 'that's in the Director of Drama's hands not mine. He's now back from the States and I believe has some news for you, if you'd care to go along and see him in the office.'

'What, right away?' I asked astonished.

Moray McLaren nodded vigorously, springing up as if about to mount the concert platform and perform a recital that very moment.

'No time like the present,' he said.

Val Gielgud had two beards, one sprouting from each corner of his chin. His office was very dark although it was daytime, and in the gloom he gave the impression of a character in an Edgar Wallace who might turn out to be someone else disguised. He stared at me severely through a forbidding pair of spectacles during a short silence which I broke by saying: 'I believe you have some news about a play of mine called *The Stars Foretell*.'

'I have,' Val Gielgud said abruptly. He had a deep brusque voice, 'Not good news, I'm afraid.'

'I'm sorry to hear that,' I said.

Val Gielgud said: 'The script has somehow been mislaid. Even after an extensive search it has not been found.'

'D'you mean you've lost it?' I asked.

'We hope it may yet come to light.'

'But it arrived here all right. You sent an acknowledgment.'

'My secretary did,' Val Gielgud corrected me. 'I was in America at the time. When I returned, the script was no longer in the file awaiting my attention.'

'What does your secretary say?'

The secretary was called in and interrogated by her employer, plainly not for the first time. She showed us the file concerned and even opened it for our inspection as if hoping the script might be still inside. The script was not inside, but then we were already aware of that.

'However,' Val Gielgud said dismissing the secretary, by now close to tears, 'you no doubt have a copy, so no great harm will have been done.'

'I haven't a copy,' I told him.

'But surely you keep a carbon?'

'I do my own typing, and I've no time to bother making carbons.'

'That, if I may say so,' Val Gielgud said severely, 'is a trifle careless of you.'

'More careless than losing typescripts?'

There was another silence, this time broken by Val Gielgud saying: 'Of course you realise that, while every reasonable care is taken of MSS submitted to this Department, the Corporation cannot assume responsibility in cases of loss or damage?'

'Has every reasonable care been taken,' I asked, 'in this particular case?'

That went unanswered also, then he said: 'Perhaps you'd like to send us the original MS? From what I have seen of your handwriting…'

I said: 'The MS would have to be entirely rewritten first. I made all corrections and alterations while typing, and I couldn't undertake to do it all over again unless I were commissioned to do so.'

Val Gielgud at this rose to his feet, smiling faintly for the first time since I'd entered his office: 'That, as you'll understand,' he said, 'would be quite out of the question.'

Not long after, I received by the same post two letters from the BBC Drama Department. One was from Val Gielgud saying that, although further enquiries had been made, my script still remained missing, and he feared there was nothing more that could be done.

The other said that they had much pleasure in accepting my play *The Stars Foretell*, for which a fee of £25 would be paid on production. This letter was not signed by the Director of Drama but by a producer into whose hands the script had passed in some manner which was never quite cleared up. Having been filed under Acceptances, it was in none of the places where it should have been, hence the confusion which arose. The producer in question afterwards committed suicide, and I never found out whether or not he first produced *The Stars Foretell*.

Nor was *A Gun for Sale* so far as I know ever produced. The early date unerringly chosen by the BBC was September 1, 1939, and considering the play's subject the broadcast was naturally cancelled: since, two days later, we really did have war in our time.

A Story in *Horizon*

*   *   *

A FLYING BOMB LATER KILLED THE GIRL CALLED BOBBIE WHOM I kissed in the back of the car, and Di who drove it is dead as well: though of natural causes, if you can call cancer a natural cause.

But that morning in March 1940 these young women were both very much alive: Bobbie's crimson lipstick tasted like scented soap in my mouth, she drew back to arch provocatively her pencilled brows over bold dark eyes, and to slap lightly with her wedding-ringed hand one of mine which may have reached too far under the rug covering her knees; while Di at the wheel, with the back of her cloud of blonde hair turned to us but her eyes intent on the driving mirror, called out gaily: 'Now then you two!'

The car was a Riley painted red, with a detachable hood which at this moment was up, and in it I was on my way to London, where I'd been invited to call on Cyril Connolly, who had recently accepted a story of mine for publication in his review *Horizon*.

GREEN FOLDERS, GREEN INK

Cyril Connolly's book *Enemies of Promise* remains a landmark to members of my generation, standing up as such today, the cautions which it contains still valid: though most of us, Connolly included, have fallen into the snares which he foresaw, while a warning 'not to capitalise indolence and egotism' reads oddly now from the author of *The Unquiet Grave*.

In the Thirties I'd known Connolly's name only through his stimulating reviews in *The New Statesman* and Desmond MacCarthy's eulogistic *Sunday Times* notice of his novel *The Rock Pool*, then un-obtainable in England: though I'd tried hard to get a copy of the Obelisk Press edition, having spent my own early youth not far from those parts of the French Riviera featured in *The Rock Pool*, among characters not dissimilar from those evidently described therein.

Then quite by chance I discovered *Enemies of Promise* in the local public library, about a year after its publication during the Munich crisis. I was still on the Assistance and very dispirited; the outbreak of war seemed to put the lid firmly on any chance of a literary career, and finding a book like this was a tremendously invigorating experience.

Part of its appeal lay I suppose in the author's having read and appreciated all the contemporary novelists that I myself enjoyed (not by any means usual at this period, still less in the backwater where I lived), also some novels which I'd not read at all, such as *Living* by Henry Green and Christopher Isherwood's *The Memorial*. Here, I felt, was someone who might see merit in my work, if merit was indeed there to be seen, which I was seriously beginning to doubt: I'd even ceased to send my stories out, and there still weren't enough of them to make up a volume.

If only Cyril Connolly were an editor, I thought, and a few days later the first advertisement for *Horizon*, a Review of Literature and Art, edited by Cyril Connolly, appeared like an answer to prayer in the sixpenny weeklies.

'One last chance, if this doesn't come off I'll pack it in,' I told Jaeger who had finished his novel and, like me, was awaiting call up while signing-on the Labour; Lydia his wife parcelled up the green spring-board folder containing the stories, their daughter now aged two was handed a label to lick; and addressed to *Horizon* office the parcel was posted off when the price of a ninepenny stamp had with difficulty been rustled up between us.

Soon a winter even worse than the last one tightened round our bungalow its rigorous icy grip, every day the postman trudged through snowdrifts to the door: bills, demands and threats from unpaid tradesmen lay unanswered on the mat but, except for a printed acknowledgment, nothing from *Horizon* came through the letter box.

Against the advice of everyone I knew, I finally in mid-February wrote a postcard to the editor asking for the typescript's return. In prompt reply came a postcard written in green ink and Cyril Connolly's own handwriting: 'Hold on, MSS filed in error, just been found, now being read,' but I'd long ceased to be an optimist and merely gave a hollow laugh.

That weekend we were asked over by friends in Littlehampton; a play reading of Julius Caesar was held while a snow-storm whirled round the house; Jaeger, who was in the title rôle and suffered from recurrent bouts of asthma, suddenly turned blue and fell off his chair; and we had to stay the night since the storm had stopped all traffic on the roads.

Sunday, back at home, we found all pipes frozen, the water off, and our credit frozen also; I retired to bed with a streaming snorting cold, woke on Monday with rigid limbs and head stuffed up. A burst pipe had instantly blossomed out in icicles, and Jaeger throwing me a letter from the doorway said: 'From Connolly I think'.

My fingers had chilblains on and I found the letter hard to open. It was from Connolly all right, the green handwriting covered both sides of the page. I read the opening paragraphs and tried to produce a shout of elation, but the strangled sound that came instead was mistaken for my death rattle and brought all the Jaegers rushing in.

Particularly gratifying was the fact that the main story mentioned and accepted was one called 'A Bit of a Smash in Madras' which nobody, certainly not the Jaegers and perhaps not even myself, had believed would ever be published; moreover Connolly also proposed to print in future issues 'Five Finger Exercises', the first short story that I'd ever written and one hitherto rejected by editors with cries of distress, since it described a girl of sixteen being seduced by a man of thirty in a seaside town; and 'Happy as the Day is Long', around which the Denys Kilham Roberts controversy had raged. Last but not least, *Horizon* paid two guineas per thousand words, 'A Bit of a Smash in Madras' was in length at least 8000, and Connolly wrote that a cheque for half the fee was on its way.

'Julian's bloody well done it at last,' Karel Jaeger shouted, wringing my chilblained hand; little Karel his daughter caught the spirit of rejoicing and did an elephantine dance around my bed; and Lydia Jaeger was sent forth into the snow with the *Horizon* letter, to unfreeze further credit from the shops.

The reasons for the delay in deciding were explained in the letter as well. Apparently *Horizon*'s office was also the flat of Stephen Spender, then associated with the Review and in the Fire Service at the time, and by the sort of coincidence by no means unique in my life, the type-scripts of his poems were bound in green folders exactly similar to those I used. A girl secretary of the species that has haunted me throughout my professional career, beginning with the BBC, had found my stories lying on a desk and, without looking in the folder, filed them away with the rest of Spender's work in his study, where they remained until on receipt of my postcard a search was made. (This incident taught me a lesson which all young writers should learn: never to be afraid of sending editors a reminder once a reasonable length of time has elapsed: 'a maximum of, say, two weeks,' to quote again from the excellent precepts outlined in Edmund Wilson's *Literary Worker's Polonius*, a copy of which should hang over the desk in every editorial office.)

A cheque for nine guineas duly arrived from Connolly, and with it another letter: now he wanted me to write a long 10,000 word story about the South of France and was not inimical either to considering the short vacuum-cleaner salesman novel with which I'd been wrestling, and which at that time I reckoned would run out at about 25,000 words.

'A whole issue of the magazine maybe,' Jaeger said in awe as he took the cheque to a chap he knew who would put it through his bank, and that evening we celebrated with a real bottle of wine instead of the noxious patent stuff in which we usually indulged when the dole paid out on Fridays.

But suddenly there began to be trouble at the *Horizon* end. 'A Bit of a Smash in Madras' concerned a motor accident in the city of that name and the legal intrigues consequent upon it; and, for fear of a possible libel suit, the locale had to be changed to E.M. Forster's imaginary state of Chandrapore and the words In Madras were cut therefore from the title. (Actually, when the story appeared, the sole legal repercussion was a letter of praise from a retired judge in Bombay wrongly identifying by name all the protagonists in the case, which he believed he had tried himself.)

Even so, two sets of printers flatly refused to print, objecting to several expressions in the text and to the opening sentence in particular, which originally read: 'Absolute fact, I knew fuck-all about it,' and was not acceptable even when the offending words were altered to 'Sweet F.A.' Stephen Spender took up the struggle with the printers and sent me a list of the expressions for which substitutes had to be supplied and which ended, in the form of a short poem:

'Pissed-up'

'By Christ'

'Balls'

'Bugger.'

This list was in my pocket when I set off in the Riley with Di, who was driving up for a day's shopping in London with her friend Bobbie. I was lucky to get the lift, for £1 was all the cash I'd been able to raise.

BOBBIE AND BURMESE CIGARETTES

Bobbie said: 'But I don't know you well enough,' her eyes opening wide at a suggestion of mine; then later on she said: 'Well not yet,' and later still: 'We'll have to see.'

It was true she didn't know me well enough, I'd never set eyes on her until that morning. She was about thirty, a long-legged brunette, slender, with sleek hair almost black and these bold brown eyes. She had been a model before her marriage and was very well made up, using a shade of cream and powder that gave a matt, tanned-looking surface to her skin. Her mouth was painted in a crimson curve that looked hard but in fact was soft and smooth. The moment we met antagonism crackled like electricity between us and a residue remained even after we'd begun kissing in the back of the car.

Di had brought chicken sandwiches for our lunch, a bottle of sherry, and even glasses to drink this out of: the sherry went slightly to Bobbie's head and on the last lap of the drive her leg pressed hard against mine, the rug was cast aside; her wedding ring cut into my fingers which were twined in hers, and after all this time I can smell her scent mingled with the petrol fumes one always got inside that car whenever the hood was up.

Antagonism evaporated too and when we reached High Holborn where they were to drop me off, Bobbie opened her mouth for a final kiss that obliged me to wait for passion to subside before I could climb out of the car. It was then that she said: 'We'll have to see.'

Di, a born matchmaker though herself unmarried, beamed as they drove off, the blonde and the brunette, towards the City where Bobbie's husband worked. I walked elatedly up Southampton Row, stopping at a tobacconist's to break into my pound note and buy some Burmese cigarettes which seemed appropriate to the occasion. I soon found these almost unsmokable, and wished I had stuck to my usual Brazilians but I had to go careful with only nineteen shillings now to last the day: though

Connolly in his letter of invitation had promised to let me have the remainder of the fee, this would take the form of a cheque and the banks were already closed.

A clock said 3.15, my appointment was 3.30, and first I entered a big Bloomsbury hotel, with green cupolas on the roof like a Russian church, to wash off Bobbie's lipstick in a basin down below, little knowing that years later I would live there eighteen months.

Lansdowne Terrace was easily found and not far off, a row of small smoky dun-brick houses built all alike, with big blank front windows facing a children's playground on the other side. No 6 had no plate outside, or indication that the *Horizon* office was to be found within: the stairs were uncarpeted and stone. I climbed them and knocked at random on a door. This after a stealthy pause came open, a dark face peered cautiously through a crack, then the door was banged-to in my face.

I climbed higher, knocked, another Indian appeared, small and shrivelled like the first: one look at me and his door too was smartly shut. A third occupant, Indian also, seemed to know no English; I asked desperately: '*Horizon*? Spender? Connolly?' even producing the Burmese cigarettes to make him feel at home, but helplessly he shook his head and retreated bowing through the doorway.

No 6 was plainly on the fanlight but it was equally plain that *Horizon* didn't hang out there, and I tried the house next door. Here none of the occupants would answer, there was hollow silence except for my footsteps echoing up and down; if this went on I would be late; in a panic I rushed along the row, up more and more stone stairs: Indians in every flat, either unable or unwilling to give any information, and the last one, a woman in a sari, shrank in terror when she saw me and almost slammed her door upon my hand.

Baffled, hot and bothered in my teddy bear coat I came out on to the pavement, and my hand seeking cigarettes touched a crumpled piece of paper in my pocket. Stephen Spender's list, and at the top the correct address which I'd not troubled to check. No 6 Selwyn House, Landsdowne Terrace: first one in the row, I'd passed it on the Guilford Street corner and now stood right outside.

The front door was open, a carpeted hall inside, on the ground floor right another door, with the names Spender and *Horizon*. Cyril Connolly himself answered the bell.

CYRIL CONNOLLY AT SELWYN HO.

Connolly at the time must have been thirty-six or seven years of age. The only photograph I'd seen of him was one which formed a frontispiece to the first edition of *Enemies of Promise*, where he is wearing an Eton suit and a top hat that rests on rather protruding ears; and the only clue to his grown-up appearance was the last paragraph of the book where he tells us that his face is round.

His face was round. Plump and pale, his shoulders sloped from a short thick neck, and dark hair was fluffed thickly out behind the ears that seemed no longer to protrude. He had a short snub Irish nose and under shaggy Irish brows his eyes, set far apart, looked both hooded and alert. A startled expression, instantly veiled, had entered them when he saw me standing at the door and it was clear that I was not what he had pictured (pith helmet and white ducks: a pukka sahib? Capped and collarless, with muffler round the neck: the dole? A blazer and rope-soled shoes: the South of France? Or a salesman, wearing a raincoat and porkpie hat with feathers in the band?).

Under his speculative gaze, I launched into an apology for being late, describing my peculiar reception by the Indian tenants of the Terrace, which I was still at a loss to account for. Connolly explained. Apparently a new regulation that all Asiatics should be rounded up had that day been passed: something to do with subversive activities and the war, and the unfortunate Indians had mistaken me for an official come to enforce the order.

'But of course you were able to reassure them,' Cyril Connolly was saying.

'How?' I said. 'None of them could speak English.'

'But with your knowledge of their native language, Hindustani, or is it Tamil?'

'I don't speak Tamil or Hindustani.'

'What?' A slightly sharp note became perceptible in Connolly's soft bland voice. 'Not after all those years out East?'

This was going to be a let-down, but it was too late to bluff it out. 'I've never been out East,' I told him.

'Nor to Madras?'

'No.'

Connolly said: 'D'you mean that story's pure imagination? With all the background detail?'

'Not altogether,' I said unhappily. 'I had a friend who used to tell me stories of his life out there. I picked most of it up from him.'

We were standing in the front room which overlooked the Terrace and had been Stephen Spender's study: his books were in a glass-fronted case by the cabinet containing the green springback folders among which my stories had been filed in error. Now, to cover an awkward pause, I bent closer to the bookcase and immediately saw inside copies of *Living* and *The Memorial*, which ever since reading *Enemies of Promise*, I'd been trying to obtain.

'I suppose I couldn't borrow these?'

Connolly said: 'If you're good at bringing books back. I don't think Stephen would mind, but they are his you see.'

I promised faithfully to return them (which I did), adding: 'You haven't also got *The Rock Pool* by any chance?'

Connolly said: 'Not a single copy left, I'm sorry. At one time you might have found one in a rubber goods shop but not, I fear, any longer,' and I was to find again the phrase about the rubber goods in the preface to the original edition of *The Rock Pool* when later I did obtain a copy.

Zipping the two novels up in my briefcase, I asked what Henry Green was like, since I'd just read *Party Going* and been enormously impressed.

'A nice quiet private detective in a book by Nicholas Blake,' Connolly replied.

'Nigel Strangeways?'

Connolly said: 'If Henry was an actor he'd be ideal for the part.'

Walking as if with slippered feet though in fact he wore suede shoes, he led the way into his own office at the back. The house-master's outfit affected by many writers of the Thirties—tweed jacket, woollen tie, grey flannels baggy at the knee—gave him an unbuttoned rather than an informal air as he slumped back in the armchair opposite me. His movements like his voice were indolent, one had the impression that he should have been eating grapes, but at the same time his half-closed eyes missed nothing. He was a formidable person.

I asked him if he knew G.S. Marlowe, who had not yet been lost in Norway; Connolly not only knew him, but he told me his real surname, which was unpronounceable and might have belonged to any Central European, though Connolly thought that he was Viennese.

'We used to stay in the same country house near Marlow, and that's where he took his name from, adding an E on the end for good measure. He used to boast a lot about being a fisherman, but we never saw anything he caught.'

'That's curious,' I said, 'He once told me much the same about Hemingway, only it was shooting not fishing.'

'I doubt if he ever knew Hemingway,' Connolly said.

'What about Greta Garbo?'

Connolly made a dismissive gesture. 'Tales from the Vienna Woods,' he said, reaching out for the folder with my stories which lay upon his desk. He spoke about the father in one about childhood called *The Snows of Yesterday*, saying: 'My father was quite like yours, all regular army men are really much the same.'

'My father wasn't in the regular army,' I said. 'He was only a captain in the Boer War.'

'But you say here he was a colonel in the Indian army.'

'That's just the father in the story,' I said.

Connolly shifted in his chair; he seemed positive that all my work was autobiographical, and I realised that this was tantamount to contradicting him. So I added quickly: 'My grandfather was an Indian army colonel though.'

'Perhaps the character was based on him?'

'No, he died before I was born. He wrote books on big game hunting. Quite well written. They were published by Chapman and Hall.'

'So writing runs in the family?'

I let this ride, though quite certain my grandfather never thought of himself as a writer, and Connolly said: 'I suppose you'll be going into the army yourself now?'

'I'm expecting the call-up any time.'

Connolly nodded. 'The Indian army,' he said. 'Then you'll be able to go to Madras. That reminds me, I have a cheque for you somewhere.'

The cheque, already made out for nine guineas, was finally found clipped to the stories in the folder, and he said: 'Just take it to the bank in the morning, they'll cash it for you before we meet for lunch.'

'Lunch? Tomorrow?'

'Yes, I thought the Café Royal if that suits you.'

I said: 'Of course I'd love to, but I'm afraid I must go back this evening. Frankly I can't afford to stay the night.'

Connolly said: 'But that's all arranged, everything paid for. Bill Makins our business manager has fixed up a room for you. He'll be here presently and you can go out for drinks together, unfortunately I'm engaged myself tonight.'

I muttered my thanks; I was touched by his kindness and consideration, and had a sudden urge to tell him what receiving his long friendly letters had meant to me in my unrecognised and exiled state. But I'd the sense not to embarrass him with such a speech, for I felt that beneath his immense sophistication he was very public school.

'Unless of course there's a wife at home waiting for you?' Connolly was saying.

'There isn't a wife.'

'You've never been married?'

'Once, but it didn't take. Only lasted six months.'

'Six months. You were very unlucky,' Connolly said. 'In marriage, if even moderately lucky, one can expect at least seven years of happiness. And if exceptionally lucky, why then,' he smiled benignly, 'another seven': a dictum which twenty years later I attributed, with other sayings of his, to a film producer in a novel, though I'm glad now to acknowledge their proper source.

'I'll look forward to that next time,' I told him.

'Do you mean to marry again?'

'Not if I can help it, but these things sometimes happen. As you've pointed out, the pram in the hall.'[1]

'You're not yet thirty?'

'Nearly twenty-eight.'

Connolly sighed, 'Nearer Bill Makins' generation than mine. In fact I think you must be just about the same age.'

'1911,' a voice said, as if on cue from the passage outside: 'I'm a year ahead,' and into the office came William Cooper Makins, a man who afterwards died twice: as I will tell.

---

1   See *Enemies of Promise*, Penguin Modern Classics edition, p. 127.

GOAT'S BLOOD IN RUSSELL SQUARE

'Two minutes to opening time,' Makins announced glancing at his watch outside the office; then as we turned into Russell Square he pointed at a skyscraper-type building visible above trees on the farther side: 'D'you see that? London University, but it's now the Ministry of Information. Graham Greene works there!'

'Does he?' I said.

'He does,' Makins said. 'He may be in there working at this very moment.' It was a solemn thought: we stood there looking towards the Ministry as if it were a shrine or cenotaph. Makins said: 'He's just finished a new novel. About a Mexican priest. It'll be published in the summer. You'll have whisky of course,' leading the way down into an underground bar with barrels round the walls.

I was not loth to accept; at this early stage of the war spirits were easily obtainable, and he'd told me going along the street that he was amply provided with expenses and that, as a guest of *Horizon*, I was not allowed to pay.

Hitherto I'd known the name William C. Makins only from seeing it on the *Horizon* letterhead, with Business Manager printed above, and Cyril Connolly told me that as a business manager he was extremely efficient: before this he had worked in advertising I believe.

Makins in the flesh was a redoubtable figure: tall, gaunt, with a fierce Highland high-boned face and a dark Elizabethan beard jutting from his chin. I borrowed his appearance for a film director in the same novel which embodies some of Connolly's aphorisms, and gave him a monocle much as Gabriel Marlowe added the final E to his surname: Makins, however, did not need a monocle, his eyes were piercing enough without. They were electric eyes and deep sunk in their sockets, causing his head to be even more haughtily held.

He outdid Karel Jaeger in looking like a Scottish tribal chieftain, though his accent was incisively English and he did not affect national dress. Whenever I saw him, which seemed always to be in cold weather, he was tightly buttoned in a black business overcoat and wore outdoors a stiff brimmed black hat tilted back rather in the manner of Graham Greene, whom he resembled a little in height and build and who was the novelist he admired above all others.

His admiration for Greene's work exceeded even my own, and moreover he always knew whatever Greene was doing or writing at any given time; I forgot whether he knew Greene personally, but rather fancy he did not.

It was by recounting my experiences with Greene and the adaptation of *A Gun for Sale*, thus adding to his store of information, that I became accepted by Makins as a friend, the friendship being cemented that evening with much grain and malt.

Over the scotch with beer chasers, he pointed out what I'd already noticed: the curious omission of Graham Greene's name from *Enemies of Promise*, though *It's a Battlefield*, *England Made Me* and *Brighton Rock* had already come out when the book was written; this, however, Makins told me, would soon be rectified in *Horizon*, and it was: by Arthur Calder-Marshall's excellent analysis of the novels, the first critical article on Greene to appear anywhere, in which the phrase 'Greene Land' was first coined.

But Greene was not the only writer about whom Bill Makins had inside information: there was also Evelyn Waugh. I think it was on this occasion that I heard from him about the unfinished novel *Work Suspended*: 'It's told in the first person by a chap who writes very superior detective stories, he's very proud of these detective stories but he gradually becomes human, and the book's about the humanising process he goes through.' (I don't know whether Evelyn Waugh would approve of this précis, which I remember word for word, my interest was so great; later on when the book had appeared in a limited edition only, and I wanted to write a critical article about him, he replied asking me to wait until he was dead: I respected his wish, but this was long before the spate of articles that began to be written after *Brideshead*, by critics who didn't wait for him to be dead.)

Anyway, according to Makins, at this time *Work Suspended* was to be published in *Penguin Parade*, taking up a complete number of the miscellany; and I was able to pass on the story of Denys Kilham Roberts and 'Happy as the Day is Long', which after all that had been accepted by *Horizon*. Makins, who'd been laughing at the story, stopped suddenly to pass a hand down his beard. He said: 'The one about the Count in Chelsea?' but made no further comment then, going on to relay some further advance publishing news.

He knew more of what was going on behind the literary scene than anyone I ever knew. Not the sort of malicious personal gossip that poets indulge in, but real hard facts. His finger was constantly on the pulse, moreover he meant it to remain there. He'd no intention of being railroaded into the bloody Forces, which would mean he'd years to make up after: despite his aggressively vigorous exterior he not only had genuine pacifist convictions but also an incipient stomach ulcer which had already caused one medical board to turn him down.

'If I continue to keep out,' he said putting down money for more drinks, 'I plan to start up as a literary agent, apart from my job at *Horizon*, real live-wire stuff and you can be one of my very first authors.' Real live-wires seemed to spark out of his eyes: 'I'll handle your output and push the stories to their best advantage, which you won't be able to do when they shove you in the army, right?'

'Only too right,' I agreed with whisky burning my throat, and Makins seized my hand in a powerful grip.

'Then we're in business, or rather we ruddy soon will be. Promotion, publicity, that's the thing. Tell you what I'm going to fix up for you,' and, as he proceeded to promise, the issue of *Horizon* in which 'A Bit of a Smash' eventually appeared was advertised with my name and the title of the story alone, bordered in black, instead of all the contributors being listed as previously: a matter of great pride to me at the time.

'We've got to keep your name always to the fore,' Makins explained, emptying his glass and thrusting out his beard for emphasis. 'Impress it on the public mind. I've already been working on some of the chaps, they'll be here presently,' and while toasting the new venture we were joined by two of the chaps, both of them already familiar with my name and apparently eager to be introduced.

'You see?' Makins said. 'You're famous before you've even been published,' and another round of scotch came up: whisky didn't seem to upset his ulcer, he said, or if it did all the better as he was due for another bloody Board soon.

More of the chaps appeared, I hoped some of the girls might show up as well, but the party remained all male and the conversation became a lot less literary. All at once it turned on a woman, evidently much given to experiment and well known to all, who'd been the victim of an accident, perhaps to her leg, certainly on a remote Italian hillside, and had had to have a blood-transfusion on the spot. Since none of the people roundabout belonged to the proper blood group, the doctor had been compelled to accept as blood donor some mountain animal: here my memory begins to falter, although a goat seems the most probable in such surroundings and comes most readily to mind as the kind of quadruped concerned.

Anyhow the transfusion had been triumphantly successful, and the brightest of the chaps began to declaim a limerick that he'd made up, in which the patient subsequently rejected as stimulants various sexual deviations, also gin and heroin: at this point everybody joined in chanting the last line, the bar resounded with 'I must have goat's blood —under the skin!'; protests arose from the management, and a general move was made through the blackout towards a delicatessen and wine store that stayed open late, the idea being to carry on the party at Makins' place in Guilford Street.

At the delicatessen they started laying in a typical Bloomsbury meal: potato salad, loaves of French bread, paté and salami (not affected by meat rationing which had just come in), bottles of red wine and beer. I insisted this time on paying my whack, only to find that at some previous point I had dropped my one ten shilling note, probably in the tobacconist's where I'd bought Brazilian cigarettes on the way to the bar, having given up attempting to smoke the Burmese some time before.

I immediately wanted to go back there and search, but was dissuaded on the grounds that the shop would now be shut: I remember that, in an effort to divert my attention, one of the younger men pointed wildly into the darkness ahead, shouting: 'Look, down there's Doughty Street. Where bloody old Dickens lived,' while another leant over some railings to show me an area in which he'd once either had a fight or else been sick, dropping in the process a bottle of pale ale which shattered below.

A GOOD NIGHT IN GUILFORD STREET

Another of the chaps was worried for fear he might be sterile. The one who did something scientific and may have been a bio-chemist said: 'That's easily settled, old boy. Just take a sample of your spunk along to a hospital, and they'll soon tell you one way or the other.'

'How'm I supposed to get it there?'

The brightest of the chaps said: 'Simple. All you've to do is toss yourself off into a bottle.'

Makins managed to wrench the conversation away from the medical turn it had taken, and back to literature.

We were sitting over the remains of the meal in his large bedsitter, which had masks hung on the walls and a big box containing marionettes in one corner. A marionette play of his had been performed at a theatre club which specialised also in plays where the protagonists wore masks, and he was now writing one with four masked characters in it, entitled *The Unknown*: the latter being a fifth character who did not actually appear in the play.

Two incomplete acts in typescript were passed round the company for criticism, while a refugee antique dealer, who'd been waiting for Makins (or a free meal) outside the door when we arrived, sneered quietly to himself in the armchair nearest the gas fire, with his chin resting on the top of a tasselled cane. The food had sobered me up, and I remembered Gabriel Marlowe telling me about a play by Karel Câpek, also entitled *The Unknown*, which Marlowe had produced in some foreign capital and which was narrated by a man in a mackintosh wearing a mask; but it was unlikely that Makins had heard of this play, never to my knowledge translated into English, and I held my peace.

The antique dealer, when the typescript came round to him, had no such inhibitions. After he'd finished explaining that all worthwhile drama, indeed all art, had originated somewhere in Central Europe, eaten the last piece of salami and made sure that there was no more wine, he climbed with Makins' assistance into a fur-collared overcoat: there was a curfew for people like him, Golders Green was a long way off, and he looked hopefully round in search of someone going in the same direction who might pay for his taxi; but no one was, and bad-tempered he left.

'Poor fellow,' Makins said. 'He's been through a lot,' and even I nodded sympathetically: none of us being used to this type of person at that time, though we were to become amply familiar with it in the years ahead.

The antique dealer was, however, the only jarring note in the whole evening: the chaps were all nice cheerful intelligent young men and I regret, during all my future nights in Bloomsbury and Soho pubs, that I never came across any of them again; nor did I ever run into the woman who had been transfused with the blood of the goat. Perhaps they were all killed in the war, though I hope not.

Now we sat round drinking beer and looking at the typescript of a very long story by another of Makins' future clients, which included a complete description in blank verse of the film *The Petrified Forest*: some of the characters visited a cinema where this was showing, and while the chap who did something scientific and may have been a bio-chemist was having a pee on the landing, Makins told me that he was the original of one of the key personages in the story.

I asked him whether the story was to be printed in *Horizon*, but he said no: the reason for its rejection seemed to be that the author had a beard. But he himself had a beard, I pointed out. Yes Makins said, he had a beard but this author's beard was reddish, and wearing it he had called on Cyril Connolly and attempted personally to persuade him to publish his poems. The moral seemed to be: never employ the personal approach with editors, still less when in an aggressive mood; on the other hand there was the precedent of Wyndham Lewis reading a MS to Ford Madox Ford while Ford was having a bath. Parts of the red-bearded poet's story seemed stylistically influenced by Lewis, but Connolly was evidently less easily stampeded by shock tactics into accepting material than Ford had been.

It was all fascinating to me, but there I had to leave it, for I was afraid that the digs Makins had procured for me (themselves in Guilford Street) might refuse to let me in if I made it any later, also none of us had another shilling for the gas fire. So we all trooped down into the blackout, Makins having first opened the windows to let out the smoke.

The room he'd booked for me was in a house owned by Belgians and it too was heated by a gas fire which, lacking a shilling, I was unable to light. So I got into an enormous brass bedstead while Makins, who'd accompanied me upstairs, sat by it in hat and overcoat, to have a last smoke.

He said: 'After Rudi's valuable criticism, it might be a good idea to revise my play along less expressionist lines and call it *The Unseen* instead. What d'you think?'

At this, fatigue and drink sandbagged me suddenly, the noise of the pub and the party still went on in my head but with a soporific effect, as the sound of train wheels might lull a traveller; then the noise faded like background babble in a radio play and Makins' voice alone came clearly through, saying: 'Of course Cyril often changes his mind.'

'About what?' I asked sleepily.

'Stuff he's accepted.'

'Not like *Penguin Parade*, it's to be hoped,' I laughed, but Makins was unsmiling.

He said uncomfortably: 'Well, you know how editors are.'

'No,' I said, 'I don't,' then waking completely: 'What's all this about?'

'Your stories,' Makins said: 'Didn't you tell me Cyril had accepted the one about the Chelsea Count?'

'Yes I did. He has.'

Makins passed a hand down his beard, like he had done in the bar.

He said: 'I'm afraid it might be my fault. I told him I didn't consider it quite up to the standard of "A Bit of a Smash".'

'You mean,' I said, sitting up, 'he's not going to print it after all? What about "Five Finger Exercises"? He said he was taking that story too.'

Makins shrugged: 'Well, there again. But there's nothing definite either way.'

'Connolly's letter was definite enough. And he didn't mention any of this to me today.'

Makins said decisively: 'Then I wouldn't mention it to him when you meet tomorrow. Keep in touch and I'll keep you posted. It may never happen and anyway, when "A Bit of a Smash" comes out, you may feel differently about wanting to publish the other two.'

I was about to tell him that I wouldn't feel differently about having to forfeit the fees, which would help to keep me going more comfortably until the army took over from the Assistance; but he had spoken as agent to author, and I was too tired to argue any more now.

'We'll see,' I said, sinking down on the pillows: 'It was a good night, Bill.'

'A bloody good night,' Makins agreed clicking the light off at the door: 'Sleep well now.'

I did.

CYRIL CONNOLLY AT THE CAFÉ ROYAL

The bank cashier was counting pads of pound notes when I appeared at his grille next morning. He carefully examined the amount and signature on the *Horizon* cheque, all of it in Connolly's green ink, then asked: 'What d'you want to do with this?'

'Cash it,' I said.

'Have you an account at this branch?'

'I haven't, no. But Mr Connolly has. He said you'd cash this for me.'

'Sorry,' the cashier said. 'I can't cash it, you've no account here,' and he pushed the cheque back under the grille.

'Why can't you cash it?' I asked. 'Here's my name, quite clearly made out.'

'It's a crossed cheque,' he told me. 'It's not been opened. You could put it through your own bank, would be the best way.'

'I haven't a bank.'

The cashier went back to counting pound notes. People without banks did not interest him.

'What d'you mean, the cheque hasn't been opened?' I asked.

He glanced up, surprised to find me still there: he'd thought the matter settled.

'A crossed cheque can only be paid into a banking account,' he said patiently. 'It cannot be cashed unless it's been correctly opened.'

'Against banking regulations otherwise,' said a second, older cashier, who'd come up to listen.

'And if this cheque were opened? Would you cash it then?'

The second cashier in turn took the cheque and examined every inch of it. 'But this hasn't been opened,' he said at last.

'Suppose Mr Connolly was to open it for me. I'm having lunch with him today.'

The second cashier said: 'Could I see your identity card, please?' He seemed to have taken over entirely. The first cashier had meantime got through counting a couple of hundred. The second cashier went over my identity card with equal care, even reading the regulations on the back; then he said: 'Well we don't naturally like cashing opened cheques as a rule, but in this case we might stretch a point. If you can persuade our client to open it of course.'

'Of course,' I said. 'What's the procedure?'

'Well these lines here, which make it a crossed cheque, must be crossed out and the words Pay Cash written in between. And this must also be signed or initialled by the drawer.'

'I get it. Thank you.'

'Always glad to be of service,' the second cashier smiled. 'Good morning.'

'D'you mind if I have the cheque back?'

'Please forgive me,' he handed it over with a bow: 'I was quite forgetting, ha ha.'

'See you later,' I said, 'Ha ha,' then had to return for my briefcase which I'd left behind and which had not, luckily, been pinched. The first cashier was still counting: he must have got up to a Monkey by now.

I didn't realise that this incident would recur like a nightmare through-out my career, editors being what they are and banks even more so. Nowadays opened cheques as well are subjected to suspicious scrutiny and may even be refused, but that morning I'd more important things than bank officials to worry about.

I was mainly worried as to whether Connolly meant to turn down the other two stories that he'd accepted, as Makins had hinted the night before. I thought perhaps he would pay me for them even if he didn't print, though I ought to have known better than that; and on my way to the Café Royal I was determined to ask him right out, despite my prospective agent's advice.

But at sight of Connolly my resolve at once began to falter. He was in the upstairs bar as arranged, sitting on a sofa near the door with a bulging leather satchel beside him and galley proofs unfurled upon his knee. His round plump face looked mild enough and he even smiled as he saw me, nonetheless he was clearly not a man amenable to direct questioning (though fond of it himself), and had indeed a built-in resistance to such an approach.

Waving to a waiter and pointing to an armchair opposite with the thick editorial pencil in his hand, he said as I sat down: 'I hope you had a good evening, was the room all right? Did you get your money at the bank?'

'Actually, no,' I replied to this last bit.

Connolly's shaggy eyebrows shot up in surprise. 'No? Why not?'

'The cheque hadn't been opened you see.'

'No,' Connolly said his eyebrows coming down in a slight frown, 'I don't see. I made it out to you, it can be cashed across the counter surely?'

'Not unless these lines are crossed out and Pay Cash written in between. Otherwise absolutely not. Against banking regulations.'

'Never heard of such nonsense,' Connolly said, 'but of course I'll alter it at once. What did you say I had to do?'

The waiter interrupted with our drinks and while Connolly fumbled for change I looked round the bar, which I'd not been in since an evening just before my marriage. I'd sat over by the ticker-tape drinking Corpse Revivers with a man called Mooney who could quote Gibbon off by heart. We were waiting for my future wife, and at a table facing us sat a startling blonde with legs crossed so high that Mooney said one could almost read the time.

That was October 1936: now the tape ticked out war news, the bar was full of uniforms, Corpse Revivers were off the cocktail menu, and the blonde's clock had surely been stopped.

Connolly said: 'There, I've crossed out the lines and written Pay Cash, how's that?'

'I'm sorry, you're supposed to sign the Pay Cash bit.'

The galleys slipped from Connolly's knee and unfurled across the floor, I hastened to pick them up, and muttering indignantly about the officiousness of bank clerks he signed the alterations with his satchel for a desk.

'D'you think they'll cash it now?'

'Thank you. I'm sure they will,' and they did.

'You must be sure to get to the bank before three,'[1] Connolly told me, then tapping with his editor's pencil the proofs which I'd passed back to him, he said: 'Maugham'.

'I beg your pardon?'

'Somerset Maugham.' His article on the Detective Story for *Horizon*.

'When's it coming out?' I asked. The article had been advertised as a future attraction in *Horizon* itself, and I'd been looking forward to its appearance.

Connolly did not directly answer. Instead he asked: 'D'you know anything about detective stories?'

I said: 'As it happens, quite a lot.'

'Then tell me what you think of this?'

'You want me to read the article?' I said surprised.

'A quick glance through should be enough.' Connolly said and sat back impassive with hands folded on his satchel top while I read.

Maugham's article was the one afterwards published as 'The Decline and Fall of the Detective Story' in a book of essays entitled *The Vagrant Mood*; though, since only one novel by Raymond Chandler had been published at this date, the version I saw cannot have included the references to Philip Marlowe: spelt throughout by Maugham as if he were the town from which G.S. Marlowe took his name. But otherwise the material must have been substantially the same.

'Well?' Connolly asked as I again handed back the proofs.

'D'you think it's a good article?'

'Of course. Don't you?'

---

1 I got there before three, for it turned out Conolly had another appointment at 2.15, and I must have misinterpreted 'Lunch *time*' as 'Lunch' the day before. Later I ate Welsh rarebit in the buffet car of the train taking me back to the South Coast.

Connolly had folded up the galleys and was thrusting them deep into his satchel from which other proofs protruded. He succeeded at last in pulling the straps through the fastening buckles, the satchel by now at bursting point was rolled aside like an antagonist whom he had bound and gagged, and he settled himself more comfortably on the sofa. Only then did he reply.

'No,' he said. 'I don't think it's a good article.'

'You don't?' I echoed in dismay.

Benignly smiling, Connolly shook his head. 'In fact I've decided not to print it.'

'Not print it,' I gasped, 'But it's by Maugham!'

'I have the greatest respect for Maugham as a novelist,' Connolly said in his soft bland voice, 'and I don't say this is a bad article. It's good enough to be accepted for *Horizon* but not quite good enough for me to publish.'

Then, not quite changing the subject, but dropping that of Maugham, he began to discourse on the distinction between the detective story and the thriller: a theme already examined in his early *New Statesman* essays.

I knew by the blandness of his smile that I'd been given an oblique answer to a question not yet asked. It was now plain that if a long article by an author of Maugham's eminence, obviously commissioned and already heralded in the magazine, could thus be rejected out of hand, my other two stories, irrespective of acceptance, stood little chance of appearing in *Horizon*, and indeed they didn't. I dared not ask if Maugham had been, or would be, paid.

'Of course the detective story is in decline,' Connolly was saying. 'Its great period, its golden age, really ended with *The Glass Key* in 1931.'

I said: 'Aren't you quoted as saying that in *The Face on the Cutting Room Floor* by Cameron McCabe, whoever he is?'

'Why yes,' Connolly said, 'I believe I am. A brilliant book don't you agree?'

I did agree. *The Face on the Cutting Room Floor* was a strange sophisticated off-beat crime novel, by its very nature pseudonymous, which came out in 1937. 'You don't happen to know who really wrote it?' I asked.

'No I never found out. Who would be your guess?'

I said: 'I'd thought of you, actually.'

'As Cameron McCabe?' Connolly stared at me astonished. 'What gave you that idea?' Well, knowing your interest in this type of book it occurred to me you might have had a go at writing one under another name. Whoever wrote it has from internal evidence read a lot of detective stories, and your own reviews are so often quoted in the Epilogue that…' Here I broke off embarrassed, conscious too late of the brick I'd already dropped.

But to my relief Connolly had begun to laugh. 'I see,' he said. 'You thought I was giving myself a pseudonymous boost. Well I'm sorry, I'd like to have written that book, but I didn't. The author's obviously an experienced film technician for one thing, and I am not.'

Our glasses were empty, he flapped a hand at the waiter, then said: 'Now tell me, how did you get on with Bill Makins last night?'

'Excellently. Though I was scared stiff of him at first sight.'

Connolly laughed. 'Yes he's very fierce looking, but wouldn't he be more so without the beard?' and we discussed Makins' beard, Connolly believing that he wore it because his face would otherwise seem to stark and Scottish, I taking the view that it added to his fierceness. Both of us discounted the possibility that it might conceal a weak chin.

Connolly said: 'But a lot of young men seem to be wearing beards these days. There's another young man who comes round to the office occasionally with a reddish beard, trying to argue me into publishing things of his. Poetical plays,' he sighed: 'I suppose I'll have to give in eventually, I'm very weak that way,' but he wasn't weak and he didn't give in, for I cannot remember anything by the red bearded author ever appearing in *Horizon*.

I drank a fresh drink very quickly to give me courage, then asked: 'I suppose there's no more news from the printers about "A Bit of a Smash", for when I saw Maugham's proofs first I'd hoped they were my own, but now I'd begun to fear this story wouldn't come out either. But I was wrong.

Connolly seemed to rouse himself: 'I'm glad you reminded me, yesterday I forgot to ask. The substitutes for what the printers termed "offensive language". Have you decided yet what they're to be?'

'I have them here,' I said. 'You'll see I've put "sewn-up" for "pissed-up" as you suggested.'

'"Sewn-up", yes,' Connolly said reading rapidly down the list: '"Holy Smoke" instead of "By Christ", "Bunk" for "Balls", "Bleeder" for "Bugger" and "Damn-all" for "Sweet F.A." That seems all right and the word "bainchut" can stay in because they don't know what it means. It's a shame to emasculate your story like this, not my fault, all these printers are such damned puritans you know. Almost an occupational disease. But never fear,' he smiled tucking the list away, 'I'll get that piece out in *Horizon* if I have to bring printers over from Madras to do it!'

And, for all I know, he may have done. That might explain why, when the story did appear, part of my surname was misspelt 'Maclaryn': an error which partly reduced the pleasure I felt at seeing something of mine in print at last.

They Can't Give You a Baby

*　　　*　　　*

A BIG LAKE

'THEY CAN DO ANYTHING TO YOU IN THE ARMY BAR GIVE YOU A baby,' the old London-Irish porter who'd had varicocele and served in four campaigns told me as I got aboard the train in July 1940. 'But keep your trap shut and your bowels open you can't come to no harm.'

So I reported as ordered to the Infantry Training Camp at Blandford, Essex, and was there enlisted as No. 6027033 Private Ross J.

Further advice was offered me on arrival by an older recruit who said: 'Take my tip, mate, when they put you down for the range don't go on the piss the night before and don't go with no woman neither 'cause you can't shoot proper with a shaking hand,' but this advice was wasted because the only drink available in the camp was Naafi beer which certainly resembled piss but was not drunk-making enough to send one on it; no women were allowed in; and we for the first fortnight weren't allowed out.

Besides, going on the range was out of the question as none of us had so far been issued with rifles: since Dunkirk, in short supply.

The survivors from Dunkirk had been billeted for a short time in the camp on their return, and the latrine walls were decorated with drawings of a death's head above a grave-mound, underlined with the caption: 'HOW D'YOU LIKE THIS YOU ROOKIE BASTARDS? (SIGNED) THE BOYS WHO BEEN THROUGH IT.'

There was also a rhyme signed by Spokeshave the Shithouse Poet, a universal figure who seems to have served in every regiment in the British army:

'When apples are ripe
And ready for plucking
Girls of sixteen are ready for…
NOT WHAT YOU THINK THEY'RE
READY FOR YOU FILTHY-MINDED
FUCKERS.'

The camp looked from the air like a big lake, they told us, which hadn't prevented Jerry from dropping a load on it in the not so distant past, as craters in the surrounding chalk abundantly testified.

Every time a plane roared overhead, the blokes rushed joyfully to the barrack hut windows, shouting 'Watch out, boys, here comes Hitler!'; they made whistling noises like sticks of bombs falling, followed by concerted shouts of 'BOOM' to represent the explosion. But that summer Hitler seemed to have got sick of coming.

'That's on account of this new camouflage we got,' explained our platoon sergeant, who looked like the soldierly figure depicted on the labels of Camp coffee bottles and claimed that we resembled not a big lake but a big bloody shower.

So while we new recruits drilled in shirt sleeve order on the enormous sun-baked barrack square, other more seasoned soldiers sprayed the surface of sheds and buildings round about with camouflage paint that speckled our bare arms and khaki shirts with almost indelible brown and green spots as it was blown towards us on the wind.

We drilled at first with broomsticks owing to the dearth of rifles, then an actual rifle appeared and was handed round the square, though our platoon hadn't much time to learn its mechanism before a runner came to attention in front of our sergeant saying: 'Please sar'nt our sar'nt in No. 8 says could we have the rifle for a dekko over there 'cause none of our blokes so much as seen one yet.'

We had none of us seen a steel helmet at close quarters either, they hadn't been issued to us although a consignment in the stores awaited a War Office or Command order authorising distribution.

Then one afternoon, when parades were over and the blokes in our barrack hut were rattling their mess tins all ready for tea, Hitler came at last.

His coming was not heralded, as it should have been, by sirens (it turned out after someone had forgotten to let these off), and a series of dull detonations from the Artillery Camp across the valley caused little stir, as things were always going off over there. But this time the hum of an engine could be heard, the blokes began their whistling and booming then stopped abruptly, dropping their mess tins, as real whistles and crumps duplicated outside the sounds they'd made.

Through the window, from the hillside on which the Artillery Camp was built, a tall brown flower of earth could be seen blossoming while we watched: it expanded outwards like a firework in all directions and afterwards many swore they had seen swastikas on the wings of the lone raider that was now heading straight towards us.

There were no NCOs present, still less an officer; we dashed to the side doorway, got jammed in the entrance, then threw ourselves flat beneath a whitewashed wall outside as Jerry zoomed over low, chips of whitewash flew; and we heard for the first time in earnest the DUH-DUH-DUH of the machine gun that had been so often mimicked in jest.

The plane dived, again the DUH-DUH-DUH, then it banked and headed towards the Gunner camp while we made crouching for the trenches: there was no one to lead the way there but we knew that already since we'd helped, ourselves, to dig them in the chalk, pissing on our palms to harden them as it was said that navvies did.

More bombs whistled down, one sounding like a direct hit; and the Nazi plane returned, circling silver and so high above our heads it could hardly be seen; voices from adjoining trenches shouted: 'Where the bleeding bloody officers?' and 'Why'nt we got tin hats?' while somebody shrilled hysterically: 'Shut your row he'll hear us, he'll hear us I tell you shut your bleeding row.'

The Jerry pilot didn't hear them and soon ceased to hear anything at all, for he flew away to be caught in the Bournemouth barrage and shot down in flames so we were later told.

Directly he'd gone everyone clambered out of the trenches and began to utter guffaws of relief and bravado, then suddenly a young subaltern appeared panting, to mutters of 'Bout time too' and 'Joy your tea, mate?', and red in the face ordered us back in until the All Clear was blown, which happened after we'd stood tealess for another thirty minutes in the trenches.

There were no casualties in the Artillery Camp, indeed we almost wished Jerry had chosen us instead, for the direct hit had demolished the Gunners' empty gym whereas ours remained intact and there were many who hated PT, above all the Horse.

But the upshot of this baptism by fire was that we were issued with tin hats and small arms shortly followed. First to be given a rifle was our barrack-room NCO, a lance-corporal who'd been an insurance clerk in civvy street and now felt the chance had come to show his mettle as a leader of men.

To demonstrate the efficacy of our new steel helmets and the protection they afforded, he clapped on his own tin hat then handing his rifle to a huge recruit, told this man to strike him with the butt.

The recruit, a gentle timid soul despite his size, demurred. 'That's an order,' the lance-jack rapped out, 'You either hit me or go on a 252,' there was a pause while the nature of a 252, the minor offence report, was explained to the huge recruit who could expect seven days to barracks if he went on one for disobeying an order; then down came the rifle butt, blood spurted from under the tin hat's brim and the corporal sank slowly down, the sound of his fall swiftly echoed by a heavier thump as the huge recruit followed suit, having fainted at the sight of blood.

It appeared a loose screw inside the corporal's helmet had been driven into his scalp by the blow; we agreed that a screw had also been loose inside the corporal's head, and he was carted off to hospital, where the huge contrite recruit visited him every day: being unable, himself, ever to handle a rifle with confidence thereafter.

Meanwhile the barrack-room radio played records of Judy Garland singing 'Over The Rainbow' or a tune called 'I Was Watching a Man Paint A Fence'; and the camp must have ceased to look from above like a big lake, for Jerry took time off from the Battle of Britain to bomb us day and night.

Planes came over in droves, it was no longer necessary for the blokes to whistle and boom, all leave was cancelled, and when not a lot of the ITC was left we were abruptly evacuated, destination unknown to all other ranks.

On arrival, after a roundabout train journey so long that we'd believed ourselves bound for Scotland, we were assembled on an enormous desert of asphalt and addressed in pitch darkness by the Commanding Officer of another ITC in Suffolk.

'Now you men have been through a bad time,' he told us, 'blitzed and strafed right and left by the Hun, and you've stood up to it well. But you'll be glad to hear that Jerry hasn't smelt us out so far ha ha, so you can get on with your training in peace,' and at this prospect searchlights suddenly probed the sky, a German engine nosed chugging somewhere overhead, and the sirens started to wail.

X COMPANY

Now what I always think of as the Brown Period began. Browned-off was the phrase one heard most often in X Company, the other recruits owing to difficulty in finding any skirt started jocosely to talk of having Bits of Brown (buggery), the RAF blokes stationed next door called us Brown Jobs, it was autumn and the leaves were brown, and everything was uniquely brown.

The Biscuits on which we fell, exhausted after all day training, were also brown and a great source of grumbling as at Blandford we'd had real iron beds with sheets to sleep in: here we kipped down on bare boards with the three brown Biscuits beneath us, wrapped in brown blankets which had been recently fumigated and stank for weeks on end; on the other hand we couldn't spend much time in them since Jerry visited us regularly every night.

Indeed, Acky the barrack-room clown and butt kipped always fully clothed and wearing boots, so's to be ready he told us 'for when the sireens start dropping their shit'. Nothing could persuade Acky that the sirens were not the cause of bombs being dropped; only dimly aware that aircraft existed, he believed that the warning was a special device which Hitler himself operated by remote control, anticipating the doodlebugs and V-2 rockets yet to come: perhaps like many simpletons he possessed the gift of prophecy.

The worst of the raids was not stumbling to the trenches through black night occasionally lit by bursting incendiaries, searchlight beams or flashes of ack-ack fire, but waiting in the iron cold when winter came for the All Clear to go, for until it went we were not allowed to return to our blankets, which by this time had ceased to stink.

I remember one night standing in a trench next to a corporal when all sounds of strife had long since faded and any danger was clearly past, both of us frozen to the bone despite long woollen underpants, battle dress, greatcoat, balaclava helmet and woollen gloves: we'd ceased for some time to feel our feet except as blocks of ice we stood on; but when I cursed our lot the corporal stolidly replied: 'Could be worse mate.'

I said: 'How could it be worse? We've been here two bloody hours frozen solid while Jerry drops stuff all round us, now he's gone but that bastard siren still won't blow maybe till reveille, so how could it be worse?'

The corporal said stolidly: 'Could be bleeding sight worse mate. Could be pissing down with rain as well.'

It was an unpleasant sensation after such a night to rise at six with the sky above still black and stars out over the wash-house where we shaved in icy water: the cistern of the latrines, liberally sprinkled with the works of Spokeshave, having also frozen so the plug wouldn't pull.

At these times the sense of helplessness was strong. Jaeger, who despite his asthma had been allowed into the Artillery, could at least defend himself: in fact he had done more. Manning a gun during an alert on the coast one night, he'd got bored and fired off a burst at random, bringing down by a lucky chance a Jerry plane that happened to be flying over at the time.

For this feat he'd been forthwith promoted bombardier; and by the same post that brought his letter announcing this came under separate cover a copy of his first novel, out that week.

Nobody promoted me, I remained unalterably a private and had temporarily given up any attempt to write. I had however sent my green folder of stories, returned finally by *Horizon*, to a new anthology called *English Story* which was due to be published twice a year in hard-cover book-form, giving the ITC address without knowing that its editor, Woodrow Wyatt, was stationed as a subaltern in this very camp.

So one evening when we got back from shovelling snow off the rifle range where, owing to weather conditions, we'd still not fired a single shot, I received word that an officer wanted me to report urgent over at his bunk.

WOODROW WYATT IN THE ARMY

Last time I heard of Woodrow Wyatt MP (Lab.) he was chasing out of his house burglars who'd been incautious enough to break into it. By that time he had been not only an MP but a Parliamentary Under-Secretary and Financial Secretary to the War Office, and I hadn't seen him, except when he was interviewing someone on the Telly, for twenty years.

The photograph appended to the *Evening Standard* account of the abortive burglary told me little of what he looked like now save that it looked as if he'd put on flesh.

But when I saw him first, as a second lieutenant in the Suffolks, he was a short slender young man, precocious though not pompous, about whom everything seemed to be polished: his Sam Browne and ox-blood shoes, the buttons of his service dress, his round cheeks and reddish nose. He had a small neat head and, brushed flat across his forehead, black or very dark hair that seemed polished also, or at any rate to shine. His eyes shone brightly too behind horn rims, the lenses of his spectacles were thick and so were his lips, which pouted as he spoke or puffed a cigar.

At that date he must have been twenty-two, six years younger than myself, but was apparently a qualified barrister or anyhow had studied for the bar. Altogether a bright young man and bearing already the hallmarks of one who'd far to go. But though a socialist he'd no political ambitions then, his ambition was to be himself a writer and to make a really good anthology out of *English Story* which he co-edited with his wife.

We sat smoking cigars in his bunk where a small stove burned, blissfully warm after shovelling snow all day, there may have been some drink as well and it was pleasant to talk of other things than training and what we were down for on tomorrow's detail, though I was at first nervous of being discovered there, as the Battalion took a dim view of fraternisation despite Hore-Belisha: especially between officers and other ranks, since even a newly made-up lance-jack was not allowed to 'walk out', as they put it, with a private soldier.

'Like a bloody courting couple,' Wyatt chortled when I told him this. 'Honestly they are a pack of bloody twerps.' He had a loud angry-sounding laugh and a complete contempt for routine and regulations. 'I'd damn soon send them packing if they came sniffing round my private quarters, don't you worry.'

He told me he'd accepted my only other story about Madras, much shorter than 'A Bit of a Smash', and entitled 'The Hell of a Time': it would be coming out in the next volume of *English Story*, and he planned to publish another of mine in the volume after that only they hadn't chosen yet.

He said: 'Any story except one called "Happy as the Day is Long". I've not read that so far, but Susan's dead against it so that rules it out.'

'Your wife?'

Wyatt nodded. 'I rely implicitly on her judgment.'

I said: 'But that's a good story. Connolly nearly printed it, so did *Penguin Parade*. Read it yourself and see.'

He said: 'No, no, Susan says it's no good at all and Susan can't be wrong, so I'm afraid that's that,' but that wasn't that, for much later he read the story for himself and was so enthusiastic that he sent me a telegram of acceptance: though this was after he separated from his wife.

He asked what I was writing now, I said under army conditions it was impossible to write, he said Balls, I should put in for a pip, then I'd be more comfortable and also be able to do something for the men.

I said I'd a hard job to do anything for myself let alone the men, he said Utter nonsense, he'd have a word with the Old Man; and when I got up to go it was slightly surprising to find he didn't know what time Lights Out was for Other Ranks.

But then he'd not been commissioned long, no rubbish about going through the ranks, but straight from school OTC and University to be commissioned almost on the outbreak.

I saw him twice more before he was transferred to an orderly-room at Ipswich: once in the Company Lines, where he showed signs of wanting to stop and talk, but with my CSM watching, I saluted him and hurried on; then when he was doing duty as Orderly Officer in the cookhouse.

There he tasted a spoonful of rice pudding, pronounced it perfectly foul (which was an understatement) and tried to egg us on to make complaints, though even I buried my face in my tin plate: since to say anything against the food amounted to a Frivolous Complaint and I'd nearly done jankers for that already.

Then came his transfer to Ipswich, where I later followed him: by that time he'd been posted for special training at the Staff College, but terrific tales persisted of his prowess as a Defending Officer at Courts Martial, for which he'd become much feared and respected in the Regiment.

Accused soldiers from far and wide asked for Mr Wyatt as an American in trouble might send for Perry Mason. His clients were always acquitted, he'd succeeded in getting off a chap who'd burned down his tent during an exercise under canvas and had even secured an acquittal in a case of what sounded uncommonly like murder. When, in London on leave, I asked him afterwards how he'd managed this, he merely laughed out loud and said the Prosecution Officers opposing him were such dimwits it was just a piece of cake. He was by then a staff captain at the War House and tried to get me a job there, though he failed.

But he must have put a word in for me somewhere at the Suffolk ITC, for suddenly I was brought before my Company Commander and put on the roll of OCTU candidates as a potential officer.

The major was ex-Indian army, enormously tall with a shaggy black moustache and he wasn't stuck on having haircuts either, though where his men were concerned it was a case of 'Don't do as I do, do as I tell you'.

He said to me in his subterranean rumble, which all of us imitated though with respect: 'Now look here Ross I've had one or two complaints about you, insubordination and so on, but I'm prepared to believe you're doing your best and so I'm recommending you to see the Commanding Officer with a view to obtaining a commission. After all I suppose soldiering must be damned difficult for you just as writing books would be for me. Couldn't write a book to save my ruddy life. However there's a war on and we're all having to make sacrifices and do things we don't care for. Take me for example, my real life was in India, been there since I was a boy, but the war was being fought in Europe so I went and got myself shot up at Dunkirk, too badly for them to ever have me back out there I'm afraid. No, when this show's over I'll be kicked out with a tiny pension, won't even be able to afford to hunt, which was the only thing I enjoyed doing in civilian life over here. I was shot in the arse too, which makes it worse. Hard to sit a horse and looks as if I'd been bloody well running away.'

OPPENHEIM

The Commanding Officer was a very small colonel sitting behind a very big desk. He screwed in an eyeglass and said: 'Educated in the South of France eh? D'you speak French?'

'Yes sir,' I said.

The CO said: 'Not much use, French, now that France has fallen unfortunately.'

Then he looked at my paper again and said: 'What's this, "Civilian Occupation: Author". Are you an author?'

'Yes sir,' I told him.

'D'you write spy thrillers?'

'No sir.'

The CO said: 'Pity, that. E. Phillips Oppenheim now, he writes damn good spy thrillers. Lived in the South of France too. D'you ever come across him down there?'

'As a matter of fact I did sir. At a party once.'

'Very interesting,' said the CO. 'And tell me what did he talk about?'

'Well sir he talked about agents mostly.'

'Agents!' the CO exclaimed. 'Well of course, fellow like that would know all about secret agents. Wonder to me they haven't made him Head of MI5.'

'I'm sorry sir,' said. 'It wasn't secret agents he talked about, it was literary agents.'

'Literary agents?' the CO said. 'What the devil are they?'

I said: 'Well sir, they place the work you've written with editors and publishers you see.'

The CO said: 'Do they now.'

I said: 'Not in my experience sir.'

The CO said: 'Oh, thought you said they did. Well anyway it's most interesting to've talked to you,' and turning to my Company Commander, who stood massively beside his chair: 'Well of course he's passed all right, an author, knows Oppenheim and that, eh? Why hasn't he got a stripe?'

The major rumbled: 'No vacancy on establishment sir.'

The CO said: 'Oh, pity that. Well all right Ross, Brigadier next step, keep your fingers crossed, gooday'; the sergeant-major entered shouting: 'Private Ross, Private Ross SHUN. Left wheel, quick march, left-right-left-right-left,' and in getting past the CO I was luckier than many OCTU wallahs, one of whom had been failed for the following reason.

He was an instructor, young, fighting fit, two stripes, splendid record as an NCO and would have made an even better officer, but at one time he'd been stationed in Scotland and the CO had therefore asked him: 'How long is the Forth Bridge, Corporal?'

'I'm sorry sir,' the corporal answered, 'I couldn't say.'

'You mean you don't know?'

'Yes sir.'

'How long were you in Scotland Corporal?'

'Six months sir.'

'And you don't know the length of the Forth Bridge?'

'No sir.'

'Thank you Corporal, that's all,' and the corporal was marched out, to be marked unsuitable as officer material. But the real reason for failing him had nothing to do with the length of the Forth Bridge, it was because of his strong Cockney accent, which the CO didn't feel would make him welcome in the Mess.

Giles Cooper, now one of our best TV dramatists and certainly the best we have on radio, was as a young lieutenant attached to the ITC for a time, though of course owing to our CO's rigid segregation of officers and men I never met him there.

Giles, as he afterwards told me, also found disfavour with the CO almost on arrival, for a reason even stranger than that which caused the rejection of the corporal.

On his first evening in the Mess, the CO had said to the Adjutant: 'That new young fellow just been posted to us. Cooper, isn't it?'

'It is sir.'

'He wears an eyeglass.'

'Yes sir. Astigmatism I believe.'

'Damned impertinence you mean,' the CO said. 'I'm the only one who's allowed to wear an eyeglass in this Mess. Have Mr Cooper posted elsewhere please, soon as you can, overseas if possible,' which is how Giles came eventually to serve in Burma, which provided the setting for one of his finest TV plays.

BOOM

But I never became an officer.

It was at the WOSBE, the War Office Selection Board Test, that I came unstuck. I'd been doing splendidly until the very last exercise when, being for the moment in command, I decided to save the lives of my men at the expense of my own.

It was a dodgy situation, all the umpires had gathered round to watch: we were retreating with imaginary Jerries on our tail, imagining bullets were whining round our heads and the only means of escape was over a bridge (non-imaginary) which we'd built across a bottomless chasm below. The chasm was not imaginary either but it was hardly bottomless, being about fifteen feet deep, so ordering my lot ahead of me across the bridge I decided to blow this up with our imaginary grenades and ammunition so the Jerries couldn't follow, thus also destroying the ammunition which might otherwise have fallen into their hands.

Therefore, straddling the tree trunk we'd stretched across the gap, I tugged it loose from the bank and clasping it in my arms fell to my death in the chasm: I'm not certain I wasn't riddled with German bullets for good measure as I fell.

Anyhow in my opinion I deserved a posthumous VC and a hero's grave at the very least; yet to my surprise, when I'd scrambled out of the chasm, the umpires were all walking away and the following day I was returned unsuitable to my unit, the report to my Company Commander saying that I'd not taken the Test seriously enough to merit recommendation for OCTU.

'Not seriously enough?' I cried. 'When I died to save my men? What more do they expect?'

I was no longer at the ITC and this Company Commander was not the major:[1] in fact he was a captain.

He said: 'You died for your men?'

I said: 'Greater love hath no man,' and told him about the bridge.

The captain said: 'Seems to me you behaved with great presence of mind. Don't know what they can have found wrong.'

'Nor do I sir. Except for one thing?'

'And what was that?'

'Well you see sir, when I blew up the bridge and myself as well, I shouted BOOM as I fell into the chasm. That's what may have upset them.'

The captain said: 'You shouted BOOM? But why?'

I said: 'Sound of the explosion sir. You see everything was imaginary, the Germans and the bullets, the grenades and ammunition, so I thought we ought to have a little realism when it came to the bang, otherwise it all seemed a bit too much like a game of tin soldiers if you understand me sir.'

'I do,' the captain said dubiously, 'But all the same,' he added shaking his head, 'you shouldn't have shouted BOOM.'

---

1   The major, now a Lieut. Col., had also left the ITC and was my CO instead of OC in the new battalion.

The Double Death of
William Cooper Makins

*   *   *

BUT IN THE AUTUMN OF 1941 BILL MAKINS HAD NOT EVEN DIED once, nor had I yet shouted BOOM. As a potential officer (though still without a stripe) I'd been transferred to orderly-room duties at the Ipswich HQ where Woodrow Wyatt had secured his sensational acquittals, and Makins, as my self-appointed agent, was trying to find me a publisher in London.

Previous to my being enlisted, when 'A Bit of a Smash' appeared in *Horizon*, a publisher had however found me.

30 BEDFORD SQUARE AGAIN

Rupert Hart-Davis was then a junior director of Jonathan Cape and soon after receiving his enthusiastic letter I was seated opposite him in a different, smaller office from that in which I'd been interviewed two years before by Mr Cape himself: now in America on business and prevented from returning by the outbreak of war.

Hart-Davis in those days was a large loose-limbed young man, blond with small shrewd blue eyes in a big fair face: smooth shaven except for the fair moustache clipped square above a humorous mouth. He had a deep hearty voice, lounged easily in hairy tweeds and swivel chair and although he did not, like Norman Collins, actually put his feet up on the desk, gave the impression of being just about to do so.

Perhaps all young publishers affected these relaxed postures in the office, though the way Hart-Davis sat may have been due to the length of his legs, for he was perhaps two inches taller than myself besides being four years older.

One of the first things he asked me was my age, and when I told him 28, stated his own, adding that I'd been quite right to publish late.

'It's much better not to publish anything until one's properly mature,' he told me and as two properly mature men we beamed at each other across the desk. The Thirties writers were like pop singers are today, adolescent publication was if not the rule at any rate no exception, and I'm always surprised when nowadays the thirty-year-old author of some first novel is treated as if he were an infant prodigy.

I took care however not to tell Hart-Davis that my apparent wisdom in publishing late was really due to my work being hitherto rejected right and left; then we talked of Simenon, whose first books to be translated into English were just being issued by Routledge, two Maigrets in one volume to make up the 80,000 words then de rigueur in the trade.

Hart-Davis said: 'Of course all this business about length is absolute tripe. The Maigret novels are good precisely because they're short. In France 40,000 words is quite acceptable for separate publication, so he's able to cut out all the boring bits and is therefore much more readable. In England detective story writers are obliged to pad, their publishers insist on 80,000 because of the libraries, and that's why ours seem so damned dull.'

I said: 'But would you as a publisher accept a detective story or any other novel of 40,000 words if it were sent to you? Wouldn't the same restrictions apply?'

Hart-Davis swivelled sideways in his chair, stretched his legs out further, then said well they didn't publish detective stories anyway, and of course they'd done *The Postman* and other short American novels that'd been successful: he nevertheless admitted frankly that owing to pressure from the lending libraries publication of anything under 70,000 was a risk not lightly to be undertaken.

However, he said, it might be different now, with wartime paper rationing, and if ever I wrote a novel, even underlength, they'd be glad to consider it, and at parting he clapped me on the back. Despite his heartiness and genuine good fellowship I sensed he was a shrewd man besides being a likeable one, it showed in his eyes, and I thought I'd be lucky to have him for a publisher.

Since our meeting, in spite of army conditions, I had indeed written a short novel; but unfortunately Hart-Davis had been called up like everyone else, except Makins whom they still hadn't managed to enrol, and who wrote me that Rupert was now a Coldstream Guardsman.

TOO SHORT

The short novel I'd managed to complete had started as the 10,000 word South of France story which Connolly had asked me to write for *Horizon*, but ended up at treble the length.

Naturally *Horizon* couldn't print it, as it would have more than filled the entire magazine; Oliver Warner of Chatto and Windus, approached by Makins, had shown interest and then backed down because of the length: even shorter than the minimum mentioned by Hart-Davis; Allen and Unwin had rejected it for the same reason, mislaying for a while the second half of the MS during the period of consideration.

They were however much more interested in my vacuum-cleaner novel, originally estimated at 25,000 words but evidently destined to be much longer, since Part One alone comprised 20,000: already written and now in the hands of Makins.

'Congratulations! It is becoming richer,' he wrote to me and promised to show the MS to Philip Unwin, nephew of the Chairman, at the earliest opportunity, adding as a postscript: 'Unless the ruddy army gets me first'.

Meanwhile my second Madras piece only appeared in Woodrow Wyatt's *English Story* No. 2 and had a reasonable reception when this was reviewed: I'd also managed to sell at last 'Five Finger Exercises' (always difficult, in those pre-*Lolita* days, to place because of its subject)[1] to another miscellany called *Fortune Anthology*; though 'sell' is not quite accurate since *Fortune Anthology* couldn't afford to pay a fee: Makins suggesting when he heard this that the *Anthology* should appear in future under its initials only as these seemed appropriate enough.

MUSEUM STREET

Philip Unwin, suave and greying at the temples, shook his head roguishly at me: 'When I read "A Bit of a Smash" I said to myself "Ah, these Sahibs from out East certainly know how to tell a story,"' and paused, looking in his black jacket and pin-stripe trousers like a Harley Street psychiatrist or an aesthetic member of some government department, preferably the Colonial Office.

---

1 I was consequently surprised when a *TLS* reviewer later dismissed it as a conventional magazine story, out of place in an avant-garde miscellany like this.

Then he went on: 'It was a disappointment when Bill Makins told me you'd never been to Madras, but you know how to tell a story all the same I must admit.'

The implication was of an imposture or false pretences good-humouredly exposed, but I was glad Makins had passed on this information as I wasn't feeling in the least like a Sahib that afternoon. I was passing through London on leave, had not yet been able to change into civvy clothes and even in my best battle dress, brightened by the yellow and red Suffolk flashes, felt no match for Unwin's formal elegance.

I was particularly self-conscious about my heavy army boots, and glad that these were hidden beneath his desk in the office at Ruskin House: Other Ranks not being allowed to go about in shoes at this stage of the war.

Unwin smiled, the psychiatrist for the moment uppermost. 'Curious this fixation, however, in the novel also the narrator returns to England from Madras. Is there some psychological explanation I wonder.'

'None,' I told him. 'I just like the characters to have backgrounds that are not my own.'

'Ah yes,' Unwin nodded, 'I understand. It reduces the autobiographical element certainly,' and aligning on his desk top the MS books that Makins had passed to him, went on to say the firm was willing to make me an advance in order both to secure an option on the novel and also encourage me to continue writing it.

His smile had switched to the administratorial, his tone became more suavely diplomatic, and I felt like a small native tribe on whom a disadvantageous treaty is about to be imposed.

'How much?' I asked.

Unwin said: 'We were thinking in terms of a total advance of £25. Of which ten would be payable on signature of contract.'

I said: 'It's not an awful lot.'

Unwin explained: 'My uncle, our Chairman, does not believe in making large advances to young authors. He doesn't believe that this practice lends encouragement to their industry.'

I said: 'You mean they're more likely to work if they're broke?' not knowing that this is an illusion which all publishers entertain.

In his book *The Truth About Publishing* (7th edition) Sir Stanley Unwin LLD states: 'The hardest bargain he (a financially sound publisher) may drive is likely to prove more profitable to you than the most alluring contract with an insolvent firm.' Nonetheless I felt that, while Allen and Unwin were undoubtedly solvent, this particular bargain was a trifle too hard for me to accept.

Philip Unwin smiled thinly and spread his hands: the natives had proved less ignorant, or more cunning in their primitive way, than the administrator had expected.

I said: 'I'm sorry, in any case you'd better negotiate with Bill,' and soon found myself outside Ruskin House under the smoky autumn sky of Museum Street, to which summer seldom comes.

Dusk moreover was encroaching as in my heavy boots I clumped along to the corner where Makins waited in the saloon bar of the Museum Tavern where I was to spend many evenings during the Flying Bomb period: but even then, in June 1944, the skies above that street were always overcast and autumnal, the sun never shone, allowing the Doodlebugs to slip through our defences under cover of the cloud drifting overhead.

CHAMBER MUSIC

I'd called for Makins, as arranged by letter, at the *Horizon* office earlier that afternoon. I didn't see Cyril Connolly, but he apparently caught a glimpse of me, for Makins wrote afterwards that he'd said I looked very much a soldier in my uniform, which would have surprised the Suffolk sergeant-major.

Makins immediately took me on a conducted tour of the Bloomsbury bomb sites, for I'd not been in London since the Blitz, and during it they wouldn't give me leave (I must emphasise this point, since in a taxi once I was called 'a Soho non-blitzer' by a very stout young woman known to us as Are They Real Or Are They False).

We inspected stretches of rubble from which rose shells of blackened brick that seemed to stay upright only by an effort of will. In one of them the privy was revealed complete with undamaged lavatory bowl, cistern and chain, halfway up a landing under which stairs had collapsed with the outer wall that bomb blast had neatly stripped away.

Makins reported that Graham Greene himself had been seen staring with peculiar intentness at this particular ruin, and from this deduced that he might be writing something about London in the air raids: though at the moment Greene was said to be going to Africa on some Top Secret Foreign Office mission, or had perhaps already gone.

Africa combined with Top Secret rang a bell, and I described to Makins how at the ITC, not long after my Oppenheim interview, I'd suddenly been summoned by the Adjutant, who proposed that I should volunteer for Special Service with a cipher department somewhere on the Gold Coast, starting with the rank of Sergeant, allowances, and several rates of additional pay.

'It's the White Man's Grave,' the Adjutant told me. 'Pretty ropey billet, terrible heat, malaria, leprosy and cholera plague, you've got a week to think it over and I won't blame you if the answer's no.'

I said instantly: 'I'll take it sir'; 'What?' the Adjutant cried disconcerted, 'Better not decide anything in a hurry you know, White Man's Grave remember, it'll be too late once you're on the roster,' but I told him: 'I've decided sir. You can put me on it right away,' then went down promptly with pneumonia and according to the MO service in Africa was out for me, at any rate that year.

So I was struck off the Special Service roster, reinstated on the roll of OCTU candidates, and posted to the Ipswich HQ on my return from convalescent leave.

'Christ you must have been delirious already,' Makins exclaimed, 'to volunteer for duty in a place like that'. 'Anything to get away from the Home Front,' I told him, 'My dear Bill you've yet to find out what the army's like.'

'Yes and I'll make ruddy sure I never do,' Makins retorted: Evelyn Waugh was in the army too, he told me, a novel with a wartime setting due out soon, and we arrived at the hall where a concert was being held and Makins' wife, whom I'd not previously met, awaited us.

Carlotta Makins, plump, short and Spanish-looking, had shiny black hair and wore black with gipsyish adornments; inside the hall instruments were tuning up, people anxiously consulted scores and several heads craned round startled to see a private soldier clumping in and taking up a seat on one of those fragile little chairs.

My awkwardness at being in khaki, temporarily forgotten, revived at this: the concert too turned out to be chamber music, which I support only with difficulty, but I attempted to look appropriately soulful until the last item, when Mrs Makins immediately left us and it was time for my appointment with Unwin.

'Well?' Makins asked ordering scotch as I entered the Museum Tavern. 'Far from well,' I answered and he stroked his beard soberly while I described the interview.

'Not to worry, they'll come round to paying more in time,' he told me, and come round in time they did: though not for another two years, when Philip Unwin over the telephone offered me an advance of £50 on a volume of army stories which I'd already sold for twice that amount to Jonathan Cape.

'Drink up, my round,' I told Makins, who emptied his glass at a gulp; luckily before going on leave I had drawn some pay which I'd managed to save and had thus been proof against Unwin's proffered tenner.

Makins' beard bristled with optimism as he downed a toast to our future; he was coming up for yet another bloody Board but they'd not a chance of nailing him; and in a haze of whisky fumes I clumped off through the blackout to pick up my kit and catch a train for the South Coast.

OLD BILL

Catastrophe followed swiftly on, for they did nail Makins after all. X-rays at the Medical Board showed his stomach ulcer to be either healed or non-existent, he was re-graded as A1 and a terrible letter of farewell, such as one might receive from a lamb on its way to the slaughter, arrived announcing his departure for an army training depot somewhere in England: the worst being of course that he would have to shave off his beard.

Silence supervened, and almost simultaneously I was myself re-posted as clerk to the Second-in-Command of a Young Soldiers Battalion on the Suffolk Coast: billeted in a requisitioned hotel facing the seafront where mines bobbed about like buoys beyond the coils of rusty Dannert wire.

The Young Soldiers were delinquents to a boy, always deserting or committing robbery and rape; the Regimental Jail, also in our building, had a 'FULL UP' notice on it like a Bloomsbury hotel, and all winter I was kept fully occupied typing out reports of various offences.

Then once more I heard from Makins, and opening the letter was dumbfounded.

Makins liked the army. He'd received top marks on his training, given up drink and tobacco ('Must keep fit you know'), wrote in praise of discipline, and couldn't understand what I'd got against routine and regulations, without which after all the army couldn't function. The loss of his beard seemed more than compensated for by corporal's stripes, and he wound up by saying I'd given him a completely false impression of a damn fine outfit.

After receiving several letters in this strain I replied sharply saying I'd have to think of him as Old Bill if he carried on like this any further: unperturbed Makins replied that he'd just returned from an MT course and been promoted Sergeant.

By this time it was Spring and in charge of his platoon he was shot off to North Africa where, according to Lydia, Bombardier Jaeger had preceded him.

CAIRO

And then for the first time he died.

He was burnt to death in Egypt. I heard the news from Carlotta Makins, whose handwriting I remember was enormous and who wrote in crimson ink. She enclosed the MS books of the vacuum-cleaner novel, left behind at their flat when he joined up, also a press cutting from a Cairo newspaper describing how William C. Makins, a journalist on leave from the Middle East Forces, had died from asphyxia in a hotel bedroom set on fire, apparently, by a cigarette left alight whilst he was asleep: thus he shared the same fate as Louis Joseph Vance, author of *The Lone Wolf* novels so popular during the First World War and which, adapted as films featuring Warren William, were circulating in cinemas at the very date of Makins' death.

That summer I seemed surrounded by death: my mother had just died, returning from the funeral I received Mrs Makins' letter, and I'd nearly died myself: a live round fired on the range had struck my steel helmet while I was marking in the butts, and for years I carried this bullet about as the One With My Name On It: possession of which, according to army superstition, guaranteed immortality at any rate for the duration.

I packed away the MS books together with all Mākins' letters and the other completed portion of the vacuum-cleaner novel: it was as though a file had been marked closed or as if the death of Makins had for the time being severed a thread binding us both to this book, and not until four years after was I able to work on it again.

TALES OF ARMY LIFE

Meanwhile Tobruk had fallen; my boss, the Second-in-Command, sauntered about in white flannels carrying a tennis racket or cricket bat; the Young Soldiers set fire to the Gym; and having failed the WOSB Test I gave up any hope of active participation in the war.

Instead I started writing a series of army stories and typing them in the evenings on my portable typewriter which I carried with me throughout my service: on this I also did the Second-in-Command's paperwork while he played cricket or tennis and arranged various fixtures as Battalion Sports Officer, a position which no one envied him since the Young Soldiers didn't take kindly to organised games.

I wrote the stories after duty in a large café restaurant on the sea-front, always full of handsome Wrens vying with each other about the RAF officers who'd taken them out the night before. RAF officers rated tops, being classified in turn by rank and number of decorations; naval officers came second and Brown Jobs a long long way behind. In any case it was Officers Only though the Wrens were not themselves commissioned: one presumes that those who were went out only with admirals and air-vice-marshals.

To my amusement, many years later one of these young women, having read my book of army stories, wrote to me and said she had recognised my description of the town, that she'd herself been stationed there, and claimed to have seen me often writing in the café. In fact none of the Wrens even looked in my direction, for a private soldier was not so much beneath their notice as practically invisible.

But while they enjoyed briefly their brightest period, before the claims of suburban home and kitchen sink enclosed them, I wrote grimly on; and when the first of these stories, 'I Had to Go Sick', published by *Horizon*, brought a letter of congratulation from Evelyn Waugh, I thought how pleased poor Makins would have been.

There were, in that peak year of 1942, excluding *Horizon* and *Penguin New Writing* where I was also published, no less than 16 markets for a short-story writer to choose from, unlike today; and stories of mine came out in all these periodicals and magazines including *Lilliput*.

Kaye Webb, one of the *Lilliput* editors, who afterwards discovered and married the artist Ronald Searle, told me later how they came to publish me.

I'd submitted three stories, two months passed with no reply; so, bearing in mind my initial experience with *Horizon*, I wrote a letter to the editor reminding him of my existence. In answer came a note from Kaye Webb's secretary saying she was sorry my stories had got caught up in the back drawer, but they'd now been found and she was returning them herewith as not suitable for publication.

The stories, however, were not returned therewith; instead on the following day a letter of acceptance arrived enclosing with apologies a cheque for all three stories.

What had caused this change of mind was that Kaye Webb had been lunching with a man who complained how few humorous stories of Forces life were appearing in her magazine. She replied that they were not receiving many, citing mine as some that had been mislaid and were now being sent back as she really had not had time enough to look at them.

Her luncheon companion said: 'Maclaren-Ross? But haven't you read his army story in *Horizon*? Don't mean to say you're turning him down?'

Kaye Webb, who in fact had never heard of me, since editors do not really read a lot, returned to the office, went swiftly through my stories and dictated at once the letter of acceptance: thus beginning a long and, for me, profitable association, since Hulton Press periodicals paid twice as much as anybody else.

Hitherto I'd been selling some of my best early stories to the new paperback miscellanies, such as Reginald Moore's *Modern Reading* and *Selected Writing* or the short-lived *First Eighteen* (edited by the intriguing and attractive Patricia Joan Bruce) for as little as three guineas flat: a guinea of course being worth double in those days, nonetheless I did not become exactly rich.

At the same time I was fulfilling my ambition to earn a living by my work, and the appearance of the stories caused Rupert Hart-Davis, now a captain and adjutant in the Guards, to contact me again and arrange for their later publication in volume-form: so it came about that after all my first publisher was Cape.

I often remembered Makins at this time when I didn't need an agent, and reflected on how glad he'd be that my name was undoubtedly before the public now.

Then, in the winter of 1944, I heard again from him.

A DEAD LETTER

It was a horrid winter; that night all traffic had been stopped and the Edgware Road, which I had to cross to reach my flat, was an empty stretch of polished ice. I was the only pedestrian afoot in a frozen world, crossing the road I fell down twice, and awaiting me at home was Makins' letter.

The angular handwriting was unmistakable, besides his name rank and number were written on the back. The postmark on the envelope, bearing Middle East stamps, was obliterated but, from the amount of re-addresses including old army units scrawled thereon, it had obviously been following me about for years.

It was a thick letter, crackling I thought with the optimism and future hopes contained inside, and I surveyed it with misgiving. I'd been fond of Makins, had mourned him already in my way, and I didn't feel at that moment up to reading a letter from the dead. As I put it away unopened a V2 rocket exploded dully, I remember, in the distance like a gun being fired over a soldier's grave.

Then when the war ended, one evening at the Wheatsheaf pub in Rathbone Place, I became aware of a tall pale man wearing a long pale mackintosh and grey hat, from under the straight stiff brim of which he'd been staring fixedly for quite a while.

'D'you remember me?' he asked.

'No,' I replied, sighing inwardly Here goes, for his long shaven chin jutted like a boot and he looked formidable and severe, bearing all the signs of a fellow seeking an argument or fight.

'Makins,' he announced abruptly, 'You've surely not forgotten? I'm Bill Makins.'

'No,' I said backing away alarmed, for a fight was one thing and a ghost quite another. 'Not possible. You are dead.'

'How can I be dead,' the ghost of Makins asked. 'When I am standing here?' and despite the beardless chin I recognised that piercing stare and eyes. 'You know bloody well I didn't die, you must have read my letter.'

'But the press-cutting,' I stammered. 'Carlotta sent it me, burnt to death in Cairo.'

'A mistake,' Makins explained with a long arm waving this away. 'It was a bloke called Makin, William C. Makin, who died not me.'

'W.C. Makin,' I cried, 'Who wrote a book called *Red Sea Nights*.'

'*Red Sea Nights*,' Makins nodded, 'and it was he who burned to death in that hotel,' then while I called shakily for scotch, he went on further to explain.

W.C. Makin was a journalist and war-correspondent; at the time of his death Makins was Missing Believed Killed, when actually he'd been taken prisoner by the Eyeties, and the similarity of names had caused this confusion that in a work of fiction would have strained the bounds of possibility.

So the resurrected Makins and I began to drink together, gradually his austerity relaxed and he became once more his old dynamic self; it was a memorable reunion: cut short only because the supply of scotch at this period was hardly inexhaustible, and also Makins was due up North that night.

He'd escaped in the end from the Eyetie POW camp, had however in the meantime learnt Italian, a language on which he'd always been keen; and now that he was repatriated, out of the army and prospectless, a job in Rome had cropped up for which he had to apply in some Northern city.

'I'll let you know what happens,' he said at closing time and the tails of his long mackintosh vanished into a taxi en route for Euston Station.

But he didn't let me know, and ten years went by before he wrote to me again.

ROME

In 1955 I published in *The London Magazine* a memoir of Frank Harris, and on its appearance received a letter from Makins whom I'd begun to give up once more for dead.

But no, he was still alive and domiciled in Rome. He'd a new wife now and lived in a wing of a converted marble palace where they sometimes held private concerts of chamber music and where, should I ever come to Italy, I would be welcome as their guest.

Makins also said that he'd been asked by the editors of *Botteghe Oscure*, an Anglo-Italian miscellany then published twice-yearly in Rome, to write his memories of the old *Horizon* days, and could he have permission to describe my first appearance there.

I replied 'Of course'; then seeing a copy of the current *Botteghe Oscure* in a Charing Cross Road bookshop sometime later, opened it at the Contents to see if his *Horizon* piece was in.

His name was certainly there but appended to three prose poems only, and underneath in brackets were the dates, writing *Finis* to the story of William Cooper Makins: (1911–1955).

Calder-Marshall and
the Reverend Todd

*   *   *

'SO YOU'RE OUT OF THE ARMY AND YOU'VE SOLD YOUR BOOK,' Arthur Calder-Marshall said depositing the drinks on the table. 'What d'you intend to do now?'

His voice was slightly nasal and although in the vast anonymous pub acres of bare floor and empty tables surrounded us, he spoke conspiratorially from the corner of his mouth as if we were convicts in danger of being overheard by the screw.

We'd met by appointment, it was six p.m. at the Horseshoe Tavern, next to the Dominion Cinema in the Tottenham Court Road; and for once I can even be certain of the date: the Thursday before August Bank Holiday, 1943.

'Get a job,' I told him.

Calder-Marshall's eyes narrowed, he seemed about to make some comment which he however withheld: instead picking up his pint of bitter, which was served in a straight-sided glass without a handle and seemed one of the biggest pints I've ever seen.

As he drank a straight lock of hair like that shown in the early photographs of W. H. Auden fell across his eyebrow and he looked not unlike these photographs, although never having met Auden I cannot say whether a resemblance in fact exists. Calder-Marshall's face was of a smooth uniform pallor including the lips, the eyes were webbed at the corners with tiny lines, his expression was that of one squinting against strong sunlight; and like other Left-Wing writers of the Thirties—Randall Swingler in particular—it was arranged to look like the face of a working-man without the features in themselves being all that rough-hewn. He wore a brown suit, was thick-set with broad shoulders shrugged up high and had about him an air of great circumspect wisdom and self-imposed control.

He was a novelist whose early work I'd much admired, *About Levy* especially being a technical tour-de-force and a remarkable study of anti-semitism in which the phrase is never actually mentioned.

Eyeing me narrowly over the pint glass rim he asked: 'And Cape is doing the book? Who are you dealing with there?'

'Hart-Davis,' I said, 'but now he's gone to America as a King's Messenger I'm dealing with Mr Wren Howard.'

'How d'you get on with Rupert?'

'The book's dedicated to him.'

'And Wren Howard?'

'Less well,' I said.

Calder-Marshall nodded but no reflection upon Mr Wren Howard was implied: it was rather that he did not really expect me to get on with anyone. The rôle which I'd been assigned at our very first meeting was that of a wild intransigent clever but foolish young man unable to cope realistically with the world and its ways; and this part was one in which I'd been unwillingly cast so often that I assumed it almost as second nature. Besides my admiration for Calder-Marshall's novels was such that I wouldn't have dreamt of contradicting him by behaving out of character.

Now he said: 'Go easy with Wren Howard and you'll be all right, when dealing with publishers you have to compromise,' though his tone contained no hope that I'd take this advice to heart. 'Did they give you any money?'

'A hundred quid,' I told him, 'but it's started to run out a bit now.'

'I can well imagine,' Calder-Marshall said, his narrow glance taking in the clothes I'd recently bought since those I'd had before joining up were not many and had moreover got too small. His glance was not approving, nor did he approve of my attitude towards the army or the manner in which I'd got out of it: via the glasshouse, which excited in him no surprise, since he considered some of my stories, particularly one called 'Dodging the Column', had also gone too far.

He himself had been in the army and had got out of it too, but in a much less sensational fashion. When in the ranks he had written anonymously for *Horizon* a bitter indictment of the system entitled 'Ours Not to Reason Why'; but later as an OCTU cadet his views had become modified and another piece called 'Marching', published under his own name in *Life and Letters*, ended on a Kiplingesque note in praise of discipline, not this time satirically intended. Not long after he had been transferred to the Films Division of the Ministry of Information, where it was felt, quite rightly, that his talents could be better employed.

'What sort of job had you in mind?' he asked.

I swallowed my whisky and said: 'Well actually Cyril Connolly thought you might get me one.'

'I?' Calder-Marshall said startled. 'How?'

'In films. With your Ministry.'

Calder-Marshall recovering seemed again about to make some comment which he once more withheld, or perhaps rephrased as: 'And what d'you think you'd do there?'

'I could do scripts,' I said eagerly, 'and I've got a lot of ideas about films in general.'

Calder-Marshall said dryly: 'I don't doubt that, but whether they'd be ideas that would find favour with the powers that be,' and at this we were joined by his wife Ara, who also worked in Documentary and was employed by a company called Data.

'Julian wants a job,' her husband told her, she nodded smiling wanly, and while he went to get her a beer shook back her curtains of blondish hair which she wore shoulder-length in a style much affected in those days and which indeed she may have originated.

Ara Calder-Marshall was a slender woman of considerable chic and beauty, genuinely serene where her husband seemed banked-down, his calm rigorously imposed by an effort of the will in which he was a great believer. She had a lovely wryly-drooping mouth and chiselled features like a statue yet gave an effect of great sympathy and warmth. She wore a black tailor-made business suit and spoke in a husky voice so low as to be almost inaudible: once in a crowded pub I had a long conversation with her at the end of which I was mortified to find I'd been inadvertently supporting fascism.

'The routine,' her husband said to me returning with replenished drinks, 'the Ministerial red tape wouldn't suit you at all you know.'

'I got used to red tape in the orderly-room,' I said.

Calder-Marshall said: 'Another thing. I doubt whether they'd let you do scripts straightaway. They might if you qualified as an assistant director first, but I don't think you'd care much for that either.'

'What does being an assistant director entail?'

Calder-Marshall said: 'A sort of general dogsbody,' his wife nodded confirmation, I on the other hand shook my head, then Ara suddenly said quite loud and clear: 'Why don't we all go to the Highlander?'

I felt like saying 'How will that get me a job?' since she had spoken as if a solution to this problem had been provided: her husband glanced quickly at her, she smiled serenely back and receiving some unspoken message he said: 'Yes but d'you think he's likely to be there?'

'He'll be there,' Ara murmured nodding with conviction.

'Who'll be there?' I asked.

'Never you mind m'lad,' Calder-Marshall told me, by now on his feet and intent on lowering his pint in one long draught like a lorry-driver would a quick wet, having succeeded he said: 'Just drink up and come with us,' and with his arm linked in mine on one side and Ara's on the other I was frogmarched in friendly fashion out into the petrol-fumes and pink evening light of the Tottenham Court Road.

'D'you know the Highlander?' Ara asked me as we cut past the Astoria across Soho Square.

'Yes I know the Highlander but no one goes there until half-past ten.'

'That's where you're wrong my boy,' Calder-Marshall, who now appeared thoroughly relieved and in high spirits, told me; and wrong I was.

The Highlander in Dean Street, which until then I'd believed to be a pub where one went only after those on the other side of Oxford Street closed at half-past ten, was jammed to the doors. This early evening clientèle was composed mainly of people younger than myself: the boys in tweed jackets with leather inserts at the elbows, the girls in white blouses and slacks with shoulder-slung bags. These I afterwards found out were university-educated assistant-cameramen, sound technicians, secretaries and continuity-girls from various documentary companies affiliated to the Ministry.

A pint of bitter was immediately waved in greeting at the Calder-Marshalls by a febrile young man slightly older than the rest and seeming not to belong among them although on friendly terms, whom Ara introduced in her husky murmur, made even less audible by the clamour in the bar, as the Reverend Todd.

The Reverend Todd did not look especially clerical, yet there was something curate-like, a suggestion of primness and precision, about the long straight mobile mouth from which issued with great rapidity a loud strident voice. He seemed able to conduct several conversations at once and to have ears in the back of his head: frequently firing over his shoulder a retort to someone at the opposite side of the counter, as a gunslinger in a Western might carelessly drop an opponent who is drawing a bead on him from behind.

He had a shock of black hair piled high above a narrow pale wedge-shaped face and the side struts of his large square-framed spectacles were the thickest I'd yet encountered. It was impossible to see whether he wore a dog-collar, as his navy-blue woollen pullover cut him off at the point where the knot of a necktie might have been.

He was evidently not the mysterious person whom we'd come there to meet since the Calder-Marshalls were still watching the open door, then through it there stepped in from the street a bulky man of middle height, conservatively dressed and wearing a bow tie, who came towards us smiling.

Into his hand Calder-Marshall at once thrust a large whisky which he appeared to have in readiness, at the same time saying: 'Donald this is Julian, he's out of the army and looking for a job, I thought you'd better get together.'

The man with the bow tie had thick arched George Robey eyebrows, his smiling face was blue chinned, round and bland. He made a formal almost foreign jerky bow, though without quite clicking his heels.

'Taylor,' he said in a deep pleasant voice that was not at all foreign. 'Donald Taylor.'

'Maclaren-Ross,' I said.

Donald Taylor said: 'I'm happy to meet you,' his smile curving now to resemble that of the Cheshire cat. Like the Reverend Todd he had thick black hair and dark-rimmed spectacles but his hair was swept back smoothly into a curved mane at the back and the rims and struts of his spectacles were of ordinary thickness and shape.

Taking a sip of whisky he said: 'So you're looking for a job Arthur says.'

'Yes,' I said. 'Can you give me one?'

'Documentary films?'

'Yes.'

'Scripts?'

'I can do scripts, yes.'

'Then I'll be happy to give you a job,' Donald Taylor smiled. 'As a matter of fact I've been hoping we would meet. Here is my card, come to the office about 10.30 tomorrow morning and I will sign you on then. Sorry I have to dash now, good-night,' and replacing his empty glass on the counter, he gave again his jerky bow and stepped back through the doorway out of sight. His Cheshire cat smile had not faded throughout and I expected to see it lingering in the air even though its owner had disappeared.

Convinced this was some kind of joke, I turned to the Calder-Marshalls for an explanation but they were no longer in the pub, and as I was about to examine the card given me by Donald Taylor I was startled by hearing the Reverend Todd use a most unecclesiastical expression of contempt close to my ear.

'And what d'you think about it?' he said sensing someone behind him and swivelling his spectacles towards me like the sights of a .45.

'About what?' I asked placing the card unread in my breast pocket.

The Reverend Todd was occupied in tipping back a fresh pint of bitter, unlike Calder-Marshall it took him two goes, then wiping foam from his lips, he said: 'Poetry.'

'I don't know anything about poetry.'

The Reverend Todd said: 'Then you must be a poet,' emitting a strident peal of laughter. Sweat stood out like pimples on his pale cheeks and forehead. 'Are you a poet?'

'No,' I said. 'Are you.'

'Of course I am.'

I said: 'Well there are precedents, Donne for instance.'

'Donne?'

'John Donne. He was a clergyman too.'

'I know he was a clergyman,' the Reverend Todd began then broke off to shout behind him, in answer to some remark I hadn't caught: 'No, no, I write my own novels not anybody else's, thank you.'

I asked him: 'Are you a novelist as well?'

'Two novels,' he told me and I tried to think of a precedent for this, but clergymen who wrote fiction were fewer and only one name came to mind.

'S. Baring Gould,' I said.

The Reverend Todd repeated 'Baring Gould?' blankly, his mouth open in what seemed to be bewilderment.

'He wrote *In the Roar of the Sea.*'

'I know that. So what?'

'Well he was in holy orders.'

'Holy what?'

'Orders. He was a parson.'

'What,' the Reverend Todd demanded and his voice rose to hitherto unclimbed heights of stridency, 'is all this about bloody parsons?'

'Well aren't you a parson. The Reverend Todd?'

'Reverend Todd be damned,' shouted Todd, 'I'm Ruthven Todd.'

There was a short silence during which he glared and I in turn drained my glass, for I knew the work of Ruthven Todd who was a good poet, also the author of an excellent book on William Blake and an allegorical novel called *Over the Mountain*: one of the first in the neo-Kafkan manner to be published in this country.

But before I could apologise for having misheard the introduction, Ruthven Todd, who now held a whisky in his hand, said: 'I didn't get your name either. Who the hell are you anyway?'

I gave my name, Todd's whisky went down the wrong way, and when I'd patted him on the back he spluttered: 'But I discovered you!'

'I thought Cyril Connolly discovered me.'

'On my recommendation,' Todd shouted, his voice still pitched to carry above a crowd though the pub had now emptied around us. 'I happened to be in the *Horizon* office when your stuff came to light, I sat down and read it through, then I went straight to Connolly and told him: "Whatever else you do you've got to publish this bloke," and he did.'

There was no denying that, although the name of Ruthven Todd did not figure in the story as Connolly had told it to me by letter or on the occasion of my first visit to Selwyn House.

Meantime dusk had fallen outside and, anticipating the landlord who was eyeing him as if about to refuse further service, Todd said: 'Come on, this place'll be dead now until the others close. Let's push off to my flat, I've got some food and beer in and we can carry on drinking there.'

Todd's flat was in Mecklenburgh Square, not far from the *Horizon* office, a wall of books confronted us as we entered the narrow hall and in the living-room there was hardly space for the truckle-bed on which he slept.

'Borrow anything you like,' he shouted from the kitchen where he was clattering plates and glasses, so I detached a blue and silver paper covered Obelisk Press copy of *The Rock Pool* followed by an Alfred Knopf edition of Dashiell Hammett's first novel, *Red Harvest*, not then available in England; and began with awe to examine what appeared to be a complete signed set of Wyndham Lewis on a lower shelf.

Todd, returning with salami, French bread and a gallon jug of beer, told me how, when he first came to London from Edinburgh, Wyndham Lewis had not only presented him with the books, but when he was broke put him up in the basement of his flat, bringing down the breakfast himself every morning for a week before introducing Todd to his wife, after which they all breakfasted together upstairs.

It was not a story which confirmed the popular view of Lewis as everyone's implacable enemy, but Todd was full of tales like this: famous names erupted rapidly from him, he seemed on friendly terms with every conceivable literary figure and, although still in his late twenties, to be himself a figure more of the Thirties than of the Forties.

Now he worked as a bookseller's assistant at Zwemmers in the Charing Cross Road but also acted as a consultant on antique furniture to a feature film company which paid him a small retainer, and had a new novel coming out from Wrey Gardiner, who owned the Grey Walls Press.

Mention of the film company reminded me of my own search for a job, and I said to Todd: 'D'you know a man called Donald Taylor?'

'Of Strand Films?'

'Yes that's it,' I said taking out the card Taylor had given me in the Highlander. 'Strand Films, No. 1 Golden Square. Is he really a producer?'

Todd shouted: 'Good God of course he is. Strand's the best documentary company in London.'

I said: 'Well he told me if I called there tomorrow he'd give me a job doing scripts. D'you think he might?'

Todd shouted: 'Of course he will. For God's sake go and see him. Dylan Thomas works there as well.'

The Polestar Neighbour

*   *   *

> On almost the incendiary eve
> > When at your lips and keys
> Locking, unlocking, the murdered strangers weave,
>
> > One who is most unknown,
> Your polestar neighbour, sun of another street,
> > Will dive up to his tears.

('Deaths and Entrances')

DYLAN THOMAS IN 1943 DID NOT GREATLY RESEMBLE THAT MUCH-reproduced early photograph known to him as the Fucking Cherub. Certainly I failed to recognise him from it on the morning we first met.

It was the day after August Bank Holiday: the date when I was to start work at Strand Films, where Dylan was already employed as a documentary script-writer. He was then going on twenty-nine and I had just turned thirty-one.

We travelled up together in the lift at No. 1 Golden Square without speaking, neither knowing who the other was. Dylan wore a green porkpie hat pulled down level with his slightly bulging eyes: like the agate marbles we used as Alley Taws when I was a boy in France, but a darker brown. His full lips were set low in a round full face, a fag-end stuck to the lower one. His nose was bulbous and shiny. He told me afterwards that he used to rub it up with his fist before the mirror every morning until it shone satisfactorily; as a housewife might polish her doorknob or I the silver-topped malacca cane that I affected in those days.

Dylan's gaze lit on this cane and he huddled back into the very soiled and much pleated raincoat worn capewise round his shoulders. He had his left arm in a sling, and judging by the greyness of the linen had evidently carried it thus for some time. He later told me that, although his sprained wrist was now all right, he had become attached to the sling and hoped to wear it until it turned completely black.

Side by side we stood while the lift creaked upward in a series of jerks. It was a very old, capricious lift with a great deal of personality, but it did not on this occasion give up halfway as happened one evening in the weeks to come when Dylan and I were trapped in it between two floors for twenty minutes, until someone working late below pressed the button to release us. Now we jerked slowly past a sign advertising the manufacture of Free-Japanese Lampshades, and Dylan's eyes rolled sideways in alarm as through the open grille we saw an actual Japanese in native dress emerge from the door that bore the sign. Dylan's glance took in also my white corduroy jacket and he turned his head discreetly away as if at some obscene sight: indeed, I looked hastily down to make sure my flies were buttoned.

At that moment the lift gave out a sigh of exhaustion, rose a few inches above floor level, then sank to a stop facing the double doors marked 'STRAND', against which Dylan, clashing the lift-gate back, launched himself at a fast lick. By the time I had finished closing the grille he had disappeared, and the lift followed suit down its shaft at double the speed with which it had ascended.

I in turn passed through the Strand doors, still swinging back and forth like those of a saloon in a Western, and was brought up short by a switchboard desk and behind it a good-looking red-haired young lady, who later married a feature-film producer with whom I, long after, became associated. But before I could announce my name, a buzzer sounded and the disembodied voice of Donald Taylor, the boss, asked whether I had yet arrived.

'Reporting for duty,' I said and was waved towards an office on the right where Dylan had preceded me and Donald Taylor now introduced us.

Divested of hat and raincoat, though still wearing the sling, Dylan was revealed to have on a very respectable dark blue suit and a white shirt with a bow tie and celluloid collar, too tight round the neck and giving the effect of someone strapped in the stocks. In these clothes he might have been a young provincial tradesman or perhaps a farmer up in London for the day on business. He was stockily built and robust-looking rather than fat, though beginning to put on a bit of a pot. His hair, light brown in colour and not dull gold as the romantics would like it, was no longer centre-parted and wavy, as in the cherubic photograph. Now it covered his round skull in tight woolly curls. His full cheeks were carefully shaven. He replied in a rapid mutter to the introduction that seemed acutely nervous and uncomfortable. Of course it was my general get-up that embarrassed him; I had on a cream silk shirt and peach-coloured tie besides the white corduroy, but I didn't realise the cause until much later; and Dylan was by nature far too polite to make any comment at this stage.

Meanwhile Donald Taylor was speaking: 'Well you boys had better get to know each other as you're going to work together'—at this Dylan visibly recoiled, and it came as startling news to me as well— 'You can share that office through there, Dylan show him where it is, I'm sure you can sort out between you the best method of working.'

'What are we going to work on?' I asked.

'The Home Guard script. Feature length, Dylan will explain. I expect it to be a most fruitful collaboration.'

Donald gave his Cheshire-cat smile and little jerky bow. The interview was over, and in the office assigned to us Dylan and I stood uneasy and shame-faced, like two strange children sent off to play alone by a benevolent adult, in the belief that because they are contemporaries they're bound to get on well. We looked out of the one long window, which had a splendid view right across the rooftop to the blitzed church of St Anne's in Old Compton Street, Soho. The weathervane on the spire was still intact and glinted, a golden arrow, in the sun.

'Have you been in the Home Guard?' I asked.

'Never.'

'Neither have I. I was in the Infantry.'

'I know. I've read your stories.' He didn't tell me, nor for a long while did I find out, that he'd read the stories aloud to Donald Taylor, insisting that I be taken on at Strand when discharged from the army: that, in other words, I owed my job to him.

He said: 'One of the directors here was in the Home Guard, but he's doing the script about the RAF.'

'Haven't you an RAF man?'

'Yes, but he's doing a script about the Tank Corps.'

'How many are there in the Script Department?'

'Only ourselves and Philip Lindsay. The rest are directors who sometimes write a script. You can see them all on this.'

He led me to a large coloured cartoon framed on the wall behind the big broad desk, captioned 'A High Wind in Golden Square' and showing various members of Strand Films personnel being blown about in all directions. I recognised the work of John Banting, a painter and illustrator whom I'd met once or twice in bars.

'I didn't know Banting was on the staff.'

'He's not any longer,' Dylan said. 'Bit of a disagreement, don't know the details. See, there's Phil Lindsay, that little bloke floating away over the trees.'

'I'd like to meet Lindsay.'

'You're certain to sooner or later. If you spot a little leprechaunish chap with a big bump on his forehead and dried blood all over his face, that'll be Phil for sure. He was born with the bump I believe, but the blood comes from falling downstairs. He's always falling down, old Phil.'

'Is that how you did your wrist?'

Dylan nodded delightedly. 'Trying to hold Phil up. I was sober too, makes it seem more silly.' It was then that he told me about his wrist and how long he planned to wear the sling.

'Coming along nicely, ought to be jet black soon. They wanted me to go along to the hospital for treatment twice a week, but I said to myself No bloody fear. Start going to hospitals and you never know what they'll find wrong. Might begin taking my liver out and scraping it again.'

'Again? Have you had your liver scraped?'

'Every so often,' Dylan said with relish. 'Get it put back afterwards and sewn in of course. I'm always scared they'll leave out a bit. Whenever the boys here get a tough piece of liver for lunch, and there's a lot of it about just now, they always say Now we're eating a bit of bloody old Dylan. Actually they'd have a job to eat mine.'

'But what's wrong with your liver?'

'Cirrhosis I expect.' When he laughed his cheeks puffed out but the cigarette remained squarely in the centre of his mouth. 'Hard as bloody leather. It's the booze. D'you drink at all yourself?'

'When I can get it.'

'Beer?'

'Scotch.'

'Oh of course. Your national drink.' He added: 'You don't seem much like a Scotsman though. I thought you'd be very small and tough, with steel-rimmed specs, that sort of thing.'

'A kilt?'

'No, not a kilt. But a Scots accent, Glasgow perhaps.'

'My parents didn't come from Glasgow.'

'Have they got accents?'

'They're dead. But they hadn't accents.'

Dylan flushed and muttered 'Sorry'. His cigarette waggled up and down as he spoke and his face was screwed up in a frown against the smoke, but he removed the fag end only when it was burnt right down. But even when he mumbled you could understand every word, though his voice was low-toned and he spoke fast. I've heard people who should know better do imitations of him with a sing-song Welsh accent, but a slight intonation on certain words—'Daughter', for instance—was all he really had.

'You haven't an accent yourself,' I said to him.

He puffed out a laugh. 'Cut-glass, they'd call it down in Wales.' I didn't know this expression but rightly assumed it to be the equivalent of talking pound-noteish or having a half-crown voice in the army. 'I don't speak Welsh either,' he added, pulling open a drawer and searching inside. 'Now where's this bloody script got to. Ah here we are. Home Guard,' coming up with a green foolscap folder which we were to get to know too well. 'I expect you'll want to start work right away?'

'We could discuss it over drinks. They'll be open time we get there.'

Dylan seemed delighted with this suggestion, which he'd plainly not wanted to be the first to make. He told Donald Taylor afterwards that it was the first sign he'd had that I was halfway human; until then, he'd seriously considered saying he couldn't work with me at all, as for some reason never stated, and quite apart from my appearance, I reminded him of Gaudier-Brezska.

'We mustn't get tight though,' he added.

At that time when drink-shortage was starting it was not easy to get tight, nor even to get scotch; the back bar of the Café Royal had, however, Irish in abundance. As I lowered glass after glass, while Dylan rationed himself to a single pint of bitter, his anxiety increased; but we regained the office at two o'clock with me sober enough to join in roughing-out the Home Guard story outline: the shooting script we swore to start next day.

Meanwhile that evening Dylan did get tight. In the back bar he abandoned beer and went on the hard stuff himself; as we worked our way up Soho in search of scotch, towards the Wheatsheaf where we were certain of Scotch ale at any rate, his celluloid collar seemed to be constricting him more and more until when we reached the Highlander and there discovered gin, he was scarlet in the face and I suggested he should take the damned thing off.

'Why don't you take that bloody jacket off?' Dylan said.

'What's wrong with my jacket?'

'Fucking dandy. Flourishing that stick. Why don't you try to look more sordid. Sordidness, boy, that's the thing.'

'If you'd just come out of a glasshouse you wouldn't want to look more sordid.'

Dylan paused with a double gin suspended. 'The glasshouse?' he said. 'That where you've been?'

'They called it a Detention Barrack, but the glasshouse is what you'd call it.'

Dylan set his gin carefully on the counter, and reaching up wrenched the celluloid collar from its stud. 'Jesus boy,' he said, 'I'm sorry.'

'That's all right. You weren't to know.'

'Why didn't you tell me?'

'No reason why I should.'

Dylan stood there gulping and goggle-eyed, the celluloid collar dangling from his hand. 'But Jesus, the glasshouse,' he said.

He remained abashed for the rest of the evening and later on I somehow lost him.

But when next morning I arrived at the office he was there before me, hunched up over the desk as if he'd been stabbed at it. Like one of those characters in films who when touched slump stiffly back with a knife handle sticking out in front. Then I saw that he was moving. He was grasping a pencil and attempting to insert it in the holes of the dial-telephone, but without success owing to trembling of his hand.

'What on earth are you doing?'

'Jesus you made me jump. I'm trying to dial TIM, what d'you think?'

'Tim?'

'To get the time. Find out if they're open yet.'

'They're not. It's only half-past ten.'

'Oh God another hour.' He groaned. His eyes were globular, rimmed with red right round, nor had he shaved. His left arm was still in the sling but this morning he wore a brown check tweed jacket and grey flannels, these remaining his office uniform from then on, except when he was in shirt sleeves. 'Was I rude to you last night?'

'No.'

'I bloody was. I was rude to you about your coat. Is the coat all right? You weren't sick down it or anything?'

'No.'

'What about the stick? Don't say you've lost the stick?'

I showed him the stick and he seemed genuinely comforted. Henceforward he adopted the cane and jacket as though they were his own especial properties, making sure I didn't leave the cane behind in pubs and becoming belligerent himself when a chap in one of them took exception to the jacket. When one day as we walked along the street soot fell from a roof all over the white corduroy, he was horrified, and insisted on rushing me to a firm of cleaners who restored it as good as new within 24 hours, a miracle in that time of war.

Now he started suddenly to sneeze. Sneeze after sneeze convulsed him and he tried to smother them in a large red bandanna snatched from out of his sleeve.

'That's a nasty cold you've got.'

'Not a cold. It's the drink coming out.'

The drink was also coming out in sweat, and I said: 'Look here Dylan, I don't feel too good myself. Why don't we have a bottle up here, guard against these hangovers in future?'

'A bottle?'

'Whisky. We could go halves. I know a fellow can get it on the black market, I'll ring him now if you like.'

'Whisky? In the office?' He seemed absolutely appalled.

'Don't be silly, why not?'

But Dylan firmly shook his head.

'Not for me. You please yourself of course, but I won't if you don't mind.'

So the bottle was not imported. Actually, one double Irish when the back bar opened and a pint of bitter over lunch were sufficient to pull Dylan together and enable him to work that afternoon; incidentally this was one of the few times when I saw him eat anything bar a ham sandwich or a sausage roll.

Lunch was Spaghetti Bolognese at Fava's Restaurant in Frith Street, much frequented by our staff, especially junior members and minor technicians, most of whom had been at Cambridge and enjoyed trying out their Italian on the waitress. Dylan did imitations of all these, including the waitress, as we strolled along outside: a considerable feat since he himself spoke no Italian; but first he led me across the street to examine in a shop window what seemed to be a woman's severed head, also tresses of hair, cut, apparently, from the decapitated head: itself dimly visible beyond the dusty pane. By the time we had discussed the disposal of the body, involving goulash and stuffed heart served off the ration to gourmets in a black market basement, we'd arrived in Soho Square, where Dylan said he'd something even more gruesome to show me.

'See that doorway on the other side? That's Film Centre, that is!'

'A sort of documentary club?'

'In a way.'

'Well what's so gruesome about it?'

'Don't you know?' He sank his voice to a hollow graveyard whisper: 'It's where we go when we've no jobs.'

For the time being, however, we did have jobs and it was on my first payday with the firm, when I happened to be alone in the office, that a large bulb-shaped head, with a big carbuncle on the forehead, was poked cautiously round the door jamb. The nose was noduled with purple veins, clots of dark dried blood surrounded the carbuncle, and I said: 'You must be Philip Lindsay.'

'That's right. Not seen a huge tall woman armed with an axe anywhere about, have you?'

'Not today. Why? D'you want one?'

'No, but she wants me. To chop my ruddy block off.' Lindsay now came all the way in, the rough swagman's face and short skimpy frame might have belonged to two different men, and I saw that he too was carrying his left arm in a sling.

While I was introducing myself, Dylan appeared in the doorway. His eyes rolled at sight of Lindsay's sling, with a shrug he stripped off his own and dropped it in the waste-paper basket by the desk.

'Can't all go round looking like a bunch of bloody cripples,' he said. 'What happened Phil? She catch up with you at last?'

'No, or I'd be lacking a head. Missed my footing going down the gents that's all. They say it isn't broken, though.'

'How's Crippen? Crapping?'

'Just about to bump off Belle.' Lindsay said in his hoarse staccato voice. The phone rang and he skipped back in alarm: 'Christ suppose that's her,' but instead it was Donald Taylor asking for him on the inter-com.

'Phil's on the Crippen script, one of Donald's feature projects,' Dylan said when Lindsay had answered the summons. 'Works at home nowadays and only shows up Fridays to collect his dough.'

'Doesn't this woman with the axe know where he lives?'

'No, he's safe so long as he stays indoors.'

Then Dylan told me how, some weeks before, the backers of Strand had held a board meeting at which Donald Taylor as Managing Director presided, but apparently beforehand they had called a sort of script-writers' roll-call at Golden Square and Philip Lindsay had been marked absent on parade. Donald had been asked the reason and replied that he never insisted on writers clocking in daily, so long as they delivered the goods on schedule that was all he was concerned with.

But an accountant said: 'Surely it would be preferable Mr Taylor if these, er, writers performed their duties in the office like any other employee?'

'Yes it would,' Donald said.

'Thank you Mr Taylor,' the accountant said in triumph. 'I thought you would agree.'

But Donald said: 'I'm sorry, you didn't allow me to finish my sentence. It would be preferable—if we were making let's say sausages. Instead we are making documentary films, or am I mistaken?'

'Well no, Mr Taylor, but...'

'Thank you,' Donald said, bowing jerkily with his blandest smile, 'I thought you'd agree,' and there was no more question of compulsory attendance for writers at the office after that. Nonetheless Dylan and I did come in every morning, and the Home Guard script was proceeding apace.

This script was never completed, and it's hard to tell what the Ministry officials who'd commissioned it would have said had they seen the sequences we wrote. Neither of us having served in the Home Guard we'd had to invent our own, like Kafka's *Amerika*; and what we concocted was a lively comedy-thriller set in a village 'somewhere in England', stuffed full of eccentrics and containing also a fifth column group, a delayed-action bomb, and a German parachutist who'd been in civvy street a music hall Master of Disguise. Those ruled sheets of Government foolscap might even be worth money should they ever come to light; for Dylan with his usual unselfishness did much of the actual donkey work in longhand, while I dictated from the other side of the desk the dialogue of the characters assigned to me: an old sweat who'd served in several wars, etcetera.

Dylan wrote in soft pencil with a BB lead, and carried a sharpener about in his trouser pocket; long coils of cedar-wood filled the ashtray and the blotter on his side of the desk was covered with quick sketches, some highly amusing if obscene, made while he was thinking out a scene. He often bought sketching blocks of cartridge paper, but these were used exclusively for writing poetry: also in pencil, in those days before the invention of Biro or Bic; and he was determined that his handwriting, already neat and clear, should eventually become smaller than my own.

Contrary to what is often said, he was extremely interested in the film medium while I at that time was obsessed by it, though it's doubtful whether we either of us had the true Documentary Mind. What we really wanted to script were features, and together we planned among other subjects a mystery film to be written in collaboration, entitled *The Whispering Gallery* or *The Distorting Mirror*. We both had a penchant for pictures of this sort and spent much time in tracking down the vintage examples all over London; a typical dialogue when we met in the morning would run like this:

'Dylan have you seen *The Cat Creeps*?'

'No but I've seen *The Crimson Claw*.'

'D'you recommend it?'

A violent shuddering shake of the head. 'NBG. Was your cat creepy?'

'Don't go anywhere near.'

Our own film was to be a deliberate throwback to *Caligari* and *The Cat and the Canary* in its original Paul Léni version, and Dylan provided the basic idea. A party of assorted people are being shown by a guide round the whispering gallery of a stately home open to the public, when suddenly a voice says out loud: 'I'll have this place'. Owing to the acoustics no one can tell who spoke, camera pans the various faces, and the film begins, with the heir many times removed ironing out methodically and by remote control all those in his way. He was to recruit his murderous accomplices in a deserted amusement park, and to be seen unrecognisably reflected in the Hall of Mirrors, hence the alternative title. We could never decide whether this super-villain was to be male or female, and Dylan was in favour of both: i.e. a character whose sex was changed by an operation halfway through, even though this meant censorship trouble and at very least the 'H' Certificate which then did duty for the present day 'X'.

We also shared another ambition, which was to write a film-script, not a treatment as the story-form is called, but a complete scenario ready for shooting which would give the ordinary reader an absolute visual impression of the film in words and could be published as a new form of literature. Carl Meyer, the co-author of *Caligari* and creator of many of the great early German silents, who invented the mobile camera or rather caused it to be moved about, is said to have written such scripts; but neither Dylan nor I could get hold of a script by Meyer, and the only ones we knew which almost succeeded in doing what we had in mind were those printed in *The Film Sense* by Sergei Eisenstein.

The rules we laid down ourselves were that the script had to be an original specially written in this form and not any kind of adaptation, and that actual film production must be possible. Our main obstacle consisted in the camera directions, which if given were apt to look too technical, and if omitted would lose the dramatic impact of, for instance, a sudden large close-up, which Dylan however hoped could be conveyed by one's actual choice of words. In fact we were attempting the well nigh impossible, as anyone who has read the printed versions of *Marienbad* or *L'Immortelle* by Robbe-Grillet will realise, and perhaps Dylan himself in *The Doctor and the Devils* came as close to it as any writer ever will.

Donald Taylor encouraged us in all this; he too wanted to make features and was trying to persuade our backers to make this financially possible. Apart from *Dr Crippen* and the Burke and Hare film, which even then kept cropping up, one of his pet projects was to put on the screen Dylan's novel *Adventures in the Skin Trade*, and I read with much enjoyment the portion which was published posthumously and which he had written some time before. The book, Dylan told me, was to end with the hero shivering stark-naked on Paddington Station, having lost all his clothes at strip poker in the course of the story, and in the last shot of the film-version the bottle caught on his finger was to slip off and shatter on the stone-cold platform.

Donald had had typescripts made and bound up, only two of these remained, and Tambimuttu the editor of *Poetry London* borrowed one of them with a view to obtaining an advance for Dylan from the firm he worked for. Anything involving Tambi took more time than anyone could possibly have to spare, months, maybe years could go by with nothing done, and when Dylan terribly hard up finally had another offer for the book, it turned out Tambi had lost the typescript, or at any rate this could not be found. It was the only time I ever saw Dylan angry, the scene took place in the Wheatsheaf and one could not help overhearing it. Luckily I remembered borrowing the other copy some months before, so I took Dylan home quickly in a cab and gave him the typescript which I had there, thus enabling him to draw his advance next day: or so I hope, publishers not being renowned for speed in this connection.

Meantime we were still stuck with the Home Guard, and Dylan wanted to incorporate the Free Japanese who made lampshades below our office. He said he had heard of Free French, Free Poles, Free Dutch, Free Italians and if not actually Free Germans at any rate Free German-speaking people, but never, no never Free Japanese; and he tried very hard to have them in the script, while I objected on the grounds that their kimonos might lead to their being lynched in a typical English village and which of us would write their bloody dialogue?

These questions were debated often in the office, and occasionally, when we'd done a good morning's work, in an afternoon drinking place called the Horseshoe Club, which now no longer exists in Wardour Street. This was approached by the most sordid staircase that I've ever seen, on either side were leprous walls, and it was down these worn stone steps that Philip Lindsay most frequently fell. The club also had a Judas window in the door. Dylan led me proudly up to this, a panel slid aside and the eye of the proprietor appeared at an aperture which had previously seemed to be a knothole in the wood.

'You see?' Dylan hissed. 'Like a speakeasy or an opium den,' but behind the spyhole nothing much went on: bookies' touts or ageing lesbians sitting on leather settees and sometimes some elderly character such as an art critic famous when President of the Union for subtle deadpan wit, of whom Dylan was particularly fond. I personally found this man a thumping bore, with his strange furry cap of hair, round staring eyes, and thread-like lips from which issued at long intervals a tiny insect voice; one strained one's ears in vain to catch some smart crack that never came, but then of course his Oxford days lay far behind. Dylan liked elderly men as a whole, he spoke often of his old mentor, the senior reporter so affectionately described in *Portrait of the Artist as a Young Dog*, and seemed generally to equate age with sage; in the early days he'd drag me off to Tidal Basin pubs to meet decaying ship's doctors or potato-nosed skippers who must have sailed with Bully Hayes; sometimes these were also present in the Horseshoe, and in the end I largely cried off the club.

We gradually evolved a system of holding the fort on alternate after-noons, he spent his in the Horseshoe and mine were taken up with various young women, as my love-life was getting rather complicated and I had to be sure that in the evenings nothing overlapped. Dylan was too discreet to ask me any questions, though he knew the names and, when it was his turn to stay behind, answered the occasional phone calls without divulging information, as indeed I would have done for him.

Dylan was said, when fire-watching one night on the roof at Golden Square, to have smuggled a girl up there in his sleeping bag, but when asked point blank he replied with equal blankness: Then she must have been a very little girl.

He would talk bawdily about sex in general but never about any woman in particular. For example, I once had a girl, a great admirer of his poetry, whose pride it was that she had slept with Dylan when she first came round Soho. Being less discreet than he, I asked what it was like. She said that he undoubtedly knew what to do, was gentle, considerate and even tender, but oh the guilt when morning came. In her opinion the only woman he ever really cared about was his wife Caitlin, and that is also mine.

Anyhow, in due course I brought this girl to the back bar where Dylan was, he greeted her with great formality and afterwards, when she'd gone to make a phone call, said: 'Congratulations, she's a sweetie. Course I used to know her slightly and don't mind telling you I tried a pass, only she wasn't having any, and that's what most of the boys have found. Lucky bugger, I hope you'll both be happy.'

We weren't happy for long, but that was hardly Dylan's fault, and in his place how many could have foreborne to boast, or drop a winking innuendo? The only woman I ever heard him speak about at length was his wife, and of her he said: 'I managed to marry the prettiest girl I knew, and can a bloke do more?'

Caitlin was indeed pretty, pink-cheeked with brilliant blue eyes and a few blonde strands always straggling loose from an otherwise neat hair-do: Dylan's Irish Rose, I never got to know her well, she didn't often join us and may even have been away, though I remember a quarrel one evening at the Café Royal and another time in the Antelope at Chelsea when Augustus John, expected, failed to appear. I was alone with her only once, in the Mandrake Club after Dylan's death: it was the night *Under Milk Wood* was to be broadcast for the first time. She spoke mainly of her children and a trust that was being set up for them, then I gave her a lift in a taxi to the George, the BBC pub where Roy Campbell was to be. Campbell however didn't show, and without him Caitlin suddenly said she couldn't face the broadcast. Louis MacNeice and Dr Daniel Jones, who'd done the music for *Milk Wood*, then tried to carry her bodily off to Broadcasting House but she kicked out at MacNeice, twisted free of Dr Jones and they had to go off without her. Caitlin said to me with dignity: 'Now Julian we'll go and see some nice Irishmen I know. There'll be a party at their place. Just wait here while I ring.'

Happily Margaret Taylor (no relation to Donald but then married to A.J.P. Taylor the historian), who'd been a good friend to the Thomases in Oxford and elsewhere, came in just then and promised to look after Caitlin when she got back from the phone. I slipped off out, rather pleased since I couldn't have felt less like a party with nice Irishmen that night; and I've not seen Caitlin since.

But back to Strand, the autumn of '43 advancing, and Dylan still alive.

Suddenly we were taken off the Home Guard script. The subject of course was out of date to start with—Dylan told me that the Ministry of Films Division had sat on the proposal for two years before okaying it—and abruptly it was cancelled by higher authority. The green foolscap folder was stuffed away in a desk drawer and did not re-emerge. Philip Lindsay started coming to the office again, Crippen had been hanged and Le Neve acquitted, also the woman on his tail had abandoned her axe and married someone else. This oddly enough piqued Phil instead of pleasing him, perhaps he missed the excitement of being a hunted man: though he often proclaimed, Dylan and I disagreeing, that Terror as a literary theme was Out.

'You boys sit tight,' Donald Taylor told us. 'We'll be making features soon.' He was often called to board meetings with the backers these days and an acrimonious correspondence with the Ministry had started up. Winter was soon upon us; fog enveloped the golden arrow of St Anne's, which could no longer be seen out of the window, and the office began to fill with directors and cameramen who'd been taken off the subjects they were preparing to shoot.

The air was thick with coughing and tobacco smoke and the young red-headed lady from the switchboard desk, who had not yet married my future producer and had to make and carry in the cups of tea, often complained that Strand had not been like this in the days of Reg Groves, a documentary man of the old school and formerly Head of the Script Department: headless now since his departure some months before.

Dylan: 'It's become like bloody Film Centre,' not realising how near to Film Centre itself we all were heading: for before the spring Strand Films had folded.

* * *

What else do I know about Dylan and what more can I say? That he had a horror of moths and was an authority on the Giant Sloth: both of which are true?

My close connection with him ended with Strand, though I saw him often after that. Once, notably, in the Mandrake Club, dead sober and more utterly depressed than I had ever known him; they were about to foreclose a mortgage on his house and his publishers would not advance the £50 he needed, on the grounds that he'd already had too much. I was able on this occasion to repay a little of what I owed to him by advising Graham Greene, then Managing Director of Eyre and Spottiswoode, to make him an immediate advance on a prospective travel-book, and so the day was saved.

Latterly I saw him less, for he was much mixed up with BBC people for whom I cared as little as they cared for me; or else, after his first trip to the States, with American poets who thought him the Most, to one of whom, when this was voiced, he sharply said: 'Poetry is not a competition.'

The last time we met was in the Mandrake Club after *The Doctor and the Devils* came out in book form. Again he was very sober, we talked on Donald Taylor and all that he had done for Dylan in the days of Strand and after, and finally we talked of our old ambition: the film-script which would be an entirely new literary form.

Dylan said: 'I didn't pull it off in *The Doctor*, I'm afraid. Perhaps you'll pull it off one day.'

'Yes, and perhaps again I won't.'

Someone said: 'Mr Thomas wanted on the phone.'

'Hold on there,' Dylan said to me. 'We'll have another drink.'

'Can't. I've got a date. Tonight, maybe?'

Dylan called out over his shoulder: 'I'm flying to America tonight.'

'Have a good trip,' I said. 'See you when you come back.'

Tambimuttu and the Progress
of *Poetry London*

*   *   *

J. MEARY TAMBIMUTTU, POET AND FOUNDER-EDITOR OF *POETRY London*, was according to himself a Prince in his own country. He was an Indian like his friend the short-story writer Alagu Subramaniam, but both of them came from Ceylon: the nearest parallel being perhaps the Glasgow Irish, Subra was a Hindu, Tambi a Christian, and some said that the initial preceding his name stood for Jesus. I never found out what it actually stood for.

A girl known as Kitty of Bloomsbury told me that Tambi's family seat was called Tambimuttu Towers. She said that at one time he used special crested writing paper, with a picture of the Towers embossed in the top left-hand corner. This was when he first came to London, abdicating his territory to become a literary pundit and famous figure of the Forties.

'A poet,' he would say, 'is a citizen of the world. All mankind is his country,' or 'My principality is everywhere. The Principality of the Mind.'

When Kitty came down from Oxford and was looking for a job, he took her to a bare basement room containing a half-collapsed camp bed, a kitchen chair and a wooden table on which were a bottle of blue-black ink, a chewed post office pen-holder, and stocks of the embossed crested paper.

'This was my office,' he said. 'Now it is yours. I engage you as my secretary and poetry-reader.' Squashing a cockroach on the sweating wall with a rolled-up copy of *Poetry London*, he waved this at a chaos of accumulated MSS in a corner.

'Poems,' he said. 'Contributions. You know? I have not time to read them. If they're no good perhaps they should be returned. They have been here a long time, the rats have eaten some. We have no typewriter yet but there is ink and paper to write the authors. You will be paid fortnightly, on Fridays. Do you have any money?'

'Yes thank you. I've got £5.'

'That is good,' Tambimuttu said. 'I am a Prince in my country and princes don't carry money, you know. Give me the fiver and later the firm will refund you. I am going to lunch with T.S. Eliot. You know who is T.S. Eliot?'

'Yes indeed.'

Tambi stowed away the fiver. 'He takes interest in me and in the quarterly,' he said.

This was true, On arrival in England (completely penniless according to legend: there was garbled talk of privation and an open boat) he secured an introduction to Eliot, who had been impressed by him and helped in the starting of *Poetry London*. The great grandson of a great Victorian novelist helped the most, and Tambi was no longer penniless though the grandson as a result became relatively so; but the tale has many versions and there are many more competent to tell it than I. The grandson had enlisted in the army and gone overseas during the war, and I only saw him once, in the uniform of a captain and looking ineluctably sad: as well he might if the stories are true.

Kitty's £5 was supposed to last her a week. She slept on the camp bed in the basement, living on bread and cheese: not an ideal food as it attracted the rats who'd got bored with gnawing a way through the poetry contributions and needed a change of diet. But Kitty survived without being eaten and when after ten days Tambi returned, he surveyed with approval the pile of stamped addressed envelopes that almost hid his secretary from sight.

'But the stamps?' he said, 'Where did you get them? I did not think that there were any.'

'I bought them.'

'Then you still have some money?'

'An aunt sent me £3.'

'That is good. Give me what remains, I am tonight entertaining Edith Sitwell. You know about Edith Sitwell?' He added, dropping the money into his pocket: 'Remember, next Friday is settlement day. Payment every fortnight.'

But when he did look in, after a further fortnight, he found a polite note of resignation written on the embossed stationery and the basement floor deep in peevish letters from rejected contributors addressed to K. Banks, Esq, Banks being Kitty of Bloomsbury's surname. She hadn't been able to send back all the poems, having no more money left to buy stamps, so she'd gone and got herself a job in the foreign office.

'All the same,' Kitty concluded, telling me this in 1943, 'he's a great editor. No stop laughing, he is. He has such flair.'

By that time the basement had long been abandoned to the rats and beetles, and *Poetry London* was subsidised by Messrs Nicholson and Watson (a publishing firm now defunct), who allowed Tambi a free hand in running it, plus salary and expenses as editor. He now had an office in Manchester Square, had published a very slim volume of his own verse called *Out of this War*, and was sometimes commissioned by the BBC to speak on poetry in wartime.

Every night he was to be seen in the pubs and cafés of Soho, wrapped summer and winter in the same blue melton overcoat buttoned to the chin and with the collar turned up, for he keenly felt the cold and in December slept every night in a Turkish bath (Subramaniam wrote a story in which Tambi died in one, having had too much to drink beforehand: he was convinced that this would one day be his actual fate).

Tambi's blue-black hair was bobbed like a woman's and curled up at the corners; his extraordinary hands, with fingers that bent right back, apparently boneless and like a lemur's only longer, flickered mesmerically as he talked in rapid tones with an accent that on the wireless sounded Welsh, white teeth and eyeballs flashing meantime in the dusk of his face.

It was really Tambimuttu who introduced me to Soho or, as he called it, Fitzrovia. One night, soon after I'd been discharged from the army and before I was signed-on at Strand, he came up in the Swiss pub which I'd already found, and asked if I'd a book for sale.

'I'm not a bookseller,' I said.

Tambi said: 'No no I mean a book you have written yourself. I am empowered by my principals to offer a one hundred pounds advance.'

'Sorry,' I said.

Tambi said: 'One hundred and fifty.'

'Not possible,' I said.

He said: 'Two hundred. That is the top.'

I said: 'We're not in the bazaar.' Tambi's prehensile pink tongue darted out like a chameleon's from between his purple puckered lips. 'I will have to consult Nick and Wat,' he said, 'before I can go higher.'

When I explained that I was already under contract to Cape, he said: 'A pity. My imprint would give an added lustre to your work.' He was very fond of this phrase, which he used as a sort of slogan, like 'It is impossible not to be thrilled by Edgar Wallace': though in those days he had not actually got a publishing firm of his own.

Then he said: 'So you have already had an advance? That is good, you must be rich, we will go on a pub crawl,' and at these words masses of his supporters gathered round, they seemed to grow up all at once from out of the floor.

'Well I thought of finishing some work tonight,' I said.

Tambimuttu said: 'Yes work is good but you are a writer, you must meet people and it is better you meet them under my aegis. That is so isn't it?' and the supporters raised a sullen murmur of agreement like a lynching mob getting ready to string someone up at the behest of a rabble rouser.

'Only beware of Fitzrovia,' Tambi said quelling the mob with a flicker of his amazing fingers. 'It's a dangerous place, you must be careful.'

'Fights with knives?'

'No, a worse danger. You might get Sohoitis you know.'

'No I don't. What is it?'

'If you get Sohoitis,' Tambi said very seriously, 'you will stay there always day and night and get no work done ever. You have been warned.'

'Is this Fitzrovia?'

'No, Old Compton Street, Soho. You are safer here.'

'Why won't I get Sohoitis in Soho? Or is Fitzrovia in Soho too?'

'Fitzrovia's really a part of Bloomsbury,' said a supporter called Steven. 'But the borough is St Pancras.'

'Sounds complicated,' I said, whereupon he asked me if I came from Streatham.

'No he doesn't come from Streatham,' Tambi said sharply before I could reply.

'And Steven if you are rude you must buy beer for us all.'

Steven retired hastily to the back of the crowd like a boy who's been rebuked in class, and Tambi said: 'Now we will go to the Black Horse, the Burglar's Rest, the Marquess of Granby, The Wheatsheaf, then the Beer House and after 10:30 back to the Highlander which closes later at eleven and after this eat curries in St Giles' High or steak at the Coffee An'.'

'Steak,' Steven echoed his eyes snapping.

'Be quiet Steven,' Tambi told him and we set off up Dean Street outside.

'Where are all these pubs?' I asked him.

'In Fitzrovia. The other side of Oxford Street.'

I said: 'I know the Fitzroy of course.'

Tambi said: 'Ah that was in the Thirties, now they go other places. Wait and you will see.'

He loped along beside me in the soft late summer evening which was still light, and the supporters formed a rearguard, Steven often lurching out into the roadway then back on to the sidewalk with movements apparently un-coordinated, while Tambi pointed out a pub on the right-hand side where only negro GIs went, as the other publicans had put up the colour bar: now in consequence the negroes had established their own bridgehead which none of us might pass. A huge one standing in the open door, tunic unbuttoned, pint glass in hand, ready to repel invaders, shouted: 'No white folks allowed in here,' in a Southern accent as we straggled by.

'And here,' Tambi indicated ground-glass windows on our left, 'is the Highlander but we don't drink there until half-past ten. This way round Soho Square,' then on the corner before reaching the post office he suddenly halted. 'Do you have a bank account?'

'Yes,' I said.

'Where?'

'Barclay's, Piccadilly.'

Tambi said: 'You should bank here, Martin's Bank,' pointing to it. 'It's one of the Big Five,' he added encouragingly, 'You should transfer your account here, I bank with Martin's myself.'

'At this branch?'

'No no, in Baker Street near my office, but this branch is better for you, near the pubs and you can come quickly down to cash a cheque if you are short or any of us needs money. And when the bank is shut, landlords will more quickly cash one for you if the branch is near.'

The supporters chorused agreement, I determined to disregard their advice and across Oxford Street, up Rathbone Place, the first step of our pilgrimage, the Black Horse, was reached. We visited that night all the places Tambi had promised we should visit, these I will describe elsewhere, then the Highlander at closing time with a cellar-restaurant to follow; and I remember Steven being ripped untimely from his steak by a powerful Greek waiter who'd had enough of him, and holding it still impaled upon his fork he was hurled into the outer darkness.

I remember also getting back to my room determined to finish the work which I'd neglected, and waking fully dressed on my bed with the room full of smoke from a cigarette which had burned away a whole corner of a new leather brief case which I'd just been given: I was lucky not to have been burnt to death as Bill Makins was said to have been.

It was the first night of my many in Fitzrovia and perhaps Tambi had been right in warning me against Sohoitis, although he was himself a demonstration case of the disease to which, however, we neither of us succumbed in the end.

A long time later he said to me: 'You know, Julian, somebody showed me a story of yours the other day, I don't read much prose, only poetic prose you know, but I read this right through and you know it was very good? I was surprised you wrote so well.'

'D'you mean you'd never read anything of mine before?' I asked astonished. 'Why, you offered me two hundred advance on a book, remember?'

'Did I?' Tambi was only momentarily disconcerted, 'Ah but you see,' he said recovering, 'my instinct told me your work was good, and my instinct cannot fail.'

'There now!' Kitty exclaimed in triumph when I reported this conversation, 'He didn't have to read you, he knew. He is a great editor, I told you he had flair.'

But Tambi had decided to become a great publisher as well. After long deliberation Nicholson and Watson were prepared to issue a separate non-commercial line of books, both verse and prose (poetic prose of course) to be selected and edited entirely by Tambimuttu.

The general title that this series should have gave rise to much cogitation on Tambi's part, and everyone was called in to help. He originally wanted something very succinct, with the hint of a telegraphic address conveyed in the title of his quarterly, and the metropolitan emphasis was to be retained: in the Forties there was no nonsense about regionalism or Liverpool or Salford being the centre of the arts, London was the centre and that was bloody well that.

Tambi read out with dissatisfaction a list of alternatives written on the back of a beer mat: Tambimuttu London Books, Poetry London Library, Poetry London Editions, Poetry Editions London. What else?'

I said: 'How about Prince Tambimuttu Poetry London Books?'

'Too long. Also perhaps,' reluctantly, 'too undemocratic-sounding. You know?'

I then suggested Editions Poetry London, as if the books were French. To my surprise Tambi pounced on this with enthusiasm as if the suggestion had been his own, though without the French *accentaigu* which he couldn't pronounce; and the series eventually appeared under this name: most people, however, referring to them as PL Books, so we need not have taken so much trouble.

Tambi at once commanded a larger salary, and commandeered larger offices which were staffed and stormed by aspirant young poetesses who hoped to have their verse published by Editions Poetry London and, wearing mackintoshes and black leather, made the mode which the Sixties followed (then a mark of ineffectual arty bohemianism).

Tambi let them hope, the hopes were unfulfilled for he was not a fool; he in turn entertained concerning them hopes of another sort which frequently were fulfilled, for he was extremely fond of women sexually without caring for them much as a sex.

He had already been married and his former wife Jacqueline, who now went around with the poet and journalist Charles Hamblett was a permanent feature of the pubs that we frequented. A docile sweet-faced girl with long silky yellow hair and a head which rose to a point at the top like the skull of a spaniel. They were either separated or divorced but still on friendly terms, and later Jackie died: I don't know of what cause.

Tambi in fact must have been married more than once, for he had a brother-in-law who didn't seem to be the brother of Jackie and was a regular Indian army officer who together with the Great Victorian's great-grandson had supplied some of the initial *Poetry London* backing and then been booted out by Tambi, disappearing afterwards to Burma with his regiment.

But Tambi if he could have afforded it would have had not only two wives but a harem. His attitude, to most things Europeanised, was to girls exclusively Oriental. I remember once we were with two suburban young women, new to Fitzrovia, whom he'd picked up in the Wheatsheaf and who were both uninteresting and interested only in being bought a meal in some newly-opened restaurant which they'd heard was good but which was off our usual beat. Tambi was becoming increasingly worried as we stumbled over cobble-stones further and further from the territory that he had made his own; he glanced longingly at strips of light visible through the blackouts of pubs where the girls refused to stop.

'Nearly ten o'clock,' he muttered. 'In an hour they'll be closing and this restaurant has perhaps no licence,' and suddenly he caught up the girls who were walking ahead arm-in-arm, giggling and whispering together, convinced that they'd achieved their objective in finding a pair of suckers who would foot the bill.

'Listen you must tell us please, my friend and I wish to know, do you do it or not?'

'Do it?' they chorused. 'Do what?'

'You know. Sex.'

There was a pause for shock to register then outraged gasps of 'Oh how dare you,' came in unison.

'You mean you don't?' Tambi asked.

'Certainly not. The idea!'

'Then be off!' Tambi shouted, banishing them with a gesture into the blackout: 'You are wasting our valuable drinking time,' and we retraced our steps to Rathbone Place.

I said: 'I could have told you those girls were NBG.'

'How did you know?'

'Well they were nurses or something weren't they?'

'Don't nurses do sex?'

'Yes but only with doctors whom they hope to marry after.'

'Only doctors? Is that all?' Tambi was silent for a moment then asked: 'Only medical doctors? A doctor of literature would not be any good?'

'Are you a doctor of literature?'

'Not yet. But I could have a degree conferred, Honorary you know. From Oxford, I know many professors there, and then I could fuck with all these nurses. What do you think?'

Actually I would not have been surprised if some university had awarded him an honorary degree but he lost interest later in the idea of using his contacts to get him one, as there weren't really, he explained, so many attractive nurses about just then.

This was in 1943–44, at the height of my intimacy with Tambimuttu, when with Subramaniam we ate curries almost every night in one of the Indian restaurants roundabout. After this, intimacy declined but he had great plans for me round about that time.

He thought it would be good for my career to marry a girl called Diana Gardner, whose excellent collection of short stories *Halfway Down the Cliff* he later published in PL Books. She too had made a big stir in *Horizon* with a documentary piece 'The Land Girl', and her first story

'Crossing the Atlantic' had a harsh impersonal cynicism seldom found in feminine fiction at this period; Tambi felt that as presumably kindred souls we should make it a *Horizon* wedding, with Cyril Connolly to give away the bride and famous contributors outside the church to hold copies of the magazine over us when we emerged, as Guardees form an arch with their swords over a newly wedded comrade and his wife. The fact that I wasn't yet divorced was held to be a minor detail, but actually I never even met Diana Gardner, who had the good sense to not come round the pubs.

Another big plan Tambi had was that I should edit the PL *Book of French Short Stories*; he himself knew no French so he could hardly edit it himself, as he admitted with disarming candour; and at least £200 was offered as a fee for taking on the job, more if I did the translation work as well. This was just what I needed to replenish my bank account: somewhat depleted since my introduction to Fitzrovia, though not transferred to Martin's Bank in Soho Square.

Tambi assured me that this, was certain to come off: an added publishing inducement being that authors included in the anthology would not have to be paid just yet, as France was still in the hands of the Germans; and one day I was actually summoned to Nick and Wat Headquarters for discussion of the project with his principals.

I saw a Mr Roberts. He said little but stood behind Tambi's chair as befitted a power behind the throne, scratching his ear with dark Welsh wisdom, then looked shrewd as money began to be mentioned, finally when it came to the question of some being paid out in advance he smiled indulgently as one who listens to the fantasies of a child and quietly left the office, closing the door as if it were a nursery.

To say that I was displeased is to put it mildly, but Tambi said that was only Mr Roberts' way and could be got round later, now he'd take me to lunch on expenses at a good restaurant nearby. Nicholas Moore joined us, perhaps some joint-venture with Grey Walls Press, where Nick worked with Charles Wrey Gardiner, was in the wind, I don't remember; but after the meal it turned out that Tambi as usual was without cash despite his increased salary, and we had to pay each for our own, splitting the price of Tambi's lunch between us; then he asked us for the receipted bills as these could be added to his expense sheet under Entertainment to Authors, and the French Anthology was never spoken of in my presence: besides, with the liberation of France it became uneconomic, as the authors would all have to be paid.

Tambi had about him something of the snake-charmer to which I was impervious, and after this incident I could never be persuaded to join him in any business scheme. I've always been proof against anything of the hypnotic order; on the other hand Stewart Scott, who'd had political differences with the army and been repatriated from Burma, had implicit faith in the poet-publisher's occult force.

He told me that once he and Tambi were eating a curry at an Indian café where East Indian sailors were also served; Tambi for some reason loathed and despised Lascars who, though all mankind was his country, did not to him belong to mankind, and it was not long before trouble arose.

All went outside to settle matters, Stewart Scott a dauntless fellow of only apparently frail physique took on several Lascars who luckily hadn't knives, but Tambi like President Wilson was too proud to fight: he stood by with folded arms and mesmeric stare fixed upon the fray, calling to Scott as his tongue flicked in and out: 'Don't sully yourself Stewart by fighting with this scum. Let me look at them with my eyes, and they will flee abashed,' and Scott telling me the story added: 'And they would have, too, if Tambi could have only got his eyes on them.'

Which didn't prevent Scott from being thoroughly done-up and having to have stitches in where his head had been thumped against some railings. But he bore no grudge either for this or for being thrown out of the original PL set-up; and now that he was back in circulation became one of Tambi's most loyal supporters.

Yet despite the episode of the Lascars Tambi had plenty of physical courage: it was simply that he shared Scott's belief in his power to subdue the enemy by the naked eye alone. This was all part of his Holy Fakir of Poetry side for which I personally had no use. In a different kind of dangerous situation he showed great sang-froid, as I will tell later: also of his kindness and generosity in the case of Gerald Wilde the painter, whom he did, against all odds, attempt to help.

I remember too one night when after closing time I was showing to a group of his supporters, in the light of someone's torch, the bullet which had struck my steel helmet in the butts and which I carried always as a good luck charm in my hip pocket. As it was being examined, the twisted shard of metal, shaped like the business end of a scorpion, slipped from my hand and fell through the grating of a drain beside the kerb. Horror-struck I called on everybody to help me recover it; the torch was shone upon the grating below which the spent bullet could just be seen glinting, caught up by some obstruction at the side, though all attempts to salvage it with the ferrule of my cane completely failed.

The other fellows got fed-up after a while and were for moving on, but Tambi detained them crying: 'No no, you don't understand. It's his bullet, his talisman, while he carries this he cannot die, we must help him get it,' and on his instructions the grating was levered up and one of the supporters (surely it was Steven?), removing his jacket and rolling up his shirt sleeve, lay flat on the kerb, thrusting his arm down into the drain until his fingers reached the bullet, but unfortunately it was dislodged by his touch and vanished into water with a final plop: now beyond recall short of a descent into the St Pancras sewers.

Tambi mourned the loss as I did myself, but 'Never mind,' he said later, 'you will not die Julian, your work will make you immortal,' and recovering fell heartily to eating a horsemeat curry: all the same he did understand the way I felt.

Meanwhile *Poetry London* had ceased to come out quarterly, indeed to appear at all, and items announced on the Editions Poetry London were also overdue pending. Tambi pleaded all the standard wartime publishing excuses: paper shortage, trouble with printers, the binding bottleneck, but nonetheless rebellion was in the air.

John Banting, who afterwards did very striking jackets for two of my books and whose own *Little Book of Fishes* had been held up for eighteen months, cornered Tambi in the Swiss one evening and, clenching a large turpentine-stained fist under his nose, demanded a definite date or else.

Ignoring the fist, Tambi simply said: 'We will do our best, John. But you see I haven't a European conception of time.'

This pleased Banting so much that he was pacified, and Tambi signed to one of the supporters to buy him a pint of bitter, his sovereign cure for all ills. But not withstanding Banting's *Little Book of Fishes* remained among forthcoming publications. In the end even some of the supporters, who'd not yet received advances for books or payment for poems accepted but not printed, began to cut up rough.

To keep them quiet Tambi brought out an enormous omnibus volume of *Poetry London*, costing the earth to buy and known to us as Chums. I nearly got into it myself. While drinking around Soho with Keidrych Rhys and Dylan Thomas, who'd mislaid his hat, I'd made up a bit of verse which epitomised the situation and also, we'd drunkenly decided, the poetic climate of the time. Tambi hearing that I'd composed a poem asked me to recite it. I declaimed:

> Oh pisspot brimful to overflowing
> with milk of Keidrych-curdled kindness;
> My hat's in the Highlander
> crying with Wheatsheaf voice
> oh time gentlemen Police
> bearing Tambi
> > downwards
> > > Muttu
> > > > to Tube.

'Marvellous,' Tambi cried. 'I didn't know you were a poet, repeat this please,' and only the repetition of his own name, betraying the send-up, prevented its inclusion in the monster volume. All the supporters were represented however; but when Antony Brown, a young poet now turned television newsreader, who had several unpaid-for poems and poetic-prose pieces in Chums, was unable to pay his electric light bill and the supply was to be cut off in consequence, I urged him to approach Tambi and insist on some cash down.

From across the Wheatsheaf I watched Tambi's tongue and fingers flickering as he talked and Tony listened, but no wallet was produced or cheque made out: instead a brimming pint not unlike that in my poem appeared on the counter and Tony, returning to me with this clutched in his hand, explained that the expenses of production precluded any payment of fees at present.

Other contributors remembered a colossal banquet given by Tambi about a year before, where many beakers of his special cocktail had been drunk, the guests after receiving separate bills: later collected by the host and pinned to his entertainment account like those settled by Nicholas Moore and myself; and rumours began to circulate that this function had been to celebrate the sum given him by Nick and Wat to pay for poems printed in the omnibus PL. Tambi threatened to sue for slander, lost many supporters in the process, and then a setback occurred which would have knocked a less resilient man flat out.

Nicholson and Watson went bust. They however were responsible for any debts incurred, royalties to authors, etcetera, which must have made Mr Roberts smile less and look more Welshly wise; while *Poetry London* and its Editions were registered under a separate title in the name of Tambimuttu.

In no time a new patron was found, with money believed to come from coal and prepared to put up backing. This was a young man named Harold Musson, big, tall, broad-shouldered, heavy-faced and gentle, also with the reputation of a wit. Unlike other Wheatsheaf wits he did in fact once say something funny. When asked where he'd been for the last week or so, he replied: 'Farming. You know, Chalk Farm. The agricultural life.'

Brand-new supporters, secretaries and poetesses collected round Tambi, his salary went up again though he seemed to have less on him than ever, if that were possible; and he discovered a work of genius, both neo-surrealist and existentialist in tone, entitled 'Bymus'. I never read this book but gather it was about a man with three legs who came to London and had a long talk about semantics with a policeman in Piccadilly. Musson was reputed to have paid out at least two hundred and fifty to secure the rights, some even said five hundred: although years later the author, a small bearded Beat whom I encountered in a club, told me that twenty-five was all he'd had from Tambi.

But suddenly a terrible thing happened. Musson decided to become a Buddhist monk. For some time, apparently, he'd been brooding over Hiroshima and not even Tambi could dissuade him from this course.

My second wife, whom I knew by sight but didn't meet until ten years later, saw a lot of them during the period of attempted discussion. Tambi had some forlorn hope that her mother being Leonard Woolf's sister might succeed Musson as a backer, and there was a night at the Imperial Hotel when Diane suffered some un-monastic behaviour on the part of Musson, who seemed reluctant to relinquish his secular privileges until the last moment; however, being herself six feet high though only seventeen, she managed successfully to repulse him.

After this he took vows, had his head shaved and left for a lamasery in Tibet with a schoolfriend equally tall who used to drink with us also but had never been known to speak. I remember being shown newspaper photographs of them both: they were sitting cross-legged in their robes among other neophytes, and Musson's name was given as something like Brother O-Kai-Lung.

For a time Tambi didn't know where to turn. He even considered returning to Ceylon and showed me a letter from his father urging him to do so and offering money for the fare. The letter was written in impeccable almost Biblical English and a beautiful copperplate hand:

it spoke of the Prodigal Son, was extremely moving and the writing paper did not bear any family crest or reproduction of the ancestral home (Subramaniam told me that Tambi's father, like his own, was a retired High Court Judge although of course he may have been a Prince as well). Tambi however managed to hold out until yet another backer took over his firm in more ways than one.

Richard March had been, perhaps still was, in the Diplomatic Service and had written two rather good books, a collection of allegorical stories a little in the fashion of Rex Warner and a novel about a Upas Tree, both published by the Fortune Press. In looks he faintly resembled Tambi's original patron, the Great Victorian's great-grandson, with regular features and distinguished diplomatist's greying hair, but though quiet in manner soon showed signs of wanting to take a more active part in the PL administration than his predecessors had ever done: especially Harold Musson, to whom the word of Tambi had been, if not law, at any rate to be instantly complied with.

A dispute was not long in breaking out, many of Tambi's secretaries, poetesses and supporters went over to the other side: it was then revealed by a firm of lawyers that he had signed some papers without reading them and that *Poetry London*, Editions and all, belonged lock, stock and barrel to Richard March.[1]

Tambi was out. He tried to organise a rally, a protest march with banners inscribed 'UNFAIR TO TAMBIMUTTU!' but by now there were no supporters left to carry them.

The climate of poetry too was changing. Already from the academic desert of the Fifties a dry cold wind was blowing, the red brick Doctors were drumming in the distance and talk of Consolidation and the Critic as Poet could be heard. Tambi fought hard, he slept on studio floors, twice spending the fare sent him by his father in efforts to regain his former position as Prince of Poetry Pundits, but he had to give up at last.

Back to Ceylon he went but not, it seems, for long. I recently heard from Stewart Scott, who'd just come over from the States, that he's now firmly established in Greenwich Village, with fresh patrons, poetesses and a new poetry review at his disposal.

Good luck to him.

---

1 March died unexpectedly soon after, and the title to *Poetry London* presumably expired with him, for it never reappeared.

I remember on the last occasion we met standing him a hamburger and chips in some Charlotte Street café just before his departure; and he said then to my girlfriend that, being a Prince in his own country, he would arrange for us a truly royal reception, should we ever decide to visit his part of Ceylon.

'A feast,' he said, 'and the food will be served on plates of gold.' His tongue flicked out to absorb a last morsel of hamburger clinging to the corner of his mouth. 'Gold dust will be smeared upon the meat.'

'And can we have a castle to live in?' she asked, accommodation in London not being easy to obtain at that time.

'A magnificent castle,' Tambi replied.

'With servants?'

'Certainly with servants. To do your every bidding.'

'And elephants?' she went on. 'Can we have elephants as well?'

'If you insist,' Tambi agreed but with, this time, perhaps a touch of restraint in his tone. Then he added: 'That is Nancy Cunard who has just come in. You know Nancy Cunard?'

We knew Nancy Cunard and Tambi, having finished his meal, hastened over to greet her: failing to return, subsequently, to our table. Asking for the elephants had evidently been too much.

Fitzrovian Nights

*   *   *

PUBS OF RATHBONE PLACE

A FORMER PROPRIETOR OF THE BLACK HORSE IN RATHBONE PLACE had, so the story went, drunk himself literally to death.

The Black Horse was a sombre Victorian pub, as befitted the suggestion of plumed hearses implied by its name, with a narrow tiled passage leading to the various bars divided by partitions of scrolled and embossed glass, including a Ladies' Bar (no gents admitted) where old dears in dusty black toasted departed husbands with port and lemon from black leather settles. The funereal atmosphere had so affected the late proprietor that he had set out deliberately to commit suicide by drinking solidly for three days and nights behind closed doors, and when these were eventually battered down by police his dead body was found surrounded by empty bottles on the saloon bar floor. The exact amount consumed was never stated in the story, nor exactly what kind of alcohol the bottles had contained.

The Horse was the first pub to be reached, though usually the last to be visited, entering Rathbone Place from Oxford Street. Next on the right, round the cobbled curve of Gresse Street, stood the Bricklayers Arms, better known as the Burglars Rest because a gang of burglars had once broken into it and afterwards slept the night on the premises, leaving behind them as evidence even more empties than the dead landlord of the Horse; but the burglars did not die and, incidentally, were never caught.

The Burglars was a quiet house, useful for a business talk or to take a young woman whom one did not know well, unlike the Marquess of Granby at the foot of Rathbone Place where at that time the most fights broke out despite the efforts of the landlord, an ex-policeman, to keep order and put down disorderly conduct. Gigantic guardsmen went there in search of homosexuals to beat up and rob and, finding none, fought instead each other: one summer evening, in broad daylight, a man was savagely killed by several others in a brawl outside while a crowd gathered on the pavement to watch and was dispersed only by the arrival of a squad from Goodge Street Police Station nearby, by which time the killers had made their getaway in someone else's car. (Entering the Wheatsheaf shortly after this incident, I was surprised to find it empty except for a local tart known as Sister Ann, who told me equably: 'Oh, they've all gone to see the bloke being kicked to death outside the Marquess dear,' and added that the sound of the thumps was somethink awful.)

The Wheatsheaf was the last pub on the right of Rathbone Place, next to the cosmopolitan newsagent on the corner of Percy Street; and branching off diagonally past the Marquess was a roofed-in passage known to us as Jekyll and Hyde Alley because it was the sort of place through which Mr Hyde flourishing his stick rushes low-angle on the screen: this passage contained a pub called the Beerhouse because spirits were not served there, and behind it, to the left, was a warehouse yard piled with cardboard boxes into which one sometimes guided girls in order to become better acquainted.

Along Rathbone Street, past the passage, was yet another pub named the Duke of York, much patronised in the middle Forties by the more Bohemian types among whom beards and fringes abounded and who would now be called Beatniks whereas they were then called, more correctly, Bums. The proprietor of the Duke announced himself, on a large placard hung behind him in the bar, as:

MAJOR 'ALF' KLEIN
THE PRINCE OF GOOD FELLOWS

but the Prince (or the Major) did not particularly care for me, and in the end would not allow me to be served in his pub, about which I can therefore say little.

Running parallel were the restaurants and cafés of Charlotte Street which made up the district of Fitzrovia and comprised also the Fitzroy Tavern from which at an earlier period the district had derived its name. But fashions, and rendezvous for writers and artists, change; and the Wheatsheaf of all the pubs in Rathbone Place and its environs had become in the Forties the most popular.

It was a Younger's Scotch Ale house and the door to the saloon bar was down an alleyway dominated from above by a perspective of tall tenement buildings with steel outside staircases in the Tottenham Court Road beyond, and often blocked by motor milk-vans owned by two stout Italian brothers who ran a small creamery business round the corner of the alley.

When the milk-vans were parked too high up and customers had difficulty in squeezing past to enter the bar, the Wheatsheaf landlord would fling wide the door, and slapping the sides of the vans, shout with flailing arms at the Italian brothers who grinning good humouredly would shift their vans further down. The name of the brothers was Forte.

THE WHEATSHEAF AND MRS STEWART

The Wheatsheaf landlord was known as Red, not because he had red hair (in fact his hair was grey) but because his Christian name was Redvers. Also he was not the landlord but the manager appointed by Messrs Younger, though it was his unmarried sister Mona who actually held the licence and whose name as licensee was lettered small on the lintel of the public bar door in Rathbone Place itself. Mona, short, plump and meekly dressed with her hair drawn back in a bun, helped behind the bar with Red's wife Frances, who was tall, lean and in appearance strict, wearing rimless pince-nez and a tweed coat and skirt, while her husband supervised them both: portly and as a rule in shirt sleeves and braces except on Sundays when he wore a snuff-coloured suit. Nonetheless it was Mona who got rid of awkward customers by simply ordering them to leave with a quite astonishing display of authority; and once barred by Mona you never got in again, whereas Red and even Frances were inclined to be much less inflexible.

The saloon bar of the Wheatsheaf was not large but cheerful, warm in winter, and always brightly lit, good blackout boards fitting tightly over the windows of armorial glass and the floor spread with scarlet linoleum. It had mock-Tudor panelling and, inset round the walls, squares of tartan belonging to various Scottish clans. An important feature was the large china swan, hollowed out inside and sometimes used by vandals as an extra ashtray, which stood in the big bow-window above the long settee at the bottom of the bar and was frequently smuggled out, on very busy evenings, for bets: it was always however returned next day, as the bar would not have been the same without it.

As Tambimuttu had told me, everyone or almost everyone came sooner or later to the Wheatsheaf; even the very eminent paid a passing after-dinner call, for the posh restaurants of Percy Street, where rationing was less rigorous, were only round the corner; also it must be remembered that as bottles of drink became in wartime and after more and more difficult to buy, and wine well-nigh impossible, fewer and fewer parties could be thrown and social life for most people began to revolve round the pubs at night.

Curtain-up on the evening was signalled by the arrival on the dot of six of Mrs Stewart, who lived on her old-age pension in one of the tenements at the foot of the alley and was collected by her married daughter towards closing time or when the pub became too noisy. Mrs Stewart was a very small elderly lady dressed in black silk with yellow-white hair and she arrived always carrying two evening papers in which to do the crossword and an alarm-clock to time herself by. She always drank bottled Guinness and having assembled her alarm clock, evening papers, spectacle case, purse and other properties on the table, sat in front of them on a leather-covered bench which ran along the right-hand wall by the corner of the bar.

It was in this corner, propped up against the wooden partition of the seat, that I stood for many years (though not, as has been said, underneath my own tartan), having displaced from this strategic position a Central European sports writer on a daily picture paper by the simple expedient of arriving each evening earlier than he was able to.

The sports writer was furious and hated me virulently because of this, since for years before my arrival on the scene he'd been able to lean there, wearing a brown porkpie hat and camel hair coat of inferior quality, speaking to few but hoping always that tourists would say: 'Who is that interesting-looking foreign man over there?' as he struck a Napoleonic pose and stared superciliously ahead with his pouched eyes through the smoke of a nonchalantly puffed-at cigarette.

Having permanently dislodged him, however (for if prevented by business from getting there in time, I would have someone else to hold the corner), it became my duty in turn to keep Mrs Stewart's place, to pass over the Guinnesses in exchange for the exact money produced from her purse, and to see that well-intentioned idiots did not try to help her with the crosswords, a thing she hated above all. Great care had to be exercised in offering her a drink, it could only be done by split-second timing when her nightly ration was running low, but she was very proud and from certain people who plonked down heartily before her an open bottle, with the words 'Have that one on me Ma,' she would not accept anything at all.

She was spiky and occasionally irascible. Happily she approved of me, but Dylan Thomas and the poetess Anna Wickham she could not stand at any price. Red and Frances shared, originally, her dislike of Dylan, Mona to a lesser extent (luckily, or he wouldn't have been allowed in), but later when he had begun to broadcast they chanced to hear him on the radio and from then on nothing was too good. Mrs Stewart either didn't own a set or was perhaps too deaf, for her opinion of Dylan remained unchanged, despite the attempts of Red and Frances to win her over to what was now their side.

And yet she was no stranger to people of this sort. In Paris as a young woman she had lived in Montparnasse where she'd known Pascin, Hemingway and Joyce, also Denis Corrigan who'd once been my uncle's partner on the Côte and later hanged himself with his necktie in a prison cell awaiting trial (a paperback thriller called *Hangman's Tie* was found lying below the bench from which he'd kicked off).

Corrigan Mrs Stewart had met mainly on the racecourse, but her encounters with the painters and writers had been in Paris cafés and her stories about them always ended with her saying: 'And there they were, my dear, staggering about just like you and the rest of the young fellows are doing today.'

She was unlike other old ladies in that she never spoke of the past in a personal angle, so nobody was told what she had been doing in Paris at this period. Nina Hamnett, who was better at painting old people than she was the young, did a superb portrait of her, which for some time after she died hung above the spot where so long she'd sat, though I don't know what happened to it in the end.

The death of Mrs Stewart—in the late Forties or early Fifties— marked, as writers of memoirs are fond of saying, the passing of an epoch, and it might have pleased her to know that she'd become a symbolic figure to a whole generation now no longer young: for there are few former Wheatsheaf habitués whose eyes fail to light up in the memory of her name.

REGULARS, WITS AND BUMS

Alan Ross, then a junior naval officer on leave, used to come round, among others, about this time. As a promising young poet he had been discovered by John Lehmann, whom he was later to succeed as editor of *The London Magazine*, and Lehmann also printed in *New Writing* and *Daylight* portions of a novel which alternated brilliant scenes of civilian and naval life but was never completed.

Ross in the navy had served with the triple murderer Ronald Chesney but he did not know that yet, since Chesney so far had only murdered once: his own mother, for which he'd been tried and acquitted at the age of 17 under his real name of John Donald Merrett.

Ross was very young and ingenuous in manner: clean shaven in those days with a dark complexion and black sleek hair which showed up handsomely against his blue and gold uniform, and he had brown eyes which peered with unabashed interest at everybody and every-thing and took in a very great deal; as was revealed when he re-created from memory, with remarkable precision except for the high nasal voice allotted to me, the complete Wheatsheaf scene in a *London Magazine* editorial last year.

He described of course an evening on which absolutely everyone was there but the point was, as he said to me recently, that such an evening could and indeed sometimes did, take place.

But there were other figures whom he did not mention and possibly did not notice, without whom the Wheatsheaf wouldn't really have been complete: they made up the background and the unsung chorus and occasionally, on an off-night, the entire cast.

These fell roughly into three categories: Regulars, Wits and Bums.

Regulars, of whom Mrs Stewart was the doyenne, included the old Home Guard who though extremely old wore on his tunic medal ribbons of more campaigns than even he could possibly have served in: it was thought that the tunic or the ribbons had been handed down to him by his grandfather, and I was using him as a model for the old sweat in the Home Guard film which Dylan and myself were then writing. Then there was the Central European sports writer, now relegated to the middle of the counter from which it was not so easy to get a drink; the orange-faced woman (so called because of the many layers of make-up which she wore which made it impossible to assess her age), whose presence in the pub made it sound like a parrot house in the zoo and who was reputed to have green silk sheets on her bed (though no man was brave enough to investigate the rumour); and Sister Ann, the tart who was more respectable than many other female customers: she mostly moved in a no-man's land between public and saloon bars and patronised both as it suited her.

Sister Ann was short and wholesome-looking and always wore russet-brown tweeds and a round russet-brown hat in shape like a schoolgirl's. She used no make-up except for two round red spots on her round apple cheeks, for she was no common brass and her chosen clientèle wanted nothing loud or flashy, consisting as it did of middle-aged or elderly businessmen from up North who liked the sort of girl that might have been a sister to them (she was shocked when I suggested this relationship was incestuous and said she was surprised to hear a man of my education using nasty dirty words like that to a woman, and she certainly never did anything of that sort, thank you dear).

When later I started going to the little afternoon clubs in Wardour Street, I often saw Ann having a quiet talk with one of her clients before or after, it was hard to say which. She never drank anything except brown bottled ale.

Ann's beat was under the Guinness clock in Tottenham Court Road: 'You catch them going into the tube or coming out for a day up in London dear, and maybe they're lost and don't know where to go or they don't want to catch a train home just yet awhile, either way they're glad to spend an hour or two with a girl they can talk to quiet like, poor blokes.'

Wits came in various shapes and sizes, but could be distinguished by the fact that none was ever heard to say anything witty: indeed one elderly Irishman, who wore a grey wideawake hat and was supposed when young to have written a very witty book, never said anything at all. Sometimes however he gave vent to a very loud laugh addressed to no one in particular, so possibly some pearl of wit too precious to cast before swine had passed through his hoary head beneath the wideawake brim.

He was a lone wolf whose laughter was sufficient unto himself; but on the whole wits tended to assemble in groups in order to laugh at the witticisms of other members as well as their own. The leader of the main group was a scenic artist who described himself as a painter, and his wit was exercised at the expense of the film producers who employed him and whom he would not have dared to criticise face to face for fear of causing offence. He was a baby elephant character, big and burly with grey hair ruffled up into a crest at the back and dangling over his fleshy nose as he lurched unsteadily about, one arm semaphoring the air, the other pointing to the ground, while his high piping voice re-enacted some scene that had taken place at the studios that day, in which according to himself he had shown the stupid bastards where to get off. When drunk he was aggressively and grossly rude, when sober extremely timid, the high piping voice was seldom heard, and if attacked in this rare condition by victims of his previous rudeness, he would flee the pub altogether, no witticism apparently coming to his aid. I only heard one sample of his wit myself, and that was repeated to me years later by an admirer who had been part of the group, now of course long disbanded. Apparently he had been taken to a pub outside his usual orbit, the name of which he didn't know; and when told this was the Adam-and-Eve, he cracked back—quick as a flash!—'Ah, I thought I saw an old bloke just going out with a halo and a long beard'.

Members of the group led by the scenic artist were always making ineffective passes at women with the object of afterwards humorously proclaiming their sexual frustration: some had literary aspirations and these passed round proudly newspaper cuttings relating to their arrests for being drunk and disorderly; it was the only chance they had of seeing their names in print, and once when the entire group was run in while searching in a cemetery, after closing time, for Hazlitt's grave, there was as much excitement as if they had won, collectively, the Nobel Prize.

Bums (some of whom under their new designation as Beats are still about), were of two kinds: (1) young men and women just down from provincial universities and wrapped in college scarves which after going several times round the necks were still long enough to hang down behind: these were known to us as the Slithy Toves since members of both sexes resembled facially the curious corkscrew-like creatures depicted by Tenniel in his illustrations to *Alice*, and (2) a number of shaggy bearded types who had managed to dodge the Services and lived communally in the cellar of a blitzed building, where they made lamp-shades and toy animals out of pipe cleaners while dealing in the black market on the side for a living. Their leader was known, for obvious reasons, as Robinson Crusoe and they called themselves the Young Anarchist Movement. None of them had any political convictions.

The Metamorphosis of Peter Brooke

*　　　*　　　*

HE CAN'T HAVE BEEN MORE THAN TWENTY-FIVE WHEN I FIRST SAW him, but even at that age he seemed sublimely unconscious of anyone except himself.

It was during the summer of 1931, at the Salle Mercier in Nice. This was a dance hall for hire, situated behind the boulevard Tsarevitch in the Russian Quarter, not far from the Orthodox Church. Unorthodox activities, however, not infrequently took place at the Salle when younger members of the Russian Colony held a dance there, and on that particular evening, just before Brooke appeared, I was wondering how to get out of the place alive.

The cabinet gramophone with its amplifying horn was temporarily silent, the dance floor had been cleared for an interval, and on either side of the empty space two rival Russian factions were drawn up making ready for civil war. Into this electric atmosphere strode Peter Brooke, entering the line of fire much as in later life he was wont to cross the barrack square bang in the middle of a battalion parade.

Irina Petrovna, by whose invitation I had come and who was also apparently unaware of the tension at present building up, exclaimed: 'Oh here is that other Englishman, Brooke. You must meet him, he too is writing a book. He has just come all the way from Spain on a bike.'

Attire as always on Russian occasions was fairly formal, a grande tenue was not de rigueur but all the girls at any rate wore evening frocks. Brooke had on rope-soled canvas shoes, tarpaulin trousers stained with axle-grease and a white open-necked shirt the sleeve of which had been partly ripped away, showing the blade of a broad shoulder burnt almost black. He had a rugged face the colour of dark tan Kiwi shoe polish and his rough straight hair, falling in bangs over the forehead, was absolutely black. He advanced upon us with deep-set dancing eyes and a smile of enormous geniality.

'Did you say bike or hike?' I asked Irina.

'Bike,' she said and Brooke bowed over her hand. He wasted no time on me but immediately drew himself up very tall and with head flung back began, smiling inexorably, to survey the young women nearby in a manner that betokened business.

At this moment the gramophone burst forth with the Stein Song and the prospective combatants reluctantly claimed partners without ceasing to exchange belligerent stares over their heads, while the amplified disc bellowed of undying campus comradeship, exhorting all to sing until the rafters ring. Brooke's glance had lit upon a placid pretty girl sitting with blonde hair braided round her head and eyes cast demurely down. It was not true, as he afterwards wrote, that I was ever his rival for this girl, whom I knew to be heavily engaged. Marousya would not in any case have been my type. On the other hand she was very much Brooke's; and after circling the floor a few times he steered her away through the open French windows towards the fairy lights of the garden beyond.

This gave me an idea. Taking Irina Petrovna in my arms and explaining the situation in a rapid undertone, I propelled her in the direction of the door, reaching it just as the Stein Song stopped abruptly and the fight broke loose. We made our getaway on the running board of somebody's car, and I often wondered what Brooke's reaction had been when, returning after his romantic interlude, he found the furniture reduced to matchwood, blood and broken bottles on the parquet floor, and the police in possession.

Long afterwards he told me that he'd always imagined I was in some way responsible. He described me as very pale, watchful and withdrawn; I wore an orchid in my buttonhole, another sinister trait according to the movies of the time, and moreover was smoking a Turkish cigarette through a long holder, the mark of at least a gang-leader if not a master criminal.

But next time I saw him he was himself smoking through a holder, and even flourishing it elegantly about on the stage at the Casino de la Méditerranée. He had somehow acquired a lounge suit and was playing Algy in *The Importance of Being Earnest*, produced by a woman with three names who ran something called the Anglo-American Repertory Company. A friend of mine had been slated to report the matinee for the *Monte Carlo News*, a weekly paper printed in English for British residents. He had no literary or journalistic aptitudes, it was his father who'd got him on to the staff, and I had offered to do the review for him; thus it came about that the first notice of Peter Brooke ever to appear in print was written by me.

It was also the first time Brooke had ever acted professionally, but he put up a rousing show. Great panache and aplomb, and his voice carried easily to every corner of the theatre, while the actor playing Ernest was barely audible over the footlights. There was only one thing out of place: Brooke had forgotten to shave. He also dozed off at times during Ernest's long explanation of his predicament, but awoke always in the nick of time, rising to come in on cue with a tremendous shout.

'Is that chap tight?' asked my friend. 'What d'you suppose he'll be like by tonight?' and I wish we had attended the evening performance instead; for, as I was told by those who did, Peter Brooke, delivering an epigram with a careless wave of his hand, stepped backward off the stage and was buried up to the neck in the jazz drum which in the orchestra pit awaited the negro musicians booked to appear on the following night.

After this I saw him no more for thirteen years, nor did the blonde Marousya ever mention his name to me.

At the Café Madrid, corner of Dean and Old Compton Streets, good strong cups of black French coffee could be had in 1944, not like the frothy Italian mud that's served up now. Outside was winter, inside was warm, and Philip Toynbee often came there to write part of a novel or Paul Potts to read a book of verse. Neither of these was present on the afternoon I met Peter Brooke again.

This time he was dressed as a corporal and wore an army greatcoat buttoned to the neck. His tan had faded slightly, his rough lamp-black hair comprised already streaks of grey, but the deep-set eyes still danced beneath brows that had grown bushier with every year that passed and the smile of set geniality remained. He was not a figure one forgets, and I said: 'So they dug you out of that jazz drum in the end?'

This greeting startled Brooke, who went through a quick routine denoting the double-take, passing a hand over his face, rubbing a finger across the nose and pushing the hair back from his forehead. Then he shouted: 'Why good God. You're that fellow who smashed up the Russian dance hall in Nice.'

By the time this was straightened out and several rounds of coffee had been swallowed, I'd found out a good deal concerning Brooke: never reluctant in any case to talk about himself. His father was a Bavarian Count born in England and a British subject, who had changed his family name and ended up as a film actor in Hollywood, and there was an elder brother who'd written several novels, including one about the private life of Jack the Ripper.

I had often seen the father as an eccentric millionaire or mad scientist on the screen, and used to play Parc Impérial tennis with the brother, a fashionable type who hobnobbed with the King of Sweden, so I was in a sense a sort of family friend and when we reached the Swiss pub across the way, where sloe gin or arak could be drunk instead of coffee, Brooke had adopted me as such.

'Would you say I'm like my brother?' he asked, choosing arak because he'd lived in Tangier where Kif was smoked and after Ramadan orgies of sex ensued.

'To look at, d'you mean? It never occurred to me you were related.'

'Well I don't think I look like him either, but a funny thing happened. Right here. In this very bar.' He pointed to the bar where the man had come up to him. The man had said: 'Brooke?' 'Yes. Your name is Brooke?' 'Certainly,' Brooke replied and with that the man had socked him in the face.

Brooke drove a fist into his palm to illustrate the blow, which it turned out was intended for his brother. 'Silly sod had got the two of us mixed up. I asked what my brother had done to him but he simply wouldn't say. Finally I got fed up and grabbed hold of him to make him talk, so they told us both to go, and in the blackout the bastard got away. I've never set eyes on him since. Most extraordinary, though. No one's ever taken me for my brother before. And he couldn't have ever seen my brother or he wouldn't have made the mistake, so how could he have been injured by a man he never saw.'

It was an insoluble mystery, but things like this were always happening to Brooke: his future career was to be founded on the fact that he was dogged by misadventure. He himself had written a novel but of course its publication coincided with the outbreak of war, which effectively killed any sales there may have been. He enumerated with a shout of contemptuous laughter the kind of Resistance novel on which public interest had centred at the time: 'The Moon is Down, The Night is Ending, Fucking Dawn Broke,' and I heartily agreed that this type of book had long outlived its day.

Brooke's own novel, which I'd read but not connected with the young man I'd so briefly met in Nice, had been far better. It was extremely accomplished and original: a macabre fantasy with cosmopolitan backgrounds, about the Aztec wife of a famous French aviator converted from childhood to vampirism, and the pages as one turned them had the authentic dry rustle of leathery wings. At the same time extravagantly comic passages belied the gruesome theme, and the technical structure of the book alone merited much more critical attention than it got.

Brooke told me about the original of his character, with whom he'd once been in love. She was also the wife of a famous French aviator and claimed to be of Aztec origin though not a vampire. As in the novel, she actually came from Mexico.

'Of course you've been to Mexico?' I said, but he said no, that part was all imagination: apart from Tangier he'd been to America, Australia, New Zealand, France, Italy and Spain, several of these continents he had crossed on foot, but he had never got to Mexico. He'd joined the army hoping to go abroad again but although he spoke three languages at least, would the bastards send him overseas? Not a bloody chance, and now he was being shunted round the bugger like a lost truck: a phrase he'd used as opening sentence of a story which no editor would print. Eventually his company commander, a man who looked like a shark, had compromised by transferring him to Intelligence, so here he was, with six more days of pending-posting leave to go.

At this prospect his eyes began again to dance: the effect, I realised, was due to the way his high cheekbones seemed to make them slant, also to short sight, so extreme that he would have often to peer closely into several people's faces before he could identify a friend. The eyes themselves were yellow.

Brooke would have none of this, however. According to him, his sight was equalled only by that of a hawk; and when the colour of his eyes was commented on, and this was done frequently by girls: 'I have golden eyes,' he would correct them sternly.

Arak had by now run out and was succeeded by rum, sloe gin being also in short supply. Together we sang the Stein Song which had been playing at the Salle Mercier on the night we first met. We sang until the rafters rang, and having no steins clinked our glasses of rum as the song required when undying friendship was being pledged. The glasses were not really up to these repeated shocks and when they broke the barman, who'd probably been on duty when Brooke was mistaken for his brother, said rum had run out as well. So we sang the Stein Song stumbling along the blacked-out streets until a couple of red caps suddenly flashed a torch on Brooke and asked to see his pay book. He then cursed all the way to Rathbone Place, with occasional indignant shouts of 'Fighting for Freedom, my God!' or 'Might as well have the bloody Nazis here,' but on entering the Wheatsheaf, where strong ale and even whisky were plentiful and girls also quite abundant, his geniality returned.

He made several dates which next day he did not keep, when the pubs closed it turned out he'd nowhere to stay, and soon he was tucked up on the couch in my upstairs sitting-room, after having eaten half a pot of jam out of the jar with a spoon. His greatcoat was spread over him and he started to snore before I switched off the light.

A few seconds after, or so it seemed, the light was switched on in my bedroom and Brooke stood over me stark naked, shouting: 'Wakey, wakey, rise and shine. It's past four in the afternoon and I could eat a horse. I could eat fried cat.'

I said, perhaps a little crossly: 'Better ring up the Ritz and find out if they've any,' and Brooke forthwith seized the phone: 'That the Ritz? Put me on to the restaurant please. Restaurant? This is Colonel Sebastian Moran speaking. Have you any fried cat on the menu for tonight? What, no fried cat? Damn it sir what's England coming to I'd like to know. No fried cat indeed.'

So we ate spaghetti at the Scala Restaurant, and at the close of another evening in the pubs Brooke told me about his current love affair, which was going far from well. I tried to concentrate sympathetically but, after two heavy nights of drinking plus the fact that I'd been working late for weeks, a cloud of fatigue descended halfway through. I would drift into a semi-doze as Brooke had done while playing Algy, then abruptly start awake to the sound of his voice declaring that the air, whenever he saw his love, was like a perfumed thunderstorm. I managed to assimilate the really important bits, such as the salient facts about the husband, but these only strengthened my conviction that he should pack it in as hopeless; and eighteen years later he wrote that I'd been profoundly shocked by his recital, not being myself interested in sex and unmoved by any sort of beauty.

Brooke did nothing by halves. Love to him was either a Florentine tragedy or an affair of ineffable enchantment. Nightclub hostesses, unscreened starlets, suburban typists were transmuted by his powerful imagination into nymphs, goddesses and legendary queens, apt to revert overnight to their true selves when the light of reality was shed upon them, as Dracula could be dispersed by a single ray of sunshine. His more mundane appetites were prodigious. Great gallons of beer, large measures of spirit, were poured upon mountains of whatever food was available, with the action of one trying to put out a fire. He could also smoke with apparent enjoyment any kind of tobacco, even the sinister nameless wartime brands or fags for the Forces made from sweepings off the Nazi floor.

He was not perhaps the perfect guest. He woke noisily, with yawning, coughing and stretching that shook the house, sang flamenco while shaving and splashed water, soap and lather in all directions: the bathroom after he'd used it was always awash as if a brontosaurus had wallowed in the tub. For the last weekend of his leave I took him down to the house of my current girlfriend's parents who lived near Windsor. On the morning after we arrived he stayed in bed until after eleven because his sinuses were playing him up, then rose suddenly and, draped in my dressing gown that had Chinese dragons on it, strode through to the dining-room where he consumed at one go all the bacon, eggs, butter and marmalade rations for the week, finally throwing down his napkin and exclaiming to the hostess: 'What a wonderful breakfast. Really pre-war standard, one so rarely gets enough to eat these days. Pity I couldn't taste any of it with this confounded sinus trouble of mine, but you're not to blame for that.'

After dinner he imitated for us the fever bird of Whakarewarewa, NZ, drank several pots of coffee and half a bottle of the host's scotch, and read aloud two acts of *Hamlet*, playing all the parts himself with stupendous verve and brio.

Next day there was nothing much left for breakfast, so he didn't get up until it was time to assemble his kit, find his forage cap and gloves, which had been mysteriously mislaid, and get not without difficulty on to a train bound for the Intelligence Corps Depot, where he was promptly clapped under close arrest.

It seemed that all his papers had not been sent on and the Intelligence people, having discovered he was a Dual National, decided to play safe.

'Your dad was a Jerry, that makes you a Jerry, mate,' a stalwart sergeant said, locking Brooke in a guardroom cell. 'Chances are you'll be interned under 18B, less of course you're a Nazzy spy, when you'll be bleeding well shot.'

Brooke's papers did not arrive for several days; in the meantime he was interrogated by security officers, then they let him out and apologised, but said the experience would be useful to him on the course where he had to learn the technique of querying prisoners and suspects. Halfway through the course, however, they said he really shouldn't be in Intelligence, not with a German father he shouldn't: paradoxically another point against him was that he couldn't speak German, so he was returned to his unit, where the shark-like OC again sent him on leave pending another posting.

'Perhaps they'll boot you out of the army altogether,' I said when he turned up in the back bar of the Café Royal, this time wearing civvy clothes: at first I thought he had been discharged. 'You'd be much more use in a Ministry, or writing documentary films,' but it turned out Brooke had already been in documentary films, and Donald Taylor said later that he would have to overcome a certain amount of opposition before getting a job in the industry again.

I was between jobs myself, it was just before Donald's new company started up, and money was short, to put it mildly.

'Look at my paybook,' Brooke said, thrusting this into my hand when the situation was explained to him.

'Why should I want to look at your paybook?'

'Feel underneath it you fool,' Brooke whispered, and thus a fiver changed hands. John Collinses came up, soon Brooke was engaged in a contest of insults with one of the back bar regulars, and acquitted himself more than well; for he had studied rudeness under the Master in Paris, having shared a flat with Brian Howard on the boulevard St Germain. He had also adopted many of the Master's mannerisms, the sidling approach, one shoulder slightly hunched, which I was to recognise several years after I met Howard himself in the Mandrake Club.

'No more spirits, sorry,' Frank the barman called out when Brooke's antagonist reeled away, routed by a parting volley of invective, and Brooke said, eyes still dancing with the light of battle: 'Let's go and look for the Pebble Man'.

One of his favourite fantasies centred round the personality of this Pebble Man, a perhaps semi-mythological character whom I certainly never saw. With his double-lensed pebble glasses, his loud hectoring voice, authoritarian opinions and obvious position of power, he epitomised everything that Brooke had a hatred for, though apparently they had never spoken. Brooke had once heard him in a Soho café, bullying the waitress and laying down the law to a group of subdued satellites, and longed ever since to teach him a lesson.

He had an idea that the Pebble Man belonged to the film world, was perhaps a leading producer or distributor, so we tried the Wardour Street pubs and then the Highlander, where I pointed enquiringly at a large man wearing a sort of Stetson and spectacles, the look of whom I personally disliked. But Brooke, having sidled up to and peered closely at my candidate, said: 'No, no, nothing like him at all,' and the search was resumed without success, even though we had a meal in the café where the Pebble Man had first been seen.

Brooke's blood, however, seemed still up the following morning and, straightening his bow tie before the looking glass in my flat, he said: 'Now we'll go and find someone to persecute.'

In the tube train he threw back his head and looked round for victims rather as he had surveyed the girls at the Salle Mercier. The person he picked on now was a dark-suited prim-faced clerkly man, carrying a briefcase, perhaps a low-grade civil servant. Brooke, nodding slowly as if in satisfaction, said to me in accented English: 'It is he, Karl,' and took a seat farther down the compartment but facing the man, at whom he stared fixedly, while whispering audibly to me in what sounded like a foreign language. The clerkly man fidgeted, first in embarrassment then with increasing nervousness, and Brooke said in a louder tone, as if I'd disagreed with him: 'I tell you Karl. That is the man, I have here the description that they gave me, the papers are there in his portfolio, soon will come the moment, not yet.'

The clerkly man clutched his briefcase in mounting agitation; at Oxford Circus he made a bolt for the doors, but Brooke marched stiffly, like a Prussian officer in mufti, down the platform on his tail. The quarry dived through an arch and on to the escalator, we followed close behind; at the top the clerkly man, glancing about in desperation, trotted towards a policeman standing by the entrance, whereupon we stepped on to the escalator going down and boarded a train for the Tottenham Court Road.

'That put the wind up the little bastard,' Brooke said at the other end. I can't bear these stinking pin-striped mice,' and he broke off to pour derision and abuse on a tube wall poster, which showed a squeezed lemon grinning wryly and got up as an aircraftman, to advertise a brand of squash.

'They've even got to put the bloody lemons in uniform,' he shouted angrily. 'It's making fun of the Forces,' then outside the station stopped short at sight of a big Ministry safety precaution placard which said: 'GOING OUT? LOOK OUT—BLACKOUT!'

Brooke at once became a foreigner again, but this time a timid refugee baffled by alien customs and this cryptic pronouncement in particular. The aid of passers-by was enlisted to explain it to him: 'Pliz to tell me sir, what is meanink this?'; he became more and more excitable: 'Goink out lookink out blackink out? But is not yet the blackink-out, is sun shining now!' then indignant: 'Black—out! Not negroes then allowed? Is Britain not democracy?' etc until a small crowd had collected and the Guinness clock announced 11.30. Then he said in his normal voice: 'Come on Julian, they'll be open now,' and we quickly crossed the road to avoid being lynched by the crowd, which seemed not to enjoy the joke.

In the Horseshoe he asked: 'How are we now for cash? Less than a quid? Not much use that, drink up and we'll see what the Charing Cross Road has to offer.'

My opinion was that in the way of money it had nothing to offer, unless you'd some books to sell, but Brooke, saying: 'Wait here,' strode through the doorway of a music publishing shop. I stared at song sheets and piano accordions in the window, wondering whether he could be already tight, when out he came with ten pounds flourished in his hand. Apparently, years before, he'd written the lyrics for a pop song about a gypsy and the ten pounds represented accumulated royalties.

Song writing was one of the ways by which he planned to make a living when discharged from the army, another was writing trailers for films: often the most exciting part of the programme, as he very truly said. He devised many trailers during the days that followed, also a complete documentary of the 'This is My Job' type then in vogue, which featured the occupation of a Lavatory Man called Dan. It was to end with Dan patriotically foiling a Nazi agent whose code messages were disguised as graffiti on the walls. In the struggle the gallant latrine-wallah was to die for his country and the last shots showed a monument being unveiled to his memory, a giant lavatory pan inscribed with the legend: 'WE ALL HAVE TO GO SOMETIMES'.

'In Latin, of course,' Brooke said emptying his pint with a shout of laughter in which the whole of the Wheatsheaf joined, and he was invited to write the script forthwith by a man who could get the backing if Brooke himself put up a hundred on the spot.

Another, more serious proposition he received was from Charles Wrey Gardiner of the Grey Walls Press, who was present when Brooke outlined a projected fantasy novel called 'The Monastery of Information'. The basic elements included an astrally projected Tibetan lamasery, controlled from the forbidden city itself and invisible to all except those in a state of ecstasy: drunks, lovers etc; there was also a London bank which financed the nefarious operations of the Tibetan fifth-column with phantom money and was manned by cashiers stuffed with straw. Murders of people who knew too much were committed by a band of trained commando midgets, and the conspiracy's total aim was world domination, narrowly averted.

Wrey Gardiner, impressed by what he called a poetic variation on thriller themes, actually offered to advance something on a synopsis if I collaborated on the writing of the book; and, as the music publishers' tenner was running out faster than the spirits in the pubs, we got down to work that night, but Brooke fell asleep over the table just as we reached the first murder by midget.

Next day deafening shrieks both male and female, and the sound of feet scampering downstairs, awoke me. The front door banged and Brooke gave another wild yell from the sitting-room above, which I reached just in time to restrain him from throwing himself bodily through the window.

I'd forgotten to warn him that the woman who came in once a fortnight to clean the flat was a kind of pixie-dwarf. Brooke had woken up to find, staring at him from the doorway, what seemed to be one of his own murderous midgets come to life. She on the other hand had assumed from his posture that he was dead. Both started simultan-eously to scream, Brooke's panic-stricken roar causing the cleaning woman to decamp so quickly that he thought he'd imagined her in a fit of lunacy or the DTs, hence his attempt to end it all.

The shock to his nerves was such that he was quite unfit to continue work on the synopsis, and later that morning a loud knock on the downstairs door further unmanned him. It was a telegram recalling him to his unit for posting, so 'The Monastery of Information' remains unwritten to this day, although Wrey Gardiner still talks about it at times.

A long Brookeless lull ensued. He never wrote letters, and I began to fear he'd been drafted overseas and fallen during the Normandy landings.

Then one late autumn day I was passing a Charing Cross Road bookshop and heard a voice raised angrily within. It came from a tall smart subaltern, with polished Sam Browne and one brass pip on each shoulder strap of his service dress. He was swishing his swagger cane and standing over the short blonde young woman who worked in the shop and was very efficient, impersonal and self-possessed.

Her close-lipped Mona Lisa smile seemed to infuriate the subaltern. He sidled nearer with one shoulder hunched and said: 'Of course, if you want to play cheap chess with me ...'

Though his back was turned, the voice was unmistakable. 'Mr Brooke!' I snapped out in a tone of command. The subaltern wheeled round startled, snatched from his pocket a pair of horn-rimmed spectacles, and inspected me through them as though they were a lorgnette. Then his eyes began to dance like yellow dervishes beneath the bushy black brows and the peak of his service dress cap, and he strode forward to embrace me.

'You old bastard,' he said. 'I thought for a moment you were my colonel. One never knows what voice you'll put on next.'

I said: 'So they fitted you out with specs at last. As well as all this,' indicating his officer's uniform.

'Yes I had to have my eyes tested before going to OCTU. We were on an exercise with live ammo and I led my chaps into a minefield by mistake. Signs all round saying DANGER, apparently. Curious thing, always thought I'd perfect sight, but the eye specialist didn't agree. Anyhow I can hardly see through the damn things he gave me, and they won't fit behind my ears.'

During this speech the short blonde young bookshop woman, who had not ceased to smile close-lipped, started unhurriedly for the stockroom below.

'My wife,' Brooke explained, nodding towards the wooden steps down which she'd disappeared.

'I didn't know you were married.'

Brooke said shortly: 'Been separated years,' and in the street outside: 'We met today to talk about the future of our son.'

'I never thought of you as a family man.'

'Neither did I,' he replied with his shout of laughter, and that was the only time we mentioned his marriage, except when much later he told me they were divorced.

Being commissioned, he said, made no difference to him except that he was now able to cash cheques at Coutts' Bank and could no longer be stopped with impunity by red caps in the street. All the same he was different, much more debonair: the awkward squad corporal had given place to the dashing young officer, a new rôle which his protean personality automatically absorbed.

His grand passion seemed to have burnt itself out, and the latest girl was a small brunette dressed in black with lace collar and cuffs, who did part-time typing and whom he used to take out to tea. I began to believe he must like them small, Marousya had been short and his estranged wife was exceptionally so: both these too were of outwardly placid temperaments and the brunette hardly spoke. But then she vanished abruptly from the scene and was replaced by a strapping turbulent wench who had a mad husband hidden somewhere, like Rochester in reverse, so I was apparently wrong about Brooke on both counts: the only link remaining was that Marousya, the wife and the strapping one were all of them blonde, and the brunette hadn't stayed the course.

I too had meanwhile acquired a new girlfriend and a new, much smaller flat, but later on Brooke settled down without comment on the new sitting-room couch, and in the Wheatsheaf greeted the new girl with as much warmth as if she'd been the old. It's doubtful indeed if he knew the difference, since happily for our relationship we didn't share the same taste in women. But he was less boisterous on this leave and perhaps found the new couch not so comfortable, for soon he sloped off to the country with the hulking blonde, whose husband I believe was left locked up in the cellar.

Again a long interval elapsed.

I'd changed my address again to a one room Mayfair flatlet, and one night came home to find a figure huddled, apparently asleep or drunk, upon my doorstep. The figure scrambled upright as I drew level and, gripping me firmly by the shoulder, said: 'Sorry but I've my duty to perform. As an officer of His Majesty's army I'm arresting you for subversive activities as per War Office instructions and my advice is don't resist.'

'Come in Peter,' I said, fitting latchkey into lock.

Brooke was tighter than I'd ever seen him. He didn't say where he'd got the skinful or how he'd found out where I lived. He slumped in the armchair which was the only bed I had to offer him, looking baffled and bull-like: his hair had begun to go grey at the temples though his eyebrows remained very black. He now had two pips up and had been put in charge of a camp for Italian prisoners, a duty he detested. He cursed women, fate, war and the army for a while, then shouted: 'Sartre! A man writing an enormous newspaper!' and snatching up a copy of *John O'London's Weekly* started scornfully to read aloud an article on Existentialism, but subsided halfway through and lay snoring on the floor.

Even the steady thunder of bomber planes on the way to Germany overhead failed to wake him, but just before dawn he had a fight with himself in his sleep. I watched from my ringside seat: himself seemed about to win but just in time he knocked himself out. I counted ten but he lay stiff and silent, not even snoring now; and in the morning we were roused by the ringing telephone. It was my girlfriend to say that Germany had surrendered, which places this meeting in early May 1945.

Brooke was once more recalled to his camp and discharged not too long after the war ended with the rank of full lieutenant. A War Office letter told him that he was quite entitled to style himself Lieutenant Brooke in civilian life, which as he said was a fat lot of good, since you couldn't even get a job as secretary of a golf club unless you were at least a captain.

He decided to become an actor instead. With his gratuity he bought new clothes and appeared among us in a very elegant navy blue suit, wearing a carnation in his buttonhole. With his greying temples he looked immensely distinguished and actorish; he had several photographs taken and acquired an agent who was a wonderful person.

But all this came to nothing, because in the course of making theatrical contacts he encountered a mid-European composer who persuaded him to collaborate on a musical which would make a fortune for them both. The composer was a wonderful person too and their future was assured. Brooke sang flamenco often in the streets at closing time—the musical was set in Seville—and it was months before the composer became a bastard who had done him down, the agent was also consigned to the ranks of the enemy and Brooke ceased altogether to be able to buy a drink.

When it came to his round he would take out all his money, usually adding up to three-and-six, squint closely at it in the palm of his hand with head cocked to one side, then replace it in his pocket, humming a phrase from perhaps *La Traviata*, as if completely dissociated from the proceedings in the bar. All but a few understood, but it was a dark period of disillusion during which civvy street seemed to lead only to the Labour Exchange and the pawnshop, into which Brooke's elegant suit eventually vanished.

One winter's day, wrapped in his army officer's greatcoat with the badges of rank removed, and having said that Neville George Heath was England's most representative post-war citizen, he told me he'd decided to turn short-story writer.

'I've just been reading a couple of your collections. That's clever, the way you present yourself as an innocent shrinking chap who just blundered into these absurd situations through no fault of his own. It gave me an idea. No reason why I shouldn't do the same, I could easily turn out that sort of thing, a series of autobiographical adventures, after all we're both incident prone,' so he bought several dark blue duplicate order books and sat writing in them every afternoon over a cup of Turkish coffee at the Scala Restaurant.

The restaurant cat had recently given birth, and while writing he was festooned with tiny kittens swinging from his shoulders and clinging round his neck. When one of them dug in its claws too hard, he would reach up and remove it gently without lifting his eyes from ballpoint pen and paper; and the kitten, placed upon the floor, would start once more to clamber up his leg. The horn-rimmed spectacles, which had finally been adjusted to fit and which he wore for work, lent him the scholarly look of an eminent eccentric don. He never referred to the kittens as kittens, but always as little cats.

The stories he wrote were fast-moving, economical and extremely funny. He'd long ago shed the strapping blonde and now had another typist in tow, who wore flowers round her hat and when off duty typed the MSS, which I did my best to place with magazines on Brooke's behalf. Editors however had relapsed into their pre-war habit of taking ages to decide; the public too had largely given up reading now that there was no blackout and its members were again able to dash about in motor-cars, and new writers were no longer being eagerly looked for as in the early Forties.

Unprompted by me, Brooke embarked on a round of personal visits to ginger the editors up. I began to get telephone calls beginning 'Look here old chap, that fellow what's his name whose story you sent me,' and the stories themselves came back en bloc.

Brooke didn't connect these multiple rejections with his appearance at the editorial offices; he believed that they were due to some confusion about his name. It seemed there was another Peter Brook, who wrote long sagas called Arden Vales and had already protested by letter about his near namesake's first novel, pointing out, in a paraphrase of Cassius during the quarrel scene, that he was an older writer if not a better and that he considered the name as his copyright however differently it might be spelt.

Brooke in turn felt much the same about the stage director Peter Brook, at that time more than a coming man, and he frequently dilated on what he would do to this new, upstart namesake if ever they should meet, and very soon they did.

I'd known Peter Brook when he'd just come down from university, having made a film version of Sterne's *Sentimental Journey* which attracted a lot of comment from the critics. Short, chubby-faced, with a schoolboy crest of hair, he was often to be encountered at the flat of Marcella Salzar, an actress who afterwards married the poet Clifford Dyment, and whose advice Brook used to ask about the course that his career should take: he was at this period undecided whether to continue in pictures or direct plays upon the stage.

One evening I was with Brooke at the Scala, having vainly tried to cheer him up by joining in another fruitless search for the Pebble Man, when Peter Brook appeared suddenly before us, perhaps after a visit to Marcella, who lived not far away.

Peter Brook said to me: 'Patrick Hamilton has a new novel out called *The Slaves of Solitude*. It's bound to be a flop, no novel with an alliterative title has ever been successful.'

Peter Brooke, not knowing who this was, nonetheless fired back: 'Sense and Sensibility, Pride and Prejudice, The Pickwick Papers, Nicholas Nickleby, Anthony Adverse?'

'Mrs Miniver?' I added, and Brook was about to retire in defeat when I quickly introduced them, getting ready for retreat myself should hostilities break out.

A truce however was immediately declared, Turkish coffee drunk by all; and Brook, detecting in Brooke some affinity with Nöel Coward, ended by urging him to write a play.

This more than ever decided Brooke to send out his stuff under a pseudonym in future. He'd just been given a journalistic assignment about which he was annoyingly mysterious, and when he reverted to the question of a choice of name for about the hundredth time, I said: 'What about your real name? Foreign books are all the rage just now, and there can't be anyone else writing called von Bohr.'

To my surprise this provoked a sudden denunciation: 'That's a bloody bright idea, when we've just finished fighting the bloody Germans. Exactly the sort of cheap flippant crack that I'd expect from you, anything to be clever at your friends' expense, unless as I suspect you'd really like to sabotage my work,' and with that he stormed out, for the next few weeks remaining absent altogether from our usual haunts.

Then one lunchtime my girlfriend rang me on the Wheatsheaf telephone. 'Have you seen this week's *Leader*?'[1]

'Of course not.'

'There's an article in it about Soho pubs and so on, attacking all of us as wasters. Somebody we know must have written it.'

'Nobody we know would write for the *Leader*,' I said loyally.

She said: 'You are described as a pistol-packing Oscar Wilde.'

I said: 'The article's not signed?'

'It's obviously pseudonymous, but if I didn't know better I'd say it was by Peter Brooke.'

'Brooke!' I exclaimed, realising she'd hit upon the truth. 'What name's it written under?'

'Anthony Carson,' she replied.

---

1 A popular weekly, then of low literary standard, now defunct.

Painters

*　　*　　*

JOHN MINTON

ONE OF MY LAST MEMORIES OF MINTON WAS CONNECTED ALSO with a poet, W.S. Graham. It is not the most pleasant memory I have of him, but before this happened I had already found that Graham in some way contrived to promote unpleasantness around him. Unpleasant things tended to happen in his vicinity.

Graham himself was not unpleasant, just inordinately prickly. If one entered a club or pub where he happened to be and acknowledged him simply with a nod or a smile, he would call out 'You didn't say good-afternoon to me,' making out of this an issue which could, unless ruthlessly cut short at the start, last for what was left of the day. If on the other hand you greeted him by saying 'Good afternoon,' he would morosely reply: 'What's good about it,' making you feel that you had tactlessly interrupted his meditations on some unfortunate mishap that had overtaken him a few moments earlier.

Or else you had omitted to add his name to the salutation, another terrible offence (if this were done he would affect to believe you were addressing someone else, and glance all round in search of this non-existent other person), or alternatively you had added his surname instead of calling him Sydney as his friends did, thus publicly proclaiming that you'd no wish to be considered a friend of his.

Even if the difficult hurdle of the initial greeting were successfully surmounted, any chance remark could give rise to a fancied slight, and endless argument would ensue or reproaches if not actual abuse would be heaped upon your head.

Graham was of sturdy build, dressed as a rule in blue-grey tweeds and had light brown curly hair, a snub nose and protuberant grey-blue eyes. My first introduction to his work came through Kitty of Bloomsbury who had a great belief in it and gave me his second volume of verse with the prophecy that he would become another Dylan Thomas; and I see that the above description of him sounds as if he physically resembled Dylan, which was not the case. The total effect was quite other, being predominantly Scottish: his lips moreover were a very different shape, always twisted or prehensilely thrust out to accommodate themselves to his accent, which was also Scots to a degree.

His expression was that of one stolidly bearing up under constant injustice or undeserved misfortune, and an atmosphere of brooding perpetually surrounded him. He sat over his beer as though reviewing every insult he had ever received with the purpose of devising effectual retorts for the future. In fact nobody insulted him at all and most people had a great respect for his poems.

Sydney Graham was quite the most competitive poet I have ever met: and this in a profession where competitiveness and rivalry by far surpasses any existing among writers of prose. Prose-writers in England, until lately, did not form themselves into groups; consequently among them there was far less deification and hero worship, and, since few idols were built, less chance existed of their turning out to have feet of clay: a flaw of course always discovered eventually by disciples who have decided to take over in turn as Master.

In the Forties internecine strife between individual poets and, on a larger scale, the various schools to which they belonged was at its height and Hemingway's warning never to praise one general to another, given apropos Gertrude Stein and James Joyce, more than applied to the world of poetry at that period. (Those poets encountered in pubs today —Kensington and Fulham are now the areas in which to encounter them, or else the BBC—seem to concentrate exclusively on who has won or is likely to win something called the Guinness Award, when not discussing some incident—usually detrimental to another poet or showing him in a ridiculous light—which occurred at the last prize-giving party: they themselves at the same time drinking Guinness, presumably to boost sales of the product from which the prize derives, though not all of them Irish.)

But Dylan Thomas might well have had W.S. Graham in mind when declaring that poetry was not a competition. I remember mentioning, on the particular occasion which I'm about to describe, that Charles Causley (a poet whom I never knew but whose work I have always liked)

339

had in correspondence given me leave to use part of a Ballad of his as epigraph for a future novel of mine, and not only this: he had actually given me the lines in question as a sort of present.

Graham was immediately aroused, his glaucous eyes glowed with the light of battle and he asked me to quote the lines concerned, saying after I'd done so: 'I will write you a better poem than that right now, and if you agree you can keep it for your very own.'

This was a Saturday morning in winter, we were in a pub in Fulham: already the poetic area was moving South-West. Above us on the wall hung a full-length portrait of John Macadam the sports columnist, who presumably before his death had been a regular customer, across the table sat John Davenport, whom I'd specially sought out as a companion most likely to soothe and help me cure an hysterical hang-over brought on by drinking all the previous day and night; and beside him was Graham's wife, whom I was meeting for the first time and who seemed to me also soothing and a thoroughly nice person, whose presence until now had prevented her husband's prickles from rising in hostility or dispute of any kind.

Now, as Graham pulled out pencil and paper and was about to settle to his self-appointed task, John Minton waved and grinned at us from the centre of a group at the other end of the bar.

I'd known Minton since the early Forties when he was a young promising painter who had, I think, some kind of art-teaching job, and I'd always found him exceptionally pleasant. He did not then have the tormented El Greco expression which Alan Ross effectively hit off in a *London Magazine* editorial, but looked more like a Modigliani or the archetypal young man whose portrait Nina Hamnett always painted irrespective of the actual subject. Tall, bony and attenuate, his face swarthy and elongated, he had protruding white front teeth which caused the mouth to remain open in a slightly awkward oval.

There was a Spanish quality about him, had he been an actor he'd have been a natural for the rôle of Don Quixote, and that face could equally have topped the ruff of a young hidalgo at the Court of Philip II or scanned the ocean for sight of undiscovered land at the time of Pizarro: a more modern maritime association being brought to mind by the blue reefer jersey which he usually wore.

In those early days he was boyishly diffident, yet affable and very ready to talk, always genuinely gay and smiling, full of energy and go without the febrility animating his movements in later years, when he would dance a sort of fandango in the streets or stand clicking fingers and tapping his feet before a bar counter, seldom still and the gaiety only simulated.

I remember one party of John Lehmann's when he stood alone by the chimney-piece, looking acutely embarrassed but self-consciously ignoring his complete isolation. This was before the days of lionisation and promising young painters at that party were two for tuppence. I was as glad to come to his rescue as he seemed that I had done so, since it enabled me to escape from a South American delegate who spoke no English and whom the host had mischievously inflicted on me.

Minton did occasional book jackets, and one of them, for a novel called *The Soldier Room* published by Rupert Hart-Davis, depicts the central figure in a pose which in my second wife's words resembled me in a Vincent Price-like mood and the features not unlike either. He had said more than once that he'd like to do a jacket for a book of mine, and therefore when a new one was due I got my publishers to write to him, adding a personal request for good measure.

We heard nothing for some time, until it became imperative to get another artist, then one afternoon I came down into the Mandrake Club, almost empty just after opening time, and Minton sitting alone over a drink on a settee jumped up and coming over explained that he'd been abroad and had not received the letters until his return, therefore had not been able to fulfil the commission as he would have liked. He was very bronzed and healthy looking and said he'd got a lot of painting done under the influence of his new surroundings on the trip.

It was soon after this that the exotic canvases which made him generally known were exhibited, and from then on it was rarely that he was seen alone. The raffish crowd that encompassed him made communication scarcely possible, though he remained unspoilt by success in his overall attitude. A creative person (horrible phrase but how else to put it?) must however be armoured against the supporters who at successful periods immediately accrete like barnacles on the bottom of a ship, unimportant in themselves but capable of causing erosion if not from time to time scraped off. Minton was incapable of scraping anybody off and the sight of him latterly brought another image to my mind: recalling the story, told to me by a man who had served in the Chindits, of a comrade who'd been torn to pieces by tiny marmosets which, descending suddenly from the trees, swarmed all over him and pulled him down by sheer weight of numbers. When they were dispersed by small arms fire, nothing of the unfortunate soldier could be found except a few shreds of flesh and khaki drill.

Only once, in the late Forties or early Fifties, did I come across Johnny Minton without a colossal cohort in attendance: Christmas was in the air, plans for parties being made, and down Dean Street towards the Colony Club he danced, his long loose-jointed figure in a sort of petty officer's pea jacket skipping ahead on the cold bare winter pavement, with bony fingers snapping like castanets and gaunt hollow face alight in the neon glow. He seemed in a state of euphoria rather than drunk, though he'd been drinking more heavily than I'd known him do before.

Since then I'd not seen him until that Saturday morning in the Fulham pub. Sydney Graham, seeing him also, forgot for the moment about writing the poem which would outdo Causley's ballad and crossed the saloon bar to swell his group. I'd seen them often together in the Wheatsheaf and Minton's equable temper was probably proof against any quarrel engendered by Graham's touchiness.

Mrs Graham then told of her husband's secret desire to make a friend of me, until now frustrated by his Scottish pride and certainly hitherto admirably concealed: the gift of the poem was a gesture intended to consolidate this new relationship. Davenport talked about Norman Douglas; closing time approached and I'd begun to propose going round the Soho clubs, when Graham reappeared at our table saying that Minton was giving a party at his studio right away and we were all to come.

He'd gone ahead to prepare for the party, Graham said, nor were we to bring any drink as there'd be plenty on the premises; and in the taxi on the way he handed me a sealed envelope containing the poem which he'd apparently written after all and which he asked me not to open until we were actually in the studio: then, if I liked it better than Causley's lines as Graham confidently expected, I should read it aloud to the assembly.

At this point we dropped off Davenport near his flat in Flood Street, Chelsea, he was to rejoin us at the party later, and for the rest of the journey Graham's Scottish pride seemed overcome to the extent of allowing him to be amicable and relaxed for the first time since I had known him.

I myself began however to have doubts about crashing a party to which I'd not been directly asked; and when the taxi stopped facing the studio, which I remember as a sort of small pavilion and was certainly the last house in a short cul-de-sac somewhere behind Battersea or Albert Bridge, I refused to go in at all unless invited by Minton personally.

But after a moment both Grahams emerged from the house and told me I'd be more than welcome, Johnny was downstairs getting something ready but he'd said to come right in. So I paid off the cab and entered a little lobby where other guests, not known to me but obviously just arrived, were standing rather respectable in overcoats: the lobby being, in my memory, white painted and done up with brass like a ship's cabin, but I may have got it wrong.

There was a steep flight of steps like a companion way, leading down on the left, and up these at top speed, leaping two at a time in haste (I thought) to welcome me, came Minton. My hand was outstretched and I'd got out a few words of congratulation on some recent work of his when advancing quickly from the head of the steps he shouted: 'Maclaren-Ross you're interfering with my sex life. Get out at once, d'you hear?'

I was dumbfounded, I could feel my mouth hanging open like a half-wit's, but promptly turned about and stretched my hand towards the latch of the door. Nobody else said anything and I hadn't time to see the expression on the Grahams' faces though they were standing by.

For Minton had followed close behind and shooting out a long arm to turn back the latch with which I was fumbling, he tore open the door with one hand and, catching my shoulder in a hard bony grip with the other, he thrust me through the opening with all his strength.

My back had been turned to him, I'd not expected any such move, and I staggered off balance and almost fell. Then, recovering, I turned just as the front door was slammed to in my face. By now in a murderous fury I thumped the door first with my fist, then with the knob of my heavy malacca cane, shouting for Minton to come forth; but not a sound could be heard from inside, it was as if they'd all been struck dumb and rigid there, and I succeeded only in denting my stick's silver top, though some damage was inflicted on the door as well.

I stumbled furiously away and was soon on the Chelsea embankment with a nightmare stream of enormous trucks clanking by like dinosaurs and not a cab in sight. My hangover returned in force, I took nearly an hour getting a taxi, when inside it found I was out of fags: having moreover paid everybody's fare to Minton's on top of the astronomically expensive night before plus that morning in the pub, I'd barely enough silver left to settle up when we got to Meard Street, Soho, and in the Mandrake had with difficulty to cash a cheque from *The Times* which I luckily had on me.

My rage had not, in consequence, abated when John Davenport showed up later in the afternoon.

It was tempered only by astonishment since I'd never known Minton be violent or pugnacious nor seen him lay a hand on anyone. Why had he chosen to make me an exception? There could be no question of a grudge being harboured since we'd not met for a year or more and had on the last occasion parted on friendly, even affectionate, terms. And how could I have been interfering with his sex life when he was homosexual and sailors were not my cup of tea?

Also why had he told the Grahams to fetch me in when he meant bodily to fling me out? Or had the Grahams deliberately retailed a wrong message with the object of seeing me humiliated in front of a pack of strangers? And if sex or some kind of orgy were taking place below, why were guests invited? Those I'd seen did not look at all like people who'd relish being involved in this type of situation or enjoy seeing an all male exhibition staged.

All these queries I put to Davenport, who sat impassive as a Buddha but was unable to supply the answers. His sole comment was: 'You fared better than I, I didn't get in at all, knocked and knocked, no one opened, so I thought you'd all have come on here.'

We sat there grimly waiting for Minton to appear and give an explanation, but of course he did not. I'd unfortunately torn up in my fury and scattered from the taxi window the envelope handed me by Graham, which might have afforded some clue such as a message inside reading: 'SOLD AGAIN! HA HA!' but he didn't seem the kind of chap to play such jokes and it might after all have contained a poem surpassing that given me by Causley. I wouldn't know because I've never since set eyes on him in London or any other place.

I did, however, see Minton twice more, both times in the Mandrake Club.

The first time he was standing dead sober by the cash desk very late one night, and once more alone: the supporters with their rat-like nose for impending disaster seemed all to have fled as from a sinking ship.

Emerging from the closed bar I came on him abruptly and at once asked what the hell he'd meant by behaving as he had. Minton drooped dejected, had simply no excuse, a sudden brainstorm or else too much drink; he agreed that I could not have interfered with his sex life for reasons I've already stated, also that throwing me out of his house had been unpardonable: nevertheless he hoped I would forgive him, shake hands and have a drink.

I shook hands but refused the drink because I'd a young woman outside getting her coat from the doorman whom I was anxious as quickly as possible to take home, and to join him in a drink just then would be interfering with my sex life.

Minton laughed, though not heartily, and next time I saw him he was not dead sober but almost the reverse, alone again and late at night, swigging red wine out of a bottle in front of the closed bar grille. He urged me despairingly to help him out, pointing to another bottle opened on the counter and saying he couldn't get through all that alone; but again I'd to refuse or lose my last train to Oxford, where I was staying at the time.

A few days later I heard of his death by suicide or accident, and wished I'd had that final drink with him.

GERALD WILDE

There's no truth in the assertion, sometimes made, that Wilde is the original of Joyce Cary's Gully Jimson in *The Horse's Mouth*.

At the same time certain aspects of his work and attitude to life have Jimson-like attributes, though one cannot imagine him painting a large biblical subject crowded with human figures nor has he served a sentence in gaol.

The Horse's Mouth appeared in August 1944, some years before Joyce Cary in Oxford met Gerald Wilde who was staying there and had already read and enjoyed the novel. Some people, while admitting Gully is not meant for Wilde, claim to have heard Cary declare that, had he not previously invented his eccentric painter, Gerald might well have served as a model; but I personally never heard him say anything of the sort when Wilde was under discussion, and Cary's characters were not constructed that way in any case.

Cary, however, could not fail to find Wilde entertaining, admired his work; and, being a kind and generous man, helped him out financially by buying some of the canvases he painted during his stay in Oxford. He also wrote an article on Gerald published in a 1956 issue of the excellent but short-lived review *Nimbus* which contained reproductions of Wilde's work and other appreciations of it. If I remember right the Jimson connection is specifically denied in this article, though I haven't a copy by me and cannot check.

I have seen pictures by Wilde at Cary's house in Parks Road; behind the bar of the Victoria pub in Walton Street (one of Gerald's drinking haunts down there) hung an arrangement of orange and black stripes giving the effect of a cage beyond the bars of which an imprisoned tiger prowls; and a drawing of a magnificent toad could be seen, too, on the panelled wall of Professor Ronald Syme's college rooms: toads playing the same rôle in Gerald's life as owls do in the work of Francis Rose.

At my request Gerald once drew a toad on the Wheatsheaf counter, first with his finger dipped in beer, then with a stub of crayon on a crumpled scrap of paper which he gave to me but which was unfortunately lost during subsequent confusion: usually attendant on any of his appearances in the Wheatsheaf, which is where I first met him.

Entering the pub one October evening in 1943 I was immediately confronted with Tambimuttu who, thrusting towards me someone else's hat upturned, exclaimed: 'Ah Julian, just in time to contribute to the cause. I am getting up a fund for Gerald Wilde the Mad Artist, he's starving and with no money, you know?'

I'd never until then heard of Gerald Wilde the Mad Artist, but I put something in the hat and was then introduced to the Mad Artist himself: sitting at a table guarded by Tambi's supporters, with only a glass of mineral water before him and seeming not noticeably insane: just pale, dispirited and sad.

He sat motionless, without speaking, until Tambi had been all round the pub collecting; then stretched out wordlessly a hand, trembling no doubt with hunger, towards the hat which jingled by now with coins and silver. Tambi slapped the hand reprovingly, as one who corrects a too-presumptuous or greedy child, and Gerald Wilde relapsed remonstrating in a rapid inaudible mutter, this incipient mutiny being quelled at once by a glance from Tambi's celebrated eyes.

'Gerald's on the wagon, you know?' he told me. 'It's not good for him to drink and he has work to do. Gerald!' he like a lion-tamer shouted and Wilde shrank back cowed: 'Gerald go back to the flat and paint. Steven you go too, lock him in, bring back the key, I will return later Gerald with some food.' He pointed with a prehensile finger fiercely to the door and Wilde obediently rose and shuffled out, the tails of a grey overcoat too long for him trailing far below his calves.

Steven followed and Tambi watched the pub door close behind them, his pose gradually relaxing as might that of a tamer whose lion has gone successfully through the flaming hoop.

'Lock him in?' I said incredulously.

'Yes, you must be severe with Gerald, a firm hand you know,' Tambi told me. 'If you give him money he buys drink with it, then he's drunk and does not work,' buying a round himself with money taken from the hat. 'But I am keeping him a prisoner now, locked in my flat, he can't get out to drink so he is painting much.'

'Hasn't he a studio of his own?'

'No no, he has no place not even to sleep, so I am putting him up, he has brushes, paint and canvas there, all he needs to work.

'Is he really any good?'

'Good? He is a genius, Kenneth Clark says so, you know who is Kenneth Clark? Well a White Hope he says, you know? But soon we will hold a Gerald Wilde exhibition, then you'll see,' and soon, too, the hat was empty and Tambi once more reverted to his regal state of not having money on his person.

It was closing time by then and Steven had returned with the flat key, reporting that Gerald Wilde was safely locked in after two attempts to escape into pubs on the way and obtain credit therein.

Tambi said: 'Let us go to the Coffee An' and there eat steak,' Steven's eyes lit up and at the Coffee An' Tambi insisted that all of us scrape a portion off our plates into a paper bag which he pulled from his overcoat pocket, scattering several MS poems from contributors in the process; then he toured the cellar as he had earlier the pub, proffering the bag instead of the hat and demanding: 'A donation of food, please, for Gerald Wilde the Mad Artist who is starving you know?'

The idea of a Mad Artist, and starving what's more, appealed strongly to the tourists who in those days flocked to the Coffee An', and the bag was speedily filled to bursting: the response indeed being so big that Tambi was emboldened to go round for a silver collection with yet another hat, the contents of which paid the bill for steaks eaten by himself and his supporters (I don't know if either of the owners ever got their hats back).

But outside the Coffee An' Tambi lost his temper suddenly and flung the bag of food at the head of one of the supporters who'd been slow off the mark in executing some command: however, enough steak and chips was recovered from the pavement to assuage the appetite of Wilde, by now presumably paint-stained and ravenous locked in Tambi's flat.

Tambi was ceaseless in his vigilance at this time, reporting to us regularly the progress of his protégé and the increasing number of paintings that had got done; and a show was being arranged—when, alas, all came to naught.

One Friday Tambi went away for the weekend, leaving Gerald locked in as usual. Unfortunately it proved to be a long weekend (perhaps the one when he stayed at Whitstable with Jaeger's patrons, which I'll tell about), anyhow on the following Tuesday he returned to find the flat door open and askew upon its hinges, a chair lying shattered on the floor nearby, and all his books gone from the shelves. Nor, needless to say, was Gerald Wilde inside: also all his paintings and painting gear had gone.

What had happened was this. Gerald, feeling hungry after four days without food (Tambi on his own admission having forgotten to lay any provisions in) got tired of painting: the creative impulse needed a re-fuel so first he collected Tambi's books in a kitbag which some PL contributor from the Forces had left behind in the flat, then he gathered together canvases and painting gear, then smashed in the lock having telephoned for a taxi, and descended to the waiting cab, which he directed to Subra's bookshop.

When Subra had bought the books, Gerald got back into the cab and was next seen eating and drinking in cafés and pubs belonging to a different area.

Subra had to give back all the books (as happened with someone's Gauguin souvenirs sold by Manolo the Spanish sculptor on a similar occasion described by Alice B. Toklas, which is doubtless where Wilde got the idea), but both he and Tambi forgave Gerald freely ('You know how it is,' they said, 'when you're with no money') and Tambi even went on trying to help him whenever possible with commissions for book jackets etcetera (I think, though I wouldn't be certain, that Gerald was responsible for the cover design of *Chums*, the omnibus *Poetry London*).

But the prospective show had to be abandoned, for Gerald had either sold the paintings in order to prolong the bender that he'd embarked on or simply given them away to strangers in the pub because he was sick of carting them around. He himself could not remember, and that particular relationship with Tambi came to an end: Tambi couldn't in any case continue to lock him in because the door was never repaired; and the shattered chair, left lying on the floor of the flat like the relic of a crime reconstructed in a museum, was seen there by many visitors and caused Gerald to acquire a quite undeserved reputation for violence, adding to the legend of his madness already blazoned forth by Tambi.

It may be for these reasons that his overcoats were always so long: perhaps they were given to him by very big men met round the pubs; it's inconceivable to imagine Gerald actually buying an overcoat of his own and, owing to the stories that were current, only outsize men would have had the courage to invite him home where they had overcoats to spare. Since I've known him he has had three overcoats, one grey tweed, one black (with a large rent just below the collar) and one dark brown, which is the one I last saw him wearing, though he wore the black one with the rent for a very long time. All three overcoats had cuffs coming down over the knuckles though his arms were long. I have also seen him wearing a pink shirt and he never appeared without a bootlace tie, usually black and turned partly inside out.

He was not tall, had sloping shoulders and a long neck, his spade-shaped face was also long and his head flat at the back. There used to be a portrait of him by Wayland Dobson in the window of Subra's bookshop, showing Gerald with a scarlet face and one eye about to burst from its socket, to symbolise the feeling of something frustrated, shut in, but about to break out which is present in his own work: arrangements of bold colour patterns in the depths of which some form, not necessarily human, can be dimly discerned attempting to emerge. Dobson's portrait therefore was a better likeness than one more representational would have been, though in fact Gerald's skin was extremely pallid and he showed signs when I first knew him of once having had ginger hair.

His hair now was brownish, carefully brushed back but often growing long on the nape though with a tonsure on top, his lips, eyelashes and eyebrows were almost colourless and his eyes also pale, large and salient, one of them indeed protruding outwards and not quite in alignment. He spoke when sober in a subdued gentle voice, not easy to hear unless one knew him well, and when drunk in a loud slurred inarticulate shout.

Gerald was not a drunkard nor anything approaching it, but alcohol, especially spirits, affected him with extraordinary speed and after a glass or two of scotch he would begin to whirl his arms with a curious clockwork motion as if drink wound up some mechanism inside him. His speech became incoherent and his movements jerky but rapid like those of a lizard. He never lost the use of his legs. Later would come the stage of staggering and clutching painfully at people's arms while shouting imaginary grievances into their faces, if he could reach up far enough or they were sitting down.

He developed a persecution complex, not apparent when he wasn't drinking, part of which centred round policemen who, he was convinced, were out to insult if not actually to molest him. In fact they behaved good-humouredly when he got into their hands and in Oxford, where he speedily got to know the whole of the Force, would indeed lead him back to where he was staying after a cup of tea at the Station, instead of shutting him in a cell or beating him up as he dared them to.

After he got to the shouting and staggering stage few landlords would have him in, and I have seen him many times burst through one door of a double entrance pub and promptly be ejected, then immediately reappear in the second doorway, same result: a performance he could keep up, scuttling from door to door, for hours, not getting a drink in consequence and ending the evening almost sober.

This happened only when he sold a picture and had, as he would put it, the wherewithal. At other times he was a quiet charming companion with beautiful manners, fond of reading and the cinema: I remember him telling me once of seeing at some film society an unexpurgated version of Pabst's *The Love of Jeanne Ney* which showed, during the orgiastic sequence, a close-up of a Tsarist officer's prick. Gerald was very disappointed since, this being such an unusual sight on the screen, he had not recognised what it was until told by the man sitting next him, by which time the prick had been flashed-off.

He was capable of working for long hours with immense concentration whenever he had somewhere to paint in and sometimes talked of holding an exhibition, not as any painter might but as if consciously indulging a fantasy or recounting a daydream. For he knew that, when enough work was done, he would again sell the canvases for nugatory sums when drunk or simply give them to any bystander who showed appreciation, which he once said gave him a feeling of being liberated.

The sense of imprisonment conveyed by his painting was certainly very strong and perhaps of psychological origin since Gerald found the greatest difficulty in understanding the sources of his confusion and was not a ready talker. Perhaps it was the vision of his own interior chaos that was struggling to break through the cryptic coloured patterns that enclosed it, as he had broken out of Tambi's flat.

Impossible to tell, for Gerald never discussed the problems of his painting though often willing to discuss the problems of how to get it done without a place to live. This problem was never solved except for short periods, since Gerald's talent for self-organisation was non-existent.

One apparent solution was found when somebody got him a job designing scarves for one of the biggest textile firms. The salary was enormous and Gerald's designs were the most beautiful and original I have ever seen on any woven fabric of this type, but in the end it didn't work out, supplementary or bread-and-butter jobs being for second-rate artists only: since having less to give they put only half of themselves into any activity they are engaged in, leaving plenty over for other purposes, which is why they're second rate.

Although the textile designing could be done quickly and easily, Gerald like all first-rate talents put as much into it as he would have into his painting and was left too exhausted and emptied out to embark on anything else in his leisure time, of which he had plenty.

So despite the salary he quit and went back to the nomad life which to him was normal; then came one night in the late Forties when he'd nowhere to stay and asked me for a bed, which living in a single hotel room I could not supply. Standing nearby was Dan Davin the New Zealand novelist, by then an executive at the Clarendon Press. He said: 'Why not come and stay with us in Oxford, Gerald. And down there you'll meet Joyce Cary.'

ROBERT COLQUHOUN AND ROBERT MACBRYDE

I once asked Fred Urquhart the short-story writer, a friend of both painters and of course a fellow Scot, if he ever meant to write anything about Colquhoun and Macbryde. I thought he was perhaps the only writer who could do them justice because he had in an early short story a line of dialogue reading 'Wha quair clae they farriners hae,' which interpreted[1] is a let down but which epitomised to me the way the Roberts talked: Macbryde perhaps more than Colquhoun.

---

1 'What queer clothes these foreigners have'.

Fred Urquhart frowned and pursed his lips with head on one side, then said in his soft cooing and not so broad Scots accent: 'Ah well, you know Julian it's not so simple to do Colquhoun and Macbryde. They may look easy but they're difficult to do.'

I agree with Fred but all the same I'm going to try, only since I hate using phonetics myself their accents are beyond my power to reproduce and readers will just have to imagine these for themselves.

Actually, the first time I met Robert Colquhoun, in 1943, I was pulled up sharply about my own accent.

He was sitting on a bar stool in the Highlander, darkly glooming with a pint of bitter in his hand, and his words were these: 'If you're who you say you are, why've you no a proper Scots accent like a man?'

I answered: 'Possibly because I was brought up in England and France.'

I had come up to congratulate him on a show of his pictures which I'd visited that afternoon, but now wished I hadn't done so.

Colquhoun made a hissing contemptuous sound between his teeth, his expression that of one about to spit, 'England and France eh?' he said. 'And you call yourself a Scotsman?'

'I never said I did.'

A short pause ensued, during which Colquhoun took a swallow of beer, then he asked: 'Are you sure you're not just some phoney trying to show off? You look like a bloody phoney anyhow,' at which I gave up, not yet having learned to reply in kind to this type of thing with the ease I was shortly to acquire.

Dylan Thomas told me he'd much the same experience sharing a taxi with Colquhoun and Macbryde on the way to a party: they'd upbraided him thoroughly for not talking like a Welshman and he too as a result had been declared a phoney.

Before this I'd already met Robert Macbryde without realising his connection with Colquhoun. It was in the Coffee An', Macbryde was wearing a fringe and a kilt, and when we were introduced he'd said to the cellar at large: 'I don't doubt he's as scared of me as I am of him.' Again I had no answer, such remarks were new to me in any case; and after a silence during which Macbryde continued quizzically to smile, I excused myself and moved away.

In those days both Roberts, round about their early thirties (they never seemed afterwards to age), were fervent Scottish Nationalists, sported kilts, and felt strongly about the accents Celts should speak with. They were then accompanied everywhere by a third, huge blond-headed smiling Scot called Shawn, who'd been a blacksmith, also sported a kilt, and seemed a permanent fixture, though he later got married and dropped out altogether, returning to the village forge from which he'd come.

Later, too, the Roberts ceased to be Nationalists or to wear kilts and, as they gradually lost the need to defend their origins and the feeling of inferiority which had to be concealed under an outward sporran of racial pride, they became more bearable and even at times quite human. They retained however their accents, though Macbryde told me once that when they went back to Glasgow they were often accused of having become bloody English and people were not always able to understand what they said.

Macbryde was the more friendly and sociable, Colquhoun the wolf-ishly lean and sullen one, who conspicuously didn't run with the pack. Like Macbryde he'd a swarthy skin but his sombre face was hollow-cheeked and lantern-jawed, with regular features and curling brown hair that became ringlets at the back of his head and neck. In his appearance there was something of the handsome hell-fire Calvinist preacher, as if he might at any moment call down the wrath of the Lord on the Sodom and Gomorrah that surrounded him. Spinsterish girls nearly swooned at sight of his ascetic mouth, so masterful and clamped determinedly tight, as one of them described it longingly to me.

Colquhoun was the taller of the two and indisputably the leader; when they loosely loped along the street, always in single file and wearing pullovers (Colquhoun's a tawny red, Macbryde's thicker, dark blue, and naval-looking) Macbryde devotedly followed. Once, when asked what he'd do if he came suddenly into a lot of money, he replied first that this was 'no likely', then that he'd give it all to Colquhoun to further the cause of his painting.

Macbryde had a round blue-chinned smiling face, thick straight black brows that crinkled wryly, a fag wobbling Dylan-like between his lips, and as a rule a cowlick of hair on the forehead instead of the fringe he'd worn when I first saw him. He had the reputation of being a wit and, though this was scarcely deserved, was certainly wittier when being rude than Colquhoun. He could also talk eloquently about the height of rhododendrons in his native land, but like his confrère and so many other denizens of Soho and Fitzrovia he was rude and eloquent only when full of beer, and at sober moments silent, subdued and even polite.

One day I said to him as he leaned his elbows silently on the bar counter beside me: 'What d'you think about when you're sober, Macbryde? Do you prepare apologies for the people you've been rude to the night before?'

Macbryde after a pause replied: 'Maybe I'm thinking up a new lot of rude things to say next time I'm drunk,' by which he scored a point.

Colquhoun also had a sense of humour of the grim, gallows type; but he was at all times morose of mien, though after a lot of scotch he would occasionally throw back his head and give vent to a strident savage contemptuous laugh, directed apparently at the world in general, and gnashing his teeth in a manner that had possibly endeared him in the first place to Wyndham Lewis, who approved of him both as a painter and a person, and many of whose more sympathetic characters were given to teeth gnashing and laughter of precisely this sort. At a later stage Colquhoun's laugh became more savage until it was merely a snarl and the nearest person who would stand for it (and it was amazing how many would) was turned upon and torn verbally to pieces.

The Roberts did command devotion. There was a constant stream of young women yearning to cook, clean, sew, look after and generally make them comfortable, though in fact they were perfectly capable of doing all these things just as efficiently themselves.

Both were excellent impromptu cooks and I've seen them clean and tidy from top to bottom a flat in which they'd passed out cold the night before, taking over two hours to do so and also making all the beds although the host had gone off to work and no obligation was laid on them to clean up at all.

Nonetheless the devoted ladies persisted: the most zealous of them, and the one who lasted the longest because more resolute than the rest, being Cedra Osborne, secretary to Annigoni, about whom she wrote a long article in a woman's magazine, besides translating Maupassant.

The Roberts had actually lodged for some time in her house, but even after they left she continued to be concerned about their welfare and to look after them all she could. Cedra was a striking young woman with dull gold hair and earnest intense ultramarine eyes, built generally along the lines of Caitlin Thomas but with a straight instead of an aquiline nose and even better looking.

I fancied her myself, but whenever we had a date she would talk earnestly about psychiatry and the electra complex, as though she were a head shrinker's secretary instead of a portrait painter's; then she'd start to wonder how the Roberts were getting along, could we just look in and see as otherwise she'd worry all evening, but once we arrived at the pub or club, Macbryde, usually by that time singing or stamping in a Scottish reel if not reeling tight, would without a word reach an arm round Cedra's shoulders, sweep her into their circle, and that was all for me that night. I don't know how Cedra reconciled her daily duties and undoubted loyalty to her employer with the very different artistic tenets propounded by Colquhoun and Macbryde.

But throughout all this the relationship of the Roberts to each other never altered. They had come from Glasgow together and they stuck together, whatever young women came and went around them. It was truly a case of David and Jonathan and perhaps this was what attracted the girls of Soho, always subconsciously eager to break something up. But if that were so, they were doomed to disappointment.

Colquhoun and Macbryde quarrelled occasionally of course, and I have seen them fight: careering in a clinch the whole curve of a long bar, with all the club members skipping out of their path, until they reached the doorman at his desk, who then toppled them, still gripped together, into the street. Perhaps this incident was symbolic, since basically nothing could separate Colquhoun and Macbryde except what finally did: against which not even they were proof.

A period which promised to be particularly fruitful as regards their work was when they shared a studio in the Notting Hill area: a period written about by Wyndham Lewis in his satirical but affectionate sketch of them in the stories *Rotting Hill*. (Though Lewis implies here that they never read anything and Macbryde is shown regarding books with fascinated horror, this was certainly the reverse of true where Colquhoun was concerned. When drunk, for instance, he could quote long passages of Shakespeare by heart, not only from the familiar plays but from *Timon of Athens* and *Pericles*, and he always quoted accurately.)

Colquhoun and Macbryde were going through a sober, industrious phase, one hardly saw them about, they'd got a lot of work done and a measure of security at last seemed within their grasp. Then came a black stroke of bad luck, from which they were not to recover for years. While they were out of London on a well-earned holiday, teenagers or local yobs broke into their studio, wrecked everything, mutilated and defiled their pictures, and on top of that the Council decreed that the property should in any case be demolished. Colquhoun and Macbryde were evicted with nowhere to go and no means of earning a living since all their work for months, maybe years, had been destroyed.

The obituary writers who so smugly stated that Colquhoun had not developed much as a painter during his last few years were not apparently aware that for some of them he was virtually homeless, or else did not realise that it's difficult to develop or even paint at all without a studio to do it in. The rich dilettantes and art-fanciers who claimed to admire his work so greatly when it was too late could have shown their appreciation better by putting a place to live at his disposal, though I believe that this was finally done.

I'll not forget the day on which I heard the news. It was an afternoon in September 1962 and I was engaged in hurrying towards the Bayswater tube a lady who was for private reasons not at all keen to be observed in my company at that time or in that district. As we glanced round guiltily before the station entrance, another young woman known to both of us and one of the Roberts' closest friends emerged from it, almost colliding with me though obviously too upset to notice what was going on around her.

As if sleepwalking she handed me a copy of the evening paper she was carrying, open at a news-item which announced that Robert Colquhoun had that day dropped dead.

Topolski and Picasso

*　　　*　　　*

THE ANGLO–FRENCH ART CENTRE

I SPOKE TO PICASSO ONLY ONCE AND VERY BRIEFLY, AND THAT WAS due to Feliks Topolski whom I met one summer in the mid-Forties through the agency of a strange Continental man, the secretary of something called the Anglo–French Art Centre at that time.

This man approached me one afternoon in the lounge of the hotel where I was then living and introduced himself with a faint click of the heels, saying simply: 'Green'.

'I don't quite follow.'

'Green. It is my name. Like all your English writers.'

'Writers?' I said, perplexed.

'Julien Green, Graham Greene, Henry Green, F.L. Green, G.F. Green,' this new addition to the clan reeled off. 'All of these are English writers, no?'

'Not Julien Green,' I said. 'He's an American who writes in French. Are you an English writer?'

'I have not this honour,' Green said, 'but I am devoted to the service of Art, Pictorial Art also Anglo–French relations. May I sit please and explain to you?'

'Go ahead.'

While he was explaining, I observed him closely but without coming to any conclusion as to his country of origin. He was thin, tall, sallow, spectacled: he had receding dark hair, his spectacles dark rims, and he wore a thin black moustache, but despite his pigmentation he was not, I'm certain, a Latin and certainly not French. He wore a check tweed suit not tailored over here and reminded me, though not physically, of

357

a fellow who in the Twenties started up a school for English boys in Nice and was supposed to be a Dutchman, though soon all the English boys whom he'd managed to enrol were singing lustily 'Der Tannenbaum'. This man had attempted to enrol me too and produced a prospectus of his school, but when addressed by my father in German bowed himself out with no further parley. Green had a prospectus on him too but was not a German, at least not judging by his accent, which was impossible to identify. He was an enigma that I never solved.

The prospectus he brought out was of the Anglo–French Art Centre, a gallery mainly intended for exchange between painters of these allied nationalities though other important international figures would, Green assured me, have their work displayed as well. There were plans for an Anglo–French library of books and periodicals, and he displayed an impressive list of patrons and supporters, the name of Feliks Topolski prominent among them. He'd in some semi-official capacity roped in also Rayner Heppenstall, always dead keen on anything French, who'd put him on to me.

What Green wanted was a translation of a sort of blurb for the catalogue advertising their first show: of whose paintings I've forgotten but French and abstract if I remember right. The blurb was written in an aphoristic post-surrealist French prose, a kind of corruption of Cocteau but lacking all his clarity, and not easy to translate because the meaning was itself obscure. Green wanted to print a double column, French one side, English on the other, and could I translate as soon as possible for the show was going to open and the printers were standing by.

Some valid reason was given why Rayner couldn't do the job: Green's excuse was that a celebrated British literary name should be appended to the English version of the blurb, though I believe he didn't attempt it himself because he didn't know French awfully well; I tried to get him to speak it to me but each time failed.

The Cause seemed worthy enough, though I'm not an addict to causes of any kind; but of course, Green said, he was a businessman besides being a devotee of art and Anglo–French relations, and a substantial fee would be payable on completion of the commission (this turned out to be two guineas), also I would be made an honorary member of the Centre and be invited to the opening do.

I managed the translation within the deadline, and had it snatched from my hand by Green, who'd taken to dropping in too often to see how the work was getting on. He did not however put a cheque or any money in my hand in exchange; and after that we heard from him no more, until a copy of the catalogue, incorporating my translation, arrived: also a card of invitation to the opening, on both of which my celebrated British literary name was misspelt. No cheque was enclosed with that either.

I was late getting to the Centre as my taxi driver did not know the street, the fare was prohibitive and the exact house hard to find. To my surprise no party was under way and the guests of both sexes were standing about in a bare lobby beyond which behind closed glass doors the gallery could be seen, empty of any human presence but with paintings on the walls and some sort of refreshment table in the middle.

The guests were kept from entering by a crimson velvet rope looped across the lobby as in the aisle of a cinema, and a sort of turnstile like that of a public lavatory which further barred the way. There was no sign of Green or anyone in charge.

I looked in vain for a familiar face but knew none of the guests: they did not seem particularly artistic, literary or ultra-international, though I heard a few phrases of French being spoken around me, such as 'Mais alors, qu'est-ce qui'il se passe içi?' or 'Quoi donc, est-ce qu'ils se fichent de nous?' etcetera.

Suddenly through the glass I saw the figure of Rayner Heppenstall appear inside the gallery. He stood by the refreshments table with head bent, not eating or drinking anything and looking neither at the pictures within nor the guests outside. I called out and waved, he raised his head but did not otherwise move, except to shrug helplessly in the direction of the doors and make the motion of a key turning as if he were a prisoner, himself, inside.

The sight of him was shut out by a middle-aged English woman who came through a side entrance and told us to queue up before the turnstile like a sergeant calling his platoon to attention on parade.

When I approached her asking for Mr Green I expected her to shout 'Markers—stead-y!'; instead she said: 'The Secretary is busy now. Get in the queue please.'

'I'd like to speak to Mr Heppenstall then.'

'Who did you say?'

'Rayner Heppenstall.' There he is. Look, in the gallery; but at that moment he moved out of sight and the woman said: 'The gallery is locked and not open to the public yet. Take your place please in the queue.'

'I want to speak to Mr Green about this catalogue.'

'I don't think I have your name.'

'You can see it here. On this translation.'

The woman said: 'The Secretary is very busy but an opportunity may perhaps be made for you to speak to him later on.'

'Will you kindly fetch Mr Green at once.'

A quiet-looking medium-sized man in a dark suit, standing in the forefront of the queue, backed me up with unexpected force.

'This gentleman is right. I am on the Committee and the Secretary should be here to welcome and admit us. We're guests invited to the opening of this Centre, not people queueing for a cinema.'

'Bravo!' I cried, seconding him in my turn.

There was some clapping at the back. Many guests took up the cry for Mr Green and mutiny seemed imminent. A few of the French faction began to chant and stamp as they do in a theatre when the curtain is slow going up. The English woman left by the side entrance and did not return.

The dark-suited man, who proved to be Feliks Topolski, called after her: 'I will raise the matter of this treatment when we sit on the Committee,' adding to me: 'If there's a Committee to sit on.'

'Who else is supposed to be on it?' I asked.

Topolski pointed to a list on the catalogue: 'All these. The patrons and supporters. Or so Green told me.'

'But none of these people are here tonight.'

'No and I seem to be the only painter present,' Topolski laughed. 'Do you think we'll ever get in there? To the champagne and caviar?'

'Is that what's on the menu?'

Topolski said: 'It had better be, after all this.'

The chanting and stamping broke out redoubled and he exclaimed 'Look there is Green. He's going to open up at last.'

Green with a key in his hand approached us down the gallery: sailing alongside were several large ladies apparently in mourning whose big black hats and trailing silk closed round him like a bodyguard directly he'd unlocked the doors and the turnstile had clicked to let us through.

I made a move in his direction but Topolski touched my arm: 'Come, let's see what there is,' indicating the refreshments table behind which two younger women in smocks now stood ready to serve.

Advancing upon them Topolski delivered a rapid commentary like a radio sports event: 'It's not champagne nor sherry either I don't see any caviar,' then suddenly recoiling from what I could see myself: 'This is tragic, it's terrible, no glasses on the table, only cups and cakes.'

I turned accusingly on Rayner Heppenstall, who again was standing with furrowed brow by the table, which seemed in some way to fascinate him.

'Rayner what have you let me in for.'

Rayner said disconsolately: 'It's all gone wrong. Some big bug was to open the show but he's not turned up. Everything's disrupted.'

'You might have seen to it there was something to drink.'

'There was to have been beer. Anyway I didn't organise this do. Green's the organiser.'

'Where's Green?' Topolski asked brightly looking round.

But Green was no longer present, and did not reappear even to bid the guests goodnight. The coffee had long strings of skin in it, white flecks floated on the surface and the rock cakes had been clearly bought at least a week before. They were the only evidence that the party had been in any way prepared for.

'This is a bad show all round,' Topolski said as we met again after circling in opposite directions the paintings on the walls: there were not many, not a single one can I remember, and we completed the circuit in record time.

Topolski said: 'That bug who didn't turn up had got the right idea. Let's go, I know a pub nearby.'

We tried to persuade Rayner to join us but he muttered that he'd better stay behind and see it through. He avoided our eyes when we said good-bye and the gallery was emptying all around us as we left.

A few weeks later, Green bounced in on me again, bringing a much longer translation that he wanted done in a much shorter time. I suggested an immediate advance, cash down, also payment for the last lot or no dice.

Green was first astonished, then shocked, then aggrieved; at length passed over two crumpled one pound notes but said he would have to consult the Committee before disbursing any more. I asked him to make sure Feliks Topolski sat in on the meeting when this question was debated; and later came a phone call during which Green said he'd be unable to put any further translation work my way unless I became more realistic about the manner of remuneration. And this, he explained, would be my loss, since the opportunities for increment would be enormous as the Centre continued to expand.

After this he ceased to get in touch, except to send a demand for payment for my overdue subscription, signed formally THE SECRETARY.

The Centre did not expand, and I never discovered what country Green returned to when finally it folded. Nor, in the pub on the evening that it opened, had Topolski and I been able to decide his nationality, out of many possibilities not unnaturally excluding Polish.

I didn't see Topolski for several years, but evidently he'd not forgotten our meeting, for one day out of the blue I received an invitation to a party he was giving in honour of (a) Pablo Picasso; (b) Vladimir Pudovkin, the Soviet director whose film *Mother* remains a classic of the Russian cinema.

THE PARTY FOR PICASSO

I shortly afterwards used the exterior of Topolski's studio when describing the headquarters of Stevenson's Suicide Club in a film-script I'd been commissioned to do of 'The New Arabian Nights' brought up to date.

Seen from outside the building was ideal for this purpose: big, ramshackle and dark, only small chinks of light showing as if blacked-out, and approached through a walled garden in which grass and weeds grew nearly to knee-level. It was somewhere behind Warwick Avenue and, Topolski told me later that evening, under threat of demolition by the local Council though he was fighting hard to retain it. Not far away lived Alan Pryce-Jones in quarters similarly menaced, and within the same area was my former flat where Peter Brooke had been scared almost to self-destruction by the midget char and which was under sentence of death, even when I lived there, owing to the Blitz that had shaken all these structures: rendered doubly unsafe by the explosions of the Paddington Gun and the fly-bombs that followed after.

Inside, the studio wouldn't have made a bad set for the Suicide Club-Room either. It was immense, indirectly lit and shadowy, high-ceilinged and with a huge skylight overhead. The walls, which may have been painted with murals by Topolski, were entirely in shadow, yet despite its size the studio was very warm in contrast to the cold clear winter night outside.

Neither of the guests of honour had arrived when we got there and Topolski, quiet smiling and friendly as he'd been before, at once issued us with a bottle of special scotch which we were warned to keep behind a statue on a shelf when the invasion really started.

Adair, whom I'd brought with me, was a tall striking slender girl, dressed tonight in scarlet, young, non-literary, but intelligent, unaffected and gay. Some people preferred her to any girl I've produced before or since; and Arthur Calder-Marshall, whom I hadn't seen for years and who'd joined us where we stood over by the window, seemed of this number.

I'd been earlier on to a champagne party at John Lehmann's flat; but Adair, whom I'd picked up from our place on my way to Topolski's studio, hadn't had a drink all day, during which she'd been acting as secretary to a solicitor in Whitehall, and the whisky bottle didn't spend much time behind the statue.

We were atrociously hard-up at the time, ten shillings I remember was all the money we had between us: I'd not yet been commissioned to write the Suicide Club script (which incidentally never went on the floor), there were crises in the book trade and film world and Adair's secretarial salary just paid our weekly rent. We'd not been anywhere for weeks, and were all the more prepared to enjoy this party, which bore every sign of being an outstandingly good one.

Calder-Marshall too seemed in great form. Ara his wife was not with him that night, and he'd been hot on the track of Aleister Crowley, then still alive, whom he'd never met but wanted to write a book about. I didn't know Crowley either, but I told Calder-Marshall what Joan Graham-Murray had recently recounted of his final, semi-respectable phase.

Joan, a friend of Louis Wilkinson alias Marlow, Crowley's literary executor who afterwards scattered his ashes on the wind, had gone to stay with Wilkinson in the country, taking with her a copy of my short-story collection *The Nine Men of Soho*. Crowley, also there as a guest, had idly glanced through this and, saying he'd like to see what the young men were up to nowadays, asked Joan's permission to borrow it. When he returned the book she saw that the margins had been scribbled over with rather petulant old-world comments, such as: 'Yes yes, all very well, but why doesn't he tell us what the girl's background is?! Who are her people?!!' and so on.

He also asked Joan if she knew me, she said yes, and Crowley then said testily: 'Well next time you see him, tell him to be more precise about his characters' origins. He seems to ignore all the traditional social values that make up the fabric of our civilisation,' which, since I'd always understood that Crowley's mission as Worst Man in the World was to tear this fabric down, amused me quite a lot. But then maybe all diabolists are conservative at heart, or where would be the fun?

Calder-Marshall, amused as well but slightly frowning since this didn't equate with his idea of Crowley either, asked me if I thought the story true. I answered that I'd seen the annotated copy for myself and had offered to give Joan another in exchange, to which she had replied with the best-known line of Shaw's Eliza.

Meanwhile there was a stir among the guests and at the door: Picasso had just arrived. He was instantly surrounded and too short to be seen from where we stood, though all of us were naturally intent. We caught just a glimpse of him, gesticulating gaily, before he was whisked away to the far corner of the studio facing us, where it was better lit though Picasso was hidden again from view by the same sort of statuesque black-clad women who'd formed a bodyguard for Green at the opening of the Centre, and who seemed to attend every function concerned with painting or painters.

Then abruptly these fell back as Topolski was hurrying towards us with Picasso himself in tow. Their objective was the window by which we stood, the only one on that side of the studio and Topolski, excusing himself to us, tugged at it and with the aid of Calder-Marshall finally flung it open.

Picasso, close on his heels, small, square and nimble, wearing a thick rough suit of sack-coloured tweed, was within touching distance; and as a cold blast of air rushed into the room he gave a sigh of relief, nodded vigorously and grinning at us fanned himself with both hands, blowing out his cheeks to show he'd been too hot: since he must have thought we understood no French. The female retinue had followed en bloc and waited with expressions of concern while Picasso took great gulps of air and grinned at all.

At that moment through the door Vladimir Pudovkin came, with a somewhat similar following, the few men having the air of attachés; and Topolski hastened forward to welcome him. Calder-Marshall went too, being as sold on Russia at this time as Rayner Heppenstall still is on France, besides he'd some job connected with Anglo–Soviet cinematic relations; and the stately ladies speedily bore Picasso back to their original corner.

Adair observed their departure with suddenly narrowed eyes. The scotch combined with the air blowing in from the open window was having its effect on her.

She said: 'Why don't you go and speak to Picasso? I'll bet you speak better French than any of those women. Come to that, I'll bet I do.'

This was quite possibly true. Her mother lived in Jersey and as a very young girl Adair had met Françoise Rosay, who'd taken a liking to her and taught her French. Some years after she got a job with a London distributor of French films and was sent by her boss to Paris, where she assisted at the shooting of a film by Jacques Tad: an experience which I envied her, but by that time we'd parted company.

'I dare you to go over there now.'

'Darling don't be silly. Later perhaps.'

'But you'd like to meet Picasso wouldn't you.'

'Of course.'

Adair said: 'Then I'll bring him over to you.'

'Are you out of your mind,' I said alarmed, but she was already in motion.

Too late to intervene I watched the swinging skirts of her scarlet frock scythe a way through the black silk and velvet of the female entourage, and perform a kind of pirouette before Picasso's startled stocky tweeded figure. It was a terrible moment.

Then at my elbow I heard the voice of Topolski: he'd come to present me to Pudovkin, who was now established on a divan at the opposite side of the studio. On a semi-circle of chairs in front sat his followers, including Calder-Marshall; the men with the air of attachés stood stiffly up and I had to reach over the seated women in order to shake hands.

It was clear immediately that Pudovkin spoke no English, and the only Russian I knew had been learned from exiled noblemen in Nice: how, for instance, to invite a girl to accompany me for a moonlight walk along the Promenade des Anglais, which did not seem appropriate to this occasion.

Topolski had been called away to welcome a fresh influx of guests, including some whom I'd seen at the Lehmann party but not, surprisingly, Lehmann himself; and I stood irresolute, holding a glass which I'd been handed, and wondering whether to try French. Then I noticed Calder-Marshall motioning me to look round.

I turned and saw Picasso and Adair heading straight towards me. She had hold of his arm and stood taller than he by more than half a head. Both were smiling and Picasso seemed delighted. Behind, from the corner they'd vacated, the white faces of the black-clad women glared rigid with shock and outrage.

I swallowed at a gulp what was in my glass, vodka scorched my throat, and as I went forward with outstretched hand various topics of conversation, none suitable, shot through my head, then the word Cubism; and before my inner vision appeared the walls of Tube platforms, plastered at this period with inferior imitation Cubist advertisements perhaps hastily put together to commemorate Picasso's visit. I'd been commenting on their repulsiveness only the day before.

Adair was by now performing the introduction in her best Françoise Rosay French, but I realised with horror that she'd got it the wrong way round: was introducing Picasso to me.

Hastily I interrupted to say that I was greatly honoured, addressing him as Cher Maître and remembering too late that he was known to hate this.

We both bowed, Picasso continuing to smile with steel grey hair smoothly brushed across his forehead and a face the colour of Spanish earth, oddly unlined for a Spaniard and a man his age. In his rough sack-coloured sack he looked like a well barbered version of Harpo Marx, perhaps owing to the intensity of his stare.

I said: 'Do you remember, monsieur, saying once to Gertrude Stein...'

Picasso nodded encouragingly, and I waited for him to say 'Gertrude' with the simple affection and confidence which according to Alice B. Toklas always characterises his pronunciation of the name; but he did not.

Instead he said: 'Oui, oui, Mademoiselle Stein,' his bright prominent sloe-brown eyes fixed unblinking on mine; and I continued: 'You told her, did you not, that when you make a thing, it is so complicated making it that it is bound to be ugly, but those that do it after you they don't have to worry about making it, and they can make it pretty, and so everybody can like it when the others make it?'

I was by no means sure if I'd got this quotation right or had translated it properly, it was some time since I'd spoken French; but Picasso said instantly: 'Oui monsieur, I did indeed once say something of the sort,' and I went on: 'Then, monsieur, have you as yet descended, travelled by, the Tube, our English metro?'

'Non monsieur,' Picasso replied, 'I've not so far had that pleasure,' and I noted that after all those years in France he still retained his Spanish accent.

'Then when you do, monsieur,' I said, and he nodded several times emphatically to indicate that he couldn't wait to get down the Underground: his eyes were still fixed on mine and he must have been wondering what the hell, if anything, I was getting at.

'Then,' I said, 'you will realise, from the crude imitation Cubist advertisements on the platform walls, the truth in reverse of your so brilliant axiom. For, in seeking to exploit your discovery for vulgar commercial purposes, they have succeeded only in making the beautiful ugly.'

I bowed, taking a step back to do so: sweat was standing on me as I ended, more or less as I'd begun, by saying it'd been a great honour.

'That, monsieur, is reciprocal,' Picasso said, bowing in his turn; at which Adair, whose arm all this while had been hooked in his, turned him about and led him away, completely bemused by now, to his corner, where she left him among the indignant clucking women: while I hurried back to the whisky bottle behind its statue.

At the time I thought I'd carried it off rather well, only later did I feel embarrassment and shame, and later still in self-defence began to think of it as funny.

Nonetheless, when beset by celebrity snobs, I can truthfully say that I've talked about painting to the greatest living painter: moreover Picasso made a special point of turning to smile and bow in my direction. Perhaps he really did believe he had met somebody important: on the other hand, his politeness being almost oriental in its inscrutability, he may have been dying inwardly of laughter.

WORSE THAN ALEISTER CROWLEY

Picasso and Pudovkin had gone. At the end of the evening there was only a small group left, we were over by the door with Adair animatedly talking to our host, who was standing, as I recall, with either a grand piano or a giant easel for a background.

He'd brought out more scotch as the original bottle was empty, and with us was Calder-Marshall, also Tom Driberg, the initial William Hickey whose column Jaeger in Munich Year used to read so avidly over breakfast before going down the Labour.

Driberg, very tall and broad in a brown suit, had springy dark hair and a pleasant tough impassive face like a highly intelligent rugger blue. I remember questioning him eagerly about the hands of Weidmann the mass murderer, whose trial he had covered for *The Express*, and he stuck now to what he'd written at the time, namely that 'Weidmann seemed a nice quiet chap.'

I remember Topolski asking me, as he gave us a hand with our coats in the hall: 'Do you ever think of Mr Green? And the coffee? And the cakes?' and my uncontrollable fit of laughter, which also infected Adair though she'd never heard of the Mr Green Topolski meant.

I remember flagging a taxi into which we climbed with Calder-Marshall. I remember saying that Feliks Topolski was one of the finest hosts and nicest men I'd ever met: an opinion which I've no reason to retract.

I remember developing as well a sudden great affection for Calder-Marshall: Good Old Arthur, whom it was so wonderful to see again after all this time, Dear Old Arthur who must come home with us and have a last one for the road.

No denials were brooked, and when the flat door was unlocked Rashomon our white cat, who'd come in from the balcony at sound of the taxi stopping, fled again at sight of a stranger. Because of the window left open to let him in and out, the living-room felt like the inside of a fridge. I remember all this, then comes a tiny gap.

I was kneeling down trying to light our gas fire that had an air lock in the pipe, when I became conscious of Calder-Marshall saying loudly: 'You mustn't speak to a woman like that.'

'Woman?' I said startled.

'Mustn't talk to her like that.' His Auden-like lock of hair was hanging forward and his face mushroom-pale with anger.

Afterwards Adair told me I'd said to her sharply: 'For Christ's sake shove over and let me do it,' after she'd spilt a match box at my feet attempting to get the fire lit. It was to this that Calder-Marshall had taken exception; and seeing Adair's eyes narrowing once more I said quickly, before she could tell him not give me orders in my own home: 'Oh balls Arthur, have a glass of wine.'

The bottle of white burgundy which we'd been saving to cure our morning hangovers stood open on the table. Calder-Marshall ignored this. He said heavily: 'You're a bad man Julian. A bad man.'

My affection for him was on the wane, but I didn't want to end a good evening with a quarrel, I thrust another match into the hissing fire and said lightly: 'Like Aleister Crowley?'

'Worse than Aleister Crowley.'

At that the asbestos lit at last with a sound like a bomb going off; Adair gave a startled cry and I one of satisfaction: then I heard behind me the flat door bang and looked round to see Adair standing alone, as if the explosion had blown Calder-Marshall out of the room.

She cried: 'Arthur's just rushed off, go after him quick, he'll get away!'

On the stairs I heard his footsteps running down ahead of me then the front door slammed below, and when I reached the street he was heading full tilt for the main road beyond. I gave chase shouting: 'Arthur, Arthur come back!' and from behind came the clatter of Adair's high heels and her voice calling like a light echo of my own.

But Calder-Marshall had more than a head start; down the main road towards him came a taxi with FOR HIRE lit up in the front, a thing that usually happens only on the screen, and by the time I reached the corner he was already climbing in.

I said: 'Arthur don't be a fool, come on back,' but the taxi door banged, he leaned out of the lowered window to say loudly: 'A bad man. Worse than Crowley!' and the cab drove off just as Adair drew level with me on the pavement.

We watched its tail light turn the next corner out of sight, then Adair asked: 'What got into him? Who is Crowley? He can't have meant the one you were talking about at the party, the Worst Man in the World?'

'Never mind,' I said and we walked back arm-in-arm to where our cat mewed from the balcony and the wine waited to be drunk.

I didn't meet Calder-Marshall again until this year, when I chanced upon him drinking with the fiction editor of *The Times Literary Supplement* in a Great Portland Street pub. With his hair gone beautifully silver and the Auden lock combed back, I recognised him only when he spoke. He seemed quite affable and to have forgotten completely that I was worse than the Worst Man in the World.

I don't suppose I'll ever know what got into him that night of Topolski's party for Picasso.

OTHER MEMOIRS

My Father was Born in Havana

*   *   *

MY FATHER WAS BORN IN HAVANA. WHEN HE WAS A VERY SMALL boy, a negro slave named Domingo took him to see vampire bats hanging up by their wing-hooks in a barn. It was daytime and the bats were asleep. They had faces like evil mice. Domingo took a half-smoked cigar from his mouth and placed it in the mouth of one of the bats. The bat puffed away in its sleep until, drugged by the alien tobacco-fumes, it fell, collapsed in its leathery wings on the floor of the barn like a folded umbrella.

At night these bats fed on the big toes of nigger boys. They were voodoo gods and slept in the barn by day swollen with sucked blood. Domingo was an emancipated slave and did not believe in their magic. Hence the cigar.

On the island there were also tarantulas. My father slept under a special mosquito-net as protection against them. The tarantulas were foiled and ran about on the ceiling in hairy impotent malice. From the ceiling they dropped poison that raised a blister if it scored a direct hit.

My father's first language was Spanish, but he wasn't a Spaniard. His mother was South American but his father was Scottish: an engineer who built bridges and afterwards owned ships. There was a grandfather who was not South American but from the Southern States of America, to whom General Lee said during the Civil War: 'I will leave the South only her eyes to weep with.' Or perhaps he said it to somebody else, I don't really remember.

Suddenly my father was transported from Havana, from this colourful island of Cuba, to England. Domingo doffed his palm-leaf hat and wept, waving his cigar. The folded bats hung suspended in sleep and the taran-tulas scampered furiously about dropping their poison on the empty cot.

Before he'd time to think, my father was in England, riding a horse. He was six. He fell off. The horse aimed a kick at him as it galloped away and my father was given three days to live. In point of fact he lived until the age of seventy-eight but all his life he was subject to dizziness and headaches. When he recovered from the horse's kick and the doctors had finished saying Marvellous, he was sent away to school in France. It was a priest's school because my grandmother and all her children were Roman Catholics. My father had already learnt to speak English and now he learnt to speak French. The only trouble was that in learning French he completely forgot his English, so they packed him off to a public school to learn it all over again.

The public school was a sort of minor hell, referred to by my father in later life as the happiest days of his life. The food often had maggots in it. Then there was rugger. My father had broken chilblains on his toes and these were stamped on in the scrum. He fainted and his boots had to be cut off. In summer there was cricket. A sadistic prefect used to make the smaller boys stand at the wicket while he bowled at them with all his strength. A fast ball ran up my father's bat and broke two of his front teeth.

The school was run mainly for boys destined to go into the Indian army, and a ferocious headmaster managed it. He had a huge family and various deformities: the boys composed a rhyme in his honour.

> One eye
> One lung
> Nine daughters
> And one son.

There was also an Abyssinian prince. He'd been to Windsor Castle and had kissed the hand of the Queen. This made him uneasy, because he didn't know which one she used.

My father fagged for a prefect named Tremayne, who wore side-whiskers and, like Domingo, smoked cigars. Father did his French for him and so escaped being beaten. Presently Tremayne left to become a general and my father became a prefect in his turn. His three brothers, Ronnie, Dick and Edward, were now also at this school, in lower forms. My father was the eldest son: his family was almost as large as that of the Headmaster. Besides the brothers there were four sisters: Enid, Trissie, Emily and Jane. These were being finished abroad. When my father had done being a prefect he thought he'd go abroad again too. He chose Heidelberg as a suitable university. The students explained to him kindly that, as a foreigner, it was not necessary for him to acquire a duelling-scar.

He lived au pair with a German family named Schwob. A young English peer who afterwards died as the result of a Pharaoh's curse was his fellow-boarder. They drank, gambled and got into debt. To ease the financial situation, the peer proposed a racket. They went to a tailor's and ordered expensive suits which they immediately pawned. The bills for these suits were sent to their respective fathers.

Then one day they came unstuck. Having pawned a suit without even opening the parcel, they found this really contained one belonging to Herr Dolfuss, the son-in-law of the house where they were staying. A scandal exploded: Herr Dolfuss threatened to call in the police. Only respect for the peer's title prevented him from taking this step.

Soon afterwards my father did get arrested. He was drunk in a beer-garden with a student named Keller. Keller was juggling with oranges. He balanced an orange on the end of his nose. A big man in a black suit stood up and bawled at them in German to shut their row. Keller threw an orange at him. It was over-ripe and it burst. The big man gave a roar and came for them like a bull. My father was also a big man and he got his blow in first. The man in black overturned a table as he fell. Waiters came running. Lying on his back the big man blew a police-whistle. An old lady hit my father with her parasol. The blow brought on one of his head-aches. He took the parasol away and broke it in his hands. The beer garden filled with police. My father and Keller were lodged in the jail.

Drunk and disorderly, assaulting a police officer. The magistrate looked serious. My father said: 'But he wasn't in uniform. How were we to know.' The big man shouted, enraged: 'The only time I need to wear uniform is when I come to England as a soldier, to conquer your country.' 'Yes, and then you'll wear a convict's uniform,' my father shouted back. The magistrate rapped for order and dished out a heavy fine.

My father left Heidelberg for Berlin. Here Prussian military parades were in full swing; officers were served before civilians in the shops and the best seats were reserved for them at the theatre. The sidewalks shook under Bismarck's boots. Von Moltke stepped more delicately: ascetic, like a priest. My father, slightly deafened by the sound of Bismarck's stamping, got on a train for England. He arrived to find his sister chained to the railings outside their town house. She'd become a Suffragette.

All the sisters were now grown-up: beautiful girls, all very tall and wayward. The house was crammed with crimson-faced racing men, friends of my Uncle Ronnie. Dick was away in Havana with my grand-father, on the sugar plantation. Edward played the piano upstairs in a special studio of his own and came down only to meals. He was enormously fat and very sensitive. He wanted to become a concert-pianist but was afraid to appear on the platform for fear people would laugh at him. He was a Laird Cregar character, complete with a pet Persian named Dan Leno. This cat, smoke-grey and with blue eyes, ate cheese and perched on the piano while he played.

After dinner, over which my grandmother presided wearing a mantilla, the racing men retired with my uncle Ronnie to study form. The sisters were busy being débutantes, going to balls and getting engaged. My Aunt Emily had already been engaged eight times. Being engaged runs in the family. I've been engaged a few times myself.

There was now a move on the part of my grandmother to get my father engaged. A lot of girls were asked to the house but he was wary. He was also very large and handsome. Wavy auburn hair and blue eyes. He was clean-shaven in those days: the pointed nautical beard came later. I saw a photo of him as he was then—in a curly-brimmed bowler and a check suit with narrow lapels and very tight trousers. His blue eyes, oddly enough, were inherited from my grandmother who was a blonde South American. My grandfather was dark, with a hollow high-boned face and a square preacher's beard.

My father decided to stay in London and become a masher, or man-about-town. He took chambers in Half Moon Street and kept an actress. His boon companion was a man called Percy Hall. It was Percy Hall's proudest boast that he had been saved more often at Salvation Army meetings than any other man of his age. He attended Salvation Army meetings on every possible occasion; it was the bonnets of the lassies that attracted him. He also threw boiled eggs at policemen and smashed gaslamps with his stick. He and my father started betting pretty heavily. They got into the clutches of money-lenders: a feat which I envy them, since I've never been able to get into any money-lender's clutches myself. But of course they had security. Bills were backed, IOU's dished around by the dozen, accounts run up with benevolent bookies. They staggered roaring on Boat Race night through a London of Romano's and Oddenino's; Tale Pitcher and the Pink 'Un. They popped over to Paris and broke up a brothel in Brussels.

My Uncle Ronnie was distinguishing himself too about this time. He was extremely proud of the fact that a man named Three-Fingered

Fred once said to him: 'Lumme, guv'nor, what a crook you'd have made.' With him my father attended race-meetings, backed the favourite, the outsider, the winner the loser. And they all drank ceaseless champagne. Meanwhile, in the town house, my grandmother devoted herself more and more to her Faith and the visits of her Father Confessor: a priest whom my father had once offended by asking him if he'd read Renan's *Vie de Jésus*. Upstairs my Uncle Edward played the piano and drank brandy. Occasional knocks on the door announced that Aunt Enid had been arrested once more in the cause of women's suffrage. My Aunt Jane was studying singing in Milan. My Aunt Trissie got married to a German painter. Aunt Emily got engaged for the ninth time. Marie Corelli came to dinner, and possibly Beerbohm Tree.

My father knew a lot of actors. He belonged, I think, to the Garrick. He backed a play and it was a flop. The money-lenders began to get restive. So did the hidden actress my father was keeping. She chose the moment to come into the open when my grandfather had just returned from Cuba. She announced herself at the house as my father's wife. All the bookies sent in their bills. The IOU's cropped up too. My grandfather gave his eldest son the choice of the shipping office in Liverpool, or Canada, where we had cousins.

My father chose Canada. Percy Hall came to see him off and fell in the dock. The ship weighed anchor. My father made his way to the saloon, where an American detective arrested him. Turned out to be a mistake. His description and initials tallied with those of a famous embezzler who was supposed to be on board. The mistake was rectified after they'd been some days at sea, but the detective wouldn't apologise. He said my father'd been lucky not to be put in irons.

The boat docked at New York. My father had never been to America so he got off. In New York the skyscrapers were too high: they made him dizzy. People kept asking him why he didn't wear a monocle if he was an Englishman. Oscar Wilde appeared on the stage with his hair long and carrying a lily. In a Greenwich Village bar an American suggested to my father that they should open a wine-tasting business together. They did but it went bust: they both got too drunk tasting the wines. My father, who'd forgotten all about Canada, staggered off to the South to see his grandfather. The grandfather, who had known George Washington, was now dying and his estate had been burnt down in the Civil War, so that was no good.

My father then lost all the money he had with him. It was while he was playing poker with a clergyman and the clergyman's son, on a show-boat on the Mississippi. In the end the clergyman gave him back a hundred pounds, with the caution not to play cards in future with strangers. My father had just enough to go to Cuba, where my Uncle Dick was running the sugar plantation.

An earthquake was in progress at the time. White houses crumbled quite suddenly amid rumbling and a cart full of fruit disappeared through a crack in the earth, which afterwards closed over it like a sliding trapdoor. A few frogs fell from the sky. Then the ground ceased to tremble; my father picked himself up from under a café table and made his way among wails and mounds of debris across the city.

He found the plantation practically undamaged but Domingo, like the cart, had been swallowed up by the earthquake. The bats and tarantulas were still there, however. My Uncle Dick was by now tremendously interested in sugar and had invented a machine for cutting the cane up into cubes. My father borrowed a large sum of money from him and went to Canada.

When he arrived it was terribly cold. He spat and it turned into a hailstone. There was snow everywhere. He tried to make a snowball but the snow crumbled to powder in his frozen fingers. He arrived at his cousin's office. At first he was too cold to speak. His cousin thought he was dumb. My father managed to mumble: 'I'm cold.' The cousin said: 'Well, sure. You're dressed in white drill.' This was true. White drill had been worn in Cuba and my father had forgotten to change his clothes. He bought a fur suit like an Eskimo's. Now he felt warm but the cousin's house was cold, and he couldn't wear his fur suit all the time. Then, too, he had to rise at six to attend morning service in an unheated chapel. There were family prayers four times a day and endless discussions on the sort of job my father was to have. His cousin was in favour of him starting at the bottom. My father couldn't take it. He made his way up country. He joined the Mounted Police. He was sent to a sort of roaring camp, where he had to keep order among lumberjacks accustomed to kill one another with hatchets on pay-day. My father was tough but this was a bit too tough to suit him. The proportion of murders was high and he felt he was letting down the proud tradition of the Mounted Police: A Mountie Always Gets His Man. He hadn't got anyone yet, but on the other hand one of the lumberjacks had nearly got him with a flung chopper.

He was on his way to hand in his resignation when he got caught in a blizzard and was snowed up in a hut with grizzly bears scratching at the door. Another Mountie sent as a replacement from Headquarters dug him out. Meanwhile the camp had been set alight. Nothing was left of it. My father's duty was done. He resigned and got a boat back to England.

Here there was news: my Aunt Emily had got fed up with her engagements and gone into a convent; Uncle Ronnie had made a runaway marriage; Uncle Edward was drinking himself to death, and the butler, who'd been supplying him with secret brandy, had himself developed DTs. All these things had upset my grandfather, and no alternative was now offered to the shipping office in Liverpool. My father agreed to give it a try. London didn't seem the same; Percy Hall had got married too, and his wife regarded my father as a bad influence.

In Liverpool it was always raining. The office was managed by another cousin, a short-tempered Scot who had once quelled a mutiny on board one of the firm's ships. There were board-meetings and terrible dinners with black-suited merchants who devoured whole hams and sides of beef at a sitting. My father got indigestion. He started coming late to the office. One morning there was a row. The cousin picked up a poker. My father, a short-tempered man himself, felt a headache coming on. He left the office: a pane of glass in the door broke as he shut it.

In London my grandfather listened to my father's story, stroking his beard with the same impatience that my father was in turn to assume when, many years later, he himself had to hear yet another proof of my shiftlessness and inability to adapt myself to other people's requirements. Upstairs, my Uncle Edward struck a chord and reached for his hip-flask; my grandfather crossed and uncrossed his legs: stomach ulcers were giving him hell; Aunt Enid had been locked up again; the Father Confessor was never out of the house ('Popery!'); what was to become of them all? Aunt Jane had given up singing and showed signs of wanting to marry a penniless French cavalry officer; Uncle Ronnie's father-in-law, disapproving of the runaway marriage, had refused to settle anything on his daughter; Uncle Dick, with his plantation and inventions, seemed the only industrious member of the family.

In the end my father was sent on a voyage round the world, in the hope that on his return he would settle down. He sailed on a ship called *The Scottish Fairy*; it was owned by my grandfather's firm. It nearly foundered twice: once, in a storm off the Cape of Good Hope.

According to the crew, an albatross was the cause of the storm. This bird had been blown down on the deck during a gale, and there it lay, beating one prodigious broken wing, for three days. On the third day, Captain Wilson, a humane character, brought out a revolver and shot the wounded bird dead, despite the protests of the sailors, who said this would bring bad luck on them all.

However, the ship weathered the succeeding storm and did in fact sail round the world. In Singapore my father admired the deftness of Chinese bank-tellers counting up stacks of silver dollars; in Australia he was present at a siege in which the Kelly Brothers were roasted alive in their own armour made of kettles and saucepans. He drank various kinds of drink and slept with girls brown, black and yellow. On the voyage home he read the Bible. It was the only book on board. He got to know it so well he could quote any passage from memory.

More catastrophes had occurred in the family during his absence. Uncle Edward was dead and buried: his bones would keep. Aunt Jane had married the cavalry officer and gone to live in Lille; Aunt Trissie had given birth to German twins; my grandfather's ulcers confined him to bed. After the excitements of life aboard *The Scottish Fairy*, London life bored my father, and though Oscar Wilde once spoke to him in French at the Garrick and Aubrey Beardsley had been discovered in an attic by a protégé of my grandmother's, he decided to join the army.

He became a captain in some territorial unit: was it the yeomanry? He drilled his men by the roadside and once his company went into action—against a gang of local roughs who'd jeered and thrown stones at them. Then all of a sudden the Boer War broke out and he found himself leading his men on the battlefield. He was shot in the leg and in due course invalided home. With a limp that remained with him for the rest of his life, and wearing a wide brimmed black hat which he claimed had been given him by De Wet, he returned to visit his family. Nobody recognised him at first because of his beard; he'd also put on several stone in weight. He was enormous. The London house, sunk in gloom because of my grandfather's illness and my grandmother's piety, depressed him. He went to a spa for a cure, to get his weight down.

It was in Alsace and there, in a pension, he met my mother: a girl of eighteen who'd just come out of a convent, though she was not a Catholic. She, too, had lived an adventurous life. Her father was a Colonel in the Indian army and she was born in Calcutta. Later she lived on an island in the Azores dominated by a smoking volcano. She could speak Hindustani, Arabic, French and Portuguese. She'd had the Aleppo boil and had contracted ophthalmia in Syria. One of her brothers, believed by the natives to be an incarnation of Buddha, had been trampled to death as a child by a rogue elephant in India; another brother had been carried off by an eagle. Stories of her early life used to fascinate us as children; my father was equally entranced.

His bulk, his limp, his beard, intimidated my mother, for she was young and small; but eventually she agreed to marry him. Her father approved; her mother was indifferent. An engagement ring appeared on her finger. A friend of my father's called Clarke, who wore cotton-wool in one of his ears, was the first to notice this. He was congratulating her and admiring the ring when my father came into the room. He thought Clarke was kissing her hand. He threw Clarke bodily through a french window. That was the end of their friendship: also, for the time being, of the engagement. Clarke left the next day, swathed in bandages, and refused to shake hands. A cable, announcing that my grandfather was dying, brought my mother and father together again. One could not refuse to marry the son of a dying man. They were married on the spot and left for London together.

The city was shrouded in a dense fog. My father went round to see his mother and announce the marriage. On the way back he got lost and wandered round in circles until four a.m. when the fog lifted. He arrived at the hotel to find my mother fully dressed and packing her bag. She was a girl of spirit and believed that he had deserted her.

Next day he took her round to meet the family. The gloom of the huge house, the sophistication of Aunt Enid, the gallantry of Uncle Ronnie, and the grande-dame manner of my grandmother—her lorgnette and her mantilla—were not encouraging. My grandfather, eating rusks and drinking milk upstairs, had been told nothing of the marriage for fear this news brought on a relapse. My mother felt uncomfortable. She had a further strain to undergo: my grandmother's test of her daughter-in-law's good breeding.

My grandmother was bald. All her hair had been burnt off in a fire. On some pretext she invited my mother to her dressing-room and then removed the mantilla, and with it her wig. But my mother's face betrayed neither astonishment nor horror and she was now fully admitted into favour.

My grandfather didn't die yet, after all. Soon he was well enough to come downstairs again. One morning a new footman showed my mother into the room where he was sitting. It was not the first time a girl had been announced to my grandfather as his eldest son's wife. At first he didn't believe it, and then he was glad. He said: 'I was always afraid he'd marry an actress.' But a few days later he killed himself. Peas did it. He was strictly forbidden to eat peas but he suddenly scooped a spoonful and swallowed them. A relapse and the funeral followed.

The family assembled from all over for the reading of the will; all except Uncle Dick and Aunt Trissie, who remained in Cuba and Germany respectively. Aunt Jane was there with her husband, and Aunt Emily (now Sister Emily) dressed as a nun. She got a smaller legacy than anyone else, because my grandfather disapproved of Popery.

My father should now by rights have taken charge of the shipping company, but Uncle Ronnie offered to take it over in his stead. He said: 'You two go off and have a nice honeymoon,' and winked. They did; and a year later, after the birth of my brother, the business had to be wound up. Uncle Ronnie, in an attempt to retrieve the family fortunes, went off to the Gold Rush and died, frozen stiff as a board, in the Klondyke.

There was still plenty of money, though—for the present. Money enough to bring up and educate my brother and sister, and for that matter, me. But I came later.

It was in 1912 and in South Norwood, of all places. There was a frightful storm. Lightning crackled and midnight struck. I was born. There my story begins, but this one must end.

Are You Happy in Your Work

*   *   *

GEOGRAPHY AND DESCRIPTION

THE COMPANY IS BILLETED IN REQUISITIONED HOTELS ALONG THE seafront: our HQ's on a corner, three storeys of red brick and rough plaster, tarnished gilt letters—one of them missing—spelling out a name along a balcony. It faces the rusty criss-cross of iron struts, the coils of Dannert wire barricading the mined sea. Barrage balloons dot the sky: on clear days, coming down closer, sparkling in the sun, they resemble the illustrations in a book that I read as a boy, in which the earth was invaded by the inhabitants of a planet that had the power of propelling itself through space.

Past the picquet man on duty at the door is the hall of echoing black and white tiles swabbed down nightly by defaulters; doors opening off it respectively into the Piquet Room, the Company Commander, the Second-in-Command. Beyond them a door without a handle leads out to a no-man's-land of tin sinks and taps—formerly the hotel kitchen. Draughts sweep icily through this in winter, banging the doors and bringing soot down the chimney; the whole house rattles; to step outside for a moment from a heated room translates you at once to a temperature below zero.

But in summer, sweating upstairs in shirtsleeves, it's quite pleasant to come down into the draught, and the wind which in February froze the rain on the pavement into a solid sheet of ice and caused chilblains to break out on the ear-lobes is now only the breeze.

The offices are above, up a flight of uncarpeted wooden treads one of which, lower than the rest, lets you treacherously down unless you're careful. The RSM's room, the Orderly Sergeant's Bunk, the CSM, the

CQMS (incorporating the pay sergeant who is simultaneously the Company Clerk), the Post Corporal (OUT OF BOUNDS TO ALL RANKS), the Despatch Clerk (that's me).

There's a bathroom, a lavatory, and an enormous room used for Courts Martial, all the windows of which have been shattered by enemy action, with a fitted wash-basin incongruous among the crimson blankets and Sam Browne belts when someone's being tried.

I have in my time worked in nearly all the various offices but now I have an office to myself; it has only one window and this faces a wall painted with enormous letters:

THE CREAMERY
BEACH TEAS AND TRAYS
AT POPULAR PRICES
ICES, MINERALS, ETC.

all, of course, unobtainable now. Underneath this sign, but with its entrance in the next street, is a shop which sells cigarettes and tea and buns and where the training squads congregate at breaktimes. On the wall of this shop it says: DO NOT GRUMBLE IF YOU HAVEN'T ENOUGH SUGAR—YOUR RATION IS TWO-THIRDS OF A TEA-SPOONFUL. I do not patronise the shop myself; it's run by an enormous swarthy slattern who looks like somebody's mother in a film about Italian gangsters; she is in fact very English and calls everyone Dear.

Above the offices are the rooms where we sleep and on this second landing is a loose board where all the dirt from the various rooms is naturally swept, and above this again are the Regimental Police and the guardroom, always bungful of prisoners who are constantly escaping: one man, in civilian life a cat-burglar, has just completed his fifth escape, and is still, at the moment of writing, at large.

I have a bedroom of my own. The window of it was blown out by an exploding mine whilst I was asleep and has been repaired in such a way that the room is permanently blacked-out. It contains a double-decker bed, a wash-basin and a mouse-hole. The mouse-hole had originally a mouse living in it, that used to inconvenience me by running across my face at night when, before the arrival of the bed, I slept on the floor. In the end I became annoyed and plugged up the hole by placing a saucer over it. The night visitations ceased, but the mouse presumably died down there and quite soon there was a smell. I complained, the Company Plumber came, he took the floorboards up, but by this time the mouse had disintegrated and he could find nothing. The smell persisted, I again complained, the Company Plumber finally got fed-up and said it must be me. But now the smell has gone so it can't have been.

SARMAJOR

Work for me starts normally at nine. The rattle of my typewriter coincides with the arrival downstairs of the Second-in-Command, whose clerk I am. At the moment he's on leave, so we'll leave him. Then shortly afterwards a shout of SHUN shakes the house and that is Company Evidence. CO's Evidence follows later and then you get ESCORT AND ACCUSED SHUN. While this is going on downstairs I enter despatches. There are many items to be entered, including the annoying return required urgently by the adjutant three days ago and duly despatched to him; returned by BHQ in error that evening; the next day again sent off by me marked ADJUTANT; returned the same afternoon with HQ Company on it and ADJUTANT rubbed out; redirected and returned promptly with new markings on it and moreover with one corner missing: it's beginning to come to bits. The only solution is to seal it up to ensure the adjutant gets it, otherwise he'll be raising hell. I pick up a sticky label: by the middle of the morning my mouth is sour with gum arabic and my tongue stuck to my teeth.

The CSM enters with an Offence Report in his hand. A spot more crime to add on, he says. Who's it today? Bloody Bates and Hubbard. What, again? Yeah. They'll be for the clink this time that's one comfort. We'll soon be rid of 'em. What shall I put down. The usual? AWOL? That's the ticket.

It's typed, the CSM says Thank you and goes out with a flourish.

The CSM always says Thank You, he also says Please, which is what makes him different from other Company Sergeant-Majors. His name is Denton, although recently when a phone message came through to him from Major Glover, the signaller on phone duty transcribed it as 'TO MAYOR KENTON FROM MAYOR CLOVER', where-upon the CSM said to him, If a Mayor gets more pay than I do then I am willing to be one, but my name I have had for 37 years and I'll be damned if I change it now.

CSM Denton is a regular soldier and has seen service in most parts of the world: he can talk entertainingly about them all. His attitude towards most things is one of cheerful je m'en foutisme, and is frequently expressed by him in its literal English equivalent. Tall and straight and thin, with a rigid back, a lean mobile face, a high neighing laugh, he has only one aversion: OCTU candidates. And this is natural, since you cannot expect him to willingly salute, on their return to the unit as officers, lance corporals of 19 who when sent to OCTU were probably not in receipt of proficiency pay, having less than six months service in. In any case 'CSM' Denton always says that he does not salute anything below the rank of Captain.

ROMEO WITH THREE STRIPES

Returning to his office the CSM almost collides with Sgt Legge, the pay NCO and Company Clerk, rushing down the corridor with a casualty state in his hand. Sgt Legge grins Sorry over his shoulder and roars out in the same breath RUNNER. This is the signal for everybody in the building to roar out RUNNER simultaneously. Corporal Dexter, the Orderly Sergeant, emerges from his bunk and leans over the banisters. RUNNER! RUNNER!! RUNNER!!! The shout echoes down the stairwell; it is taken up from every office, like the barking of dogs in a country-side at night.

Sgt Legge is by now in my office; big and burly, with curly hair and a large grin, he drops the casualty state on my desk. Nicknamed Smiler for obvious reasons, he speaks always explosively. Where are the expurgated runners? I don't know. Well send one of the expurgators down to me will you when they roll up.

Legge goes out, he is stopped on the landing by a corporal for a confidential talk about the tarts they met at the dance last night. What she said what I said and did you and did I, it was a proper laugh.

Sgt Legge is the Company Romeo. Once he became monogamous: it was a telephone girl. Then there was a bust up and he ceased to live up to his nickname. For days he went about looking black; blokes coming to him for casual payments got their heads bitten off. He drank all his pay and was broke by Monday. I said to console him There are more fish in the sea. He said he ruddy well knew it but in his present state of mind he didn't feel like fishing. I could understand that, having been offered the same advice in similar circumstances myself. But it is good advice all the same and later Sgt Legge took it and the other fish is blonde and wears the uniform of a WAAF.

THE RUNNERS AND ROSIE

I enter a despatch SUBJECT Discipline. It's one of the CO's special stinkers and should wake everyone up. I read it with satisfaction. Cpl Dexter puts a sick report on my desk. Look at this here.

The MO has written across it, This man was recommended for 14 days Sick Leave in hospital but states he has been given detention instead.

Some ruddy mess-up I reckon, Cpl Dexter says buttoning his blouse, I don't know nothing about it.

Then the runners come trooping in, they've been in the tea-shop. Two of them are immediately nailed down and sent out on messages. The remaining two, Wells and Williams, sit at opposite ends of the desk.

Wells comes from West Ham and plays the accordion in the unit dance-band. With his cap cocked on one side, nervous rolling eyes, a deep guttural voice, he is actually timid despite a rather raffish exterior. He is easily elated and depressed; he is nineteen years old. He starts now to write a letter in pencil but not as formerly on my best notepaper, as I have this locked up in a cupboard. Wells' letters are either Dear Mum and Dad or else to his girl. His girl is generally known as Bleeding Rosie. She has puritan instincts and is constantly repudiating the plans put forward by Wells for their wedding night. When he is on leave she wears frocks buttoned to the neck and leaves nothing to chance. Get something, Wellsy? they ask him on his return. Yerce, he tells them gloomily; a slap in the chops.

Wells's wedding is always being postponed. His Mum interfered when the banns were put up and there was a row which ended in Wells being kicked out of home. Everyone gave contradictory advice and Wells nearly went out of his mind. Eventually it was smoothed over, the wedding fixed for his next seven days, and correspondence with Mum and Dad, interrupted during the breach, continued as usual. But Rose advises Wells in her latest to bring home with him a tin opener or better still two, in case one breaks.

Williams, on the other side of the table, leans forward with a burnt-out-fag-butt in his mouth and in an accent at first unintelligible to me but which I have got gradually used to, asks if he can have one of my lights. Like most Welshmen he buys few matches and then only on Fridays. I tell him he can have the rest of the lights tomorrow. He sits back with his legs stuck straight out, puffing at his fag and smiling foolishly. As usual his jacket and collar are undone.

Williams is lanky and owing to adolescence and the condition of his skin might easily be mistaken for a case of scabies. One day he was and spent a blissful five days in hospital, where he got off with a nurse. When he first arrived as a runner I thought he was either foreign or else congenitally unable to understand what was said to him. Both turned out to be right, as in his native village he spoke only Welsh, but his knowledge of English slowly improves, although it's still confined mainly to swearing.

The other two runners are Pritchett and Dobb. Pritchett is the banker of the quartet: he lends money out to the other three at interest. He collects threepenny bits and is continually counting his money over in the kitchen. He keeps a reserve fund of half-a-crown concealed under his cap-badge in case of need. His other money is kept in two separate pockets: one for silver, wrapped carefully in a handkerchief so that no coin jingles; the other for coppers, which he brings out and displays as his entire means if approached for a loan by anyone other than his regular clientèle. He is a practised dodger and an actor of no mean ability. If sent up the town on a message he spends the afternoon in the cinema; consequently I employ him only for local jobs from two o'clock onwards.

During the winter he volunteered for the job of looking after fires; thereafter officers used to comment on him commiseratingly as he staggered manfully in with the coal bucket full to the brim. One of the officers, feeling particularly sorry to see him so laden, offered to help. He lifted the bucket; it was astonishingly light and proved on investigation to be stuffed with paper, a few knobs of coal artistically arranged on top. After this he was in disgrace and Dobb took over the fires from him. The job suited Dobb because it permitted him to be revoltingly dirty at all times without being checked for it.

Dobb is another Cockney but of a repellent kind. Almost a dwarf, he is always shadow-boxing about the office and telling about the time he knocked out a fascist with a righthander in Whitechapel. It transpired that the righthander was delivered by Dobb while three of his mates held the fascist down, one of them sitting on his head. I have tried hard to dislodge Dobb but without success. Once he was transferred but he came back; no one could handle him. Now, without the excuse of fires, he still contrives to be almost completely black; one day when he had a bath he left his boots behind in it.

RESPIRATORS WILL BE WORN: MERCER'S CAFÉ

Wells scrawls a signature in pencil and beneath it embarks on a series of crosses. I count forty-six. Wells searches among my papers for an envelope, sticks it down, writes SWALK on the flap. RUNNER is called out in the voice of the CQMS. Williams, flinging away his fag, lopes off along the corridor; Wells starts on a long yarn about his cousin who has inherited a hundred pounds and how he can go about tapping her. My head is empty of ideas.

Now there is a sudden speeding-up of work, people run in and out with papers to be sent off, the Education Officer drops two letters in front of me, the PT Sergeant wants a sports programme typed, a lieutenant asks me how to spell loofah.

Wells picked up a magazine of mine and opening it is faced at once with a reproduction of a painting by Dali. What the deleted's this? he says. It's a picture. Yerce but what's it meant to be.

A scraping of rifle butts on the landing advertises the presence of men waiting outside the CSM's for their leave passes. It must be ten o'clock. Thank God for that. At half-past I can slip out for a break. A sudden shout goes up. One of the passes, supposedly for seven days, is found to be made out for fourteen. A row begins, the guardroom is mentioned. The CSM gets the best of it, the man doesn't get his pass, Wells gives up Dali as a bad job. Can he post his letter? Yes but don't forget to come back. Garn whatcher take me for.

I examine the postage book. Somewhere there's been a ballsup. I count my remaining money and stamps. I'm a shilling short. I go over the account day by day, it goes back weeks. The total adds up wrong, I'm in a whirl. Suddenly a slip of paper hitherto unnoticed catches my eye, Respirators will be worn by all ranks today from 1030 till 1115 hours. That makes me pause. Respirators? Three-quarters of an hour? Not bloody likely. I grab my cap and the two letters dumped by the Education Officer and make for the stairs. There is no official break time for office personnel: mine is known as going to post. I do in fact go there but afterwards. First I go to Mercer's Café. It's down on the front by the Pier and is civilian, that is to say although patronised mainly by the troops there are tablecloths and the atmosphere is not that of a canteen. A stag's head, antlers on the wall, a banner: PLEASE BRING YOUR OWN BAGS AND PAPER. Black coffee can be obtained and it is good. Also chocolate cakes and hot doughnuts. There is a downstairs room for the officers where everything costs more. Once we had a sub-altern of socialistic views who objected to the implied class distinction and also to the twopence extra on tea; for two mornings he sat upstairs with the other ranks but we damn soon showed him what was what and after that he too went below with his brother officers.

There are two wicker armchairs in the corner: if you're lucky and arrive early enough you can bag one of them. I am and I do. I drink coffee, dust sugar from fingers, start to write this sketch. Gradually the café fills up: the CSM, the Messing staff, the two educational sergeants (at other times invisible), the orderly sergeant, a few corporals, the training sergeant-major in shirtsleeves with his crown strapped to his wrist like a watch, and of course Smiler, roaring with laughter and with a face like the rising sun. He is surrounded by WAAFs and one Wren, a girl with eyes staring out of her head. There is backchat with the waitresses: the big frizzy one, the smaller one in the green smock who looks always as though she had awakened from a night of love, the buxom sophisticated one that Wells has his eye on. Coppers rattle in the china bowl, cream doughnuts are consumed by the score. There's an argument over who pays. The waitress says Come on, Smiler says, I'll toss you. Who's got any sporting blood. Toss you hell, they say, pay up it's your turn. But in the end they toss for it; Cpl Dexter says Let's see them all go up same time. He loses, they all hoot, it costs a tanner.

The wireless plays Music While You Work; in the middle of this Wells suddenly appears. Rossy, they all got respirators on. So what? Well I ain't got mine, are we safe in here. Safe as houses.

I go on writing; Wells, after eyeing my black coffee with appre-hension, as though it were a potion about to turn me into Mr Hyde, orders a tea. He signals to the sophisticated one: a screwed-up note changes hands. Dating her up, Wells explains, eight o'clock tonight. What about Rosie? Well she won't know will she.

The hands of the clock point to eleven, it's time to go. I leave Wells, who's officially supposed to be taking a message to the Transport Office, and make my way through back streets to the post office. The entrance to the grocery shop which houses it is guarded by an enormous black ferocious-looking but docile-natured dog of indeterminate breed, chewing a bone that must have come from the Dental Centre. At any rate it is mainly teeth. The letters drop in the box; as it's Thursday I withdraw five bob from the savings bank.

Coming out a man bicycles past me with his respirator on, I am shaken by the sight. I crawl in through barbed wire the back way. I cower in the downstairs lavatory hearing the muffled voices of men calling out through their gasmasks. Surely time must be up now? At last! The voices begin to shout normally; I emerge, walk past a regimental policeman wiping his face-piece with anti-dim, and slide up the stairs to my office. There the table is almost completely covered with papers brought in during my absence for despatch: it looks as though there's been an avalanche.

I sit down and straighten it out: to X Company, to BHQ, Sealed PERSONAL to Adjutant, local stuff; a kit inventory to the QM, dental card, a medical history sheet to the MI Room. A completely silent man, category C, slips into the room like a shadow and removes the salvage sack from its hook on the cupboard where I keep my manuscripts. Several figures in denim suits present themselves paybook in hand and are redirected to Smiler in the pay office. Then there are men asking to see the CQMS, they want a new cap-badge, a cake of blanco, one has lost the whole of his kit. He's in his office, in the stores, in the mess, up the town, in bed asleep, how should I know, get the hell out.

Dobb puts his nose round the corner, wiping it with his sleeve. He gets the local despatches given him. I just bin out, it ain't my flicking turn. Go on, get going. Wells got the flicking bike. You don't need the bike to go round the corner. Dobb goes off moaning. It ain't his turn, it ain't fair, he gets all the flicking work, he's thorough browned-off. All the men in denims return in a body, they can't find the Colour Bloke nowhere. Well come back at two. We're on parade at two. Well come back after parade.

I struggle again with the postage account, end by putting one of the shillings from my savings into the wallet where I keep the postage money. From upstairs comes a stampede of men clattering knives forks and spoons. Dinner time. I fall in on parade outside; we march down to the cookhouse.

COOKHOUSE: GHOST STORY: DON-R

The duty officer for the day is also the Messing Officer. We are given open order march and our hands and eating utensils are inspected. Several men are sent off to wash. Suddenly after all this a gigantic MT corporal appears, in denims soaked with oil and stained with grease; he salutes the Messing Officer with a hand as black as a negro's. The Messing Officer gives up; we get Front Rank right turn quick march. We file into the cookhouse; it's in the basement of a large empty hotel supposed to be haunted. The ghost used to appear in winter dressed as a waiter. Several people saw it; there was at the same time an epidemic of pinching. Then one man shot another by accident and a third got sent to detention and the ghost ceased to walk. We drew our own conclusions but we're not sure.

The dinner is principally stew. I get a bone for my ration and lots of men begin to bark. There are also shouts of Fido and Good Dog. The Messing Officer asks any complaints. It's a rhetorical question. No answer is given or expected. After that we get duff. It's good but I am put off my portion by the sudden appearance of Dobb in front of me. Here I ain't had no flicking grub. Why not? They won't give me none not without a chitty. See the orderly sergeant. Dobb retires muttering, I finish my duff.

Back to the office. There I find the rest of the runners about to operate on Williams's more outstanding blackheads. Those on the back of his neck are now receiving attention. Williams is screaming blue murder; Pritchett, grinning in the background, has whipped a pin from his lapel and is gouging with it at something that turns out to be a mole. This pastime is curtailed at my entrance; the runners, joined by Dobb, go off after cups of tea.

I do the sports programme for the PT Sergeant: it includes a series of exercises for unarmed combat; how to disarm a sentry, Japanese stranglehold, etc. The siren goes; Jerry flies low over the roofs; ack-ack gunfire flaps like washing in a wind. Sound of aeroplane engine receding; the all-clear coincides with the arrival of today's despatch rider, a man about seven-foot tall, his height added to by his crash-helmet, who once figured prominently in a courts-martial case. I ask him What's the time. Twenty past two. The time is eternally twenty past two according to despatch riders. They are always eager to get off and twenty past two is the time scheduled for their departure. They are not so eager to come back, especially those with homes in the neighbourhood of BHQ. Of course there are always excuses—a new motorbike, hold-ups at Companies, engine trouble, a breakdown miles from anywhere. At one time all these reasons for delay recurred regularly, sometimes all at once, and Don-Rs started to roll in after dark. I then instituted a time-sheet to be sent in to the adjutant once a month, on which the names of the Don-Rs returning late were entered in red ink. Engine trouble immediately ceased, Companies dished out despatches on the dot, and Don-Rs, muttering Rotten regimental basket under their breaths, were in the office by half-past four.

But now the time is twenty past two according to the Don-R; two o'clock according to everyone else. He has twenty minutes' wait, he does it in the tea-shop downstairs. I finish off the PT programme, concluding with a a blood-curdling exercise of combined arm-lock and kidney-punch.

Again the despatch rider climbs the stairs and stands with his top boots and his yellow gloves, and despatch case invitingly open. The RSM appears at the last moment with a colossal package of Training Pamphlets to be tied on to the back of the bike. At last he's off, then everybody remembers something urgent they should have sent. Too late, save it, 'll do tomorrow.

SIX AIDS TO GOOD SHOOTING

What's that noise on the landing outside? Sounds like rifle butts again. The noise resolves itself into a shout from downstairs of EMPLOYED MEN GET ON PARADE. Pritchett rushes in with his rifle and says Rossy have you forgotten. Hell, I had. It's Thursday, when half the employed personnel do their rifle revision; the other half who do it on Monday go to the baths. Get my equipment quick. He brings it down, I buckle on belt and bayonet, sling my rifle, and we thunder down the stairs. The parade has marched off, we can't see anyone at all. There's a squad in the distance but it turns out to be the NCOs Cadre drilling under the RSM. He waves us sternly towards an even further group of men, at first invisible because they are lying flat on the ground behind bushes. As we approach they turn into familiar figures: Bentick, the one-eyed storeman, Hansford from the Officers' Mess, L/C Smith of the QM's, Kirkland and Draper. They have small targets stuck in the ground in front of them and are in the charge of a corporal new to the company.

He gives them UNLOAD, they work their bolts and stagger to their feet, Kirkland losing his balance completely and falling to the ground. Pritchett and I line up with the rest. The corporal scratches his head. What they give you usually on these bloody parades. The rifle, Corp.

Yes I know but which lesson. We was on the lying load last time. Okay well carry on with that. All of you got dummies.

Pritchett and I haven't; we get five apiece. Squad, lying—LOAD. Down we get, fumbling with our pouches. Keep your eyes on the target, look down only when inserting the rounds in the breech-charger guide. There's a further delay while I get my glasses out and adjust them. We fire five dummies, reload with a further five (imaginary). You, third man, what's your name, Draper: what's the first rule of aiming. Keep the sights upright, Corporal. Why don't you do it then. Right, rest.

We lie on our sides; the corporal squats on his hams beside us. How long's this bloody thing go on for? Three quarter hour Corp. Ah to hell. The ground is hot, there's a smell of sun-warmed grass and rifle-oil. Bentick sings out suddenly, Watch your step, Corp, here comes an officer. Righto, blokes, look as though you're doing something. The officer draws near, it's Lieutenant Stroud. The corporal says in a loud voice as he comes level: Give us the six aids to good shooting. We rattle through them, the corporal salutes, Lt Stroud passes on, switching at the long grass with his stick. We relax immediately, the time is looked at. Ten minutes to go. 34 Platoon with their towels marches past on the road, bound for the baths. There are distant shouts from squads drilling out of sight somewhere. ONE two-three ONE. ONE two-three ONE. ORDER—hup! Old Smudger Smith, the post corporal, cycles past with a sack slung over his shoulder.

What's the time now. Quarter to, Corp. Right, unload. Clip up your dummies. As I rise my equipment falls off me. But who cares, the parade's over. Squad Dis-miss! Pritchett limps along beside me telling about the gangster film he saw last week. I hand over my equipment for him to take up stairs; Smudger Smith, locking his door, says Nothing for you Rossy. There seems to be no one else about; I enter the CSM's office for our afternoon chat. He's sitting at his desk, fags are mutually offered. The conversation opens on traditional lines. Well sir how are you. Proper browned-off. So am I. Roll on the end of the war.

We count the number of absentees, read out the choicest entries in the crime-file. Cpl Dexter's latest romance, the time when the CSM was fed through his ankles. He pulls down his socks to show me the scars where tubes were inserted. And believe it or not you felt as though you'd had a blinking good meal afterwards.

A knock on the door. Come in, yes what d'you want. It's Pte Ames. Can he have his afterduty pass please sir. All right, half a tick. But when it comes to the point the pass cannot be found. We look in all the boxes, in the pay office, under the tablecloth. No pass anywhere. Are you sure you put it in. Pte Ames is positive. He has begun to sweat and to nervously unclasp his hands. He joins in the search. We look in the corners, under the table, the CSM turns out his pockets. A screwed-up ball of paper in the washbasin: ah, what this! Ames's pass is found. The list of cricket fixtures that the CSM's been looking for all morning also comes to light in this way. Ames snatches his pass, counterfoil and all, and dashes down the stairs before anyone can stop him, pursued by a shout of laughter from the CSM.

We look out of the window. About time that blasted despatch rider rolled in. A tramp of feet on the stairs. Ah, that's him maybe. But no, it's the rest of the staff back from wherever they've been. Are the despatches in. No not yet. Wells comes back from the baths with his face all covered with blood and crimson lipstick. He'd slopped a tart about in the doorway, had a fight with a sailor. The sailor, obscurely connected with the tart in some fashion, had socked Wells without warning on the snout. The story is told several times, Wells mops at his nose with the bath towel. Flicking nuisance, may spoil my chance with that waitress to-night. Dobb creeps up the staircase clean for once: he's been supervised by a lance-corporal in his bath.

Then a motorbike shudders to a standstill outside. We all rush to the window; it is, it isn't, it is. The despatch rider drops packages and receipt books on my desk. He proudly says, Dead on time; the red ink bottle is not uncorked. Everyone descends on me before I can sort anything out; I say For Pete's sake. Signatures are scrawled, the motorbike roars off up the street. The despatches are ready for distribution. WELLS WILLIAMS PRITCHETT DOBB. They appear but minus Dobb. Whose turn is it to take the stuff out. Ain't mine. Nor mine. I took 'em yesterday, it's flicking Dobb. Where is Dobb. Echo answers where, Dobb doesn't answer his name. Cpl Dexter is called in, he keeps watch and pounces on Dobb creeping out the back way.

What, me again? Cor stone a crow I done em Tuesday. Wells says Bleeding liar; gets his cap knocked off by a right-hander. Dobb dances about with his fists up, Cpl Dexter says That'll do. At last Dobb bicycles off, bent low over the handle-bars. I stuff the Second-in-Command's stuff in a special envelope and throw it in a cupboard to await his arrival from leave. Padlock off, padlock on. Key in pocket. I prepare to knock off. But no, there's a sudden outcry. It's the Captain. The urgent return to the adjutant has reappeared once more, inscribed in green pencil THIS RETURN IS INCORRECTLY RENDERED. READ A.C.I.s. A.C.I.s are thumbed through, at last the required pro-forma is found, I rattle it off on the Imperial. The men in denims are queuing up outside the CQMS. But he's gone, they're foiled again. Come back tomorrow.

Now I really do knock off. Down the road past the swimming pool and the sign STATIC WATER. Up the town.

END OF A PERFECT DAY

The town is approached only by hills. The most convenient is one appropriately named Convalescent Hill. Trees lean drunkenly sideways with the effect of surrealist landscape. I climb through a barricade, bump my head once, recover my balance and make for a café. Bacon, chips, peas, two cheese sandwiches, and a black coffee. The order is as invariable as the day's routine. The café is all right to eat in but not for any other purpose. I emerge into the High Street again, there are few people about and nothing to do. At the Plaza Mickey Rooney; at the Picturedrome Madame X. The shops close at six. There is a public library and two canteens: the YM and the Methodist. I choose the latter; too many matelots in the YM. Under the stone lintel a neon-lit WELCOME. Orange juice and sandwiches at the counter: a white-haired woman in a picture hat presides. The Minister circulates among the ping-pong players. I enter the reading room: stained glass windows, leather chairs, a bookcase containing an odd assortment of children's and religious books: 'COBBER NOB SECOND MATE', 'SIMPLE TALKS ON THE HOLY SPIRIT'.

I settle down to write, someone plays the same tune over and over again on a piano in the games room. Men step over your feet with plates of cakes and cups of tea slopping into the saucer. One trips and drops the lot. Shattered china and a steaming brown puddle on the floor. An incredibly old man with a purple nose peddles newspapers: Anyone like the latest? A lance-corporal asks me for a light; some men start singing to the piano; a girl of about sixteen, daughter of one of the servers, sits down in the next armchair and talks. I kissed her once under the mistletoe at Christmas and she's never got over it. It's impossible to work here, I decide to go back and type out what I've written.

Down the hill; along the seafront; the women's services in pairs, arm in arm, trailed by soldiers and aircraftmen on the hunt. The chase comes to a giggling conclusion among the laurel bushes and benches of the gardens overlooking the sea. I go the opposite way; in the Jazz, the huge hotel of black and blue bakelite (best appointed ballroom on the coast) there's a dance on: Smiler waltzing with his WAAF, the officers saying 'Have another' in the upstairs lounge. The signals office is surrounded by small civilian girls who've not long left school but have already the airs and graces of the Garbo. The picquet man clicks his heels at the door of HQ. There is funny business of a mock salute and requests for rude books to read. The jankermen are reporting to Cpl Dexter in full pack. What about your water-bottle? Forgot to fill it Corp. If you was in the flicking desert you wouldn't forget. Double back and report again with it full.

I sit at the window in the fading light; downstairs the blackout boards are being manoeuvred into position. I've half an hour to do some typing before lights out. Tomorrow the Second-in-Command comes back, I shan't have time. Bed and before you know it, reveille; breakfast; and then the majors bell, silent for the past seven days, starting to ring. Despatches and postage; typing and Mercer's Café; Wells and Rosie; Dobb being dirty; Williams being Welsh. The same day after day; the only change recorded on the calendar. My leave's not due for another two months.

Old Ginger

*   *   *

GINGER, OF COURSE, WASN'T REALLY OLD: WHEN I KNEW HIM AT the Infantry Training Centre in 1941, he cannot have been more than 26 at the most. His face, however, might have belonged to a man of any age up to 40: roughly rectangular in shape, with a uniform brick-red complexion, lashless and, apparently, lidless eyes, and hair, cropped very close, furry in texture and worn in a fringe at the front, of a colour that had earned him his nickname.

There was an odd prehistoric quality, a suggestion of the troglodyte, in his shambling walk, long body, bow legs and loosely swinging arms that caused orderly-sergeants at first to single him out on sight for various duties: though it was not long before they learned to recoil in horror from the thought of assigning him to even the simplest task. The sound of his voice, alone, was sufficient to make them shrink, and if he ambled up to address them they would at once start to sketch wide, shooing gestures and to yammer unintelligibly.

It is impossible to reproduce on paper the full effect of Ginger's speech: I can imitate it, vocally, to perfection, but people always complain that they can't understand what I'm saying.

We learned, in time, to understand Ginger, but it was not easy; for his utterance appeared to be impeded by the presence of some half-chewed substance in his mouth: this being partially due to the fact that he invariably started to smile when about to speak, as though the act of articulation were in itself a cause for irrepressible mirth.

In sartorial matters, particularly, Ginger proved himself to be a strong individualist. His tin hat, that was much too small, was camouflaged, instead of being sprayed with the rough grey stucco then in force at the depot. His gas-cape, on the other hand, was not camouflaged, or of the semi-transparent sort laid down in orders, but rubberised and rolled in a manner peculiarly his own. When boots were supposed to be dubbined, Ginger's shone, as his comrades paradoxically put it, like muck; his equipment was not khaki-blancoed like everybody else's, but bright grasshopper green; so were his anklets web, which he wore the wrong way round.

This may have been because he never read DO's or Company Detail. Some said he was unable to read at all, and certainly he was never seen with a newspaper or book. On the other hand he was undoubtedly able to write. Much of his time, off parade, was occupied in writing long letters to his girl, who was known as the Brown Bomber.

The Bomber lived somewhere up north, and no photographs of her were ever exhibited; if questioned on the subject, Ginger would give his special laugh, which even I am unable to imitate, and say: 'Well, mates, she's a bit of an old bag, see?'

Many of the letters, which had SWALK inscribed, several times, on the backs of the envelopes, were written while Ginger crouched close to the light from the barrack-room stove and most of us were asleep.

This was during a period when the depot was being bombed nightly and we were liable to be ordered to the trenches at any moment. Ginger sat up fully dressed, with his equipment on, waiting for the wail of the air-raid warning. He imagined this sound to be the cause of the explosions which shortly followed it: once, when asked why he didn't get into kip, he answered: 'I'm waiting for the sirens to start dropping their load.'

Once Ginger developed boils and went sick. He returned from the MI Room with a broad grin, bearing a slip of paper which he showed proudly to all of us. 'Here, take a screw at this, mates. They made me a doctor, see! MD, it got here.' Nothing would persuade him that the initials on the paper stood for Medicine and Duty instead; and for a time he sulked because we refused to address him by his new title.

Again, when placed on a charge because a spider ran out of his rifle during small arms inspection, he imagined that he'd been awarded CB; a sort of decoration, instead of being confined to barracks; and was only convinced of this latter face by the sudden appearance of regimental police in our midst, after he'd failed to appear at the guardroom half an hour before reveille.

It was a trying time for all of us, since Ginger had often to be forcibly strapped into his equipment in order to report; Ginger himself was disgruntled, and frequently muttered: 'Cod this for a game of tin soldiers'; but the RP corporal, who was obliged to receive him every 30 minutes after parades were over, found it most trying of all.

At Ginger's third appearance in quick succession, for he had little conception of the passage of time, this NCO rose clutching his head and uttering roars of distress, and refused to let him enter the guard-room at all. Thereafter, Ginger was put on no more charges.

But suddenly, after the incident of the spider, Ginger began to take great pride in his rifle, which had once had to have the gauze put through it. He cleaned and oiled it more than slightly; the shining barrel was always being presented for our inspection; he polished the wood-work and inserted peas in the magazine so that it would rattle smartly when presenting arms on parade.

It transpired that his greatest ambition was to go on the range. He wrote to the Brown Bomber all about this: but as the day approached, our platoon-sergeant was seen shaking his head dubiously. He remem-bered the time when, on grenades, Ginger was discovered just in time peering into the aperture of his pineapple to find out what made the thing work, having first extracted the pin.

In the end, however, Ginger was allowed to embus with the rest of the recruits.

On the range itself, he donned a large pair of steel-rimmed spectacles, which gave him an other-worldly appearance, and the chin-strap of his steel helmet had to be adjusted twice so that it would not strangle him. Sergeant Ames watched anxiously as Ginger's turn approached and live ammo was issued to him.

At last came the command, and Ginger charged rapidly towards the firing-point, with the air of one about to storm a barricade. He flung himself flat on the ground and inserted five rounds in the breech; then squeezed the trigger convulsively twice, before any further fire-order could be given.

This attracted the attention of the commanding officer, who'd sud-denly appeared from nowhere and now advanced on Ginger with his stick raised in admonition. 'No, no, no. That man there. Don't fire at the barrage balloon, and not at the corporal—aim at the target, man!'

The sound of his voice startled Ginger, who, like most of us, held the CO in awe. He rolled over on his back, pointing the rifle in the air. There came a sharp report followed by a stunned silence, during which the rifle slid out of Ginger's hands; luckily, this time, without exploding.

He remained staring up at the CO, who, in turn, stood rigid, staring down at him. Then Sergeant Ames, recovering, rushed forward, snatching up the rifle with one hand, and hauling Ginger to his feet with the other.

The rest of us converged on the firing-point and stood mutely round the Colonel, who himself was temporarily unable to speak. He was a man of iron nerve, but on the other hand he had not been so near death since Dunkirk.

At last he raised his stick and pointed with it towards the bus that stood empty in the background; as Ginger was led away, his voice could be heard making a muffled protest. 'But, Sarnt, I want to shoot. I want to shoot, at the target.'

'They got me down for a medical board, mates,' Ginger told us, after we'd finished boiling out our rifles that night. He looked sad, and did not smile as he spoke. 'Maybe you will get made a doctor this time, Ginge,' the blokes said to cheer him up, but Ginger shook his head gloomily. Somehow he seemed to know.

On the morning Ginger was due to go off on discharge leave, as we were getting our dressing for company drill, there came a sudden shout from the CSM. 'What the devil's that man doing here? In civvies? Sergeant, get him off the square right away! Gillo!'

All heads automatically turned to see old Ginger shambling towards us, hatless and wearing a cobalt blue suit with gamboge-coloured shoes, the heels of which clicked together as he came to attention in front of the sergeant. There was a brief dialogue, during which the CSM again shouted: 'What's the fellow want? Take him away, I tell you!' 'He says he wants to say good-bye to his mates, sir.'

The CSM had by now recognised Ginger in his unfamiliar guise. He gulped and, like the CO after he'd been shot at, seemed bereft of the power of speech. Then, after a pause during which some of us thought he'd burst, he waved his hand towards our platoon and stood back with arms tightly folded, while Ginger, like a visiting royalty, went up and down the ranks shaking hands with all of us, including the NCOs and finally the sergeant.

Then he approached the CSM himself and stopped two paces short of him, standing again to attention and saying something that sounded like 'Sah'. The CSM replied to this with a sort of bow. He still hadn't recovered his speech.

Ginger turned about, and without more ado set off across the square at a brisk marching pace, though he did not actually swing his arms.

Nor did he look back, even when the CSM called us to attention in a voice that showed his vocal chords to be once more in full working order.

The general opinion of this farewell performance seemed to be that poor old Ginger was up the pole. 'Shove him in the bin without his heels have time to touch the ground, they will in civvy street.'

I'm not so sure, myself. For, as Ginger grinned up at me and his rough, freckled hand grasped mine, one of the lashless, lidless eyes had simultaneously closed in a slow, deliberate, unmistakable wink.

Second Lieutenant Lewis

*   *   *

I

I'M NO GOOD AT DATES AND I DON'T KEEP A DIARY; SO IT MAY HAVE been spring or summer 1942, I can't really remember.

I stepped into the hall of BHQ over two janker-wallahs on hands and knees scrubbing down the chequered tiles; a smell of yellow soap steamed up all around me; the door knob of Company office fell off with a clatter as the door itself opened. Corporal Dexter came out: shirt sleeves and a big grin, scratching his chest.

'Hey, Rossy, where'd you get to? There's an officer been round looking for you,'

'Let him look,' I said. 'I'm off duty.'

'Never 'eard of it. A soldier's on duty twenty-four hours a day.'

Dexter had a whole store of these idiotic army catch-phrases, which he repeated as though each were an epigram coined fresh by him that very moment. He was permanent orderly sergeant, Category C, and underneath his bluffness and easy going air he enjoyed the authority. In civvy street he had been a manufacturer of ladies' straw hats.

He said: 'Don't give a bullock what you do, meself. All I know is he said for you to report to him straightaway, soon's you come in.'

The morning'll be soon enough,' I said. I took for granted it was one of our subalterns: the twenty-year-old school prefect type who was always asking me how to spell something, or perhaps Lieutenant Buckley who wanted some typing done in my spare time. I was on my way again when Dexter's voice arrested me.

'Ain't one of our mob. He's a Taff. One pip. Name of,' he looked at a pencilled scrap of paper in his hand, 'Lewis. Mr Lewis. Said you was to report down the road, their HQ. Asked for you very special, by name an' all.'

He broke off to bawl out the jankermen, who'd stopped scrubbing and squatted back on their heels to enjoy our dialogue. I was intrigued, I knew of no Welsh one-pipper named Lewis, and it was curiosity, not obedience to an order, that drove me out into the evening sunshine along what had once been the marine parade, past the rusty hoops of Dannert wire cutting off the pebbly beach and the sea in which mines bobbed like buoys.

A guard on the gate of the Welsh Headquarters halted me. Mr Lewis'd be eating his dinner; Officers' Mess; third house on the left, I went in there; it seemed uninhabited: bare boards echoing to my boots, flakes of fallen plaster, wallpaper peeling off. I shouted. An orderly appeared from the kitchen with a mug of tea in his hand. He said he'd see. He disappeared up some stairs. In a few moments a young officer came running lightly down these. He wore one pip and service dress, but without his Sam Browne belt, as though he were awaiting trial by court martial. He had a Welsh face, dark, with eyes set deep.

I came smartly to attention and saluted. '6027033 Private Ross J. reporting for duty, sir.'

To my surprise the face of Mr Lewis flushed even darker at this. He turned his head away and muttered something in a voice so low that I couldn't catch the words: I said: 'I beg your pardon, sir?'

He muttered, but more audibly this time: 'I'm Alun Lewis.' He held out his hand. In a second we were shaking hands heartily. I said: 'I'd no idea. They just said Mr Lewis and I was to report to you straight away.'

'The fools,' he said. 'My god, isn't that typical. When you saluted I thought you were making fun of me.' He smiled, a quick boyish grin. He spoke very quickly, too, and with a strong Welsh intonation which I found difficult at first to understand. Later this wore off and I discovered it was a mark of embarrassment. He was extraordinarily shy. He said: 'But come upstairs. There's only one fellow there, the others are all out. Gone to the dance.'

We started to climb the stairs and I said: 'How did you know I was here?'

'Your padre told me. When he said your name was Ross and you were a writer, I thought you must be Hugh Ross Williamson.'

'I never thought you were Wyndham Lewis,' I said.

That set us back again; his face flushed up and he muttered some-thing I couldn't catch. I soon learnt not to make wisecracks of that sort; they only upset him. We reached the door of the Mess and it was my turn to be embarrassed. How should a private behave when invited into the Officers' Mess? I decided it must be a social occasion and removed my cap, as if going up before the MO. This obviated the need for saluting the other subaltern whom Alun Lewis now introduced me to, and as the table was between us we didn't have to shake hands. His eyes nearly fell out of his head when Lewis asked me to sit down and have some coffee. They'd finished dinner and the orderly was clearing away. When this was served we were all at a loss, Lewis jumped up and looked out of the window. It faced on to the sea, a ship could be seen way out, we looked at this through field glasses. But at last even the ship was exhausted as a topic of conversation and we sat down again. Cigarettes were handed round and then the other subaltern excused himself: he had to do his tour as duty officer.

Once he'd gone, Lewis said: You see, I wanted to talk to you, because I thought you could tell me about India. I'm being posted there any day now. Or is that a military secret?' He smiled.

'Not to me,' I said. 'Everyone knows your mob's bound for India. But why I should be able to tell you about it I can't imagine.'

Lewis stared at me astounded. He said: 'But surely you know India well?'

'Never been there in my life.' Then, too late, I realised. At that time I'd only had two stories printed, and both of them dealt with India—or, to be precise, Madras. I now had to explain how I had acquired my material. This story is always a let down, and leaves people with a feeling that they oughtn't to meet writers whose stories they have read.

Lewis was no exception. He was disappointed. He said: 'I've just read another story of yours. In *Fortune Anthology*. It's not about India.'

'No,' I said. 'It wasn't. It was about a man of thirty seducing a girl of sixteen in a seaside hotel.'

Lewis's face had begun to flush and his Welsh accent came on again. 'I've to review the *Anthology* for *Tribune*. I wonder if you'll mind,' here he coughed and looked into his coffee, 'if I don't mention your story?'

'Not at all. Do you think it's so bad?'

'No, no. But you see it's about sex. I couldn't possibly say anything about it.'

'Because I don't treat sex seriously?'

He nodded. That sent me off into a denunciation. I particularly hate the idea of sex treated as a solemn fetish. I couldn't understand this attitude, which seemed to me puritanical, in a writer who produced a fine sensual story like *The Wanderers*. It seemed like hypocrisy. It was not that, as I understood later, and Alun Lewis was not a puritan. But his deep love and respect for women, the fact that his wife was expecting a child at the time when they were about, any moment, to be separated, made him inimical to anything that savoured of a sophisticated approach to sex. We argued for a while but Lewis remained unconvinced. He coughed and kicked the table leg doggedly. The talk switched from sex to technical problems in writing. He had a great admiration for the stories of Flying Officer X, and asked me if I knew who that was. He said he himself was writing some stories about the army and we went to his room to look at the MSS.

His room was a tiny cubby hole with a window looking out to a wall: no bigger and no better—except for the camp bed and the small table piled with army pamphlets—than my own bunk at BHQ. Lewis sat down on the bed, ran his fingers through his dark hair which had just been cut: his OC had talked about curling pins and violins. Some of the pamphlets slipped off the table and lay scattered on the floor; ABCA, WAR, Battle and Weapon Training, War Office Memoranda: Lewis looked at them with despair.

'I've got to swot all these up somehow,' he said. He'd just come back from a battle course. It'd been hell and yet he'd enjoyed it. This was what he hated: the paper work, swotting up pamphlets, reports to prepare, red tape and routine, always something to remember that had slipped the mind; he voiced the eternal hope of the soldier. It'll be different out there,' and then: 'But it's a long way to go.'

He showed me two stories called that; with a third one, as yet unfinished, they were to form a trilogy. He showed me one called Flick and gave me a bundle of MSS, to take away and read. At this moment a knock came on the door. I thought it would be Lewis's Officer Commanding, come to give him a bollock for fraternising with a private soldier. It wasn't. Instead it was our C of E Chaplain, who had been instrumental in bringing us together.

This padre asked me as a favour not to write anything about him. I have already broken my promise, so will not say any more, except that he was one of the most intelligent and understanding men whom I ever came across during my service in the army.

The padre did not stay long, but before he knocked out his pipe and went, the constraint remaining between Lewis and myself was completely gone. We agreed to go and have one in the pub. When we got outside Lewis had to rush back in for his Sam Browne: 'I'm always forgetting the damn thing.' He walked along the street beside me buckling on the belt. My RSM was passing on the other side of the parade. He gave Lewis an eyes-right and his stiff jerky salute, imitated behind his back through the battalion. Lewis attempted to return the salute and the belt fell to the ground. He stopped to retrieve it while the RSM passed on stiffly disapproving in his rubber-soled shoes.

'I made a mess of that,' Lewis said ruefully, getting the Sam Browne round him at last. 'An RSM, too.'

'That's my RSM,' I said. 'Used to be a milkman.'

'Nothing against him,' Lewis said. 'That's class distinction.'

I said: 'It's something against him when he uses his wartime authority to work off the past grievances and an inferiority complex. He's more class conscious than either of us. I bet you he votes Conservative.'

Lewis couldn't see my point, although he admitted to having had some pretty bloody sergeant-majors in his time.

Comparing notes about the sergeant-majors brought us to the pub. This was jammed to the doors. It took ages to get a drink, and then they'd only mild. We had to shout to make ourselves heard. Soldiers from Lewis's regiment kept on coming up to greet him and to offer him drinks. Eventually they shouted 'Time' and we left. Corporal Dexter, hanging on the gate chatting with the curious women who gave us haircuts, turned and saluted. This time Lewis managed to return the compliment without dropping his stick or his service dress cap falling off. Dexter stared after him open mouthed. Neither of us had the army knack of surface smartness, and by military standards we must have seemed, officer and private, a pretty scruffy pair.

'Did you ever put in for commission?' Lewis asked me.

'Failed the WOSBE test,' I told him. 'Returned unsuitable.'

'I'm not certain I shouldn't have stayed in the ranks,' Lewis said. 'I thought as an officer I'd be able to do something for the men. But one's more helpless than ever.'

The sense of helplessness and the thought of the pamphlets that remained to be swotted up in the small airless room, while the poems, the stories, stayed unwritten: these were the things that oppressed him. Had it not been for his wife, the idea of India—the jungle, the Japs, something doing at last—would have seemed a welcome opportunity: one that I myself, being without ties, certainly envied him.

I asked how his brother officers treated the idea of his being a poet. At first they'd regarded it as rather rum, made contemptuous little jokes about Shakespeare and asked him to make up smutty limericks, but then a photograph of him was found in an old copy of *Lilliput* and the Mess was impressed. Fame could reach no higher: unless, of course, the photograph had appeared in *Men Only*. Now his writing was regarded as a harmless pastime, so long as it didn't interfere with his efficiency as an officer. It was generally hoped, however, that India would knock all that nonsense out of him.

We arrived at the Mess and Lewis sighed—the pamphlets awaited him inexorably upstairs. He said: 'You must show me your stories too.'

As we were in the streets I raised my hands to salute. Lewis said: 'For Christ's sake don't do that,' seized my hand and shook it. Then he doubled inside and I could hear him running up the stairs. But my RSM had observed our parting handshake from the door of BHQ, where he was giving the Picquet Commander a dressing down.

'Ah, Ross,' he said as he came up, showing in a crafty smile his greenish teeth under the clipped white moustache. 'Going up in the world, aren't you?'

'Sir?' I said.

'Consorting with officers. Who was that? Your brother?'

'A brother writer, sir,' I said.

'Ah, that explains it; I thought something of the sort. I observed him putting on his Sam Browne belt in the street.' The RSM shook his head. 'These civilians—writers and such-like—you can't make soldiers out of 'em.'

'Sir,' I said stiffly—I was standing to attention—'I didn't know that it came within your province to comment on the dress of commissioned officers belonging to another regiment.'

The RSM opened his mouth. He gasped, and looked round to make sure the Picquet Commander was out of hearing. His eyes narrowed but he knew I had him knackered, as the saying goes. He said: 'One of these fine days you'll go a bit too far, Private Ross, and I'm warning you.'

'Yes, sir,' I said, and went on upstairs to my office. I had meant to write a short story that evening, but I sat down and read Lewis' instead. I started with 'Private Jones' and ended with 'The Prisoners'. This is not a work of literary criticism and the stories have now all been published and can speak for themselves. I will say only this: that after reading them, the army stories which I myself was trying to write seemed by contrast a joke in rather bad taste. This feeling had worn off by the next morning, but I went to bed profoundly dissatisfied with myself and my work.

I sent my stories back to Lewis next day by an orderly who happened to be taking a message to the Welsh HQ. He returned with an odd story. He had accosted a fatigue party who were coal heaving outside—why, at that time of year, I can't imagine. He asked where Mr Lewis could be found. One of the fatigue party, in shirt sleeves and covered with coal dust, had turned and said: 'Here I am.' This had so shaken the orderly that he'd delivered the packet of MSS without remembering to salute. I don't suppose that Lewis minded.

II

I saw him several times after that. We ate steak and chips together in a café along the seafront, full of snobbish Wrens talking at the tops of their voices about the RAF officers who'd taken them out. I didn't show Lewis any of my stories, except one which again dealt with sex, and part of a novel that I was writing. I think that to a great extent he disapproved of what I wrote, I remember him speaking once of the enormous responsibility which a writer should feel towards his characters having once called them into being. He spoke of this almost with awe.

I do not think that in civilian life we could have been friends. We were too different. Where he was genuinely humble and modest, I am arrogant and didactic. Where he felt sympathy and love, I feel anger and contempt. I have only a film gangster's kindness towards small things—animals, children—Lewis had a deep tenderness towards life itself: a nostalgic yearning for his Welsh village, his wife, whereas I have no roots and regard family life with fascinated horror. That doesn't mean to say I am ascribing all the virtues to Lewis, to myself all the faults. I don't necessarily consider them faults or virtues in either case. We were simply of different temperaments: even our aims as writers were violently opposed. But in the army, where the strangest friendships are struck up, it was natural for us to draw together and to talk of intimate ambitions which in civvy street—in a Soho pub or the Café Royal— we might never have discussed.

Our friendship excited much hostile comment in our respective regiments, owing to the differences in rank. Lewis, being an officer, got the worst of it. He had several open rows, whereas I only had to put up with Corporal Dexter talking about my officer pal and the RSM's innuendoes.

One night we were drinking in the saloon bar of a posh hotel. Officers were staggering about with blondies and popsies in all directions. Suddenly Lewis's Officer Commanding walked in. He gave us a terrible yellow stare and said: 'Lewis, I'll see you in the Mess later.'

Lewis flushed. He was furious. Outside in the street he cursed. Later he got a blowing up, and after that we were driven out into back streets where the OC was unlikely to see us. We used to walk aimlessly about or dodge into furtive pubs.

On the night before Lewis's mob was due to move, we sat on a rusty abandoned roller in a field of long grass, Lewis didn't talk much. He was depressed. Once he said: 'I'm not sure that I want to go really,' and later: 'But there'll be something to get to grips with out there.'

I said, 'Write to me.' We shook hands and he walked on down the road to see if they'd got his gear ready. He had his Sam Browne belt slung wrong again.

That's the last time I saw him.

'Your officer pal's gone then, Rossy,' Corporal Dexter said with relish next morning. 'See the Taffys've moved.'

'Yes,' I said. 'He's gone.'

He never wrote to me, or if he did I never got the letter.

In March 1943, I was travelling to hospital under escort, for I was at the time awaiting court martial: as the RSM predicted, I had gone a little bit too far at last. On a station bookstall I saw *The Last Inspection and Other Stories*, by Alun Lewis, and bought the book. I wondered how he was getting on; but not for long, as I had my own troubles and plenty of them. Much later, when I was a civilian again, I heard he'd been killed in action.

Kiedrych Rhys heard the news first and rang up the War Office. They didn't know what he was talking about.

'This is the War Office.'

'I am inquiring about Second Lieutenant Lewis, believed killed in action.'

'Oh, I see. At first you said a poet or something. Why didn't you say he was an officer?'

Adventures in Film (1):
Getting into Pictures

*   *   *

ONE DAY A YEAR OR TWO AGO I HAPPENED TO BE GLANCING IDLY
through a ciné weekly in a barber's shop when I was confronted by a
photograph of a well-known producer sitting at his desk in an attitude
of dejection, his hair suitably dishevelled, the floor all around piled
high with plays in typescript, novels in their dust-jackets, and rejected
scenarios in a tattered condition.

'THE STORY'S THE THING' was the caption running in large type
above the picture of the despondent executive: for the past six months,
according to the article printed below, he had been trying without success
to find a suitable screen-subject; everything else was fixed: studio-space,
distribution-guarantee, stars under contract, finance ready for release:
the whole bag of tricks in fact. But—no story; so he couldn't proceed.

I turned the page; the next article dealt with an identical theme: this
time it was actually written by a producer and director, whose name was
a Household Word. He too was at his wits' end for material: 'serious'
writers, he deplored, took no interest in the medium; the standard of
MSS submitted fell far below that of the average published novel or play
performed upon the stage; above all, they were not written 'visually',
with cinematic requirements in mind.

My heart went out to these unhappy men in their plight: by the
time my turn in the chair came and the fibrous towel was tucked in
round my neck I had determined to help them. One of my earliest
ambitions had been to write for the films; during the war I had been
employed for that purpose by a documentary company; in a drawer at
home lay a full-length feature-script, written primarily for the screen
and overflowing with visual content. The plots of books marked down
long ago as ideal for cinema adaptation; fragmentary scenes; snatches

411

of dialogue: actual camera-angles surged up from my subconscious and swirled dizzily in montage through my head—at the moment being held down by the barber's ruthless Cypriot hand. Obviously I was the answer to the problems of these distressed impresarios; nor was my philanthropic desire to come to their aid unmixed with recollections of the fabulous sums which producers were reputed to pay for film rights; for, as usual, I was not overburdened with ready cash.

So, on leaving the hairdresser's, damp, shorn, and smelling of aromatic lotion, I at once entered a telephone-box and rang up the first producer, since his need seemed the most urgent.

'Sorry, Mr Samuelson is down at the studio today,' an apathetic feminine voice informed me.

'Couldn't I contact him there?' I asked.

'If you have an appointment.'

'No, I meant by telephone.'

'Mr Samuelson is allergic to the telephone, and he never sees anyone except by appointment.'

'It's about a story,' I said, playing what I believed to be my trump-card. I was evidently mistaken. Before, the voice had sounded merely bored; now, a perceptible note of contempt insinuated itself. 'Oh, I thought you wanted Mr Samuelson himself. Just a moment, I'll put you through to the Scenario Department.'

A series of rapid clicks, one of which almost burst my ear-drum; then another voice, also female, but brusque to the point of incivility: 'Script editor speaking'.

'I have a story that might interest Mr Samuelson. I believe he's looking for one.'

'The department's always looking for stories. Just send in a preliminary outline, typed, on a postcard. That will be sufficient for us to judge. If it shows promise we'll get in touch with you in due course. Good-bye.'

'Wait a second,' I said; 'this is a full shooting-script'.

'Haven't time to read 'em, I'm afraid, unless you're somebody frightfully well known. What d'you say your name…? Maclaren-Ross? Oh. Well, outline, synopsis, skeleton-treatment, full story-treatment, master-scene, that's the procedure. Shooting-script prepared by the director himself, if and when appointed. Not an original, is it?'

'Yes.'

'Originals considered only when submitted through a recognised and reputable agency. Inflexible company rule. Sorry.'

'But I've just read an article saying Mr Samuelson's desperate for stuff.'

'Publicity Department's pigeon, that: not mine. Good-bye.'

The receiver clicked down decisively. I waited a minute for my annoyance to abate before dialling my second string: the Household Word. In the article signed by him his ready accessibility had been strongly emphasised: in frequent interviews that I'd read, this quality had also been stressed, together with insistent references to the lack of formality characteristic of him. I was certain that, in his own interests, he would listen to reason. Recalling my experience with editors, I foresaw already the invitation to lunch, the post-prandial rounds of cognac, the story retailed in synopsis over the coffee: 'Yes, that sounds the stuff, old boy. Just push it along and we'll get it done. As for the fee...'

'I don't,' I said, 'want to speak to his secretary, nor to the script-department, but to HIM in person. Is that clear?'

'Half a tick, sir. I'll connect you right away...'

'HIS personal secretary speaking.' (Female, undoubtedly, but dulcet and soothing this time. Dressed for a cert in something clinging and soft.) 'Can I help you at all?'

'By putting me on to HIM,' I said implacably.

'HE's out just at present, and I'm not sure HE'll be back this afternoon. But I can give you HIS private number at home; if you ring about seven you're sure to get HIM...'

On the stroke of seven I was again spinning the dial. A deep contralto answered: 'HIS personal secretary speaking.'

'Surely not the one I talked to this afternoon?'

'Oh no. That would be Miss Sims at the office. I'm HIS home secretary, so to speak.' (A low, gurgling laugh.) 'Unfortunately HE's left for the weekend. If you could give me a message... oh, a story! But that's wonderful, the poor lamb doesn't know which way to turn for one. Best thing you can do is to write HIM a letter, and I'm sure HE'll ring you back Tuesday morning... yes, I'll see HE gets it directly HE comes in.'

But on Tuesday my telephone did not ring at all. Nor on Wednesday or Thursday. On Friday I rang the dulcet voice at the office. 'I'm afraid HE is weekending in Paris... No reply to your letter? But that's most extraordinary... very unlike HIM indeed. Perhaps it never got there at all: lost in the post... most unreliable, the mails, nowadays. If you care to write again, though, and bring it down by hand, I can guarantee HE'll have it first thing on Wednesday when HE returns…Oh, you will? That's very kind: I do apologise for the trouble you've been put to…'

So once again I shoved it all down on paper: the names of the books I'd written, my documentary experience, agreement with the views expressed in HIS article, request for a brief interview; and enclosed the letter with a copy of my script, for which I obtained a receipt from the commissionaire: HIS secretary being out to lunch at the time of delivery.

No immediate reply came to that either. Meanwhile, in the columns of the ciné weekly, Mr Samuelson continued to tear his hair for lack of stories; I wrote to the staff-reporter relating my own experience, but received no acknowledgement: then to the editor of the paper, with similar result. Instead, another article by HIM appeared, expressing HIS grief that the appeal HE made to writers had met with so singular a lack of response; I telephoned the office and was told by an entirely new secretary—who denied all knowledge of my letter and typescript— that her employer was away on a pleasure-cruise and not expected to return for several weeks.

Three months later a bulky package was delivered to me, wrongly addressed and re-forwarded at least twice through the dead-letter office. Inside was my script, removed from its spring-binder, roughly tied together with tape, and stained abundantly with tea and lipstick, accompanied by a typewritten note as follows:

DEAR MR McCALLUM ROSE,—We are returning herewith your script which, addressed erroneously to HIM, eventually found its way to this Department. We regret that HE is too busy personally to read scenarios submitted by unknown authors, even in the rare event of these being recommended by a recognised literary agent; and though, in our opinion, your script shows ability above the average, we are not only provided with material sufficient for some time to come, but HIS personal preference is for works whose popular appeal has already been demonstrated by their circulation in volume form, rather than for plays written specially for the screen, whose chances of success would necessarily be of a problematical nature.

Yours very truly
ISOLA VAN DEN BOSSCHE
(President, Scenario Selection Board)

Adventures in Film (2):
The Shoestring Budget

*   *   *

THE LIFT WAS OUT OF ORDER: PYROTECHNIC PICTURES ON THE very topmost floor, behind a ground-glass panel blackly engraved with the Company's name and partly obscured by the shadow of many mackintoshes hanging from within. The anteroom beyond was crowded with persons of both sexes; a typewriter stopped clattering long enough for a sleek young woman with black hair centre-parted to frown up at me and say: 'Casting Director's down the studio, and anyway we're full up for now. Sorry.'

I said: 'Mr Deepcar's expecting me, if you'll tell him I'm here.' The aspirants to stardom glared round with expressions of indignation and dislike: the secretary made a tentative display of teeth, still uncertain that I wasn't an actor trying to get past by a trick. She said: 'Wing Commander Deepcar?'

'If that's his rank.'

'Well there's two of them—cousins, you see. Dennis is Pilot Officer, Deepcar. I think the Wing Co.'s what you want—he produces!'

As if to symbolise an English summer, a ray of sunshine split the rain-clouds, spotlighting the thickset Raff-moustached young man who rose, in shirt sleeves, from a swivel chair in the inner office, offering a pew and a fag with two waves of his freckled hairy hand.

'Neville's the name, o' boy,' said the Wing Co., heartily disclaiming any more formal mode of address; 'Out of the Service now, mercy beaucoup all the same.' His eyes, by no means devoid of native shrewdness, narrowed slightly as the removal of my raincoat revealed a corduroy jacket: Bohemian, artistic, impractical, he was clearly thinking; it would shortly be my duty to disabuse him of this latter notion.

The Wing Co. went into his spiel without further ado: he and his cousin Dennis had both read stuff of mine, and they wondered if I'd any original stories suitable for filming. Not scripts: just a few lines on paper. Synopsis form. Give the general outline, see? Then, providing the Distributors approved, I'd be asked to do a short treatment: scenes, sample dialogue, that sort of thing. 'And then,' I said, 'a Full Treatment, a Master Scene Script, and a Shooting-Script—always providing the Distributors approve, naturally. In fact, they really decide what's what, and not you at all.'

'Well,' the sun was quite strong now, and the Wing Co. shifted uncomfortably, 'no producer's independent these days, o' boy. You can't make a movie without a distribution contract, now be reasonable, can you?' 'I can't make movies at all, unfortunately. No capital. And talking of money, how much would you pay? Supposing my synopsis went over big in Wardour Street, I mean?'

Deepcar gulped. He'd plainly not expected this. The persuasive smile he hurriedly assumed looked, in consequence, more like a cunning leer, or the involuntary grimace caused by a sudden twinge of toothache. Well, actually, o' boy, they expected writers to take a gamble with them in that respect. With this shoestring budget they were operating on, it just wasn't possible to lash out big sums simply for stories. Oh, admitted—no story no picture; only, let's face it, a story by itself had no star-value: 'less it was by Shakespeare or Greene or Balchin, or some wizard bloke like that, and they'd never raise the ante for any of those. 'You could always ask them to gamble with you,' I said.

'I can see you've a sense of humour, ha ha,' Neville Deepcar said. 'Seriously though, what else can we do, case like yours? If you'd written some plays now, it'd be a different cup. Got a great respect for the Drama, these Wardour Street blokes. Take that play of Dennis's—they fairly ate it up.'

'Your cousin, Pilot Officer Deepcar, is a dramatist?'

'No no, it's a script he heard on radio, had a copy somewhere, now what the heck's it called?' The door opened and a breezy blond chap grinned round it pointing a pipe like a pistol: obviously back from his midday pint. '*Lawfully Deceased*,' he said.

'*Lawfully Deceased* of course, what a man, what a memory! Shut the door, Dennis, join the fold; I was just thinking—suppose we briefed Julian here to do the script? Might even manage spot cash for once—how'd that suit, Julian o' boy?'

'How much spot cash?' I asked.

'Depends on what we've to pay for the rights,' the Wing Co. said.

'Well, let me know when you've got them.' With this I started to rise, but Dennis Deepcar intercepted me. 'Just wait while I give you the gen, really hot effort, happened to listen-in one evening, there's this wizard item coming over. Type's been dead seven years, see? Brown job, bought it in the war, only he's not actually dead at all, War Office made a bullock, he'd just lost his memory for a bit. Then, bingo! suddenly it all comes back to him, hops a crate, England, home and beauty— what's he find? Missus married another bloke meantime, real Gremlin type the new hubby, just after the dough that's all. But what's this poor perisher to do: been declared dead, RIP past seven years, legally he's gone for a Burton. Now, hold it! here comes the cleverest part...'

'Murder,' I said resignedly. 'He plans to kill wife and husband, and the law can't do a thing because he's legally dead. Right?'

'Oh, you heard it, did you? Then you'll admit it's tops, bang on, right up your street too, eh?'

I couldn't have agreed less. Nor did I really expect to hear from the Deepcars again after the interview I've just described. But there I was wrong. During the following weeks Dennis called up several times, his excitement mounting progressively at each separate stage: negotiations were afoot; author being tricky; agent bluffing; distributors ready to sign: then—crescendo—they'd got the rights at last, when could I start on the script? The fee? Ah, not Dennis's pigeon, that: the Wing Co.'d take it from there. 'Neville speaking, can't go higher than a century I'm afraid, well one-fifty perhaps, but that'd be the absolute ceiling. Half in advance? Why have a heart, o' boy, you must be Scotch. Bit down on delivery, yes, but half... Oh well, we'll go into a huddle, see what can be done, hang on till you hear from us.'

Again I expected to hear no more, and for three months I was right. Then my phone rang and a faintly Cockney voice said: 'Julian Rose?... What d'you mean—not exactly?... Oh, Ross is it, must have got the name muddled somehow. Well, Ross, this is Mister Boscobel. Pyrotechnic, you know. I'm to direct *Lawfully Deceased—You Can't Hang ME*, it's called now—and there's some work needs doing on the script... What's that? Money in advance? Well the Deepcars aren't here right now, have to talk to 'em later... Oh, and catch a cab over, will you—this is urgent!'

Mister Boscobel was younger than the Deepcars and not a RAF type: more like a Company Office Corporal who'd been an insurance clerk in civvy street. Blue suit, suede shoes, polished black hair and evasive eyes. He pushed a bundle of roneoed typescript across his desk with the stein of an unlit pipe and said: 'Now here's the provisional job. Pretty sound, only the dialogue's bit slow in patches. That's what we want you to tighten up, little job anyone can do really, take it on meself if I'd the time, only we go on the floor in a fortnight's time and I'm too pushed.'

'Who,' I asked him, 'is Gaylord Lennox?' That was the name on the screenplay. 'Gaylord?' said Mister Boscobel. 'Oh, he wrote a play couple of years ago, Sunday performance, surprised you've not heard of him, as Dennis says you write yourself… They were thinking of having you do the whole script at one point, but I felt we ought to get somebody a bit more experienced—with dialogue, I mean. Gaylord's a great pal of mine, actually.'

'Yet it's his dialogue that's weak, you say, and from the lines I'm reading here you seem to be 100 per cent right. Why doesn't he revise this himself?'

'Well matter of fact he reckons it's perfect as it stands—refused to alter anything. You know how these artists are: temperamental-like.' At this, there was a tramp of feet next door and both the Deepcars entered. 'Ah, Julian, glad you and Bill have got together, we figured you were just the job to help us out. Only needs a line changed here and there, piece of cake, do it in a couple of days easy, and we're prepared to pay out all we can…' 'Such as?' I said. Neville's eyes narrowed: 'Tenner do you?' 'Deepcar,' I said gently, 'if, as I suspect, this dialogue has to be rewritten entirely, what's the most you'll run to?' Neville rubbed his chin. 'Bad as that, eh?' 'If not worse,' I said. 'Now I'll take this stuff away and read it over lunch; we'll meet back here by three. Meantime you'd better have a ways-and-means palaver, if you expect to start shooting in a fortnight.' Neville turned to look at Boscobel, whose glance became more evasive than ever under his producer's direct stare. 'Bill,' the Wing Co. said slowly, 'I believe your chum Gaylord's made a bellows of this script.'

He had. On the dot of three, with them all assembled in the office, I said: 'Bad news, I'm afraid, blokes. The whole thing needs re-doing. Not only dialogue—though that's some of the worst I've ever read—but the complete script: scenes, situations, everything. You're welcome to get another opinion if you like, but that's mine and I'm sticking to it.' Neville looked again at Boscobel: 'Bill,' he said, 'I'll talk to you later … You too, Dennis,' and turning to me: 'How about twenty-five, o' boy—or do I hear a deathly hush.' 'You do,' I said. 'Double it.' 'Couldn't we knock it off Gaylord's fee?' said Dennis. 'NBG,' said his cousin. 'We're bound by contract. My godfathers, another fifty quid!' 'And a proper dialogue credit,' I said. Boscobel looked up. 'Gaylord'll never stand for that.' 'Won't he?' said Neville. 'Why he won't even be sitting when I've done with him … Script in four days, Julian: fifty in cash?' 'On the desk,' I said; 'Friday three o'clock.' 'Boy, you've saved our lives,' Neville told me, turning grimly toward Boscobel as I went out.

But on Friday at three, the office was empty except for the black-haired secretary, who smiled up at me as I stood before her, with the completely rewritten script in hand. 'Oh yes, just leave it on the desk, will you? Sorry they couldn't be here today, but actually something rather urgent cropped up and they'd to rush off in a flap. Neville said you were to drop the script and when he'd read it, he'd get in touch … were you looking for something?' 'Yes, a cheque. Or, rather, cash. Didn't he give it to you?' 'No, I'm afraid not … expect he means to send it on if the stuff's suitable and Mister Boscobel's passed the script, you know.' 'Unfortunately,' I said, 'he won't have that opportunity until I've been passed the money.' 'But, Mr Maclaren, this is outrageous! The Wing Commander's instructions were…' I closed the office door carefully and continued on down the stairs with the script under my arm. The lift was still out of order and there were seven flights of stairs all told.

That night the Wing Co. rang up. 'Look here, m'lad, you don't do yourself any good behaving like this…' 'Deepcar,' I said, 'if you bring the dough round tonight, I'll still let you have the script for fifty. Tomorrow it'll have gone up ten.' 'Be reasonable, o' boy—where d'you think I'd get fifty this time of night?' 'Bargain's a bargain,' I told him. 'But,' he wailed, 'how do I know the script's okay?' 'It couldn't be worse than the one you had, or the play it's adapted from, and anyway that's your funeral. Take it or leave it, chum: I'll call in the morning and the sixty had better be there—no cheques.' 'This, I suppose,' the Wing Co. said bitterly, 'must be what they call the turn of the screw.'

I got my sixty quid right enough; and presumably Mister Boscobel passed the script, for the film was released a year later as a 'B' feature (written by GAYLORD LENNOX, after a radio play by DUNSTAN GOUGH: and—in small letters underneath—Additional dialogue by Ross McLaren). The new title was *I'll Get Away with Murder!*—one which seemed particularly appropriate to me after a conversation I had with another script writer in a bar: 'Know a chappie called Gaylord Lennox?' he asked. 'Hadn't heard of him meself, but seems he scripted some little 'B' picture that's going the rounds; one of the big shots happened to like it and signed him up straight away, three-year contract, eighty quid a week and expenses. Well, good luck to him, I suppose. Some people seem to have it all.'

In Their Black Books

*   *   *

I'M MOST ALARMED. A FELLOW-AUTHOR, FRIEND OF MINE, recently received a letter from his publisher containing the following sentence: 'At least two booksellers refused to take a single copy of your last novel because they said (my italics) *you had been such a nuisance in their shops.*' The publisher added a severe rebuke: 'If you go on in this way, you will soon have every bookseller and publisher against you, which won't really help at all.'

At first I was inclined to laugh the whole thing off, until I saw by my friend's frown that he was serious: 'Trouble is, I can't remember what I did. Might have been years ago...a chance remark...some assistant overheard...These blokes are like elephants, you know, and of course they all keep in touch: word soon gets around...' Out of sympathy I grew indignant, suggesting legal action; a libel suit; damages for slander. 'And be put on the black list directly the case is over?' he said acidly. 'A bright suggestion,' and suddenly I too realised the gravity of this latest threat to a livelihood precarious even at the best of times. In my cinematic mind's eye I saw a bookseller curtly banishing a contentious author from his premises: tapping out an immediate message in morse with the same finger that had pointed to the door; I heard, on a cerebral sound-track, the decoded message broadcast by grapevine telegraph to every bookshop in Britain; a montage of headlines (in trade papers, of course) spelling out the dread sentence 'THIS MAN IS BANNED': a photograph of the miscreant on every buyer's desk; travellers proffering proof-copies of his latest work turning hopelessly away from the stern headshake, the turned-down thumb.

Then a publishers' conference, the chairman speaking: 'Got in bad with the booksellers, poor chump. Pity, that': librarians crossing off titles on their catalogue cards, rejected MSS piling up in the post: the author with threadbare suit and starved hollow face staggering through falling snow towards doss-houses, the Embankment, and a pauper's grave. It was not a pleasant picture; and with a shiver of apprehension I asked 'But can they do it?'

And of course the answer was in the affirmative. Booksellers were becoming emancipated: like daily women they had awakened to a realisation of the power that had always lain within their grasp; a new dictatorship would reign over the literary world, more stringent than the benevolent despotism so long exercised by publishers and critics: the editor's decision would no longer be final, for bookstalls would no longer stock magazines including among the contributors some outlawed name. I foresaw fresh monopolies, the monthly selection by the Booksellers Society: a return to the days when servile authors bowed before the print-sellers of Fleet Street and Milton sold for a nugatory sum the copyright of *Paradise Lost*.

Yes, all these things would clearly come to pass, and feverishly I cast about in my memory for some occasion on which I myself might have caused offence to our future masters: an ironical tone of voice, a touch of brusquerie in my manner ... Even so, I have seldom been photographed and would, with luck, pass unrecognised by even the sharpest-eyed assistant.

But, abruptly, this mood of self-congratulation faded and I came over cold: for, like a recorded play-back from the past, the echo of my voice returned to me, angrily raised—and in no mere bookshop but the main showroom of Thwarte's itself: Thwarte's, whose network of branch libraries extended not only over the realm but to the very outposts of our dwindling empire; whose directors would certainly be Ministers of the new régime—if not actually in control of it. I groaned aloud in recollection of that autumn day in 1947 when, emerging from the shops with two novels in bright jackets tucked under my arm, I was politely but firmly arrested by a tall man of military bearing, belted into a grey gaberdine raincoat, who overtook me silently, in rubber soles, on the corner of the street outside. He was the store detective; in the course of his duty he'd observed that I'd forgotten to pay for the books I was carrying as I went out. An oversight, of course. Now if I'd just come back with him to the shop ...

Situations like this do not often come my way: this one seemed to offer inimitable possibilities of enjoyment. No, I said, there was no oversight, though I had not, indeed, paid for the books in question: was he definitely accusing me of theft? If so, what about a policeman? I would fetch one myself if he liked. He was opposed to this course; we argued for a time, the detective dogged but puzzled by what he took to be my brazen effrontery. Then I tired of the game and explained that I had actually bought the books a week before, as the manager himself would confirm: this being so, I saw no reason to pay for them again.

We returned to the shop together, but this, by now, was closing down; the manager had already left for his suburban home. The detective stood outlined against a pyramid of fiction, stuffing tobacco into the bowl of a bulldog pipe: a shadow of suspicion still remained in him. 'The manager served you personally? A week ago?' 'As I told you.' 'Then why, after all this time'—he thought he had me now—'are you still carrying the books around?' 'I might want to read one of them. Any law against that?' 'Well,' rubbing his chin indecisively, 'there's no actual law…' For some reason this annoyed me. 'In that case I'll be going. If you want me again I'm at the Imperial Hotel. As for my name' (and this is the part that now makes me wince), 'there it is,' pointing at a display of my new novel, which had been issued a few days before, 'and here's my identity card as further proof. Satisfied?' The detective nodded glumly: he seemed deflated. Next day I returned to see the manager, and there, with apologies from all concerned, the matter might have ended.

But a few months later I was again about to leave the shop when a boy of repellent aspect, barely above school age but wearing neverthe-less a green assistant's badge, accosted me at the door. 'Mind paying for that book you got there, mister?' The sense of being involved in a re-current nightmare seized me for a moment, but surely what they needed was a lesson. 'All right,' I said. 'I'll go quietly.' Swollen with pride, the boy led me to a small dusty office: in it sat the detective at a desk. 'Pinching, sir,' said the boy. 'Caught red-handed.' I'd expected the detective to exhibit signs of consternation; instead he gave me a cold searching glance and said without smiling: 'Any excuse to offer this time?'

It was a grand opportunity to have more fun, but, alas, a young woman of impatient temperament awaited me on the other side of London, and I was obliged to play my trump card without delay. 'As it happens I have. If you examine the book I'm supposed to have stolen you'll find it doesn't belong to Thwarte's at all. See this bookplate: there's the owner's name—one well known to you I'm sure.' The detective said 'He could have sold it here, couldn't he? Anyway, what are you doing with it if it's his?' 'Borrow,' I said. 'Ever heard of George Borrow?' They both gaped. The boy said: 'He wants his head examined, sir.'

'You want yours slapped,' I told him. 'Now listen. Take that 'phone, ring this number, and you'll find the owner of this book lent it to me yesterday. Hurry up, I've no more time to waste.' The detective began to dial; then he said: 'Let's see—what's your name again?' 'You know my name.' 'Ah, that's what you write under. But your real name—Barnaby, isn't it?' 'No,' I shouted. 'It is not.'

Barnaby was a noted book-thief, and it was not the first time this confusion had arisen; though no facial resemblance exists, back-view we might be mistaken one for the other, both being dark-haired and about the same height, while in those days we both wore teddy-bear coats, and Barnaby, like myself, carried a cane. 'Barnaby's in gaol,' I said, 'as you should know. Ring that number now.'

My eminent friend was in. He was indignant, threatening to arrive with solicitors and CID superintendents if I were not immediately released. Yes, he'd lent me the book; no, I was not really Barnaby; and if he were in my place, he'd sue. I cut short the detective's apology with a threat of proceedings should this happen again, and a baleful glance at the repulsive boy; nevertheless they weren't quite convinced at Thwarte's: for some time afterwards, bells rang like burglar alarms whenever I appeared, and sullen-faced female adolescents followed me about in the intervals of being rude to customers; pimply-faced youths with green badges watched my every move through steel spectacles as I browsed along the shelves.

Since then, Barnaby, released from prison, has published his memoirs; *Love Life of a Book-Thief* has become a bestseller and, as a large photograph of the author adorns the dust wrapper, the detective now knows the difference between us. All the same, in Thwarte's I'm a marked man: they may even black-list me as a nuisance, unless I flee the country and hope that in time they'll forget. I'd better start packing now. Right away.

Bop

*   *   *

AT THE TABLE OPPOSITE MINE, IN A SMALL SOHO RESTAURANT, they were discussing personalities unknown to me; a ministerial young man said severly, over his spaghetti bolognaise: 'I've never quite forgiven Felix for being so Bohemian. D'you know, he once took me to a *most* peculiar place—I believe it was called a *Bebop Club*.'

This phrase, italicised with the utmost disapproval and loathing, evoked, as a coincidence alone, vivid memories in an involuntary listener: for it must have been exactly two years ago, on a summer's night as hot as this, that I myself climbed into a taxicab bound for a similar establishment, which lay beyond a no-man's land of bomb-craters and blitzed buildings somewhere north of the Tottenham Court Road.

With me were two Irishmen bent on amorous adventure and a girl called Jehane. She was a Chelsea art student, at this time almost twenty-one and complaining already of the ravages of age; in the days of her youth, when she spelt her name in a more customary manner and before she'd actually set eyes on me, she had illustrated a story of mine for a magazine: the drawing depicted the narrator, wearing steel spectacles and about five feet high, flirting with a blonde barmaid of massive build, who towered at least twelve inches above him at the counter.

Jehane herself was not tall, but sturdily built, with sloe-black eyes in a round, healthily attractive face, which showed no sign of the ravages she often complained of now that her majority loomed ahead. She had black hair clipped, apparently, with a pair of shears in what I believe was called a Petal, or Urchin, cut, and wore a sleeveless white blouse with rather tight blue slacks. Her clothes seemed to me casual enough, but Jehane was not reassured; a rigid code of informality apparently reigned among the Bebop fans: her brooch was all right, it was in fact a sort of badge; but the blouse was embroidered, an unnecessary adornment against the rules. Then bracelets: these were absolutely OUT; they were taken off and given to me to slip into my pocket. *Existentialist* clothes, Jehane said, were really the only permissible kind: otherwise you might be labelled Square, and put outside the pale. As we alighted from the cab and Jehane led us to a doorless opening in one of the bombed buildings, I noticed her cast a worried glance at my carnation and silver-knobbed cane: these accessories might indeed be considered Square, and though the two Irishmen would pass muster I was afraid the club would refuse me admittance.

My fears, however, proved groundless: though Mike insisted on tossing who paid for the tickets at five bob apiece, issued by a suicide blonde of mature years through a small guichet not dissimilar from the box office of a cinema. Music pulsed up faintly from a flight of very steep stone stairs. The long room seemed windowless: a central darkness with walls bathed in low lurid red light, below which tables were set.

The band, barely distinguishable on a raised dais beside a pocket-handkerchief floor, stopped with a shiver of drums as we came in, and the dancers returned to their seats; discerning female forms moving dimly through the gloom, Shaun and Mike began to point and mutter excitedly, like hunters within whose line of fire a herd of fabulous beasts had unsuspectingly appeared. I too watched, with interest, the members; their average age-level was between sixteen and twenty; boys in drape-suits with long jackets, mainly powder-blue, and hair styles which, to my untutored eye, resembled that affected by Mr Danny Kaye; girls in what seemed to be ski-ing trousers and white gym-tunics, wearing no jewellery save a single brooch of the type pinned to Jehane's blouse, their faces severly unpowdered, innocent of make-up, in many cases without even lipstick: their hair cut either in horizontal fringes or worn shoulder-length, lank and straight. Could their clothes be Existentialist, I wondered, and were these young people acquainted with the works of Jean-Paul Sartre? Had they read Heidegger? I looked round for Jehane to answer these questions, but she had disappeared; Shaun and Mike were now demanding drink in loud voices and indicating a lighted hatch in a corner, which appeared unmistakably to be a bar: we made for this, only to learn that the club was unlicensed, soda-pop the one drink obtainable, and that to be sucked through a straw out of a bottle. I insisted on glasses, and secured them after an altercation; we returned to our table, where Shaun and Mike planned a sortie to the nearest pub while I took another survey of the faces surrounding us. A striking feature of these was their total lack of animation: the only expression visible being one of passive boredom; there was no fraternisation, certainly no flirtation, between the sexes, nor did they sit together: the boys on one side of the room sometimes drummed rhythmic finger-tips on the table, the girls on the other sat staring straight ahead, without speaking, blank and still.

Did they perhaps smoke marijuana? Sticks of tea? Shaun, who'd once studied medicine, thought it highly likely: our suspicions were confirmed when Jehane reappeared with the proprietor and the band-leader in two. These were named Archie and Flash respectively: small swarthy men in white silk singlets who twitched and grinned and trembled spasmodically, jigging from foot to foot like minor characters in a Chandler novel: the sort that end up dead of an overdose or with an ice-pick in their backs.

'That's it,' Shaun said when they'd gone; 'every symptom.'

'Symptoms?' Jehane said, alarmed. 'What of?'

'Viper's drag, darling,' I told her; 'Mary Jane.'

'Drag?'

'Drug.'

She was shocked. 'Certainly not. Nothing like that goes on here.'

And it didn't indeed: as we soon discovered when Mike, having lost the toss, was dispatched in search of alcohol and returned with three quarter bottles of gin: one apiece. As we poured a measure of spirit into our soda-pop, un-iced to begin with, by now tepid and fizzy, we found ourselves suddenly the focus of attention: a young man at the next table saw us do it and nudged his neighbour; necks were craned, eyebrows went up, there was muttering: girls shrank as if from a razor-gang which had somehow been introduced into the Royal Enclosure at Ascot.

There was a move to call Archie and we might have been thrown out, but luckily at that moment the band, resting until now, decide to go into action: there was a preliminary roll of stage-thunder, a blinding white beam shone down on the dais, and a succession of couples took the floor.

At last, I thought, I'd be in my element: after all, I'd been practically brought up on early jazz—I'd danced the Charleston, collected records of Beiderbecke, met Ted Lewis at a party, and when young myself had shouted BOOP-A-DOOP-A-DOOP with the best. But this was to be an evening of frustration, for what the band struck up was not jazz at all, as I knew it, but a meaningless reiterant jangle of noise: nor did even Mike and Shaun have the nerve to engage in the ritual we now saw enacted before us. There was no tune and, to me, no recognisable rhythm; yet without doubt, to the devotees, outwardly mechanical and dead-pan, this music communicated some kind of ecstasy, pure, apparently sexless: in their hearts they felt a hypnotic beat.

The usual functions were reversed, all the onus of energy being on the distaff side: the boys either stood still of jogged up and down without otherwise shifting their ground, acting as a sort of axis or maypole round which their partners weaved and whirled, remaining intent, preoccupied, and expressionless the while. Each dance lasted at least twenty minutes, and between them the intervals were short: the evening had begun in dead earnest. The etiquette, with its accent on informality, was nevertheless impeccable; by now we'd been joined by a friend of Jehane's called Maria, and whenever a boy came up to choose either of them for a partner, he would first lift an eyebrow at us inquiringly in case we objected: afterwards leading them back to the table and leaving at once without further parley.

Maria had a blonde fringe and wore the traditional uniform of the club; she'd refused any drink but undiluted soda-pop; an inquiry from me as to whether she was an Existentialist or had heard of Sartre met with no answer but a shake of the head. Seeing bruises on her bare arms, Mike had leeringly hinted at a boyfriend in the background, but this suggestion was received with a stare of haughty surprise that subdued him on the spot; after this none of us made any attempt to talk to her: a situation which she seemed to accept with equanimity and even gratitude. Both she and Jehane, however, threw themselves into the dance with the utmost abandon that the rules of their sect would allow; and to me it was obvious that, for Jehane, Bebop and its attendant rites had taken the place once occupied by the poems of Rilke, the works of Franz Kafka, *Citizen Kane*, and, it could be, the ambition, even, to become an artist.

Mike and Shaun had given up all hope of casual adventure; as soon as the gin bottles were empty, they proposed a move before the pubs shut. Jehane politely accompanied us into the street upstairs; as Shaun and Mike walked on ahead, I gave her back her bracelets, and leaning her head for a moment against my shoulder (unfaithful perhaps to her creed, she'd drunk some of the gin) she told me that next day was her twenty-first: age crept inexorably up on us all. I wished her many happy returns and confided that I too felt I was getting old: after this she scampered off with a wave of the hand—back to the smoky underground glow and the sweating band, itself obsessed as she with the senseless rhythm it beat up beneath the spotlight beam.

That was all: but now, in the Soho restaurant, as the ministerial young man's female counterpart talked knowingly of drugs and dipsomania among Bebop fans—'either drunk or doped to the *eyes*, my dear'—I remembered the evening almost with sadness.

For Bop, I am told, like Boogie-Woogie before it, is nearly extinct nowadays; Existentialist clothes are out of fashion, former adherents hard to find: the club may even have closed its doors. The younger generation has rediscovered jazz; there's talk of the Dorsey Brothers, a solid beat, a straight melodic line. And if the wheel comes full circle, what of Jehane?

For, with her premature feeling for period, she must—it's inevitable—become the last of the Bebop girls. And (as women of the Twenties sometimes weep, over their Pernod, in mourning for the Black Bottom, 'The Birth of the Blues', the signature-tunes of their time) so we may find her, one day soon, crying in some café; only Jehane will be denied the dubious solace of alcohol: her tears must fall—out of loyalty to the vanished customs of her lost youth—into a glass of straight, unadulterated soda-pop.

The Night Bathers

*   *   *

IN THE CAREFREE DAYS JUST AFTER THE WAR I USED OFTEN TO LEND seven and a tanner to an Irishman known as The Toucher Malone so that he could get himself a bed at the Turkish Baths. But I never went to the Baths myself until last year, and then for the same reason as The Toucher: because I had nowhere else to sleep.

A chap called Sketchy took me there. As his nickname implies, Sketchy made a living by sketching people in pubs and sometimes in drinking clubs. He earned enough to sleep at the Baths every night and had no possessions except the clothes he stood up in, which included a green tweed fishing hat and a coursing coat that he'd bought second-hand thirty years before and weighed nearly two stone.

When Sketchy first suggested the Baths I drew back in alarm. 'Can't afford it. Not with The Toucher there.'

'Toucher's in Dublin,' Sketchy told me. 'The entrance fee's gone up double since his day, but if you've got a quid it'll be ample. Tip the bloke on the desk and the attendant who makes your bed down a bob a-piece, and you'll have enough over for breakfast in the morning, that's if you can eat any, which is more'n I ever do. Best breakfast in London, mind you, and only half a dollar. Real home from home, the Baths, take it from your Uncle Sketchy.' He pushed a frosted glass door inscribed OPEN DAY AND NIGHT and led the way downstairs to the reception desk.

'This gent's a mate of mine, so treat him right,' he told the attendant, pointing at me. 'Bit skint present moment, but which of us isn't hard up at times? A good man's fortune may grow out at heels, as the Bard has it, eh?'

The entrance to the Baths proper resembled that of a mosque, all the more so because you had to remove your shoes before going in.

Even Sketchy surrendered his fishing hat and coursing coat, and we padded in our socks across a dim-lit carpeted lounge with a swimming-pool in the centre, round which ran an upper gallery decorated with a frieze of armorial bearings under a Moorish ceiling. It was one in the morning, the sound of deep breathing rose like the swish of waves from all sides, and the sight of semi-nude men reclining in deck-chairs through glass doors beyond added to the sudden atmosphere of shipboard.

'This is where we part company, lad,' Sketchy said. 'Always sleep aloft, meself. Less noise. Don't you go putting him near the Admiral now,' he told the attendant, and rolled with a seaman's gait up a staircase leading to the gallery overhead.

I was too tired to face a Turkish bath that night, and fell asleep immediately in the curtained cubicle, containing two beds, to which the attendant conducted me. Once in the night I started awake with the sound of a resounding snore ringing in my ears. This came from the dormitory on the other side of the swimming-pool and seemed to be made by a sea-lion rather than by any human agency. It died away in a shuddering sob and was succeeded by a quarter-deck voice shouting 'Steward!'

'Coming, sir!' answered a distant echo, and an awed whisper from an habitué in the bed opposite mine explained: 'It's the Admiral. Wants his tea. You'll get used to it in time, chum.' Soon a discreet tray rattled past, the Admiral grunted satisfaction, and silence settled down once more. I didn't wake again until the morning, with all the lights ablaze and the man in the next bed examining his shirt and murmuring 'Question is, will the collar do another day?' (It was a question I also might have asked my own shirt; and later, on the advice of Sketchy, I bought a nylon one which, washed in the lavabo and put to dry in the Hot room overnight, solved one problem of the nomadic existence that Bath Men are committed to.)

Breakfast—undoubtedly the best in London for half a crown: bacon, egg, chipolatas, roll and butter, pot of tea or iced fruit-juice—was served until 9.30 a.m. at tables in the foyer; while Sketchy in a woollen vest with braces hanging down his back, having first quoted *Romeo and Juliet* or delivered a sermon from the balcony, came down later and sat in an armchair under a sign SILENCE IS REQUESTED, exchanging racing tips with other habitués or telling us about the time when his special binoculars were stolen from him on the course. His two inseparable buddies were a short, wide, pink-faced Scot called Hamish who knew all about the anatomy of carrier-bags, since he carried his effects about in one; and a tall thin professional tipster known as Aussie, not because he was an Australian but because his first name was Oswald. Form was desultorily studied, selections in the daily papers laughed to scorn, and a momentary hush fell as the Admiral stalked by, walrus moustache, big red shining bald head, in a suit of impeccable cut, speaking to nobody on his way out. Then, after we'd shaved in genuine hot water and had our shoes handed back to us bearing a high degree of gloss (a welcome change from most hotels, with the present shortage of staff), we made in a body for one of the pubs nearby: open, in this district, at eleven a.m.

I was already under the spell of this predominantly male society, and came back night after night that winter; I got to know the attendants by their Christian names, was always given a cubicle well away from the Admiral, and wandered girt with a towel through the steam and marble slabs: even penetrating to the Very Hot Room where the floor burnt one's foot soles and the Africans huddled for warmth.

Then my financial position suddenly changed; moreover I had to work hard and to bid the Bath Life farewell. Months passed, meanwhile I saw nothing of Sketchy or the others; but one night, up from the country, all hotels full, I pushed the familiar door and went down the stairs expecting a big welcome below. To my surprise a strange reception-clerk stared at me from behind the desk; a new and taciturn attendant guided me to a bed; half the cubicles at least were empty, and there was no sign of Sketchy or any of the regulars. Not even the Admiral's snores disturbed my sleep; there were no shouts of 'Steward!' and in the morning I was given a brisk shake at 7.30.

'Sorry, sir, have to be out o' here in an hour's time—new manager's orders,' and in the next cubicle a vacuum cleaner started up. A few strangers sat without speaking at the breakfast-tables outside; others were already shaving briskly outside in the wash-room beyond; but the waiter who served me had a familiar face: he was, it turned out, the last remaining member of the old staff.

'The reg'lars? What—Sketchy and them? Lor bless you, sir, they don't come in no more. Got barred, the lot on 'em, Admiral an' all. Had an argy-bargy with the new manager, fair tartar he is, wouldn't let 'em pass the door after that. Said it was getting too much of a common lodging-house like. No, sir, I couldn't say what the trouble was all about

—religious differences, somebody told me, but I wouldn't know for sure.'

'Perhaps I can find them in the pub later?'

'Doubt it, sir, ain't seen none of 'em around these parts of late. Old Sketchy's down the country, I believe—broke him up proper, not being allowed in the Baths of a night...Hamish and the rest could be in the pub o' course, though it don't open till half-past eleven now the licensing law's been changed.'

There seemed nothing to hang about for. I took out my wallet and was about to pay with a pound note when I felt a hand on my arm and turned to look into the grinning face of The Toucher Malone.

Some Time I Shall Sleep Out

*   *   *

THE NIGHT-SERGEANT AT THE POLICE STATION SURVEYED ME dubiously from behind his desk. 'Not drunk, are you?' he said.

'No. But all the hotels are full and I want a bed for the night.'

'Can't book you unless you're drunk, I'm afraid,' the sergeant said. 'We're full up too, anyhow.' He nodded towards a noise of muffled shouting from the cells.

'Whitsun,' he said. 'Drunks. Not a single bit of room to spare. If you've any money, you might try the YMCA. Or the Salvation Army Hostel, Waterloo way.'

'Crammed to the doors. I've been.'

'Well, there's always Euston Station. The waiting-room.' He looked up at the clock; it was already 2 a.m. 'Might get in there if you hurry. Course, officially, you're not supposed to sleep on the station, but chances are no constable'll bother you. Got all we can cope with here tonight.'

I thanked him and wandered out into a wide empty road balefully lit by orange sodium lamps. Voices singing 'Mother Machree' died away in the distance and traffic had temporarily ceased. I'd been walking about for hours, and my briefcase seemed by now to weigh a ton. I stood on the kerb, a sudden prey to agoraphobia, daunted by the shining width of the street I had to cross.

Then, ahead of me, I saw the lone figure of a man approaching. It bore down slowly, limping a little, with the inexorable step of some symbolic character in a foreign film: one who might turn out to be Destiny, Satan, or perhaps even the Saviour. This effect of a fated encounter was heightened by his opening address, delivered as he drew level and halted.

'Bound for Euston, I daresay?'

'Yes. Are you?'

The man nodded, looking at me sadly and with compassion. He wore a plastic mac and carried a small attaché case of considerable antiquity. He himself was not young either, though his actual age in the lurid sodium glare was hard to assess.

'Euston Station,' he said. 'The only place where one is allowed to rest in comparative peace and comfort, free of charge. Come, let us make the journey together.'

He took my arm and steered me across the road towards crimson spelling out the station's name. 'Charing Cross is no good nowadays,' he said. 'Doesn't open till 5 a.m. I was an inmate of Rowton House until this evening but, alas, they don't let you remain more than three nights in succession—and besides I haven't the entrance-fee.' He paused in the vast booking-hall to remove his shoe and shake from inside it a sizeable lump of grit. 'I am an anachronism,' he said. 'An officer of the First World War.' Swiftly he whipped from his pocket a small tin box and allowed me to glance inside. It contained medal ribbons of indubitable 14–18 vintage. 'Pensioned of course, but it's not enough to live on, and frankly whenever it comes in, I blow the lot.'

At a brisker pace, as though revived by the thought of this improvidence, he moved towards the doors of the waiting-room and stood alertly surveying the terrain, 'Not too bad considering,' he said. I followed him into what was in fact another huge hall, where every cough raised a hollow echo, and where the benches, padded in scarlet leather, were almost all occupied by sleeping people: some huddled in pairs, others —fortunate enough to secure a bench to themselves—stretched out full length with their feet up. Few had luggage, though some soldiers' heads were pillowed on their packs, and many stirred awake at the sound of our footsteps on the tiled floor.

'This way,' the officer told me, heading straight in front of him. 'Avoid the Russian,' he added in a lower tone, indicating a bench on our right. Slumped half across this was an old man wearing several overcoats, a green furry cap pulled low over his ears, and a matted yellow-white beard. He also wore two pairs of boots, with folded newspaper inserted between their gaping toes, and muttered malevolently to himself as we approached.

'Verminous,' the officer hissed in my ear, steering me towards a vacant bench at the rear, on to which he sank with a sigh. I was about to follow suit, but started suddenly back in alarm. Towering above me was a gigantic figure, sightless and square-bearded, carved out of snuff-coloured stone and clutching a scroll.

'Stephenson,' the officer said. 'The Rocket, you know. Gives one quite a turn, doesn't he?'

I sat uneasily below the statue and took fuller stock of my surroundings. I saw now that round the walls, at regular intervals, were a series of large black bins resembling sarcophagi, on each of which a sleeping man lay recumbent, like a figure sculpted in relief upon his own tomb. But before I'd time to comment on this sepulchral feature of the station, the officer clutched my arm.

'Police!' he hissed. 'If accosted, say you're waiting for the 7.55 to Manchester. We'll be away by then.'

But the two constables were not aiming to question us. They were headed for the Russian, who watched them approach with rancour, scratching first inside one of his overcoats and then in his beard. 'They'll move him on for sure,' the officer said. 'Poor old devil.' He was right, but not until a spirited exchange had taken place, during which the Russian produced masses of tattered documents, some from inside his boots, and proffered them as evidence that he was a bona fide traveller. But the police were adamant: plainly the Russian was not waiting for the 7.55 to Manchester. At last he rose and shuffled away, with the two constables pacing behind, and those who had awoken settled down to sleep again.

'Now for a spot of shut-eye,' the officer said. 'Until the Buffet opens, five o'clock sharp,' and he dropped off immediately, sitting bolt upright with his attaché case clipped firmly between his ankles. I didn't find it easy to follow his example, my head kept slipping off the arm I attempted to rest it on, and the sleepless antiseptic glare of the light-globes beat down from above.

Nevertheless I woke to find the officer shaking me gently and pointing with his other hand towards the Refreshment Room, part of which was called the Flying Scot, and where signs of movement were now perceptible beyond the closed glass doors. 'Quick,' he said. 'Before the lunch rush begins. That is, if you've the wherewithal, dear boy.'

At that moment the door clanged open and the rush began in earnest. Even the sarcophagus-men rose from their death-like trance and flung themselves down to join in the stampede. But, owing to the officer's foresight, we were first in the queue, and soon sitting at a table well screened from the rest of the room, with sausage-rolls, sandwiches and cups of coffee before us.

'A welcome break,' the officer said, munching avidly. 'Bless you, dear boy. One day I may be able to repay. I haven't always been like this, not by any means. I had my own business once, but it went bust. Some people said I drank too much.' He brushed crumbs from his grey military moustache, clipped toothbrush-style. 'Malicious gossip, of course. Then I got married. Well, enough said. I daresay you've had woman-trouble, yourself. Mine, to cut it short, is a sordid simple story of domestic infelicity. She had a parrot,' he said with sudden venom. 'A parrot and a Pekinese. Also oodles of dough. But I got away from her in the end.' He dozed lightly off with his head bowed over the empty plate, then awoke to say: 'Freedom. I prize my freedom above all things. I'll never go back, never. On the other hand, I'm getting a bit ancient for this kind of life. Anno domini, dear boy. I was sixty-five last birthday.'

At this point I dozed off myself; when I awoke, to the clatter of cups being collected, daylight had broken over the hall outside, women with mops and pails were swabbing down the tiles, and the Whitsun crowd was pushing eagerly in from the booking-hall. 'Now for a wash and brush up, dear fellow,' the officer said, jumping up greatly refreshed.

Downstairs we washed and shaved; and afterwards, opening his attaché case, the officer took out brushes of various kinds, polished his shoes and brushed his clothes carefully, even combing his moustache with a tiny tortoise-shell comb. 'I've made a decision, my boy,' he said. 'I'm going back. Back to the wife. It'll mean sacrificing my freedom, but against that there's my age. It's a fact one's got to admit, getting older. Oh, she'll take me in all right. I've only got to turn up. No, no, thanks—I've saved the fare all right. It's not far, on the Tube, to her suburban mansion.'

We said good-bye at the Underground entrance, and I watched him walk away. Once he shivered slightly, perhaps thinking of the parrot and the Pekinese, but then he pulled his shoulders back and trod jauntily out of sight: as years before, perhaps, he had led his men over the top, at zero-hour, on some forgotten field.

INDEX

now read the biography

Fear and Loathing in Fitzrovia
Paul Willetts
Dewi Lewis Publishing
£14.99 softback
ISBN 1-899235-69-8; 416pp

'An inspiring read'
>JOHN KING, *NEW STATESMAN*
>BOOKS OF THE YEAR

'Diligent, painstaking and bleakly hilarious'
>*GUARDIAN* BOOK OF THE WEEK

'Historical profiling of a high order, richly and racily done'
>PHILIP OAKES, *LITERARY REVIEW*

'Very striking, very strange and altogether fascinating'
>RICHARD HOLMES, AUTHOR OF
>*DR JOHNSON AND MR SAVAGE*

'Gloriously readable'
>*MAIL ON SUNDAY*

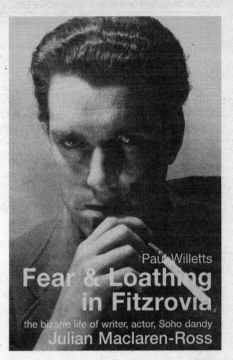

Paul Willetts
Fear & Loathing in Fitzrovia
the bizarre life of writer, actor, Soho dandy
Julian Maclaren-Ross

and the short stories

Julian Maclaren-Ross Selected Stories
Introduced by Paul Willetts
Dewi Lewis Publishing
£9.99 softback
ISBN 1-904587-17-8; 256pp

The world of Maclaren-Ross's short fiction tends to be the dingy, down-at-heel world of smoke-veiled bars, rented lodgings, blacked-out streets, and wartime army garrisons, first-hand experience lending his work a frisson of authenticity. Whether they're narrated in the breathless, slangy voice of an uneducated soldier, or the clipped cadences of a colonial 'expat', whether they're set on the French Riviera or wartime England, they're imprinted with Maclaren-Ross's unmistakable literary logo. The prevailing tone is casual, matter-of-fact and laconic, with his characteristically humorous asides failing to conceal the melancholy that seeps through their hardboiled surfaces.

The Lost Weekend *Charles Jackson*
£6.99 paperback; ISBN 0-948238-27-5; 224pp

Having cunningly contrived his own abandonment, Don Birnam begins the five-day alcoholic bender that may, just may, be the one that ends it all... Subject of Billy Wilder's classic Hollywood movie, which won four Oscars – among them best picture and best director – *The Lost Weekend* captures the atmosphere of Manhattan in the late 1930s – huge tenements, small smoke-filled piano bars, teeming streets beneath rattling elevated railways – with a haunting, cinematic vividness.

'Marvelous and horrifying... the best fictional account of alcoholism I have read' KINGSLEY AMIS

'His character is a masterpiece of psychological precision' NEW YORK TIMES

The Tenant *Roland Topor*
£6.99 paperback; ISBN 0-948238-26-7; 176pp

A masterful psychological thriller, *The Tenant* tells of Monsieur Trelkovsky, an ordinary man with ordinary desires against whom apparently ordinary circumstances conspire until he is enmeshed in an extraordinary and terrifying situation, a nightmare world of paranoia, collusion, horrifying injury and suicide – a world which, we come to feel, is separated from the normality of everyday life by the merest sliver of sanity. Roman Polanski made a film based on the book in 1976.

'hallucinatory classic of literary horror somewhat akin to a fusion of Patrick Hamilton and Edgar Allan Poe' GQ

'unforgettable, gripping' RONALD FRAME, LE MONDE

'a powerful fable set in the twilight zone' OBSERVER

'As cold and quiet and deadly as a snake in the bed' NEW YORK TIMES

The Big Brass Ring *Orson Welles with Oja Kodar*
£9.95 paperback; ISBN 0-948238-16-X; 160pp

Consciously conceived as a companion piece to *Citizen Kane*, here Welles is again concerned with the idea of the great man, and with what happens at the convergence of great talent, public ambition and the undertow of obscure, private longings rooted in the past. A film of *The Big Brass Ring*, its script heavily edited, appeared in 1999, with William Hurt in the lead role.

'The script in its present form, with its witty and extensive stage directions, gives a tremendous sense of what it might have been like in the company of the great raconteur himself... and the authors have taken great care to let us "see" what the film might have been – enthralling, sexy, funny, and politically as trenchant as anything being made today.' SIMON CALLOW

'a living, breathing, finished work on the page... one of the most remarkable and revealing works in the entire Welles canon' SIGHT AND SOUND

'playful, witty and moving' TIME OUT